D'ya Get Me Doc

ISBN: 978-0-9955726-1-4

Cover and design by SpiffingCovers Ltd.

The D'Ya Get Me series of books are books about language and communication.

The terms and expressions used in these books may offend some people, who may see them as vulgar, obscene, racist, sexist, ageist, homophobic, violent, hateful or derogatory etc. Some people will be offended but, hopefully, most will find these compilations interesting and even humorous.

The authors would like to make it clear that it is not their intention to be offensive, either directly or indirectly. We do not condone or endorse such language, or the meaning behind it, we are merely providing it for the reader. It has been our intention to present the terms and expressions objectively as examples of language used in English speaking countries across the world. We wish to show its rich diversity and believe it to be of value and interest to others in a variety of contexts.

The terms and expressions found in these books are also not meant to be a substitute for medical advice from a licensed physician. The reader should always consult their doctor in matters relating to their health.

The information presented in these books is intended to be interesting, useful and to show people different types of communication used in different settings, including healthcare. It is not presented as advice about healthcare, or deemed to help doctors or nurses improve their general healthcare practice.

The authors and publishers have made every effort to ensure that the information in this book is correct at publication. The author and publisher do not assume and hereby disclaim any liability to any party for any loss, damage, or disruption caused by errors or omissions, whether such errors or omissions result from negligence, accident or any other cause.

Crystal Clear Language Company Limited

D'ya Get Me Doc?

A **COMPREHENSIVE COLLECTION** OF *COLLOQUIAL TERMS* AND *IDIOMS* TO SUPPORT DOCTORS IN DEMYSTIFYING THE ENGLISH LANGUAGE AND ASSISTING THEM TO IMPROVE THEIR **COMMUNICATION WITH PATIENTS**.

published by

CRYSTAL CLEAR
language

Dedicated to all of the hard working staff in the NHS, who go above and beyond to save lives everyday.

Foreword

During my long career of over sixty years working in health and social care services, it has become apparent to me that medicine is an art whose magic and creative ability have long been recognised as residing in the interpersonal aspects of the patient-doctor relationship. Effective dialogue is at the core of such clinical functions and the resultant communication is the heart and art of medicine and a central component in the delivery of health care.

The three main goals of current doctor-patient communication are creating a good interpersonal relationship, facilitating exchange of information, and including patients in decision making. In my opinion, good doctor and patient communication has the potential to help regulate patients' emotions, facilitate comprehension of medical information, and allow for better identification of the patients' needs, perceptions and expectations. Patients reporting good communication with their doctor are more likely to be satisfied with their care, and especially to share pertinent information for accurate diagnosis of their problems, follow advice, and adhere to the prescribed treatment. Also it is reported that patients' who agree with their doctor about the nature of the treatment and need for follow-up is strongly associated with their recovery.

A large and compelling evidence base in communication sciences has confirmed that narrative is a vital part of the consultation process between doctor and patient. I am aware, from personal experience that despite the sterling work most medical staff carry out, there is significant carer and patient misgivings about doctors who are not proficient enough in English and, whilst they may be able to pass tests, they fail to be able to communicate in context. Many of the Royal Colleges agree with me that there are concerns in this respect and that gaining more control would improve patient care and safety. I also believe that improvements in this area would reduce costs to the Trusts dealing with complaints and litigation which arises very often as a result of mis-communication and lack of understanding, and allow this money to be re-deployed to other areas of patient care.

It is essential we accept that our country has and is changing significantly and that we now live in a diverse and multi-cultural society, where language and basic communication skills are becoming more difficult in our understanding of each other. There is much debate, in the media, and elsewhere at the current time, about immigration and the impact that curtailing this will have on the staff resourcing of the National Health Service. It is a fact that successive Governments have failed to allocate enough funding to the Education and Training budgets, in this country, to ensure sufficient doctors and nurses are trained here. The Government recently announced plans to recruit an additional 1,500 doctors each year into training, and whilst this is a step in the right direction, it will do little to address the current situation. It takes at least nine years to train a doctor to become a Consultant/Specialist and the need is now. Therefore, for the foreseeable future we have to accept that the staffing of the National Health Service, if fully resourced, will be dependent on international doctors and nurses, and we should welcome and support them when they come here to work.

I am aware that the need to address some of these communication concerns has been identified and addressed in recent legislative changes contained within the Medical Act 2014 and that these changes give the General Medical Council more powers to check the language skills of licensed doctors and has also raised the required competency skills of the International Language Testing System. I am also aware that changes are being made to the curriculum for doctor training. It is my personal experience, however, that some doctors are still struggling to make sense of the quirky and often confusing colloquial language used by patients. I believe this Reference Book will assist you in coming to grips with some of the non standard forms of English language that you might hear and I commend it to you.

Margaret Dexter, CQSW, Bristol University

Managing Director, Crystal Clear Language

CONTENTS

CONTENTS...continued

CONTENTS...continued

Abbreviations

'FOI'
*Freedom of
Information*

A&E - Accident And Emergency - My G.P. sent me to A&E to get my minor injury attended to. - *British*

AACE - Association Of Ambulance Chief Executives - The chief executive belonged to AACE. - *British*

ABHI - Association Of British Healthcare Industries - The Trust had representatives on ABHI. - *British*

ABPI - Association Of The British Pharmaceutical Industry - All of the pharmacists joined the ABPI. - *British*

AC - Audit Commission - It was widely known that the AC would be visiting next week to audit the financial records. - *British*

ACAD - Ambulatory Care And Diagnostic Centre - The doctor referred the patient to ACAD or the Ambulatory Care and Diagnostic Unit. - *British*

ACCEA - Advisory Committee On Clinical Excellence Awards - "We will refer that to ACCEA for their advice, and to gain an award for clinical excellence," said the doctor. - *British*

ACDP - Advisory Committee On Dangerous Pathogens - There was a ACDP, which reviewed dangerous pathogens. - *British*

ACEVO - Association Of Chief Executives Of Voluntary Organisations - The voluntary organisation belonged to ACEVO. - *British*

ACG - Adjusted Clinical Group - She belonged to the ACG. - *British*

ACO - Accountable Care Organisation - The health service was the ACO for the young man. - *British*

ACP - Advanced Care Plan - The patient had an ACP. - *British*

ACRA - Advisory Committee On Resource Allocation - There was an ACRA planned for next month. - *British*

ACS - Ambulatory Care-Sensitive (Conditions) - He needed to be aware of the ACS. - *British*

ADASS - Association Of Directors Of Adult Social Services - The director had joined ADASS as he thought that if he was working alongside other directors, he would get the support he needed. - *British*

ADCS - Association Of Directors Of Children's Services - She had joined ADCS when working in children's services. - *British*

AEC - Ambulatory Emergency Care - The trust had responsibility for AEC. - *British*

AFC - Agenda For Change - The government had published an AFC document of their plans. - *British*

AFPP - Association For Perioperative Practice - The hospital staff had joined the AFPP. - *British*

AGNSS - Advisory Group For National Specialised Services - The government had set up the AGNSS. - *British*

AGS - Annual Governance Statement - The school produced an AGS. - *British*

AHCS - Academy For Healthcare Science - They had joined the AHCS. - *British*

AHP - Allied Health Professional - As a podiatrist she was classified as an AHP. - *British*

AHSC - Academic Health Science Centre - She was going to the AHSC for a meeting. - *British*

AHSN - Academic Health Science Network - He was a member of the AHSN, which he found very helpful. - *British*

AIDS - Acquired Immunodeficiency Syndrome - The older man had been diagnosed with AIDS. - *British*

AIR - (Strategic Health Authority) Annual Innovation Report - The strategic health authority used to produce an AIR. - *British*

AKA - Also Known As - Bill was AKA Bernard. - *British*

ALB - Arm's-Length Body - The Inspectorate was an ALB. - *British*

ALE - Auditors Local Evaluation - The finance department produced an ALE. - *British*

ALTO - Arm's-Length Trading Organisation - The consortium was an ALTO. - *British*

AM - Assembly Member (Wales) - The man was an AM; an assembly member for Wales. - *British*

AME - Annually Managed Expenditure - The finance director was responsible for the AME. - *British*

AMHP - Approved Mental Health Professional - The psychiatrist was an AMHP. - *British*

AMR - Antimicrobial Resistance - The infection had AMR and was difficult to cure. - *British*

AMU - Acute Medical Unit - They had admitted her to the AMU for treatment. - *British*

AOMRC - Academy Of Medical Royal Colleges - It was recommended that I join the AOMRC, the professional organisation for medics. - *British*

AP - Assistant Practitioner - The nurse had been appointed as AP as she was now assisting in the surgery. - *British*

APB - Autism Partnership Board - The society had set up an APB to manage their affairs. - *British*

APC - Admitted Patient Care - Inpatients were subject to APC. - *British*

APMS - Alternative Provider Medical Services - The out of hours Doctor Service was an APMS. - *British*

APT - Anatomical Pathology Technologist - He worked as an APT. - *British*

AQI - Ambulance Quality Indicator - The ambulance service was measured through AQIs set by the government. - *British*

AQP - Any Qualified Provider - "We will accept any AQP," said the service commissioner. - *British*

AQUA - Advancing Quality Alliance - They had joined the AQUA. - *British*

ASCOF - Adult Social Care Outcomes Framework - The plan formed part of the ASCOF. - *British*

ASI - Appointment Slot Issues - The GP surgery had ASIs. - *British*

ASN - Ambulance Service Network - The Ambulance Trust had responsibility for the ASN. - *British*

ASPC - Association Of Surgeons In Primary Care - The consultants in primary care had joined the ASPC. - *British*

ASPIH - Association For Simulated Practice In Healthcare - The centre was a member of the ASPIH. - *British*

AT - Area Team - She was a member of the AT. - *British*

ATO - Assistant Theatre Operator - He was employed as an ATO. - *British*

AVR - Accredited Voluntary Registers - The charity was on the AVRs. - *British*

AWD - Agency Workers Directive - The nurses from the agency were subject to the AWD. - *British*

AWR - Agency Workers Regulations - The AWR covered the employment of nurses who worked for agencies. - *British*

B&T - NHS Blood And Transplant - She worked for the NHS B&T Service. - *British*

BAA - British Academy Of Audiology - They were members of the BAA. - *British*

BADS - British Association Of Day Surgery - They belonged to the BADS from whom they received support. - *British*

BAF - Board Assurance Framework - The board worked to a BAF which clarified their responsibilities. - *British*

BAREMA - British Anaesthetic And Respiratory Equipment Manufacturers' Association - The equipment had been approved by BAREMA. - *British*

BAS - NHS Business Authority Services - They were part of the NHS BAS. - *British*

BASICS - British Association For Immediate Care - They had joined the BASICS from whom they gained support in their profession. - *British*

BCF - Better Care Fund - They had received a grant from the BCF. - *British*

BDA - British Dental Association - They were members of the BDA. - *British*

BIS - (Department For) Business, Innovation And Skills - They had applied to the BIS for a grant. - *British*

BMA - British Medical Association - The BMA were negotiating with the government over junior doctor pay. - *British*

BME - Black And Minority Ethnic - There were a number of BME staff employed by the trust. - *British*

BNF - British National Formulary - The hospital pharmacy worked to the BNF. - *British*

BPS - British Psychological Society - The psychologists were members of the BPS. - *British*

BPT - Best Practice Tariff - The buyers were always looking for the BPT. - *British*

BRC - Biomedical Research Centre - He had been seconded to the BRC for a year. - *British*

BROMI - Better Regulation Of Medicines Initiative - The government had set up BROMI. - *British*

BRU - Biomedical Research Unit - He had gained a secondment to the BRU for six months. - *British*

BSA - British Society Of Audiology - They were members of the BSA. - *British*

BTBC - Better Training Better Care (Programme) - The course was part of the BTBC programme. - *British*

CAA - Comprehensive Area Assessment - They had undertaken a CAA. - *British*

CAG - Confidentiality Advisory Group - She had volunteered to sit on the CAG. - *British*

CAJE - Computer Aided Job Evaluation - The pay scales were set using the CAJE. - *British*

CAMHS - Child And Adolescent Mental Health Services - The G.P. had referred the child to CAMHS. - *British*

CAP - Community Acquired Pneumonia - The patient was suffering from CAP. - *British*

CAPEX - Capital Expenditure - The director of finance controlled the CAPEX. - *British*

CARU - Clinical Audit And Research Unit - He had been seconded to the CARU for six months. - *British*

CAS - Central Alert System - The CAS was available in all rooms. - *British*

CAT - Computerised Axial Tomography (Scan) - Her G.P. had referred her for a CAT scan. - *British*

CAT - Crisis Assessment And Treatment - In A&E she underwent CAT. - *British*

CAU - Clinical Assessment Unit - He worked in the CAU. - *British*

CB - NHS Commissioning Board - She was a member of the NHS CB. - *British*

CBRNE - Chemical, Biological, Radiological, Nuclear And Explosive Hazards - The health and safety officer was responsible for training staff in CBRNE. - *British*

CBT - Cognitive Behavioural Therapy - The psychiatrist was undertaking a course of CBT with the patient. - *British*

CC - NHS Clinical Commissioners - She was part of the NHS CC. - *British*

C-CBT - Computerised Cognitive Behavioural Therapy - The psychiatrist used C-CBT with his patients. - *British*

CCG - Clinical Commissioning Group - The Trust had representatives on the CCG. - *British*

CCP - Co-Operation And Competition Panel - They had set up a CCP to support their work. - *British*

CCP - Critical Care Paramedic - He had qualified as a CCP. - *British*

CCT - Community Care Team - She had been appointed to the CCT. - *British*

CCU - Coronary Care Unit - Following his heart attack, the patient was admitted to the CCU. - *British*

CDF - Cancer Drugs Fund - The hospital had a CDF from which funds were available. - *British*

CDO - Chief Dental Officer - The CDO was a member of the board. - *British*

CDS - Commissioning Data Sets - The Contracts Department used CDS to inform their work. - *British*

CDU - Clinical Decision Unit - She worked in the CDU. - *British*

CEA - Clinical Excellence Awards - The Trust valued their staff by presenting CEAs. - *British*

CEAC - Clinical And Excellence Awards Committee (Northern Ireland) - In Northern Ireland they have CEACs. - *British*

CEM - College Of Emergency Medicine - The doctor was a member of the CEM. - *British*

CEMACH - Confidential Enquiry Into Maternal And Child Health - The government had set up a CEMACH. - *British*

CEP - Centre For Evidence-Based Purchasing - The organisation belonged to CEP. - *British*

CEPN - Community Education Provider Network - The school was part of the CEPN. - *British*

CES - Care Episode Service - They worked as part of the CES. - *British*

CFH - (NHS) Connecting For Health - They worked as part of the CFH. - *British*

CFWI - Centre For Workforce Intelligence - The director of personnel was a member of CFWI. - *British*

CHC - Community Health Council - There used to be CHCs but they were disbanded. - *British*

CHC - NHS Continuing Healthcare - The district nurses worked as part of CHC. - *British*

CHCP - Community Health And Care Partnership (Scotland) - The health visitors were part of the CHCP. - *British*

CHD - Coronary Heart Disease - He had been diagnosed as having CHD. - *British*

CHI - Community Health Index (Scotland) - Their data was included in the CHI for Scotland. - *British*

CHMS - Community Health And Miscellaneous Services - She worked as part of CHMS. - *British*

CHP - Community Health Partnership (Scotland) - In Scotland they work as part of CHPs. - *British*

CHPPD - Care Hours Per Patient Day - It was important to record the CHPPD. - *British*

CHRE - Council For Healthcare Regulatory Excellence - They had representatives on the CHRE. - *British*

CIC - Community Interest Company - They were part of a CIC. - *British*

CIMP - Clinical Information Management Programme - The chief executive used the CIMP. - *British*

CIO - Chief Information Officer - He had been appointed to the CIO post. - *British*

CIP - Cost Improvement Plan - The finance director had put a cost improvement plan in place. - *British*

CIP - Cost Improvement Programme - The Trust had a CIP which all the staff worked to. - *British*

CLAHRC - Collaboration For Leadership In Applied Health Research And Care - The Trust were members of CLAHRC. - *British*

CLG - (Department Of) Communities And Local Government - He was the minister for the Department of CLG. - *British*

CMB - Corporate Management Board (Department Of Health) - The Department of Health had a CMB. - *British*

CMD - Common Mental Disorder - The patient was diagnosed with a CMD. - *British*

CME - Continuing Medical Education - The trainees were subject to CME. - *British*

CMHT - Community Mental Health Team - The social worker was a member of the CMHT. - *British*

CMO - Chief Medical Officer - He had been appointed as CMO some years before. - *British*

CNO - Chief Nursing Officer - She was the CNO and managed all of the nursing staff. - *British*

CNST - Clinical Negligence Scheme For Trusts - The Trust were members of the CNST. - *British*

CO - Cabinet Office - The prime minister is a member of the CO. - *British*

COBIC - Capitated Outcomes-Based Incentivised Contracts - The Commissioning Department drew up COBIC. - *British*

COF - Commissioning Outcomes Framework - The staff used the COF to award contracts. - *British*

COG - Clinical Operations Group - He was a member of the COG. - *British*

COG - Council Of Governors - She was a member of the COG. - *British*

COMARE - Committee On Medical Aspects Of Radiation In The Environment - The Trust was represented on the COMARE. - *British*

COMEAP - Committee On The Medical Effects Of Air Pollutants - The Trust was represented on the COMEAP. - *British*

COPD - Chronic Obstructive Pulmonary Disease - He had been diagnosed with COPD. - *British*

COSLA - Convention Of Scottish Local Authorities - The council was a member of COSLA. - *British*

CPA - Care Programme Approach - The patient had been assessed using the CPA. - *British*

CPAG - Clinical Priorities Advisory Group (Department Of Health Subcommittee) - The Department of Health run a CPAG. - *British*

CPCF - Community Pharmacy Contractual Framework - The Department of Health has a CPCF for the use of pharmacies. - *British*

CPD - Continuing Professional Development - Once a year the trainees had their CPD assessed as part of ARCP. - *British*

CPN - Community Psychiatric Nurse - She worked as a CPN as part of the mental health team. - *British*

CPPE - Centre For Pharmacy Postgraduate Education - The university had a CPPE. - *British*

CPR - Child Protection Register - The family's name was on the CPR. - *British*

CPT - Contingency Planning Team - She had been appointed to the CPT as part of her role. - *British*

CQC - Care Quality Commission - She was an inspector working for the CQC. - *British*

CQI - Clinical Quality Indicator - The medical director used CQI to assess the hospital services. - *British*

CQRS - Calculating Quality Reporting Service - He was a member of the CQRS. - *British*

CQUIN - Commissioning For Quality And Innovation - The government had produced a report with the title CQUIN. - *British*

CRB - Criminal Records Bureau - Before starting to work with children all staff were subject to CRB check. - *British*

CRD - Centre Reviews And Dissemination (N.B Note Change From Research To Reviews) - The Trust had representation on the CRD. - *British*

CRES - Cash Releasing Efficiency Scheme - The Trust had adopted the CRES in order to reduce its costs. - *British*

CRG - Clinical Reference Group - They referred the matter to the CRG for discussion. - *British*

CRL - Capital Resource Limit - The director of finance knew the CRL for the Trust. - *British*

CRN - Clinical Research Network - He was a member of the CRN which he found very supportive. - *British*

CROM - Clinician Reported Outcome Measure - The consultant used the CROM to inform the trust. - *British*

CRS - Commissioner Requested Services - The contract department followed the CRS format. - *British*

CRS - (NHS) Care Records Service - The Trust used the CRS for patients. - *British*

CSA - Common Services Agency - It was part of the CSA. - *British*

CSO - Chief Scientific Officer - He had been appointed CSO some time before. - *British*

CSO - Civil Society Organisation - They belonged to the CSO. - *British*

CSO - Commissioning Support Organisation - They belonged to the CSO and met other commissioners. - *British*

CSP - Chartered Society Of Physiotherapy - They had joined the CSP for support. - *British*

CSP - Community Safety Partnership - Each of the authorities belonged to the CSP. - *British*

CSR - Comprehensive Spending Review - The finance director undertook the CSR for the trust. - *British*

CSS - Commissioning Support Service - The Trust had its own CSS. - *British*

CSU - Commercial Support Unit - The Trust had its own CSU. - *British*

CSU - Commissioning Support Unit - The CSU was part of the Contract and Commissioning Department. - *British*

CTLD - Community Team For Learning Disabilities - The CTLD was a multi-disciplinary team containing a range of professionals. - *British*

CTO - Community Treatment Order - He had been made subject to a CTO by the court. - *British*

CTO - Compulsory Treatment Order - He had been made subject to a CTO by the court. - *British*

CTP - Care Trust Plus - They were members of CTP. - *British*

CYT - Community Youth Team - The CYT worked in the evenings with young people. - *British*

DAT - Drug Action Team - The DAT worked out of hours undertaking activities with young offenders. - *British*

DBSS - Directly Bookable Services - The department operated the DBSS policy. - *British*

DCMS - Department For Culture, Media And Sport - The DCMS had suffered severe cut backs which meant less money was available for sport. - *British*

DCO - Designated Clinical Officer - He was the DCO for the project to build a new hospital. - *British*

DCP - Division Of Clinical Psychology - He was referred to the DCP for a therapy assessment. - *British*

Abbreviations

DCS - Director Of Children's Services - He was the DCS and very well thought of. - *British*

DDRB - Doctors And Dentists (Pay) Review Body - Any pay increase needed to be reviewed by DDRB before agreement could be reached. - *British*

DECC - Department Of Energy And Climate Change - Permission needed to be sought from DECC before installing wind farms. - *British*

DEFRA - Department For Environment, Food And Rural Affairs - DEFRA was the organisation which dealt with farming and environmental affairs. - *British*

DEL - Departmental Expenditure Limit - Everyone knew the DEL and tried to keep within budget. - *British*

DES - Directed Enhanced Services - The DES had offices all over the country. - *British*

DFE - Department For Education - The DFE head office was in London and from here policy for education was developed. - *British*

DFP - Department Of Finance And Personnel (Northern Ireland) - The DFP is in Dublin. - *British*

DFT - Department For Transport - The DFT was in London and easy to get to. - *British*

DFT - Distance From Target - He asked for the DFT before he planned the course of action he would take. - *British*

DGH - District General Hospital - She was the head nurse for the DGH. - *British*

DH OR DOH - Department Of Health - He was going to a meeting at the DOH. - *British*

DHSS - Department For Health And Social Services (Wales) - They often went to meetings at the DHSS. - *British*

DHSSPS - Department Of Health, Social Services And Public Safety (Northern Ireland) - In Ireland, they go to meetings at the DHSSPS. - *British*

DID - Diagnostic Imaging Department - The doctor sent her for X-ray at the DID. - *British*

DMB - Departmental Management Board (Department Of Health) - There is a DMB at the Department of Health. - *British*

DMS - Defence Medical Services - She worked for the DMS. - *British*

DNA - Did Not Attend - The hospital had a high number of DNAs. - *British*

DNAR - Do Not Attempt Resuscitation - The patient's notes were annotated with DNAR. - *British*

DNR - Do Not Resuscitate - The patient decided that in the event of him having a heart attack, his notes should state: DNR. - *British*

DOLS - Deprivation Of Liberty Safeguards - The mental health partnership made their doctors aware of the DOLS. - *British*

DPA - Data Protection Act - A memorandum was circulated to staff making them aware of the DPA. - *British*

DPC - Dementia Prevalence Calculator - Doctors caring for the elderly may use the DPC. - *British*

DPH - Director Of Public Health - He had been appointed to the DPH role the previous year. - *British*

DPHHP - Department For Public Health And Health Professions (Wales) - They had been invited to the DPHHP for a meeting. - *British*

DPR - Data Protection Registrar - The administrator had responsibility for the DPR. - *British*

DQ - Data Quality - The DQ was quite poor and needed improvement. - *British*

DRE - Delivering Race Equality - The Equalities Department was responsible for DRE. - *British*

DRG - Diagnosis-Related Group - She was a member of the DRG. - *British*

DSO - Departmental Strategic Objective - The plan had several DSOs which staff had been made aware of - *British*

DSPH - Directors Of Public Health - There was a meeting of all the DSPH on Tuesday. - *British*

DSSA - Delivering Same-Sex Accommodation - The CQC required the hospital to DSSA. - *British*

DSU - Day Surgery Unit - He had been referred to the DSU. - *British*

DTC - Diagnosis And Treatment Centre - He had been referred to the DTC. - *British*

DTOC - Delayed Transfer Of Care - The hospital had many DTOC elderly people who were awaiting beds in elderly peoples homes. - *British*

DV - Domestic Violence - The police are now much more aware of DV. - *British*

DWP - Department For Work And Pensions - I am going to a meeting at the DWP. - *British*

E&D - Equality And Diversity - E&D was on the agenda of the manager's meeting. - *British*

EAU - Emergency Assessment Unit - The patient was admitted to the EAU for observation. - *British*

EBH - Evidence-Based Healthcare - The hospital supported EBH and had a keen interest in research. - *British*

EBITDA - Earnings Before Interest, Tax, Depreciation And Amortisation - The finance director calculated the accounts before EBITDA. - *British*

EBM - Evidence-Based Medicine - The doctors practised EBM. - *British*

EBS - Emergency Bed Service - The unit operated an EBS but they were always full. - *British*

ECA - Emergency Care Assistant - She worked as an ECA. - *British*

ECAP - Emergency Care Action Plan - They had put in place an ECAP for the patient. - *British*

ECCT - Extended Community Care Team (NHS Scotland) - She worked for the ECCT and really enjoyed her job. - *British*

ECHR - European Convention On Human Rights - He had decided to take his case to the ECHR for their jurisdiction. - *British*

ECIST - Emergency Care Intensive Support Team - He was a member of the ECIST. - *British*

ECJ - European Court Of Justice - They had taken their dispute to the ECJ. - *British*

ECN - Extended Choice Network - They were a member of the ECN. - *British*

ECSW - Emergency Care Support Worker - She had been appointed to the role of ECSW in September. - *British*

ECT - Enhanced Care Teams - There were a number of ECTs in the hospital. - *British*

ED - Emergency Department - The ED were dealing with a person injured in a road traffic accident. - *British*

EDC - Emergency Dispatch Centre - It was sent from the EDC. - *British*

EDC - (NHS) Equality And Diversity Council - They were a member of the NHS EDC. - *British*

EDD - Estimated Date Of Discharge - The doctor had written the EDD on the patient's notes. - *British*

EDS - (NHS) Equality Delivery System - The policy was part of the NHS EDS. - *British*

EFL - External Financing Limit - The director of finance was aware of the EFL. - *British*

EHC - Emergency Hormonal Contraception - The young girl was given EHC by her doctor. - *British*

EHIC - European Health Insurance Card - When I go on holiday I always get a EHIC, in case I become ill. - *British*

EHPF - European Health Policy Forum - She attended the EHPF occasionally. - *British*

EHR - Electronic Health Record - The hospital used EHR for patient's notes. - *British*

EHRG - Equality And Human Rights Group (Department Of Health) - I was a member of the EHRG at the Department of Health. - *British*

EI - Early Intervention - EI by the doctor had saved the little boy's life. - *British*

EIA - Equality Impact Assessment - The Human Resources Department had undertaken an EIA. - *British*

EIP - Early Intervention Psychosis - The physciatrist had carried out an EIP plan. - *British*

E-KSF - (Electronic) Knowledge And Skills Framework - The Training Department used an E-KSF. - *British*

EM - Emergency Medicine - She worked for the Department of EM. - *British*

ENDPB - Executive Non-Departmental Public Body - They were a member of the ENDPB. - *British*

ENT - Ear, Nose And Throat - She had been referred to the ENT Department. - *British*

EO - Employers Organisation - The hospital belonged to the national EO. - *British*

EOC - Emergency Operation Centre - They had set up an EOC to cope with the crisis. - *British*

EOF - Education Outcomes Framework - They worked according to the EOF. - *British*

EOLC - End Of Life Care - The patient was subject to EOLC and was being well looked after. - *British*

EPACCS - Electronic Palliative Care Coordination Systems - The Palliative Care Team used EPACCS. - *British*

EPP - Expert Patient Programme - The hospital had a EPP and encouraged patients to join this. - *British*

EPR - Electronic Patient Record - The hospital used the EPR system. - *British*

EPRR - Emergency Preparedness, Resilience And Response - The Emergency Team discussed EPRR on a regular basis. - *British*

EPS - Electronic Prescription Service - The G.P. had joined the EPS with the local pharmacy. - *British*

ERDB - England Revalidation Delivery Board - They were members of the ERDB. - *British*

ERMA - Emergency Response Management Arrangements - The handbook contained clear instructions on ERMA. - *British*

ESD - Early Supported Discharge - The doctor had agreed with the patient to undertake ESD. - *British*

ESIF - European Structural And Investment Fund - They were hoping to gain funds from the ESIF. - *British*

ESR - Electronic Staff Record - The Human Resources Department kept ESR. - *British*

ETP - Electronic Transmission Of Prescriptions - There was an ETP from the ward to the pharmacy deparment. - *British*

ETS - Emissions Trading Scheme (EU) - They were aware of the EU ETS . - *British*

EWTD - European Working-Time Directive - Junior doctors hours were subject to the EWTD. - *British*

FAS - Foetal Alcohol Syndrome - The baby was suffering from FAS because of his mother's high alcohol consumption. - *British*

FBC - Full Business Case - The department needed to make a FBC in order to get funding for the project. - *British*

FCE - Finished Consultant Episode - The patient was discharged and the doctor put FCE on the notes. - *British*

FESC - Framework For Procuring External Support For Commissioners - They had joined the FESC. - *British*

FFT - Friends And Family Test - They had carried out a FFT with the patient. - *British*

FGM - Female Genital Mutilation - Many young girls coming to this country from overseas have been subjected to FGM. - *British*

FHS - Family Health Services - They were part of the FHS provision. - *British*

FIMS - Financial Information Management System - The Director of Finance operated within FIMS. - *British*

FMP - Financial Management Programme - There was a FMP for the Trust. - *British*

FNP - Family Nurse Partnership - She worked for the FNP and was very happy in her job. - *British*

FNP - Family Nurse Practitioner - She had been appointed to the role of FNP the previous July. - *British*

FOI - Freedom Of Information - The data was subject to FOI and had to be carefully controlled. - *British*

FOIA - Freedom Of Information Act - The Government had passed the FOIA some years before. - *British*

FPNC - Free Personal And Nursing Care (NHS Scotland) - In Scotland, patients have FPNC. - *British*

FPPR - Fit And Proper Persons Requirement For Directors - Before being appointed they had to undergo a FPPR assessment. - *British*

FSA - Food Standards Agency - She worked for the FSA. - *British*

FSRR - Financial And Sustainability Risk Rating - The project was subject to a FSRR before agreement. - *British*

FT - Foundation Trust - The hospital had applied for FT status and were awaiting the outcome of their application. - *British*

FTGA - Foundation Trust Governors' Association - Foundation Trust Governors belong to the FTGA. - *British*

FTN - Foundation Trust Network - They had joined the FTN from which they gained support. - *British*

FY - Foundation Year - The trainee doctor was in his first FY. - *British*

FYFV (ALSO 5YFV) - Five Year Forward View - The plan contained a FYFV which enabled staff to understand the direction the Trust was taking. - *British*

GDC - General Dental Council - They had representatives on the GDC. - *British*

GDS - General Dental Services - The GDS Department was part of oral surgery. - *British*

GMB - British Trade Union - They were members of the GMB union. - *British*

GMC - General Medical Council - The GMC has responsibility for the training of doctors in the UK. - *British*

GMS - General Medical Services - He worked for GMS and enjoyed his role. - *British*

GO - Government Office (Of The English Regions) - He attended a meeting at the GO in London. - *British*

GOC - General Optical Council - They were members of the GOC. - *British*

GOS - General Ophthalmic Services - The hospital provided GOS and was separate from the district hospital. - *British*

GPC - (BMA) General Practitioners Committee - He had been elected to the GPC at the BMA. - *British*

GPES - General Practice Extraction Service - He had been referred to the GPES. - *British*

GPHC - General Pharmaceutical Council - They were member of the GPHC. - *British*

GPS - Government Procurement Services - Buying equipment was subject to the policy of the GPS. - *British*

GPSI OR GPWSI - General Practitioner With A Special Interest - He had elected to become a GPWSI. - *British*

GPSOC - G.P Systems Of Choice - He used the GPSOC for his records. - *British*

GPVTS - General Practice Vocational Training Scheme - It was agreed she should enlist with the GPVTS. - *British*

GSCC - General Social Care Council - The were represented on the GSCC. - *British*

GTAC - Gene Therapy Advisory Committee - She was a member of the GTAC. - *British*

GTN - (UK) Genetic Testing Network - They attended meetings of the GTN. - *British*

GWC - General Whitley Council - The GWC had a responsibility for the pay scales of nurses. - *British*

HA - Health Authority - They were part of the HA area. - *British*

HALO - Hospital Ambulance Liaison Officer - He had been appointed as the HALO the previous June. - *British*

HAN - Hospital At Night (Services) - They had set up a HAN service. - *British*

HAP - Hospital Admission Prevention - The social worker worked hard at HAP when working with old people. - *British*

HARTS - Hazardous Area Response Team - As part of the emergency the HARTS was alerted. - *British*

HASU - Hyper Acute Stroke Unit - The hospital had established a HASU which was well used. - *British*

HAZ - Health Action Zone - It had been designated a HAZ by Public Health. - *British*

HAZMAT - Hazardous Materials - The Health and Safety Officer had listed HAZMATs. - *British*

HB - Health Board - He was a Non-Executive Member of the HB. - *British*

HCA - Healthcare Assistant - She worked on the ward as a HCA. - *British*

HCAI - Healthcare-Associated Infection - Whilst in hospital the elderly man had acquired a HCAI. - *British*

HCHS - Hospital And Community Health Services - They were part of the HCHS and worked well together. - *British*

HCPC - Health And Care Professions Council - They were represented on the HCPC. - *British*

HCW - Health Commission Wales - They had become members of the HCW. - *British*

HDL - Health Department Letter - The hospital had received a HDL. - *British*

HDU - High Dependency Unit - He was so ill, a decision was made to admit him to HDU. - *British*

HEA - Higher Education Academy - The college had become a HEA. - *British*

HEAT - Health Efficiency Access Treatment (Targets - Scotland) - One of the targets in Scotland was HEAT. - *British*

HEE - Health Education England - The training was part of the programme run by HEE. - *British*

HEFCE - Higher Education Funding Council For England - They had obtained funds from the HEFCE. - *British*

HEI - Healthcare Environment Inspectorate (Scotland) - In Scotland they have a HEI. - *British*

HEI - Higher Education Institution - The college was part of a HEI. - *British*

HEMS - Helicopter Emergency Medical Service - The accident was so traumatic and HEMS was alerted to assist. - *British*

HENSE - Health And Education National Strategic Exchange - They were members of the HENSE. - *British*

HES - Hospital Episode Statistics - The administrators had responsibility for keeping HES. - *British*

HFEA - Human Fertilisation And Embryology Authority - The programme was subject to the policies of the HFEA. - *British*

HFMA - Healthcare Financial Management Association - The Director of Finance belonged to the HFMA. - *British*

HGC - Human Genetics Commission - They had representatives who sat on the HGC. - *British*

HIA - Health Impact Assessment - The Public Health Department carried out a HIA in relation to smoking. - *British*

HIEC - Health Innovation And Education Cluster - They belonged to the same HIEC. - *British*

HII - High-Impact Innovation - The new piece of equipment had HII. - *British*

HIMP - Health Improvement And Modernisation Plan - The policy was part of the HIMP. - *British*

HIW - Health Inspectorate Wales - She had been appointed as an Inspector with the HIW. - *British*

HLC - Healthy Living Centre - They had set up a HLC in the neighbourhood. - *British*

HLE - Healthy Life Expectancy - The HLE between areas was significant. - *British*

Abbreviations

HMO - Health Maintenance Organisation (USA) - They were represented on the HMO. - *British*

HONOS - Health Of The Nation Outcome Scales - The Department of Health kept HONOS. - *British*

HOSC - Health Overview And Scrutiny Committee - He had been invited to sit on the HOSC. - *British*

HPA - Health Protection Agency - They had received a visit from the HPA. - *British*

HPMA - Healthcare People Management Association - They were members of the HPMA. - *British*

HPU - Health Protection Unit - He had been appointed to the HPU. - *British*

HQIP - Healthcare Quality Improvement Partnership - They had joined the HQIP for support and advice. - *British*

HRA - Health Research Authority - He had been nominated to become a member of the HRA. - *British*

HRG - Healthcare Resource Group - She was a member of the HRG. - *British*

HSC - Health And Social Care (Northern Ireland) - She had been appointed to the HSC in Northern Ireland. - *British*

HSC - (House Of Commons) Health Select Committee - He was a member of the HSC. - *British*

HSCDS - Health And Social Care Digital Service - They had joined the HSCDS. - *British*

HSCI - Health Service Cost Index - They had looked at the HSCI before giving a price. - *British*

HSCIC - Health And Social Care Information Centre - The department had set up a HSCIC. - *British*

HSCT - Health And Social Care Trust (Northern Ireland) - In Northern Ireland they have HSCTs. - *British*

HSCVF - Health And Social Care Volunteering Fund (Department Of Health) - The Department of Health have a HSCVF. - *British*

HSDU - Hospital Sterilisation And Disinfection Unit - Within the hospital there was a HSDU. - *British*

HSE - Health And Safety Executive - The accident had been referred to the HSE. - *British*

HSE - Health Survey For England - The Department of Health had undertaken a HSE. - *British*

HSIB - Health Care Safety Investigation Branch - The Health and Safety Executive had a HSIB. - *British*

HSJ - Health Service Journal - She liked to read the HSJ which kept her up to date about services. - *British*

HSMR - Hospital Standardised Mortality Ratio - The administrators kept records which demonstrated the HSMR. - *British*

HSR - Health Service Research - The new service had come about following HSR. - *British*

HSRN - Health Services Research Network - They had become members of the HSRN. - *British*

HSS - Health Science Services - The department had a HSS unit. - *British*

HSW - Healthcare Support Worker - He had been appointed to the role of HSW. - *British*

HTA - Health Technology Assessment - They had carried out a HTA of the equipment. - *British*

HUI - Health Utilities Index - The administrators kept the HUI up to date. - *British*

HWB - Health And Wellbeing Board - They were represented on the HWB. - *British*

HWE - Health Watch England - They had signed up to HWE. - *British*

IAA - Information Asset Administrator - She had been appointed to the role of IAA the previous year. - *British*

IAO - Information Asset Owner - The Trust was the IAO. - *British*

IAPT - Improving Access To Psychological Therapies (Programme) - A working group had been set up to look at IAPT. - *British*

IBP - Integrated Business Plan - The policy was part of the IBP for the hospital. - *British*

IC - Information Commissioner - They carried out the policies set by the IC. - *British*

ICAS - Independent Complaints Advocacy Service - The complaint had been referred to ICAS for review. - *British*

ICASE - Integrated Care And Support Exchange - They were members of ICASE from whom they gained support. - *British*

ICD - International Classification Of Diseases - The illness was listed in the ICD. - *British*

ICO - Integrated Care Organisation - They were part of an ICO. - *British*

ICP - Integrated Care Pathway - The psychiatrist used an ICP for the patient. - *British*

ICP - Integrated Care Pilot - They had set up an ICP with joint funding. - *British*

ICR - (NHS) Injury Costs Recovery Scheme - The NHS ran an ICR. - *British*

ICT - Information And Communication Technology - She worked for the ICT Department. - *British*

ICU - Intensive Care Unit - The patient had been admitted to the ICU because he was so ill. - *British*

IDCR - Integrated Digital Care Record - The administrator kept an IDCR for the trust. - *British*

IDVA - Independent Domestic Violence Adviser - The department had appointed an IDVA. - *British*

IG - Information Governance - The Corporate Director was responsible for IG. - *British*

IGTK - Information Governance Toolkit - The Corporate Director had issued an IGTK. - *British*

IHAM - Indicative Hospital Activity Model - The administrator kept an IHAM for the Trust. - *British*

IHI - Institute For Healthcare Improvement - They often went to meetings at the IHI. - *British*

IM&T - Information Management And Technology - There was a department for IM&T. - *British*

IMAS - Interim Management And Support - She had been appointed to provide IMAS. - *British*

IMB - Integrated Management Board - They wanted representation on the IMB. - *British*

IMCA - Independent Mental Capacity Advocate - Whenever he was interviewed, he had an IMCA present. - *British*

IMROC - Implementing Recovery Through Organisational Change(Programme) - The director had presented a paper on IMROC to the board. - *British*

IP - Information Prescriptions - They produced IP as a new way of working. - *British*

IP - Inpatient - The woman was an IP and was under observation. - *British*

IPC - Integrated Personal Commissioning - The young woman operated IPC and was funded to do so by the Trust. - *British*

IPN - Infection Prevention Nurse - She had been appointed as an IPN the previous year. - *British*

IPR - Individual Performance Review - The plan was part of her IPR. - *British*

IPS - Individual Placement And Support - She was planning for his IPS. - *British*

IPSIS - Independent Patient Safety Investigation Service - They offered an IPSIS. - *British*

IQ - NHS Improving Quality - The trust had signed up to the NHS IQ plan. - *British*

IQI - Indicators For Quality Improvement - The department had clearly set out its IQI in its plan. - *British*

IQSP - Improving Quality Supporting Practices Initiatives - The Trust had signed up to IQSP. - *British*

IRP - Independent Reconfiguration Panel - She was a member of the IRP. - *British*

ISA - Independent Safeguarding Authority - They were members of the ISC. - *British*

ISB - Information Standards Board For Health And Social Care - They had sent representatives to the ISB. - *British*

ISCAS - Independent Sector Complaints Adjudication Service - The complaint had been referred to the ISCAS for review. - *British*

ISCG - Informatics Services Commissioning Group - The ISCG were dealing with the contract. - *British*

ISD - Information And Statistics Division (Scotland) - In Scotland, hospitals have an ISD. - *British*

ISMS - Information Security Management System - The administrators managed the ISMS. - *British*

ISN - Information Standard Notice - They had received an ISN. - *British*

ISP - Independent Sector Provider - The residential care home was an ISP. - *British*

IST - Intensive Support Team - The doctor had put in place an IST. - *British*

ISTC - Independent Sector Treatment Centre - The Department of Health had set up several ISTCs. - *British*

IWL - Improving Working Lives - The government had produced a document entitled IWL. - *British*

JAG - Joint Advisory Group - They were members of the JAG looking at community health. - *British*

JCP - Jobcentre Plus - He was attending the JCP, looking for a job. - *British*

JCVI - Joint Committee On Vaccination And Immunisation - They were represented on the JCVI. - *British*

JHWS - Joint Health And Wellbeing Strategy - The Trust had drawn up a JHWS with the local council. - *British*

JIP - Joint Investment Plan - Health and Social Care had a JIP. - *British*

JNC - Joint Negotiating Committee - The wages of staff were agreed at the JNC. - *British*

JSNA - Joint Strategic Needs Assessment - The working party were drawing up a JSNA. - *British*

KLOE - Key Lines Of Enquiry - The KLOE being followed were known to most staff. - *British*

KPI - Key Performance Indicator - The Director of Finance had set out the KPIs for the Senior Management Team. - *British*

KSF - (NHS) Knowledge And Skills Framework - They worked according to the KSF for the NHS. - *British*

LA - Local Authority - The LA were cutting the number of staff they employed which had a knock on effect on health. - *British*

LAA - Local Area Agreement - There was a LAA in place which they all worked to. - *British*

LAC - Looked After Children - The number of LAC had risen dramatically in the past year. - *British*

LAL - Local Authority Letter - They had received a LAL setting out the issues. - *British*

LAS - Locum Appointment For Service - The department had recruited a LAS in order to keep the service going. - *British*

LAT - Locum Appointment For Training - The hospital had recruited a LAT. - *British*

LCFS - Local Counter Fraud Specialist - The post office had received a visit from a LCFS. - *British*

LCP - Liverpool Care Pathway - The Trust had decided to use the LCP. - *British*

LDP - Local Delivery Plan - There was a LDP in place which everyone was aware of. - *British*

LDPB - Local Learning Disability Partnership Board - She was a Non-Executive Member of the LDPB. - *British*

LEP - Local Enterprise Partnership - They were part of the LEP which they found very supportive. - *British*

LES - Local Enhanced Services - The team were part of the LES which had been put in place. - *British*

LETBS - Local Education And Training Boards - There were a number of LETBs within the Deanery area. - *British*

LGA - Local Government Association - The Council was a member of the LGA. - *British*

LHB - Local Health Board (Wales) - The Council was represented on the LHB (Wales). - *British*

LHP - Local Health Plan - The project was part of the LHP. - *British*

LHRP - Local Health Resilience Partnership - They had joined up to the LHRP. - *British*

LHW - Local Health Watch - They attended meetings of the LHW. - *British*

LIFT - NHS Local Improvement Finance Trust - They were part of the LIFT scheme for Trusts. - *British*

LINK - Local Involvement Network - They attended meetings of LINK. - *British*

LIS - Local Implementation Strategy - The plan was part of the LIS. - *British*

LIT - Local Implementation Team - She had been appointed to the LIT the previous year. - *British*

LKS - Library And Knowledge Service - The Trust had a LKS within the hospital. - *British*

LMC - Local Medical Committee - He had been a member of the LMC. - *British*

LOS - Length Of Stay - The ward clerk had written on the notes of the patient: LOS. - *British*

LPN - Local Professional Network - They had joined the LPN from which they gained much support. - *British*

LPSA - Local Public Service Agreement - The Council had put in place a LPSA. - *British*

LQAF - (NHS) Library Quality Assurance Framework - The Trust had a LQAF in place. - *British*

LRF - Local Resilience Forum - She regularly attended the LRF. - *British*

LSCB - Local Safeguarding Children Board - All professions were represented on the LSCB. - *British*

LSP - Local Service Provider - He was a LSP and was regularly allocated contracts for service provision. - *British*

LSP - Local Strategic Partnership - They were members of the LSP. - *British*

LTA - Long-Term Agreement - They had signed an LTA with the local council. - *British*

LTC - Long-Term Conditions - There were a number of LTC in the agreement. - *British*

MAC - Migration Advisory Committee - They had representatives on the MAC. - *British*

MADEL - Medical And Dental Education Levy - They were expected to contribute toward the MADEL. - *British*

MAR - Monthly Activity Return - The administrator completed a MAR. - *British*

MARS - Medical Appraisal And Revalidation System (Wales) - All doctors in Wales underwent a MARS assessment. - *British*

MARS - Mutually Agreed Resignation Scheme - They had operated a MARS for some time. - *British*

MASH - Multi-Agency Safeguarding Hub - The Police Services were represented on the MASH. - *British*

MAU - Medical Assessment Unit - The patient had been admitted to MAU for observation. - *British*

MBC - Metropolitan Borough Council - There are several MBCs in the country. - *British*

MCN - Managed Clinical Network - The department was part of the MCN. - *British*

MCO - Managed Care Organisation - The company was an MCO. - *British*

Abbreviations

MCP - Multi-Specialty Community Provider - The company was an MCP. - *British*

MDA - Medical Device Alert - The MDA was switched on. - *British*

MDHU - Ministry Of Defence Hospital Unit - The barracks had an MDHU located in its grounds. - *British*

MDT - Multi-Disciplinary Team - She was a member of the MDT. - *British*

MDT - Multi-Drug Therapy - The doctor had prescribed MDT for the patient. - *British*

MEE - Medical Education England - The training was part of MEE's brief. - *British*

MERIT - Medical Emergency Response Incident Teams - The doctors had all signed up for MERIT. - *British*

METHANE - (Mnemonic) Major Incident Standby/Declared Exact Location Type Of Incident Hazards Present Or Suspected Access And Egress - Safe Routes To Use Number, Type, Severity Of Casualties Emergency Services Present & Those Required - They had practiced METHANE on a number of occasions and were well aware of their role. - *British*

MFF - Market Forces Factor - The Director of Finance had taken into account the MFF when drawing up the budget. - *British*

MHCT - Mental Health Clustering Tool - They used the MHCT when planning services. - *British*

MHLDDS - Mental Health And Learning Disability Data Set - The administrator had responsibility for the MHLDDS. - *British*

MHMDS - Mental Health Minimum Dataset - The administrator had responsibility for the MHMDS. - *British*

MHRA - Medicines And Healthcare Products Regulatory Agency - The pharmacy was regularly visited by the MHRA. - *British*

MHRT - Mental Health Review Tribunal - The patient's case was reviewed by the MHRT. - *British*

MIP - Managers In Partnership - They worked at being MIP. - *British*

MIU - Minor Injuries Unit - The patient had been referred to the MIU by her G.P. - *British*

MLA - Member Of The Legislative Assembly (Northern Ireland) - He was a member of the Northern Ireland, MLA. - *British*

MLU - Midwife Led Unit - The Maternity Department was an MLU. - *British*

MMC - Modernising Medical Careers - There was a paper which discussed MMC. - *British*

MMH - Maternal Mental Health Alliance - There was a lot of discussion about MMH. - *British*

MMHA - Maternal Mental Health Alliance - They had joined the MMHA. - *British*

MMR - Measles, Mumps, Rubella (Vaccination) - The children all had their MMR injections. - *British*

MOJ - Ministry Of Justice - He worked for the MOJ, and loved his job. - *British*

MPET - Multi-Professional Education And Training - The course was MPET, and very interesting. - *British*

MPIG - Minimum Practice Income Guarantee - The Practice Manager was aware of the MPIG. - *British*

MQI - Measuring For Quality Improvement - The research section were undertaking an MQI audit. - *British*

MRC - Medical Research Council - He worked for the MRC and really enjoyed his job. - *British*

MRI - Magnetic Resonance Imaging - The G.P had referred her for an MRI scan. - *British*

MRSA - Methicillin-Resistant Staphylococcus Aureus - The elderly man had contracted MRSA whilst in hospital. - *British*

MSC - Modernising Scientific Careers - The working group had been looking at MSC as part of their brief. - *British*

MSP - Member Of The Scottish Parliament - She was an MSP and well thought of by her constituents. - *British*

MST - Multi-Systemic Therapy - He had been prescribed MST by his doctor. - *British*

MTC - Major Trauma Centre - The hospital had recently upgraded its MTC. - *British*

MTS - (NHS) Management Training Scheme - The NHS have a MTS which you can apply for. - *British*

MUR - Medicines Use Review - The hospital had decided to undertake an MUR to try to cut costs. - *British*

MUS - Medically Unexplained Symptoms - The patient had MUS and the doctors were puzzled. - *British*

MWIA - Mental Well-Being Impact Assessment - They had undertaken an MWIA as part of the procedure. - *British*

N3 - New National Network - There was an N3 in place at the time. - *British*

NA - Nurse Assistant - She had been employed as an NA and enjoyed her job. - *British*

NAG - National Advisory Group - They had representatives on the NAG. - *British*

NAGCAE - National Advisory Group On Clinical Audit And Enquiries - She was a member of the NAGCAE. - *British*

NAMPS - National Association Of Medical Personnel Specialists - They belonged to NAMPS which gave them support. - *British*

NAO - National Audit Office - The NAO would visit the Treasury from time to time to audit the records. - *British*

NAPC - National Association Of Primary Care - They belonged to NAPC. - *British*

NARU - National Ambulance Resilience Unit - They worked as part of the NARU. - *British*

NAW - National Assembly For Wales - He was a member of NAW. - *British*

NBAP - National Booked Admissions Programme - Patients now had access to the NBAP. - *British*

NBI - National Beds Inquiry - The Government had set up an NBI. - *British*

NCAF - National Clinical Audit Forum - They were members of NCAF from which they gained much advice. - *British*

NCAPOP - National Clinical Audit And Patients Outcomes Programme - The Audit Department used NCAPOP as their guideline. - *British*

NCAS - National Clinical Assessment Service - It was part of NCAS and very helpful. - *British*

NCASP - National Clinical Audit Support Programme - NCASP offered advice to them if needed. - *British*

NCD - National Clinical Director - He worked at the Department of Health as a NCD. - *British*

NCE - National Confidential Enquiry Into Patient Outcome And Death - The failure to provide services was part of an NCE. - *British*

NCEPOD - National Confidential Enquiry Into Patient Outcome And Death - The patient's death was the subject of a review by an NCEPOD. - *British*

NCG - National Commissioning Group - The service was part of an NCG contract. - *British*

NCIN - National Cancer Intelligence Network - They were members of the NCIN. - *British*

NCRS - National Cancer Registry Service - They had elected to be part of the NCRS. - *British*

NCVO - National Council For Voluntary Organisations - She had been asked to become a member of the NCVO. - *British*

NDA - National Diabetes Audit - The hospital had taken part in the NDA. - *British*

NDIS - National Diabetes Information Service - The Trust had contributed to the NDIS. - *British*

NDPB - Non-Departmental Public Body - The organisation was an NDPB and outside of the department. - *British*

Abbreviations

NEAT - New And Emerging Applications Of Technology - The I.T. Department was always looking at NEAT. - *British*

NED - Non-Executive Director - He was a NED on the Trust Board. - *British*

NEF - New Economics Foundation - They were members of the NEF. - *British*

NES - National Enhanced Services - They were part of NES. - *British*

NES - NHS Education For Scotland - She was a member of the NES. - *British*

NEWS - National Early Warning Score - They had learnt to use NEWS to alert them to disaster. - *British*

NGMS - New General Medical Services (Contract) - The Government had issued an NGMS. - *British*

NHSE - NHS Employers - The Trust was represented at the NHSE. - *British*

NHSE - NHS England - NHSE has responsibility for the provision of Health Services in England. - *British*

NHSI - NHS Institute For Innovation And Improvement - He worked at NHSI and enjoyed the job. - *British*

NHSIC - NHS Information Centre - If necessary they get help from the NHSIC. - *British*

NHSLA - NHS Litigation Authority - When appropriate they sought the help of NHSLA. - *British*

NHSOF - NHS Outcomes Framework - It was part of the NHSOF. - *British*

NHSPS - NHS Pension Scheme - She was a member of the NHSPS. - *British*

NHSRA - NHS Registration Authority - They had representatives on the NHSRA. - *British*

NHST - NHS Trust - She worked for the local NHST. - *British*

NIA - Northern Ireland Assembly - He was a member of the NIA. - *British*

NIAO - Northern Ireland Audit Office - He worked for the NIAO. - *British*

NIC - National Insurance Contribution - All employees were required to make NICs. - *British*

NIC - (NHS) National Innovation Centre - They could submit ideas to the NIC. - *British*

NICE - National Institute For Health And Care Excellence - NICE approve all new medicines before their use. - *British*

NIGB - National Information Governance Board - He was a member of the NIGB. - *British*

NIHR - National Institute For Health Research - The NIHR awards grants to trainee doctors. - *British*

NIO - Northern Ireland Office - She was a member of the NIO. - *British*

NJR - National Joint Registry - They had contributed to the NJR. - *British*

NLIAH - National Leadership And Innovation Agency For Healthcare (Wales) - They had representatives on the NLIAH. - *British*

NLOP - National Local Ownership Programme - They had contributed to the NLOP. - *British*

NLPH - National Library For Public Health - They sometimes went to the NLPH to access reading material for their course. - *British*

NMC - Nursing And Midwifery Council - They were members of the NMC. - *British*

NMS - New Medicine Service - This was a NMS and much appreciated. - *British*

NNCPS - National Network Of Clinical Procurement Specialists - They belonged to the NNCPS. - *British*

NNU - Neonatal Unit - The baby had been taken to the NNU for care. - *British*

NOF - New Opportunities Fund - They had obtained funds from the NOF. - *British*

NOG - National Oversight Group (For High-Security Hospitals) - They were represented on the NOG for high security hospitals. - *British*

NPDG - National Pals Development Group - She was a member of the NPDG. - *British*

NPFIT - National Programme For It (In The NHS) - They were part of the NPFIT. - *British*

NPG - National Priorities Guidance - The Department of Health had issued NPG. - *British*

NPSA - National Patient Safety Agency - They had visits from the NPSA from time to time. - *British*

NQB - National Quality Board - They were represented on the NQB. - *British*

NQR - National Quality Requirement - The standard was an NQR which they needed to adhere to. - *British*

NRAC - NHS Scotland Resource Allocation Committee - She was a member of the NRAC in Scotland. - *British*

NRCI - National Reference Cost Index - She found the information on the NRCI. - *British*

NRES - National Research Ethics Service - They obtained the information from the NRES. - *British*

NRLS - National Reporting And Learning Service - They often asked for advice from the NRLS. - *British*

NRLS - National Reporting And Learning System - They had used the NRLS for information. - *British*

NRT - Nicotine Replacement Therapy - Her G.P. had recommended NRT. - *British*

NSCG - National Specialist Commissioning Group - They had representatives on the NSCG. - *British*

NSF - National Service Framework - Thy worked according to the NSF. - *British*

NSR - Next Stage Review - It was time for the NSR. - *British*

NSRC - National Schedule Of Reference Costs - The Director of Finance had a copy of the NSRC. - *British*

NSS - National Services Scotland - It was part of the NSS. - *British*

NTA - National Treatment Agency (For Substance Misuse) - They often sought advice from the NTA. - *British*

NTAC - NHS Technology Adoption Centre - They had received assistance from the NTAC. - *British*

NTAG - National Tariff Advisory Group (NHS England) - They had sought advice from NTAG. - *British*

NTD - National Tariff Document - It was an NTD. - *British*

NTDA - NHS Trust Development Authority - They were members of the NTDA. - *British*

NTO - National Training Organisation - They had representatives on the NTO. - *British*

NWP - (NHS) National Workforce Projects - The Director of Human Resources sought advice from the NWP. - *British*

OBC - Outline Business Case - They had been asked to make an OBC for the new project. - *British*

OCPA - Office Of The Commissioner For Public Appointments - Her appointment was subject to scrutiny from the OCPA. - *British*

OCS - Office For Civil Society - They had sought support from the OCS. - *British*

ODP - Operating Department Practitioner - He was employed as an ODP. - *British*

OFMDFM - Office Of The First Minister & Deputy First Minister (Northern Ireland) - She had been elected to the OFMDFM. - *British*

OGC - Office Of Government Commerce - They had been to a meeting at the OGC. - *British*

OHE - Office Of Health Economics - They had attended a meeting at the OHE. - *British*

OJEU - Official Journal Of The European Union - They contributed to the OJEU and found this interesting. - *British*

OLS - Office For Life Sciences - They were going to a meeting at the OLS. - *British*

OMB - Operational Management Board - The OMB met every week. - *British*

ONS - Office For National Statistics - The ONS collected data on Public Health issues. - *British*

OOH - Out Of Hours - Their Contract contained a clause requiring them to work OOH. - *British*

OP - Outpatient - He was an OP at the local hospital. - *British*

OPATT - Outpatient Attendance - The administrator recorded the OPATT. - *British*

OPROC - Outpatient Procedure - It was part of the OPROC. - *British*

ORSA - Organisational Readiness Self Assessment - They had undertaken an ORSA which demonstrated they still had some work to do. - *British*

OSC - (Local Authority) Overview And Scrutiny Committee - The Local Authority OSC looked at all decisions made by the local Trust. - *British*

OSCHR - Office For Strategic Coordination Of Health Research - He had been seconded to the OSCHR. - *British*

OT - Occupational Therapist/Therapy - She worked as an OT for the local hospital trust. - *British*

OTC - Over-The-Counter - You can buy lots of OTC remedies at the local pharmacy. - *British*

PA - Physician Assistant - He had been employed as a PA at the local hospital. - *British*

PA - Programmed Activity - It was part of the PA for the department. - *British*

PAB - Professional Advisory Board - The Trust was represented on the PAB. - *British*

PAC - (House Of Commons) Public Accounts Committee - He had been nominated for the PAC in the House of Commons. - *British*

PACS - Picture Archiving And Communications System - The Radiology Department used PACs to store their images. - *British*

PACS - Primary And Acute Care System - The surgery was part of the PACS. - *British*

PAF - Performance Assessment Framework - It was part of the PAF for the department. - *British*

PALS - Patient Advice And Liaison Service - Every hospital will have a PALS for patients to register their concerns. - *British*

PAM - Patient Activation Measure - The administrators used PAM. - *British*

PAR - Patient At Risk - He was known to be a PAR and needed to be closely monitored. - *British*

PAS - Patient Administration System - The office used PAS to register patients. - *British*

PASLU - (Nice) Patient Access Scheme Liaison Unit - There is a PASLU at NICE. - *British*

PASS - Patient Advice And Support Service (Scotland) - In Scotland there is a PASS. - *British*

PBC - Practice-Based Commissioning - The G.Ps had a scheme for PBC. - *British*

PBR - Payment By Results - The finance director had set up a scheme for PBR. - *British*

PCC - Police And Crime Commissioner - She had been appointed PCC the previous April. - *British*

PCIP - Primary Care Investment Plan - The scheme was part of the PCIP. - *British*

PCO - Primary Care Organisation - The surgery was part of the PCO. - *British*

PCS - Productive Community Services - Health Visiting was thought of as being a PCS. - *British*

PCT - Primary Care Trust - The local PCT has now been disbanded. - *British*

PCTPS - Primary Care Trust-Provided Services - There are no longer any PCTPS. - *British*

PDA - Patient Decision Aid - The information leaflet was intended as a PDA. - *British*

PDC - Public Dividend Capital - The money was part of the PDC. - *British*

PDD - Predicted Date Of Discharge - The doctor had written the PDD on the notes. - *British*

PDP - Personal Development Plan - She had drawn up her PDP with her manager. - *British*

PEAT - Patient Environment Action Team - The PEAT made regular visits to the hospital. - *British*

PEC - Professional Executive Committee (Of PCT) - The PEC no longer exists following the demise of the PCT. - *British*

PFI - Private Finance Initiative - The building of the new hospital was part of the PFI . - *British*

PHB - Personal Health Budget - The patient had a PHB with which to purchase their own services. - *British*

PHE - Public Health England - He had been appointed to PHE the previous year. - *British*

PHOF - Public Health Outcomes Framework - The target was part of the PHOF. - *British*

PHWSI - Pharmacist With Special Interest - He had qualified as a PHWSI. - *British*

PICD - Procurement, Investment And Commercial Division (DH) - There is a PICD at the Department of Health. - *British*

PICU - Psychiatric Intensive Care Unit - The patient was very poorly and had been admitted to PICU. - *British*

PID - Project Initiation Document - They had drafted a PID for consultation. - *British*

PIG - Policy Implementation Guide - The PIG had been circulated to all staff. - *British*

PII - Patient/ Person Identifiable Information - They had organised their records so that PII was easily found. - *British*

PIMHS - Parent And Infant Mental Health Service - The unit was part of the PIMHS. - *British*

PIMHS - Perinatal And Infant Mental Health Service - The unit was part of the PIMHS. - *British*

PIP - Personal Independence Payment - The patient had been given a PIP to fund services. - *British*

PLACE - Patient-Led Assessments Of The Care Environment - They had used a PLACE survey to ascertain how clean the ward was. - *British*

PLC - Pigmented Lesion Clinic - His G.P. had referred him to the PLC for treatment. - *British*

PLIC - Patient-Level Information And Costing - The administrator kept a record of the PLIC. - *British*

P-MERIT - Paramedic Medical Emergency Response Incident Teams - He was a member of the P-MERIT and knew he would be asked to attend traumatic incidents. - *British*

PMHL - Paediatric Mental Health Liaison - CAMHS undertook PMHL with other departments. - *British*

PMHW - Productive Mental Health Ward - He had been admitted to a PMHW. - *British*

PMI - Private Medical Insurance - The company had provided PMI for all its employees. - *British*

PMS - Personal Medical Services - They were able to offer PMS as part of the scheme. - *British*

PNA - Pharmaceutical Needs Assessment - The pharmacy had undertaken a PNA of their service. - *British*

POCT - Point Of Care Testing - The team were reviewing POCT for its efficiency. - *British*

POET - Personal Budgets Outcomes And Evaluation Tool - The Director of Finance used a POET to measure the value of the service. - *British*

POM - Prescription-Only Medicines - The pharmacy had a number of POM for patients. - *British*

POPP - Partnerships For Older People Project - The scheme was part of the POPP. - *British*

POSHH - Partnership For Occupational Safety And Health In Healthcare - They belonged to POSHH, which they found very supportive. - *British*

Abbreviations

Abbreviations

PP - Paramedic Practitioner - He was appointed as a PP just a month ago. - *British*

PPC - (Prescription) Pre-Payment Certificate - She had obtained a PPC for her medication. - *British*

PPE - Patient And Public Engagement - It was part of the PPE programme. - *British*

PPF - Priorities And Planning Framework - The Chief Executive had responsibility for the PPF. - *British*

PPG - Patient Participation Group - She was a member of the PPG. - *British*

PPI - Patient And Public Involvement - PPI is part of the Governance of hospital trusts. - *British*

PPIC - Private Patient Income Cap - The Director of Finance was aware of the PPIC. - *British*

PPIF - Patient And Public Involvement Forum - She was a member of the PPIF. - *British*

PPO - Preferred Provider Organisation - The company was on the list of PPOs. - *British*

PPP - Public and Private Partnership - The new hospital had been built with PPP. - *British*

PPRS - Pharmaceutical Price Regulation Scheme - The pharmacy was subject to the PPRS. - *British*

PPU - Private Patient Units - The Trust had a number of PPUs within the hospital. - *British*

PPV - Patient And Public Voice - The Trust was concerned that it listened to the PPV. - *British*

PRB - Pay Review Body - The increase was subject to scrutiny by the PRB. - *British*

PRCC - Principles And Rules For Cooperation And Competition - The Trust had approved its PRCC at a previous board. - *British*

PREM - Patient Reported Experience Measure - They used PREM in their planning for services. - *British*

PRF - Patient Report Form - The nursing staff gave each patient a PRF. - *British*

PROM - Patient-Reported Outcome Measure - The PROM was used to measure outcomes for patients. - *British*

PRP - Policy Research Programme - The research section used the PRP when writing policy documents. - *British*

PRSB - Professional Record Standards Body - The Trust had consulted the PRSB when developing their files. - *British*

PS - Protected Services - Some services are thought of as PS. - *British*

PSA - Professional Standards Authority For Health And Social Care - He had been referred to the PSA following his prosecution. - *British*

PSA - Public Service Agreement - They had in place a PSA with the local authority. - *British*

PSD - Patient Specific Direction - The doctor had written the PSD on the patient's notes. - *British*

PSED - Public Sector Equality Duty - All local authorities have a PSED. - *British*

PSNC - Pharmaceutical Services Negotiating Committee - The Trust was represented on the PSNC. - *British*

PSS - Personal Social Services - He was the director of PSS for the local authority. - *British*

PTL - Patient Tracking List - The administrators used a PTL for patients. - *British*

PTS - Patient Transport Service - The Emergency Department arranged for the PTS to take the patient home. - *British*

PWP - Psychological Wellbeing Practitioner - He had been appointed to the post of PWP the previous year. - *British*

PYLL - Potential Years Of Life Lost - The Research Department estimated the PYLL through smoking. - *British*

QA - Quality Assurance - The Trust had a scheme of QA in place. - *British*

QGAF - Quality Governance Assurance Framework - The Trust operated to a QGAF. - *British*

QIA - Quality Impact Assessment - The service had been subject to a QIA in the past six months. - *British*

QIPP - Quality Innovation Productivity Prevention - The hospital staff were aware of the importance of QIPP in their every day work. - *British*

QIS - NHS Quality Improvement Scotland - QIS was well known to staff. - *British*

QMAS - Quality Management And Analysis System - The Trust operated a QMAS to measure the impact of their services. - *British*

QOF - Quality And Outcomes Framework - The Department worked to a QOF. - *British*

QQUIP - Quest For Quality And Improved Performance - The Trust was always pursuing a QQUIP. - *British*

QSG - Quality Surveillance Group - She was a member of the QSG. - *British*

RAB - Resource Accounting And Budgeting - The Director of Finance was accountable for RAB. - *British*

RAID - Rapid Assessment, Interface And Discharge - The Emergency Department worked to a policy of RAID. - *British*

RAT - Rapid Assessment And Treatment - The Emergency Department undertook RAT. - *British*

RC - Reference Cost - The Finance Department were aware of the RC. - *British*

RCA - Root Cause Analysis - They had carried out RCA of the problem. - *British*

RCD - Research Capacity Development - Their RCD needed an increase. - *British*

RCGP - Royal College Of General Practitioners - He attended meetings at the RCGP on a monthly basis. - *British*

RCM - Royal College Of Midwives - She sat on several committees at the RCM. - *British*

RCN - Royal College Of Nursing - She was registered with the RCN. - *British*

RCOA - Royal College Of Anaesthetists - He regularly went to meetings at the RCOA. - *British*

RCP - Royal College Of Physicians - She regularly went to meetings at the RCP. - *British*

RCPE - Royal College Of Physicians Of Edinburgh - In Scotland there is an RCPE. - *British*

RCPSG - Royal College Of Physicians And Surgeons Of Glasgow - In Scotland there is an RCPSG. - *British*

RCS - Royal College Of Surgeons Of Edinburgh - He sat on several committees at the RCS. - *British*

RCSE - Royal College Of Surgeons Of Edinburgh - In Scotland there is an RCSE. - *British*

RCSLT - Royal College Of Speech And Language Therapists - Their training was overseen by the RCSLT. - *British*

RCT - Randomised Controlled Trial - The medication was part of an RCT. - *British*

RDAG - Rare Diseases Advisory Group - She had been seconded to the RDAG. - *British*

REF - Research And Excellence Framework - The scheme was part of the REF. - *British*

RFID - Radio Frequency Identification - They needed to access RFID before starting. - *British*

RGH - Rural General Hospital (NHS Scotland) - In Scotland they had RGHs. - *British*

RMN - Registered Mental Health Nurse - She had qualified as an RMN a long time ago. - *British*

RN - Registered Nurse - She had qualified as an RN the year before. - *British*

RO - Responsible Officer - He became the RO for the Trust. - *British*

ROCR - Review Of Central Returns - The administrator undertook an ROCR. - *British*

RPA - Radiation Protection Adviser Service - They had sought advice from the RPA regarding the new service. - *British*

RRG - Rapid Reference Group - They had referred the matter to the RRG for advice. - *British*

RRR - Rapid Responsive Review - They had undertaken an RRR of the issue. - *British*

RRR - Recovery, Rehabilitation, And Reablement (Model) - They had worked to the RRR model. - *British*

RST - (NHS) Revalidation Support Team - They had applied to the RST for advice. - *British*

RTA - Road Traffic Accident - The woman had been involved in an RTA and needed urgent treatment. - *British*

RTT - Referral To Treatment - The Doctor had used RTT for the patient. - *British*

SACDA - Scottish Advisory Committee On Distinction Awards - The decision on prizes would be made by SACDA. - *British*

SAFA - Safeguarding Adults From Abuse - They had set up a SAFA group which was inter-disciplinary. - *British*

SAM - Society For Acute Medicine - The SAM often held training sessions. - *British*

SAR - Subject Access Request - The administrator needed to get a SAR approved before proceeding. - *British*

SARS - Severe Acute Respiratory Syndrome - The boy was suffering from SARS and needed urgent treatment. - *British*

SAS - Scottish Ambulance Service - He worked for SAS. - *British*

SAS - Staff And Associated Specialist (Doctors) - He worked as an SAS for the Trust. - *British*

SASM - Scottish Audit Of Surgical Mortality - Hospitals are required to undertake SASM in Scotland. - *British*

SAU - Surgical Assessment Unit - He worked in the SAU and enjoyed the variety of patients. - *British*

SBS - (NHS) Shared Business Services - Several Trusts had adopted SBS to cut costs. - *British*

SCCI - Standardisation Committee For Care Information - She was a member of SCCI and enjoyed the work. - *British*

SCCR - Single Community Care Record - He had an SCCR which the administrator kept. - *British*

SCG - Specialised Commissioning Group - The department had an SCG for dealing with these contracts. - *British*

SCI - Scottish Care Information - All Health Organisations contributed to the SCI. - *British*

SCIE - Social Care Institute For Excellence - The SCIE often published papers which were very helpful. - *British*

SCN - Strategic Clinical Network - They were part of the SCN. - *British*

SCR - Summary Care Record - The information was noted on the patient's SCR. - *British*

SCS - Senior Civil Servants - They were employed as SCS at the Ministry. - *British*

SCVO - Scottish Council For Voluntary Organisations - In Scotland there is a SCVO. - *British*

SDO - Service Delivery And Organisation - She had overall responsibility for SDO. - *British*

SDU - (NHS) Sustainable Development Unit - She had been seconded to the SDU for six months. - *British*

SDU - Sterilisation And Disinfection Unit - Every ward has access to a SDU. - *British*

SEIF - Social Enterprise Investment Fund - They had obtained funding from SEIF. - *British*

SEN - Special Educational Need - The boy had been assessed as SEN and needed extra support. - *British*

SEQOHS - Safe Effective Quality Occupational Health Service - She had been referred to SEQOHS for information. - *British*

SES - Single Equality Scheme (Department Of Health) - The Department of Health has an SES. - *British*

SFA - Statement Of Fees And Allowances - The director of finance had developed a SFA. - *British*

SFC - Skills For Care - The college offered an SFC course. - *British*

SFH - Skills For Health - The college offered an SFH course. - *British*

SGHD - Scottish Government Health Directorates - There are a number of SGHD. - *British*

SHA - Strategic Health Authority (And Special Health Authority) - There used to be SHAs but these no longer exist. - *British*

SHMI - Summary Hospital Mortality Indicator - The clinical director was aware of the hospital's SHMI. - *British*

SHMI - Summary Hospital-Level Mortality Indicator - The clinical director was aware of the hospital's SHMI. - *British*

SHO - Senior House Officer - He worked as an SHO for the hospital. - *British*

SHOW - Scottish Health On The Web - Services were posted on SHOW for information. - *British*

SHRINE - Strategic Human Resources Information Network - The director of personnel attended the SHRINE. - *British*

SI - Serious Incident - There had been an SI and it was being investigated. - *British*

SID - Senior Independent Director - He was SID for the Trust. - *British*

SIGN - Scottish Intercollegiate Guidelines Network - They sought advice from SIGN. - *British*

SIRI - Serious Incident Requiring Investigation - It was a SIRI and the chief executive had become involved. - *British*

SIRO - Senior Information Risk Owner - The corporate director was also the SIRO. - *British*

SLA - Service Level Agreement - They had put in place a SLA for the scheme. - *British*

SLR - Service-Line Reporting - The administrator knew the SLR for the project. - *British*

SLT - Speech And Language Therapy - She had been referred for SLT. - *British*

SMAC - Standing Medical Advisory Committee - They were represented on the SMAC. - *British*

SMC - Scottish Medicines Consortium - In Scotland there is a SMC. - *British*

SMDU - Strategic Market Development Unit (Department Of Health) - The Department of Health has a SMDU. - *British*

SMR - Standardised Mortality Ratio - The trust kept a record of its SMR. - *British*

SOC - Strategic Outline Case - The medical director made a SOC for the project. - *British*

SOCF - Statement Of Cash Flows - The Director of Finance drew up a SOCF. - *British*

SOFP - Statement Of Financial Position - The director of finance drew up a SOFP. - *British*

SOR - Society Of Radiographers - The trust nominated staff to attend meetings at the SOR. - *British*

SPA - Single Point Of Access - There was a SPA for the project. - *British*

SPA - Special Programmed Activity - There was a lot of SPA involved in the Scheme. - *British*

SPF - Social Partnership Forum - They were members of the SPF. - *British*

SPG - Strategic Planning Group - She sat on the SPG. - *British*

SPI - Scientific Pandemic Influenza Advisory Committee - They were members of the SPI. - *British*

SPMS - Specialist Provider Of Medical Services - The company was a SPAMS. - *British*

SPN - Special Patient Notes - They had kept SPN - *British*

SPOR - Single Point Of Referral - The plan was to have a SPOR. - *British*

SRB - Single Regeneration Budget - The funding had come from the SRB. - *British*

SRG - System Resilience Group - They were members of the SRG. - *British*

SRO - Senior Responsible Officer - She was the SRO for the project. - *British*

SRP - Structural Reform Plan - The idea was part of the SRP for the trust. - *British*

SSA - Standard Spending Assessment - The finance director oversaw the SSA for the trust. - *British*

SSC - Shared Service Centre - They had a SSC with Social Care Services. - *British*

SSCIF - Specialised Services Commissioning Innovation Fund - They had obtained funding from the SSCIF. - *British*

SSEM - Short Stay Emergency Tariff - The cost was assessed against the SSEM. - *British*

SSRB - Senior Salaries Review Body - The matter had been referred to the SSRB. - *British*

ST&T - Scientific, Therapeutic And Technical (Staff) - They had been appointed to the ST&T grade. - *British*

STF - Sustainability And Transformation Fund - They had obtained resources from the STF. - *British*

STP - Sustainability And Transformation Plan - It was part of the STP. - *British*

SUI - Serious Untoward Incident - It had been recorded as an SUI and would need to be investigated. - *British*

SUS - Secondary Uses Service - It was part of the SUS. - *British*

SUSARS - Suspected Unexpected Serious Adverse Reactions - The doctor decided the patient was suffering from SUSARS. - *British*

TAMHS - Targeted Mental Health In Schools - They ran a programme of TAMHS. - *British*

TARN - Trauma Audit And Research Network - They belonged to the TARN, which they found helpful. - *British*

TCP - Transforming Care Partnership - They had entered into the TCP with other trusts. - *British*

TDA - Trust Development Authority - They were part of the TDA. - *British*

TEF - NHS Transitional Executive Forum - They belonged to the TEF. - *British*

TFA - Tripartite Formal Agreement - They had a TFA in place. - *British*

TLAP - Think Local Act Personal (Partnership) - They had joined the TLAP partnership and found it very helpful. - *British*

TOM - Therapy Outcome Measure - They had put TOMs in place in order to evaluate their work. - *British*

TSA - Trust Special Administrator - He was the TSA. - *British*

TUC - Trades Union Congress - They were members of the TUC. - *British*

TUPE - Transfer Of Undertakings (Protection Of Employment) Regulations 1981 - Upon re-organisation her post had been subject to TUPE. - *British*

UCB - Urgent Care Board - There was a UCB in place to oversee the work. - *British*

UCC - Urgent Care Centre - They had set up a UCC to treat patients quickly. - *British*

UECN - Urgent And Emergency Care Network - They were members of the UECN. - *British*

UKBA - UK Border Agency - The UKBA had been given increased funding by the Home Office. - *British*

UKCC - UK Cochrane Centre - They had attended meetings at the UKCC. - *British*

UKCRC - UK Clinical Research Collaboration - They had been involved with UKCRC. - *British*

UKCRN - UK Clinical Research Network - They were part of the UKCRN from which they gained much support. - *British*

ULR - Union Learning Representative - He was employed as a ULR and was enjoying the work. - *British*

UPR - Unsustainable Provider Regime - They had decided that this was part of an UPR and needed to be closed. - *British*

USAR - Urban Search And Rescue - They had signed up to the USAR Service and were deployed at traumatic events. - *British*

VCS - Voluntary And Community Sector - They were working well with the VCS to provide services. - *British*

VFM - Value For Money - The director of finance was concerned the trust was getting VFM. - *British*

VSM - Very Senior Managers - The corporate director was part of the VSM Group. - *British*

VTE - Venous Thromboembolism - The patient was diagnosed as suffering from VTE. - *British*

WAG - Welsh Assembly Government - He had been appointed to the WAG the previous year. - *British*

WAO - Wales Audit Office - The WAO would visit from time to time, to review the financial affairs of the authority. - *British*

WBS - Welsh Blood Service - She worked for the WBS. - *British*

WHO - World Health Organization - The WHO often organised international conferences. - *British*

WIC - Walk In Centre - They had established a WIC in the middle of town. - *British*

WORD - Wales Office Of Research And Development For Health And Social Care - She had been seconded to WORD for a one year placement. - *British*

WPF - Welsh Partnership Forum - They were members of the WPF. - *British*

WRAPS - Wellness Recovery Action Plans - They had drawn up WRAPS for the patients. - *British*

WRES - Workforce Race Equality Standard - The trust had a WRES in place which all staff were aware of when recruiting. - *British*

WRT - Workforce Review Team - The director of personnel chaired a WRT. - *British*

WTD - Working-Time Directive - The doctors were subject to WTD. - *British*

WTE - Whole Time Equivalent - The trust employed a number of WTE doctors. - *British*

WTR - Working Time Regulations - The doctors were subject to WTR. - *British*

WVJIP - Winterbourne View Joint Improvement Programme - Following the investigation they had drawn up a WVJIP. - *British*

LOL - Acronym: Laugh out loud - "I overslept, so I missed the bus, lol," said Finn. - *American*

YOLO - Acronym: You only live once - I'm going to go to that concert even though my Mum disapproves, YOLO! - *American*

AA - Alcoholics Anonymous, a support group for alcoholics - The support group, AA, offers help to those who may feel that their drinking of alcohol has become a problem. - *British*

B.Y.O.B. - An acroynm for: Bring your own bottle - The couple were having a B.Y.O.B party at the weekend and expected everyone to come with a nice bottle of something alcoholic to drink. - *British*

BYOB - Acronym for: Bring your own beer - BYOB parties are quite the thing. - *British*

BO - Body odour - Alan stinks, he has really bad BO, I wish he would take a bath! - *British*

ISBN - International Standard Book Number - ISBN is the reference number given to each book published. - *British*

MS - Manuscript - The MS had gone off to the publishers now, so all they could do was wait to see if the book would be successful with the public. - *British*

A.S.A.P - As soon as possible - Zoe, can you call me back A.S.A.P - *America/British*

ASAP - As Soon As Possible - We add ASAP to our communications to give the receiver an indication of the urgency with which we wish for them to act. - *British*

B.T.W. - By the way - Toni had to leave early B.T.W. - *America/British*

C.U. - Phonetic- See you, used as a goodbye - C.U later, Bro. - *America/British*

F.Y.I. - For your information - F.Y.I. Les had to leave early. - *America/British*

FYI - For Your Information - We use FYI in emails to colleagues, to bring them up- to-date with information. - *British*

Abbreviations

Abbreviations

I.M.H.O - In my humble opinion / in my honest opinion - Eve is annoying I.M.H.O. - *America/British*

N.P. - No problem - I will get the report done today, N.P. - *America/British*

N/A - Not applicable - Some of the sections on the form were marked N/A. - *British*

P.S. - Means "post script", added information, at the end of a letter, for example - At the end of a letter, people will often include a P.S. to include an extra thought - *British*

PC - Politically Correct - The older generation do not always say things that are PC in this day and age. - *British*

PPS - Post, Post Script - PPS is used at the end of a note, email or letter when PS has already been used but you realise that you still need to add another piece of information. - *British*

PS - Post Script, as previously described - The acronym PS is added at the end of a note, email or letter, when the writer has forgotten to include something. For example, PS, I love you! - *British*

Q&A - Question and Answer - The politican was reluctant to participate in the Q&A session. - *British*

R - Shorthand spelling of 'are' - R u coming out tonight? - *America/British*

R.S.V.P. - Please respond. (Comes from the French phrase: répondez, s'il-vous plait) - The acronym R.S.V.P is French for repond, if you please: 'Repondez s'il vous plait'. It is often used on invitations to parties and special events, requesting a reply of attendance of 'yes or no', from the recipient. - *British*

R.U. - Phonetic- Are you? - R u coming out tonight? - *America/British*

STFU - Acronym for the swearing phrase: shut the fuck up - Jenny, why don't you STFU? - *America/British*

TBA - To be announced - The date for the next meeting is TBA. - *British*

TBC - To be confirmed - The dates for our next meeting are TBC. - *British*

TBD - To be determined - The date for the next meeting is TBD. - *British*

TBH - To be honest - You annoy me, TBH! - *America/British*

TEAM - Together Everyone Achieves More - Motivational speakers often use the acronym-TEAM- during their speeches. - *British*

TGIF - Thank God It's Friday - TGIF, what a terrible week it has been! - *British*

THX - Shorthand spelling of thanks - this can be combined into kthx (ok, thanks), plzkthx (please, ok, thanks), and kthxbye (ok, thanks, goodbye) - Thx, John. - *America/British*

TIA - Thanks in advance - TIA for your input today at the meeting. - *British*

TIP - To insure promptness - The item is required TIP. - *British*

U - A shorthand, phonetic spelling of 'you' - I love u. - *America/British*

UR - A shorthand, phonetic spelling of 'you're/ you are' - Jim ur annoying. - *America/British*

CEO - Chief Executive Officer - The CEO of Apple Inc. is currently Tim Cook. - *British*

CFO - Chief Financial Officer - The CFO is the chief financial officer for a company, organisation or institution, and is responsible for all of the financial affairs of said place. - *British*

CMO - Chief Marketing Officer - The CMO is the person in an organisation responsible for the creation, communication and deliverance of offerings of value to their customers, clients and business partners. - *British*

EVP - Executive Vice President - The ECV is ranked third when there is an heirachy of vice presidents in a company or organisation; the title comes third from top, under: Vice President (2); and Executive Officer (1). - *British*

GM - General Manager - GMs of some supermarkets can earn around £40,000 per annum. - *British*

MD - Managing Director - The MD of a company is the most senior corporate officer who is in charge of: managing, leading and organising, the whole organisation. - *British*

PA - Personal Assistant - Most top executives will have their own PA to help them. - *British*

PR - Public Relations - There are lots of PR firms in London. - *British*

SVP - Senior Vice President - The SVP is ranked fourth when there is an heirachy of vice presidents in a company or organisation; the title comes fourth from top, under: Executive Vice President (3); Vice President (2); Executive Officer (1). - *British*

VP - Vice President - The VP is ranked second when there is an heirachy of vice presidents in a company or organisation; the title comes second from top under: Executive Officer (1). - *British*

CSV - Comma Separated Value - A CSV is a simple Microsoft file used to store tabular data. - *British*

BBC - British Broadcasting Corporation - The BBC produces excellent news coverage. - *British*

DC - Doctor of Chiropractic - A DC is a Doctor of Chiropratic, and often just called a chiropractor. These physicians diagnose and treat matters related to the body's muscular, skeletal and nervous systems. - *British*

DR - Doctor - DR. Russell works at the local health centre. - *British*

JD - Junior Doctor - A JD refers to a junior doctor, a doctor in the UK who is a qualified medical practitioner, but is also working towards their postgraduate training to become either a hospital consultant, or a GP. - *British*

BM - Bowel Movement - Have you had a BM today? - *British*

F.E.A.R - False Evidence Appearing Real - The acronym F.E.A.R is used to describe self generating fear that appears real, but has no real substance. Often used in self-help literature to discuss strategies one can use to prevent or control our fears. - *British*

BLT - Bacon, Lettuce, Tomato combination. Normally sandwiches - I'd like a BLT sandwich for my lunch, please. - *British*

GMO - Genetically Modified - Some vegetable have been GM in order to give them a longer shelf life in the supermarket. - *British*

FOC - Free of Charge - The garage had kept me waiting so they cleaned my car FOC. - *British*

FOIA - Freedom of Information Act - The Freedom of Information Act 2000 provides public access to information held by public authorities. - *British*

GDP - Gross Domestic Product. A measurement of the current state of the economy - GDP had declined in recent years due to the banking crisis. - *British*

HM - Her/His Majesty - Royalty are referred with the prefix HM. - *British*

HQ - Headquarters (The main office for a company) - The HQ was in Birmingham. - *British*

HR - Human Resources Department - The HR department are responsible for handling contracts for staff members. - *British*

HRH - Her/His Royal Highness - When my Nan turned 100 years old she received a letter from HRH. - *British*

IOU - I owe you. This is an informal contract which proposes to repay money, or used casually to mean 'I will return a favour' - Paul couldn't afford to buy a drink so, after I bought him one, he wrote me an IOU. - *British*

LHS - Left Hand Side - My car was hit on the LHS. - *British*

MP - Member of Parliament - I was not happy with the way the town council was run so I wrote to my MP. - *British*

NP - No Problem - Often used in text messages, e.g. NP I will pick you up at 8. - *British*

PC - Politically Correct language and behaviour. It is important in our culture to use language that is non offensive and does not discriminate against minority groups - Ralph was telling jokes, but they weren't very PC. - *British*

Abbreviations

QED - Quod erat demonstrandum (which was to be demonstrated) [latin] Professionally used in the fields of Law and Mathematics, to signify the logical conclusion to be drawn from the evidence - Sometimes QED is used in everyday situations to suggest you have proved your point. - *British*

RAF - Royal Air Force - My Granddad was in the RAF in WW2 - *British*

SAE - Self Addressed Envelope - Please enclose a SAE and we will return your personal documents after we have scanned them into our system. - *British*

TLC - Tender Love and Care - My nan had a nasty fall so she needs a bit of TLC. - *British*

UV - Ultra Violet - Be careful of UV rays; always wear sun cream when it is sunny. - *British*

WHO - World Health Organisation - The WHO do a great deal of work preventing the spread of diseases. - *British*

XO - Executive Officer - Frank was the XO of a large bank. - *British*

YMCA - Young Men's Christian Association - The YMCA does a lot of work supporting young people. - *British*

NHS - National Health Service - The NHS provides an excellent service. - *British*

HAZ-MAT - Hazardous materials - The safety officer did a thorough HAZ MAT assessment. - *British*

B&B - Bed and Breakfast - We have stayed in many nice B&Bs in Devon. - *British*

SPF - Sun Protection Factor (This is how sunscreen lotion is rated, according to the strength against the sun required) - It is important to use a suntan lotion with a high SPF to protect your skin from burning in the sun. - *British*

D.I.Y. - Acronym that stands for "do it yourself" decorating and refurbishment - The couple decided to do some DIY at the weekend and knock down a wall. They prefered to do it themselves, rather than get a builder in. - *British*

DOB - Date of Birth - On some official forms they may ask for your DOB. - *British*

Ave - Avenue - We abbreviate 'avenue' to 'Ave' for brevity when writing addresses. - *British*

Blvd - Boulavard - We abbreviate 'boulevard' to 'Blvd' for brevity when writing addresses. - *British*

Ln - Lane - We abbreviate 'lane' to 'Ln' for brevity when writing addresses. - *British*

Rd - Road - We abbreviate 'road' to 'Rd' for brevity when writing addresses. - *British*

St - Street - We abbreviate 'street' to 'St' for brevity when writing addresses. - *British*

c - Cup/cups - The measurement of a cup can be abbreviated to 'c'. - *British*

gal - Gallon - The measurement of a gallon can be abbreviated to 'gal'. - *British*

K - Kilo (refers to 1000 in metric system) - The metric weight of a K is equal to 2.2 pounds in imperial measurement - *British*

Km/h - Kilometres per hour is a measurement of speed used in Europe - The train was travelling at 150 km/h. - *British*

lb - Pound/ pounds - The measurement of a pound can be abbreviated to 'lb'. - *British*

Mph - Miles per hour is a measurement of speed used in the UK - George was fined for speeding he had been travelling at 60mph in a 40mph zone. - *British*

pt - Pint - The measurement of a pint can be abbreviated to 'pt'. - *British*

qt - Quart - The measurement of a quart can be abbreviated to 'qt'. - *British*

tbs, tbsp or T - Tablespoon/ tablespoons - The measurement of a tablepoon can be abbreviated to 'tbs'. - *British*

tsp or t - Teaspoon/teaspoons - The measurement of a teaspoon can be abbreviated to 'tsp'. - *British*

AIDS - Acquired Immunodeficiency Syndrome - Richard has developed AIDS and needs regular medical supervision. - *British*

GP - General Practitioner (local doctor) - I was really ill so I booked up to see the GP. - *British*

HIV - Human Immunodeficiency Virus - Richard contracted HIV through using unsterilized needles. - *British*

MS - Multiple Sclerosis. A condition which causes progressive weakening of muscles - My Auntie was really struggling with MS so she needed to have a carer. - *British*

NHS - National Health Service - The NHS provides an excellent service. - *British*

OD - Overdose. An adverse reaction to taking excessive amounts of a drugs or alcohol - Kevin OD'ed on paracetamol last night and was rushed to hospital. - *British*

PMS - Premenstrual Syndrome - The woman was struggling with her moods and so it was suggested that she had PMS, as this behaviour usually coincided with her menstrual cycle. - *British*

ATM - Automated Teller Machine (cash machine) - An ATM is a cash machine, where one can use a bank card to draw money from one's bank accounts. - *British*

P45 - The reference code for a document given to you by your employer on leaving their employment. In the US, this is known as a pink slip. - I'm waiting for my P45 to arrive so I can start looking for another job. - *British*

CC - Credit Card - Most people own a CC these days. - *British*

P60 - You receive a P60 at the end of each financial year. This details your earnings, your tax, NI and pension contributions - I'm waiting for my P60 to arrive so that I can fill in my self employment form. - *British*

PIN - Personal Identification Number - Your PIN is the number that you have to access your money from the cash machine. - *British*

POA - Power Of Attorney - The old lady gave her daughter POA with her financial affairs. - *British*

PSI - Pounds Per Square Inch - The carpet was costed at PSI. - *British*

PTO - Paid Time Off - The man was due some PTO for working loads of overtime. - *British*

AC - Air Conditioning - Please can we turn the AC off, it's freezing in here now! - *British*

AKA - Also Known As - AKA is used by people who have a legal name by which they are known but also another, more commonly known name, too. - *British*

MC - Master of Ceremonies - George is going to be the MC at Steph and Andy's wedding. - *British*

PI - Private Investigator - The PI kept close observations on the woman from his car, hoping to see her do something wrong. - *British*

POSH - Port Out, Starboard Home - The acronym POSH, means elegant and swanky and might derive from the days of The Raj, where boats sailed between the UK and India; the most expensive berths would have been port outward bound, and starboard home, hence POSH. - *British*

AWOL - Absent without Leave - The soldier had gone AWOL and had not returned after his leave for Christmas. - *British*

DOA - Dead on arrival - The man was pronounced as DOA at the hospital. - *British*

ID - Identification - We need to show ID in order to collect parcels from the post office. - *British*

IQ - Intelligence Quotient - One's IQ is said to give an idea of our intelligence. - *British*

R&R - Rest and Relaxation - We all need some R&R in this mad world. - *British*

RIP - Rest in Peace - RIP is used to mark someone's death. - *British*

SOB - Profanity: Son of a Bitch - The young man called the bus driver a SOB for pulling away from the bus stop and leaving him stranded. - *British*

TLC - Tender Loving Care - Karen had been upset all week and in need of some TLC from her friends. - *British*

VIP - Very Important Person - George has a VIP ticket for Glastonbury. - *British*

PO - Post Office - The PO is near the town centre. - *British*

PM - Prime Minister. The leader of a government - David Cameron was the PM for the UK. - *British*

MO - Modus Operandi - The phrase 'Modus Operandi' is shortened to MO, and refers to the method/procedure/ technique by which something is normally done. - *British*

SOP - Standard Operating Procedure - The SOPs for the machinery were clearly displayed on the wall of the factory. - *British*

UPC - Universal Product Code - The UPC is the universal product code for an item to be ordered or sold. - *British*

JC - Jesus Christ - I got a text message from JC last week!!!!! - *British*

ET - Extra Terrestrial (beings) - The film ET was fascinating and thought provoking; what if aliens do exist? - *British*

UFO - Unidentified Flying Object - Some people believe in UFOs and aliens. - *British*

AD - Anno Domini - AD stands for the Latin phrase, 'Anno Domini', meaning 'in the year of our lord' and is used more commonly to refer to the years after the birth of Jesus. - *British*

AM - Ante Meridiem - The acronym AM comes from the Latin phrase, 'Ante Meridiem' meaning: time before midday. - *British*

BC - Before Christ - Before Christ or BC, is a term now expunged by many academics and replaced with BCE, in order to be more politically correct. - *British*

BCE - Before the Common Era - BCE is a modern, politically correct, acronym to describe the time period historically called: BC, Before Christ. - *British*

CST - Central Standard Time - CST is the time zone used in North and Central America; it is 6 hours behind GMT. - *British*

E.T.A. - Acronym to mean "estimated time of arrival" - The ETA of the train was 10.15pm. - *British*

EST - Eastern Standard Time - EST is the time zone used in the eastern parts of the USA; it is 5 hours behind GMT. - *British*

ETA - Estimated Time of Arrival - We were expecting a visit from the boss, his ETA was after lunch. - *British*

ETR - Early to Rise - Off to bed now as we are ETR tomorrow. - *British*

GMT - Greenwich Mean Time - GMT is the standard measurement of time used in UK. Other regions of the world also follow this but adjust, either forwards or back, by a number of whole hours in order to create a similar sunrise and sunset. - *British*

MTD - Month To Date - The man looked at his accounts MTD to observe his cash flow. - *British*

PM - Postmeridiem - Mary liked to eat her lunch PM, in the afternoon. - *British*

YTD - Year To Date - The accounts of YTD were due to be submitted. - *British*

BA - Bachelor of Arts - BA stands for Batchelor of Arts, a four-year undergraduate degree awarded from university study. - *British*

BS(c) - Bachelor of Science - BS(c) stands for Batchelor of Science, a four-year undergraduate degree awarded from university study. - *British*

M.PHIL or MPHIL - Master of Philosophy - An M.PHIL is an advanced postgraduate research degree. - *British*

MA - Master of Arts - A person is awarded their MA when they have studied for a second or further degree at university. - *British*

OT - Over time. To work in excess of your contracted hours, typically for an increased rate of pay - I'm tired because I did OT all last week. - *British*

Alcohol

'Gold Watch'
Scotch - cockney

A.A. - Alcoholics Anonymous - support group for alcoholics - The alcoholic was referred to a support group known as A.A. - *British*

Alcy - A person who is drunk or an alcoholic - Fred is a bit of an alcy and nearly always drunk. - *British*

Alky - Someone who has the reputation or admittance to consuming a lot of alcohol - short for the word alcoholic - He is a bit of an alky and consumes a lot of alcohol. - *British*

Clean - To be free from alcohol - He's been clean from alcohol for 2 years now. - *British*

Cold turkey - Total Abstinence from alcohol, unsupported by professional involvement - The only way he would recover from his addiction, was to go cold turkey. - *British*

Dry out - Abstain from alcohol for a prolonged amount of time, often after over indulging - He will need a period of time, now, to dry out from alcohol. - *British*

Fallen on/ off the wagon - This is a metaphor for being safe on a journey away from drinking. People fall off the wagon, meaning they are drinking again after a period of abstinence - It's a shame that he has fallen off the wagon, he was doing so well and did not drink for ages. - *British*

Lush - An alcoholic - He's a right old lush! - *British*

On the wagon - To abstain from alcohol or drugs - Nothing for me, thanks, I'm on the wagon. - *British*

Prehab - Alcoholic - He's such a prehab! - *America/British*

Rehab - Rehabilitation from alcohol or drugs - They were an alcoholic and needed to go to rehab to get better. - *British*

Wino - Someone who consumes a lot of alcohol, possible homeless - Jennifer is a wino and lives on the streets. - *British*

Act - Foolish or dangerous behaviour or actions whilst under the influence of drink/ drugs - Under the influence of drugs, the young boy began to act. - *America*

Badload - A drunk person - Did you see that badload outside of the pub last night? - *America/British*

Bar hop - To have an alcoholic drink in a succession of bars/ pubs. Typically this phrase infers excess - The group bar hopped across town. - *America/British*

Barred - Banned from drinking in a pub/ bar because of poor, violent or antisocial behaviour - Everyone knows he's barred from that pub. - *British*

Beer belly - A distended stomach due to drinking a lot of beer over time - Have you seen his beer belly? - *British*

Alcohol

Beer goggles - A metaphorical set of glasses ("goggles") that one wears after drinking enough alcohol that the definition of sexually "attractive" declines substantially - Oh, no, she must have her beer goggles on to be interested in him! - *British*

Bend (one's) elbow - To have an alcoholic drink, or another - Can I bend your elbow? - *America/British*

Bender - An extended period of alcohol or drug use, usually more than a single night and often a deliberate action to block out the world - He went on a complete bender and ended up in Accident and Emergency! - *British*

Binge drink - To have an alcoholic drink, typically this phrase infers excess - He'd been on a binge drinking session all weekend. - *America/British*

Binge drinking - High amounts of alcohol purposefully consumed in a short period of time - He'd been on a binge drinking session. - *British*

Booze up - Party involving lots of drinking - Come to my party, it's going to be a proper booze up! - *British*

Boozy - Drunk - We had such a boozy afternoon, lazing in the sun drinking Pimms; it was heavenly! - *British*

Bottle-o - Drive through bottle shop - Pick some beers up at the bottle-o on your way home from work tonight? - *Australian*

Bottle shop - A shop selling alcohol, such as an off licence - Can you pick some beers up at the bottle shop on your way home from work tonight? - *British*

BYOB - Acronym of: Bring your own beer - I'm having a party, would you like to come? It's BYOB. - *British*

BYOW - Acronym of: Bring your own wine - I'm having a party, would you like to come? It's BYOW. - *British*

Caner - Someone who uses excessive amounts of alcohol or drugs - He's an absolute caner! - *British*

Canned - Very drunk or under the influence of drugs and have lost a sense of the norm around them - He gets canned often. - *British*

Champagne socialist - A rich person who holds socialist values - She's such a champagne socialist! - *British*

D.D. or Des - Designated driver who drinks non- alcoholic drinks, so fellow companions can drink alcohol and get home safely - Who's the Des tonight? - *British*

Dirty stop out - Someone who goes out drinking and may not come home that night - Where were you last night, you dirty stop out! - *British*

Double fist - An alcoholic drink in both hands - He had a double fist going most of the night. - *America*

Double rainbowed - Intense joy or emotions equated to an orgasm/ or a type of cocktail - He was seeing a double rainbow, I think! - *British*

Drink - Alcohol - He's on the drink again! - *America/British*

Drink like a fish - Metaphor to imply the person is immersed and surrounded by alcohol like a fish is in water/or able to consume a lot of alcohol - Do you know what? He drinks like a fish, that one! - *British*

Drink up - Phrase used to encourage people to finish drinks quickly, possibly to leave a pub/bar and go onto another or to buy more drinks - Come on, drink up! - *British*

Drive someone to drink - Distress someone so much that they become upset, angry, cross or despairing and they use alcohol to comfort themselves or give relief. Often used in a jokey fashion - She was such a nasty woman, she drove her son to drink! - *British*

Flap out - Acting loud and crazy when drunk, often viewed as annoying or stupid - He was so drunk he was flapping out all over the place. - *America*

Flushed - Pink face/neck or cheeks/ or a pink/red hue due to drinking alcohol - The alcohol flushed her face and neck. - *British*

Gary Player - All dayer- spending all day drinking or/and taking drugs - He was on a Gary Player all weekend! - *cockney*

Gasping - To be in need of something to drink-typically alcohol - He was gasping for a beer after his bad day at work. - *British*

Get (one's) swerve on - To have an alcoholic drink, typically this phrase infers excess - I'm ready to get my swerve on tonight! - *America/British*

Get a buzz on - To have an alcoholic drink, typically this phrase infers excess - I'm ready to get my buzz on tonight! - *America/British*

Had a few (too many) - Drunk - I think we had a few too many last night, didn't we? - *British*

Happy hour - An offer in pubs/bars and clubs at a particular time of day where they sell discounted priced alcoholic drinks - The pub had a happy hour, with half price drinks every evening between 5pm and 6pm. - *British*

Hit the bottle - To have an alcoholic drink, typically this phrase infers excess - He keeps hitting the bottle; it's so sad... - *America/British*

Hold (one's) liquor - To have an alcoholic drink. The ability to drink in volume - She's not very good at holding her liquor. - *America/British*

Jet fighter - All nighter- drinking and/or drugs all night to excess - They were on a jet fighter! - *cockney*

Leo Sayer - Spending all day drinking or/and taking drugs - He was on a complete Leo Sayer! - *cockney*

Liquid lunch - Preferring to drink alcohol instead of eating. Sometimes Guinness is considered to be 'food' due to its viscosity - They decided to skip the food and had a liquid lunch instead. - *British*

Lit - Under the influence of drink or drugs - Did you see how lit he was? - *America*

Lock in - Drinking in a pub after the pub has officially closed and the door is locked to paying customers - The pub had officially closed but some people were invited to stay for the lock in. - *British*

Martini girl - A female who is said to be sexually loose and will have sex with anyone, anytime, anywhere like the advertisement for the Martini drink - She's such a Martini girl! - *British*

Mash up - Party involving lots of drinking and mixing alcohol - Come to my party, it's going to be a mash up! - *British*

Mickey Finn - Alcoholic beverage tampered with to make the person ill and /or unconscious or stupefied - I think they Mickey Finned his drink. - *America*

Ned - An uneducated lout or drunkard - What a ned! - *Scotland*

On the razzle - Drunk - They were out on the razzle all night! - *British*

Pub crawl - Drinking in many pubs one after another, sometimes on a planned route round a town centre - Who's up for a pub crawl around Bath? - *British*

Sloshed - Quite drunk - Grandma was quite sloshed at Christmas from the sherry! - *British*

Spins, the - Physical sensation that the room is spinning due to over consumption of alcohol or/ and drugs - Oh, goodness, I had a bad case of the spins last night when I got into bed! - *Ireland*

Under the influence - Someone who has been drinking alcohol - He's under the influence, officer. - *British*

Wet - Permitting the sale of alcohol, the opposite of a dry country/county/state/place - The UK is described as a wet country as it is permissible to sell alcohol. - *America*

Ben Dover - Hangover - I've got such a Ben Dover, today, from drinking too much last night! - *cockney*

Broken - Hangover from drinking excessive alcohol - I am completely broken after last night! - *British*

Dads - Day after drunk shits (excrement) - I've got a bad case of the dads today after drinking so much last night. - *America*

Gut ache - Reference to stomach pains after consuming too much alcohol - I've terrible gut ache today. - *British*

Alcohol

Alcohol

Gut rot - Poor quality alcohol - I've got gut rot today after drinking that cheap wine last night! - *British*

Hair of the dog - An alcoholic drink often taken the next morning/day to try to alleviate a hangover - I need the hair of the dog to cure my hangover. - *British*

Hangin' - A headache/hangover due to consuming too much alcohol - I'm absolutely hangin' today after staying up drinking all night. - *British*

Hangover - The physical effects felt after drinking too much alcohol - I've got the worst hangover ever after last night! - *British*

Lunatic soup - Alcohol - He was on the old lunatic soup last night, I think! - *America*

Seedy - Hangover - He's a bit seedy this morning. He drank so much last night! - *Australian*

One too many - Drunk - Pauline was very drunk because she had had one too many. - *British*

Three sheets to the wind - Very drunk - Caroline was three sheets to the wind and very drunk. - *British*

Annihilated - Extremely intoxicated - He had had so much to drink, he was totally annihilated by the time he got home! - *British*

Arseholed - Extremely drunk - I was absolutely arseholed! - *British*

As pissed as a fart - Drunk - I was as pissed as a fart! - *British*

Ass out - To make a fool out of oneself whilst under the influence of drink/drugs - I was so drunk, I had my ass out! - *America*

Ass whup - Alcohol - I had my ass whupped last night...I was so drunk. - *America/British*

Battered - Extremely intoxicated - I was absolutely battered! - *British*

Bevvied - Drunk - He was completed bevvied up and out of control. - *British*

Bladdered - Drunk - I was absolutely bladdered! - *British*

Blathered - Drunk - I was absolutely blathered! - *British*

Blaze - Drunk - I was blazed! - *Scotland*

Blotto - Drunk - She was blotto by the time we got her home! - *British*

Bollocksed - Drunk - I was absolutely bollocksed! - *British*

Bombed - Drunk - I was bombed last night. - *America*

Boot and rally - To have an alcoholic drink, typically this phrase infers excess - He was completely boot and rally last night - *America/British*

Booze - Alcohol - Let's go on a booze cruise to France? - *British*

Brahms and Liszt - Rhyming slang for pissed, meaning drunk - He was completely Brahms and Liszt! - *cockney*

Bullet proof - Drunk - I was absolutely bullet proof last night. - *British*

Buttered - Drunk - I was absolutely buttered last night! - *America*

Butt-toast - Extremely inebriated - I was butt-toast last night! - *America*

Buzz - A state of mild intoxication from drink or drugs - I was on a complete buzz. - *Scotland*

Buzzed - Mild to moderately intoxicated from drugs or alcohol - I was buzzed last night. - *America*

Cabbaged - Very drunk or under the influence - I was absolutely cabbaged! - *Scotland*

Clocked out - Someone who is zonked from drugs or drink or simply just doesn't have a clue about what's going on around them - Look at him, all clocked out. - *America*

Cock eyed - So drunk, their eyes cross over and cannot focus - Look at him, all cock eyed. - *British*

Cold stone sober - Metaphor to emphasise no alcohol consumed - The thought of it made her feel cold stone sober. - *British*

Completely bladdered - Very drunk - I was completely bladdered that night! - *British*

Crippled - A drunk person - I was crippled by the drink last night; absolutely crippled! - *America/British*

Crossfade - To be under the influence of both marijuana and alcohol - I watched him crossfade; not a nice sight. - *America*

Crunched - Drunk - I was crunched last night. - *Canada*

Crunked - Crazy drunk, often with reference to getting high on drugs first, then drunk - She was crunked, wasn't she? It was hilarious. - *America*

Dead - Under the influence of excessive amounts of alcohol - He looked dead from drinking so much last night. - *America/British*

Dead (drunk) - Drunk - They were dead drunk, weren't they? - *British*

Drown your sorrows - Drink alcohol to ease your emotional pain - All I wanted to do was to drown my sorrows in wine. - *British*

Drunk - Under the influence of/ or consumed too much alcohol/ inebriated - I was drunk. - *British*

Drunk as a lord - Metaphor to describe the extent of drunkenness. In days gone by, Lords were rich and therefore had access to a lot of alcohol - I was as drunk as a lord. - *British*

Drunk as a rat - Drunk - I was as drunk as a rat last night! - *British*

Drunk as a skunk - Simile to describe being inebriated - I was as drunk as a skunk. - *British*

Elephant's trunk - Drunk- inebriated - He was completely elephant's trunk. - *cockney*

Faced - Drunk - He was absolutely faced last night. - *Canada*

Faded - Drunk - He was faded last night. - *America*

Falling down drunk - So drunk literally staggering all over the place - He was falling down drunk so the police had to be called. - *British*

Fannied - Drunk - He was completely fannied last night. - *America*

Fanny-bawed - Drunk - He was completely fanny-bawed last night. - *America*

Fart - Drunk - He was as pissed as a fart last night. - *British*

Fit-shaced - So drunk words are muddled and mixed- so shit faced, becomes fit- shaced - He was fit-shaced last night. - *America*

Fizzucked - So drunk that fucked up (extremely inebriated) doesn't cover it - He was fizzucked last night. - *America*

Forshnicked - Drunk - He was forshnicked last night. - *America*

Fucked up - Extremely intoxicated on alcohol or other drugs - He was completely fucked up last night. - *British*

Full as a tick - Drunk - He was as full as a tick last night. - *British*

Gashed - Drunk - She was gashed all weekend. - *British*

Gassed up - Intoxicated - He was completely gassed up. - *British*

Gatted - Intoxicated - He was gatted. - *British*

Gattered - Drunk - He was gattered. - *Scotland*

Get spun - To have an alcoholic drink, typically this phrase infers excess - Let's get spun! *America/British*

Greatly missed - Inebriated - He was greatly missed last night! - *cockney*

Hammed - Drunk - Dave was absolutely hammed last night. - *Canada*

Hammered - Drunk - Steve was hammered last night, wasn't he? - *British*

Hellafied - Drunk - I was hellafied last night! - *America*

Hosed - Drunk - I was hosed, man! - *America*

Housed - Drunk - He was completely housed! - *America*

Hurt - Very drunk or high on drugs - He was all hurt, man! - *America*

Hurt up - Drunk - He was all hurt up, man. - *America*

In the horrors - Drunk - By the end of the day, he was in the horrors! - *Ireland*

Alcohol

Inebriated - Drinking too much alcohol which affects one's sensibilities and capabilities - She was completely inebriated after the party. - *British*

Intoxicated - Drinking too much alcohol which affects one's sensibilities and capabilities - "You're completely intoxicated," the police officer said. - *British*

Jacked - Drunk - He was completely jacked! - *America*

Jan Leaming - Rhyming slang for steaming (very drunk) - She was absolutely Jan Leaming! - *cockney*

Jugged - Drunk - He was jugged, wasn't he? - *America*

Kalied - Very drunk - He was absolutely kalied. - *British*

Kaylied - Very drunk - He was absolutely kaylied. - *British*

Keg stand - To have an alcoholic drink, typically this phrase infers excess - She's a right keg stand, full of it. - *America/ British*

Ker plunked - Drunk - comes from the child's game where sticks and balls fall down, implies falling down drunk - They were all absolutely ker plunked! - *British*

Keyed - Really wasted or drunk - He was so keyed up. - *America*

Kootered - Extremely drunk - He was kootered at the party, wasn't he? - *America*

Krunk - To get really drunk- mix of crank it up and drunk - John got krunked after winning the lottery. - *America*

Lagered up - Drunk - The boys were all lagered up yesterday. - *British*

Lambasted - Drunk - I was completely lambasted, man! - *America*

Langered - Drunk - I was so langered. - *America*

Lathered - Drunk - I was lathered last night! - *British*

Lean - Intoxicated - I was lean last night. - *British*

Leathered - Drunk - I was absolutely leathered last night! - *British*

Legless - Drunk - I was legless after all that wine! - *British*

Lifted - Drunk - I was so lifted, I thought I could fly! - *Canada*

Loaded - Drunk - He was loaded, wasn't he? - *Canada*

Loose - Drunk - She was loose last night! - *America/British*

Lubricated - Drunk - He was well lubricated, wasn't he? - *British*

M.W.I. - Mad with it drunk, infers crazy behaviour - He was absolutely M.W.I.! - *America*

Mangled - Drunk - She was pretty mangled, wasn't she? - *British*

Mashed - Drunk - He was all mashed up. - *British*

Messed up - Drunk - He was all messed up. - *British*

Moellered - Drunk - Let's get moellered? - *British*

Monged out - Drunk - She was monged out by the end of it. - *British*

Mounted - Drunk - She was mounted by the end of the night! - *America*

Mulberry bushed - Drunk, possible associations with the children's nursery rhyme, 'here we go round the Mulberry bush' ending in falling down, therefore falling down drunk! - They were all mulberry bushed! - *British*

Mullered - To be drunk - She was absolutely mullered after the party. - *British*

Munted - Drunk - She was munted by the end of the night! - *British*

Off (one's) tits/face/arse - Very drunk - She was off her tits! - *America/British*

On the grog - To have an alcoholic drink, typically this phrase infers excess - She's on the grog tonight. - *America/ British*

One over the top - Drunk - He was a bit over the top, wasn't he? - *British*

One too many - Drunk - I think I had one too many last night! - *British*

Out of it - In a semi-conscious state as a result of excess alcohol - I was pretty out of it last night. - *British*

Out of my (their) skull - Very drunk - I was out of my skull last night. - *British*

Paralytic - Extremely drunk and unable to walk - Oh, my, he was paralytic! - *British*

Pasted - Intoxicated on drink - They were pasted. - *British*

Perve - Drunk - I was perved last night. - *Canada/America*

Pickled - Drunk - I was pickled last night. - *British*

Pickled cabbage - Drunk - I turned into pickled cabbage last night! - *British*

Pie-eyed - So drunk their eyes are unable to focus properly - Sandra was absolutely pie-eyed last night. - *British*

Piflicated - Drunk - Piflicated, that's what we were! - *Scotland*

Pished - Drunk - I think I was pished! - *British*

Piss ass drunk - Drunk - She was piss ass drunk! - *America*

Pissed - Drunk - He was so pissed. - *British*

Pissed as a parrot - Drunk - He was as pissed as a parrot last night. - *British*

Pissed up - Drunk - She was totally pissed up last night. - *British*

Plastered - Drunk - He was plastered. - *British*

Polluted - Drunk - Polluted, or what? - *America*

Poo-pooed - Getting drunk - He was pretty poo-pooed last night. - *America*

Pop - To have an alcoholic drink, typically this phrase infers excess - She's on the pop. - *America/British*

Pop my cork - Cork and bubbles from champagne or fizzy wine, but implies sexual interest in someone and the act of fizzing over like a male ejaculation - I don't pop my cork for every man I see! - *British*

Rat arsed - Intoxicated - I was rat arsed last night. - *British*

Rat-arsed - Drunk - She's so rat-arsed, she might be sick! - *British*

Rat-assed - Drunk - She's so rat-assed, she might be sick! - *British*

Retarded - Drunk - Look at how retarded he is! - *America*

Ripped - Drunk - They were totally ripped. - *America*

Roasted - Drunk - All of them were quite roasted. - *America*

Sassified - Intoxicated to the point of sassiness (over boldness) and do crazy things, such as streaking - She was so sassified she took all of her clothes off and ran around naked! - *America*

Sauced - Drunk - Look at them, all sauced up! - *British*

Saucy - Drunk - I was a bit saucy last weekend and ended up being really sick! - *British*

Scarred - Drunk - Totally scarred last night! - *America*

Schmaked - Very drunk - He was schmaked. - *America*

Schmammered - Drunk - They were schmammered! - *Canada*

Schnocked - Extremely inebriated - Absolutely schnocked! - *America*

Schnockered - Drunk - They were shnockered. - *America*

Schnookered - Drunk - They were shnookered. - *Scotland*

Schnuckered - Drunk - They were schnuckered. - *Bahamas*

Schwacked - Drunk - They were schwacked. - *America*

Shellacked - Drunk - They were shellacked. - *America*

Shit-faced - Drunk and vomiting in toilet - She was absolutely shit-faced! - *British*

Shitty - Female version of shitfaced - She was absolutely shitty! - *America*

Shmacked - Under the influence of excessive amounts of alcohol - He was completely shmacked. - *America/British*

Shnockered - Under the influence of excessive amounts of alcohol - She was shnockered. - *America/British*

Shwasted - Drunk, probably a word combination of shit faced and wasted, all meaning drunk - They were shwasted! - *America*

Sideways - Extremely inebriated - He was knocked sideways last night! - *America*

Skinful - To be intoxicated by drink or drugs - I had a right skinful last night. - *British*

Slaughtered - Very drunk - She was absolutely slaughtered and made an idiot of herself on the dance floor. - *British*

Slizzard - Drunk or high on drugs - He was slizzard, absolutely out of it! - *America*

Smashed - Extremely inebriated - Jim was absolutely smashed at the party last night. - *British*

Snookered - Drunk - They were snookered. - *America/British*

Soup sandwich - Metaphor to describe being messy, sloppy and drunk - He was so drunk, he was like a soup sandwich. - *America*

Soused - Inebriated with alcohol - I was pretty soused last night. - *America*

Sozzled - Drunk - Everyone at the party was sozzled. - *British*

Spanked - Intoxicated - I was pretty spanked last night. - *America*

Steaming - Very drunk - They were all steaming drunk by the end of the party. - *British*

Stewed - Drunk - Everyone at the party was stewed. - *America*

Stinky - Extremely inebriated - How stinky was Justine last night? - *British*

Stonked - Intoxicated - He was stonked last night. - *British*

Strunk - Intoxicated and high on drugs at the same time. A contraction of stoned and drunk= strunk - They were high on drink and drugs, absolutely strunk. - *British*

Stuck like chuck - Intoxicated or high on drugs - June was stuck like a chuck last night! - *America*

Stumble fuck - A drunk person - He was such a stumble fuck last night, staggering everywhere! - *America/British*

Swallied - Drunk - Everyone at the party was swallied. - *America*

Swilled - Intoxicated - He was absolutely swilled last night. - *British*

Tanked - Intoxicated - She had a full tank after the rugby, didn't she? - *America*

Tanked up - Drunk - I was pretty tanked up last night, I can't remember much! - *British*

Three sheets to the wind - Very drunk - I would say they were all three sheets to the wind, by the end of the day out. - *British*

Tiltered - Very drunk - James was tiltered last night. - *British*

Time travel juice - Someone who has drunk too much may have memory blackouts, hence they say they must have had too much 'time travelling juice' as they don't remember where they've been, or what they've done - I think I had too much time traveller juice last night, I don't remember a thing past ten o' clock! - *America*

Tipsy - Slightly drunk - He was a bit tipsy after going to the pub, and wondered if his wife would notice! - *British*

Toasted - A little bit drunk - I was toasted last night! - *British*

Toasty - Tipsy but not drunk - I got a bit toasty at the wedding due to drinking all the free champagne that was on offer. - *British*

Toddy stricken - Drunk from too many toddies - They were all toddy stricken by the end of the night! - *America*

Toe up - So intoxicated one falls over and is on the floor with our toes pointing up - He was so drunk he landed toe up! - *British*

Toes up - So intoxicated one falls over and is on the floor with our toes pointing up like a dead corpse - He was so drunk he landed toes up! - *British*

Tor up - Intoxicated - Jemima was pretty tor up last night. - *British*

Tore back - Intoxicated - Cath tore back last night. - *British*

Tore up from the floor up - Intoxicated - Penny tore up from the floor up, last night. - *British*

Torn down - Intoxicated - Julie was pretty torn down last night. - *British*

Tossed - Intoxicated - Peter was all tossed up last night. - *America*

Trollied - Drunk - They were all absolutely trollied! - *British*

Troubled - Intoxicated - He was pretty troubled, wasn't he? - *Scotland*

Under the table - Falling down drunk - Oh, my, she was so drunk last night she was under the table. - *British*

Wankered - Intoxicated - She was absolutely wankered last night. - *British*

Wavey - Severely under the influence of drink or/ and drugs - He's a bit wavey, isn't he? - *British*

Waxed - Very drunk or hungover - He was completely waxed! - *British*

Wetted - Ridiculously drunk so that motor skills are lost and drinks are spilt - He was so wetted, he was spilling drinks all over the place! - *America*

Wreck - So drunk or high on drugs they act out of the norm - Joan was an absolutely wreck last night. - *British*

Wrecked - Drunk or/and high on drugs - We were all wrecked at Jim's party last night. - *British*

Zoned - High on drugs and/or completely drunk on alcohol - He was zoned last night. - *America*

Zooted - Extremely intoxicated - He was absolutely zooted yesterday. - *America*

Zosted - Intoxicated - They were all zosted. - *America*

A few - Alcohol - I told my husband I was just going down to the public house for a few drinks. - *America/British*

A half - Half a pint measure of beer/ lager - Meredith ordered a half pint of beer. - *British*

A large one - A double measure of spirits such as gin - Mary ordered herself a large one. - *British*

A piss up - A party involving lots of drinking alcohol - "We are going to have a piss up," said the student, inviting his friend to a party with lots of alcohol. - *British*

A small one - A single shot of spirits - "I will just have a small one, please" said the regular to the barman, when ordering a drink. - *British*

A wee tipple/dram - A small drink, usually of spirits such as whiskey - The friends decided to have a wee tipple together, so bought a bottle of whiskey. - *Scotland*

Cheeky few - Alcohol - Fancy a cheeky few after work? - *America/British*

Cheeky one - A quick drink in circumstances perhaps one shouldn't - Fancy a cheeky one after work? - *British*

Cow and calf - Half (a pint of beer) - Just a cow and calf for me, please. - *cockney*

Larry - A partially finished cup/glass of beer - You leaving that Larry? - *America*

Shot - A small measure of alcoholic spirits - Let's do some shots? - *British*

Sip - Small, dainty drink - I'll just have a sip, please. - *British*

Sixer - A pack of six tins of beer - Get a sixer in to watch the game? - *America*

Snifter - A small drop of alcohol - Oh, go on then, I'll just have a snifter! - *British*

Three fingers - A measure of alcohol - Give me three fingers, please? - *British*

A drunkard - Someone who consumes a large quantity of alcohol - Norman referred to his wife as a drunkard because of the amount of alcohol she consumed each day. - *British*

Tosspot - Drunkard or an idiot - What an absolute tosspot! - *British*

Arethusa - Rhymes with boozer, a public house - Coming down the arethusa later? - *cockney*

Bath tub - Rhymes with pub, a public house - Coming down the bath tub later? - *cockney*

Battle cruiser - Rhymes with boozer, a public house - Coming down the battle cruiser later? - *cockney*

Bazaar - Bar, a public house - Coming down the bazaar later? - *cockney*

Boozer - A pub - Coming down the boozer after work? - *British*

German cruiser - Rhymes with boozer, a public house - Coming down the German cruiser? - *cockney*

Jack Tar - Rhymes with bar - Coming down the Jack Tar? - *cockney*

Offie - A shop selling alcohol, such as an off licence - I'm off to the offie to pick up some wine. - *British*

Waterhole - Hotel/pub - Coming down the water hole later? - *Australian*

Watering hole - Hotel/pub - Coming down the watering hole later? - *Australian*

Here's to you - A toast of good fortune or prophesy for a better future - Here's to you all this Christmas time! - *British*

Salut - A toast of good fortune or prophesy for a better future - "Salut," he said, as he raised his glass of champagne. - *French*

A toast - A toast of good fortune or prophesy for a better future - The wedding guests raised a toast to the bride and groom and wished them good fortune for their future together. - *British*

Bottoms up - A toast of good fortune or prophesy for a better future, bottoms are the bottom of glasses tipped up when drinking - "Bottoms up," she said, as she downed her champagne in one gulp! - *British*

Cheers - Salutation before a drink, a toast of good fortune or prophesy for a better future - "Cheers, everyone." he said, whilst raising his glass. - *British*

Chin-chin - A toast of good fortune or prophesy for a better future - " Chin-chin," she said, whilst raising her glass to toast her friends. - *British*

Down in one you Zulu warrior, down in one you chief, chief, chief - A drinking game/song to encourage people to drink quickly and so get drunk faster - And they all chanted together...'down in one you Zulu warrior, down in one you chief, chief', as they drank down their shots. - *British*

Down the hatch - A toast of good fortune or prophesy for a better future - "Down the hatch, old boy," he said to me. - *British*

Drink it down - Drink quickly - "Come on, drink it down," she said. - *British*

Eat, drink and be merry - A salutation often said at celebrations - Come on, it's Christmas; let's eat, drink and be merry!' - *British*

I'll drink to that! - A toast of good fortune or prophesy for a better future - "I'll drink to that!" she said. - *British*

Roll out the barrel - A song and saying about having good fun whilst drinking plenty; barrels contain alcohol such as beer - He was certainly rolling out the barrel last night! - *British*

Corked - Wine that's off and tastes unpleasant - Sorry, waiter, this wine is corked. Please could you replace it? - *British*

Irish handcuffs - Two drinks, one for each hand - He had a pair of Irish handcuffs; drinks in both hands! - *British*

Jean-Michel - Rhyming slang: Reference to Jean-Michel Jarre the French composer and performer. A play on the his surname-jarre- to mean 'jars' of drinks - Who's coming for a Jean-Michel, after work? - *cockney*

Just the one Mrs Wembly - A jokey phrase taken from a TV programme - I'll just have the one, Mrs Wembley! - *British*

Knock back a drink - Drink alcohol very quickly - Cor, you knocked that back quickly! - *British*

Let's get down to some serious drinking - A plan to get drunk - Come out now and let's get down to some serious drinking! - *British*

Liquid carnage - The aftermath/ effects of a party where people have drunk heavily - The party was absolute liquid carnage. - *British*

Mother's milk - Metaphor to imply there are positive benefits of drinking alcohol - Ooo, let's have a drop of mother's milk, shall we? - *British*

Name your poison - Say what you would like to drink - Name your poison then, guys. - *British*

Neck a drink - Drink alcohol very quickly without tasting/appreciating it and possibly with the intention of getting drunk quickly - Cor, you necked that quickly! - *British*

Night cap - Drink taken at bed time - Fancy a night cap? - *British*

Nurse a drink - Drink one drink very slowly and make it last a long period of time - You've been nursing that drink all night! - *British*

On the bottle - Out drinking, perhaps after a period of abstinence - He's on the bottle again, sadly. - *America/British*

On the lash - On a drunken binge - She's been out on the lash with her friends, all weekend. - *British*

On the piss - Getting drunk - Are you coming out on the piss tonight? - *British*

On the razz - Getting drunk - Are you coming out on the razz tonight? - *British*

On the town - On a night out with intention of drinking a lot of alcohol - The hen party were out on the town to celebrate Steph's forthcoming wedding. - *America/British*

One for the road - A last alcoholic drink before leaving a social gathering - Fancy one for the road, before you go? - *British*

Organise a piss up in a brewery - This phrase is usually used in a defamatory way to indicate that someone is so incapable of being organised, they couldn't even get drunk where there was a lot of alcohol available to drink - They couldn't even organise a piss up in a brewery! - *British*

Out of (one's) tree - So drunk unaware of what's going on around them - Julie was out of her tree after the wedding! - *British*

Out on the town - A celebration usually involving excessive drinking - Do you fancy a night out on the town? - *British*

Piss - People say they are going on the piss when they are going drinking, maybe because the more they drink the more they need to visit the lavatory to relieve themselves - Coming out on the piss tonight? - *British*

Piss up - The act of getting drunk - It was an absolute piss up! - *British*

Pissed as a fart - Metaphor to help describe how drunk a person is: farts are expelled wind from the anus and are full of hot air/bad smell. Implies to talk rubbish - Cathy was as pissed as a fart! - *British*

Pissed as a newt - Metaphor to describe being drunk - Ken was as pissed as a newt at the wedding! - *British*

Round - Buying drinks in a pub/bar for everyone in your group/party - I'll get this round in. - *cockney*

Sober - No alcohol consumed - Officer, I am as sober as a judge, I promise! - *British*

Social drinker - Someone who claims to only drink at parties or in company but not on a regular basis - Jenny is just a social drinker, she doesn't drink at home alone. - *British*

Spike - To spike a drink is to purposefully lace another person's drink with strong alcohol or drugs, with the intention of making them very drunk or ill, or causing them harm. For example, the date rape drug, rohypnol - Watch your drink doesn't get spiked, babe. - *America/British*

Stick a fork in - To be full of drugs and/or alcohol so not wanting any more at the moment - You could have stuck a fork in her, she was so done! - *British*

Alcohol

55

Alcohol

The demon drink - Metaphor for describing the 'evil' side effects of drink, getting drunk regularly or becoming an alcoholic. Implies alcohol is a bad influence and draws one into hellish ways - He's on the demon drink again! - *British*

Tiddly - A little bit drunk - I was quite tiddly last night! - *British*

Tie one on - To have an alcoholic drink, typically this phrase infers excess - Fancy coming to the pub to tie one on? - *America/British*

Tipped me over - Too much alcohol consumed resulting in adverse effects. This is often described as the effects of the last drink consumed, like I had one too many and it tipped me over into being drunk - It was that last glass that tipped me over! - *British*

To drink someone under the table - The ability to consume a lot of alcohol, more than companions, who due to drinking excessively, become drunk before you, and potentially could fall down under the table - She's able to drink anyone under the table, she is! - *British*

To hit the bottle - Someone is said to drink heavily when they are upset or distressed, depressed or an alcoholic - Jane was so depressed after her marriage break up that she hit the bottle big time! - *British*

To quaff - To drink - You quaffed that pretty quickly! - *British*

To spike - To put an illegal substance into a drink with the intention of drugging, humiliating, hurting or even raping the recipient. For example, the 'date rape' drug - Jane had her drink spiked when she was in the nightclub. - *British*

To spike a drink - To add something to someone's drink without their permission or knowledge, could be further alcohol or drugs and can potentially cause them to become very drunk, high, unconscious or ill. Can be done for 'fun' or malicious reasons - Jane had her drink spiked when she was in the nightclub. - *British*

To wet your whistle - Drink alcohol when thirsty, describes the effect of drinking as soothing your throat - Need to wet your whistle? - *British*

Toasted oats - Passed out from taking too much drugs or alcohol - Simon was toasted oats from all of the drugs and alcohol he had consumed that day. - *British*

Training wheels - Salt and a lime to accompany a shot of tequila, taken as part of the ritual for drinking tequila, but also to soften the taste, perhaps? - Have you got your training wheels with that? - *America*

Wet the baby's head - To celebrate the birth of a child by drinking - Who's free to come out tonight to wet the baby's head? - *British*

Wine o'clock - Jokey way of saying it's time to have an alcoholic beverage - Is it wine o' clock yet? - *British*

Worse for wear - Losing ability to function properly due to being drunk - Oh, dear, you were a bit worse for wear after the party, weren't you? - *British*

Alcopop - Highly sugared and sweet flavoured bottled alcoholic drinks, often targeted at a young audience - Some young people drink too many alcopops which have a high sugar content. - *British*

A cold one - A beer - Brendan asked his wife to bring him a cold one from the fridge, because he liked a beer whilst watching football. - *British*

A double - Two shots of a spirits in one drink - Petulia said, " I will have a double please," and the barman put two shots of alcohol in her glass. - *British*

A few bevvies - Alcoholic drinks/ beers - They both liked a few bevvies at the weekend so would stock up with alcoholic drinks from the supermarket. - *British*

Adult beverage - Alcohol - "This is an adult beverage and not for children," said mum, when drinking her wine. - *America/ British*

Alcopop - Alcohol - The young people usually bought alcopops to take to the party. - *America/British*

Alcohol

Amber fluid - Old fashioned term for beer - We will have a couple of pints of amber fluid when we go to the pub. - *Australian*

Ann Boleyn - Rhyming slang for gin - "I will have an Ann Boleyn, please," said Rupert, when asked what he wanted to drink. - *cockney*

Apple fritter - Bitter - beer - I'll have a pint of apple fritter," said Jess, referring to the bitter beer. - *cockney*

Baltic tea - Alcohol - Do you fancy a drop of Baltic tea? - *America/British*

Beer - A type of alcoholic drink - Fancy a beer? - *America/British*

Bevvy - Alcohol - Fancy a bevvy after work tonight? - *British*

Brewski - Slang for beer - Fancy a brewski after work? - *America*

Buckets - Large volumes or 'buckets' of mixed alcohol, usually shared, with the intention of getting very drunk - Let's do buckets tonight? - *British*

Cab - Wine - Would you like a glass of Cab? - *America/British*

Cab Sav - Short hand for the wine variety, Cabernet Sauvignion - Would you like a glass of Cab Sav? - *British*

Calvin Klein - Wine - Calvin Klein? - *cockney*

Champers - Champagne - Glass of champers? - *America/British*

Champers/ fizz/ bubbles - Champagne - Glass of fizz? Bubbles, anyone? - *British*

Cold one - Alcohol - Fancy a cold one after work? - *America/British*

Coldie - A beer - Fancy a coldie after work? - *Australian*

Dead soldiers - Alcohol; abandoned drinks - Collect up the dead soldiers, please? - *America/British*

Deep sea glider - Rhyming for cider - Fancy a deep sea glider? - *cockney*

Don Revie - Bevvy- alcoholic drink - Fancy a Don Revie? - *cockney*

Easy rider - Rhyming for cider - Fancy a pint of easy rider? - *cockney*

Forsythe Saga - Lager - Fancy a Forsyth Saga? - *cockney*

Forty - Alcohol - Fancy a bit of forty percent? - *America/British*

G and T - Short for gin and tonic - I'll have a large G and T, please. - *British*

Gay and frisky - Whiskey - Fancy a gay and frisky? - *cockney*

Giggle and titter - Bitter - beer - Fancy a giggle and titter? - *cockney*

Giggle juice - Alcohol - She's been on the giggle juice again! - *America/British*

Giggle juice/water - Alcoholic drink causing giggly effect - She's been on the giggle juice again! - *British*

Giggle water - Alcohol - She's been on the giggle water again! - *America/British*

Gold watch - Scotch (whiskey) - Gold watch for you? - *cockney*

Growler - American jug of beer/ upset stomach due to spicy food/ diseased vagina - Let's get a couple of growlers in? - *America*

Hard alcohol - High Volume Alcohol - What hard alcohol do you have? - *America/British*

Hard stuff - High Volume Alcohol - What hard stuff do you have? - *America/British*

High gravity - High alcoholic volume - That beer has a high gravity so be careful, it'll be strong. - *British*

Hooch - Illegally brewed alcohol and the name of an alcopop - Hooch was readily available at the barn dance. - *America*

Hooker - A gulp of liquor - The hooker caught him in the back of the throat making him cough. - *America*

Hot toddy - A measure of whiskey/ brandy warmed, often taken at bedtime, night-time or when ill - Fancy a hot toddy before bed? - *Scotland*

J.D. - Short for Jack Daniels - JD and coke, please. - *British*

Jack the Dandy - Brandy - Fancy a Jack the Dandy? - *cockney*

Jackie Chan - Can of beer - Pick up some Jackie Chans on your way home, please? - *cockney*

Alcohol

Jagerbombs - Jägermeister spirit mixture and drank in one mouthful - Who's up for a Jagerbomb? - *British*

Jamie - Jameson whiskey - Jamie on the rocks, please. - *British*

Jimmy - Jim Beam, a type of liquor - I'll have a tod of Jimmy, please. - *British*

Jimmy's talkin' - So drunk the alcohol is doing all of the talking. Refers to the strong liquor Jim Beam - I think that's a bit of Jimmy talkin'. - *America*

Journey drinks - Alcoholic drinks taken and consumed en route in a car/ train etc - Who's getting the journey drinks in? - *British*

Junkst - Cheap alcohol - This is junkst! - *America*

Knight Rider - Rhyming for cider - Fancy a Knight Rider? - *cockney*

Like piss - Weak/low alcohol beer - This beer is like piss, it's so weak! - *British*

Marg - Short hand for a cocktail called a Margareta - Do you fancy a Marg? - *America*

Mead - Medieval type of brew/wine made from honey - In days gone by they drank mead a lot. - *British*

Moonshine - Illegally brewed alcohol - There was plenty of moonshine to be had at the party. - *America*

Natty light - Natural light brand beer - I'll have a natty light, please. - *America*

Near beer - Light beer/non alcoholic or low alcohol - Are you having a near beer? - *America*

O.E. - Old English 800 malt liquor - Fancy an O.E? - *British*

Oh, be joyful - Home made alcohol - Fancy a glass of oh, be joyful? - *Bristol*

Oly - Olympia beer - Fancy an oly? - *America*

On the rocks - Alcoholic beverage served with ice - Would you like your whiskey on the rocks? - *America/British*

Pig's ear - Rhyming slang for beer - A pint of pigs ear! Or, to you a beer. - *British*

Pino - White wine variety- Pinot Grigio - Pino, anyone? - *British*

Plonk - Cheap wine - This wine is proper plonk! - *British*

Poison - Alcoholic drink - What's your poison, Jim? - *British*

Road soda - Alcohol - Let's pick up some road soda for the trip? - *America/British*

Road sody - Drinks brought to consume on a journey - Who's buying the road sody? - *America*

Sauce - Alcohol - He's on the sauce again! - *British*

Shots - Small glasses serving high volume alcohol intended to be drunk in one mouthful, often in a social and ritualistic way with others - Let's do shots! - *British*

Suds - Beer; refers to the head of foam found on the top of the beer - Look at the suds on that pint! - *America*

The hard stuff - Alcoholic drinks/ spirits with a high alcoholic volume - Let's have a drop of the hard stuff? - *British*

The real/ good stuff - Branded expensive alcohol/ high alcoholic volume, good quality - Oh, that's a bit of the good stuff, isn't it? - *British*

Time travel juice - Alcohol - He's been on the time travel juice again! - *America/British*

Tin - Alcohol - Fancy a tin? - *America/British*

Tinnies/ tin - Cans of beer - Pick up some tinnies on your way home, please? - *British*

Toddy - An alcoholic drink often served warmed with sugar, and thought to be of medicinal value and comfort if someone is ill or cold - I'll get you a toddy, that'll sort you out. - *Scotland*

VAT - Vodka and tonic - I'll have a large VAT, please. - *British*

Vino - Short for wine - Fancy a vino later? - *British*

Wounded soldier - An abandoned, partially consumed, alcoholic beverage - There were wounded soldiers all over the flat after the party. - *British*

Yack - Cognac, a type of brandy - Fancy a yack? - *British*

Body

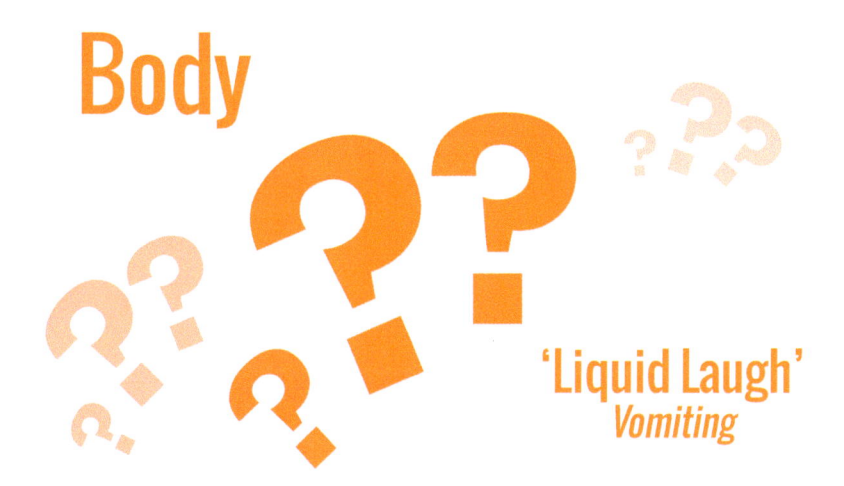

'Liquid Laugh'
Vomiting

Back door - The anus - He had a problem with his back door. - *America/British*

Back end - The anus - He had a problem with his back end. - *America/British*

Back passage - Anus - He had a problem with his back passage. - *British*

Balloon knot - The anus - The anus is sometimes referred to as the balloon knot, because of its shape. - *America/British*

Brown eye - The anus - Look me in the brown eye. - *America/British*

Brown spider - The anus - He tickled my brown spider. - *America/British*

Brown star - The anus - He touched my brown star and I didn't like it! - *America/British*

Bunghole - The anus - He's got a problem with his bunghole. - *America/British*

Butt hole - The anus - He's got a problem with his butt-hole. - *America/British*

Chocolate starfish - The anus - He liked the shape of her chocolate starfish. - *British*

Corn hole - The anus - A crude name for the anus is the corn hole. - *America/British*

Cornhole - The anus - Another crude name for the anus is the cornhole. - *America/British*

Cornholer - The anus - Some people call the anus a cornholer. - *America/British*

Fleshy fun bridge - The perineum - Some people refer to the anus as the fleshy fun bridge! - *America/British*

Freckle - The anus - Some people call their anus, the freckle. - *America/British*

Gary - The anus - I made Gary sting after that spicy curry! - *America/British*

Ham flower - The anus - Another way that the anus has been described is as the ham flower. - *America/British*

Hershey highway, the - The anus - The Hershey highway is the anus. - *America/British*

Jacksy - The buttocks or anus - He was taken up the jacksy. - *British*

Matako - The anus - The word matako means anus to some people. - *America/British*

Mussy - The anus - The mussy is a word for the anus. - *America/British*

Old dirt road, the - The anus - The phrase 'the old dirt' road refers to the anus. - *America/British*

O-ring - The anus - The phrase 'o-ring' is the anus. - *America/British*

Poop chute - The anus - The poop chute is the place where we excrete waste, the anus. - *America/British*

Puckered brown eye, the - The anus - The puckered brown eye refers to the anus. - *America/British*

Puckered starfish - The anus - The puckered starfish refers to the anus. - *America/British*

Ring - Anal sphincter - If you eat spicy food, you can get a sting around your ring! - *British*

Rusty bullet hole - The anus - I had a rusty bullet hole after a bout of diarrhoea. - *America/British*

Shit box - The anus - The shit box is a crude phrase for the anus, where shit means excrement. - *America/British*

Shitter - The anus - The shitter is a crude word for the anus, where shit means excrement. - *America/British*

Starfish - The anus - The starfish is the anus. - *America/British*

Turd cutter - The anus - The turd cutter is the anus. - *America/British*

Two-hole - The anus - The two-hole is the anus. - *America/British*

ACDC - Bisexual - Kevin is ACDC, he likes men and women. - *America/British*

Beer bi - Bisexual - Sammy is a beer bi, he likes men and women. - *America/British*

Bi - Bisexual - Andrew is sexually attracted to men and women, he is bi. - *British*

Heteroflexible - Bisexual - Miranda is heteroflexible, she likes men and women. - *America/British*

Swing both ways - Bisexual - I think she swings both ways, liking both men and girls. - *America/British*

Ass - Buttocks - I fell over and hurt my ass. - *America/British*

Backside - Buttocks - I fell over and hurt my backside. - *British*

Ball bag - Scrotum - I have an itchy ball bag. - *British*

Between the legs - The groin - He put his hand between my legs. - *British*

Booty - Buttocks - That girl has a hot booty. - *America/British*

Botay - Buttocks - That girl has a hot botay. - *British*

Bottom - Buttocks - I fell over and hurt my bottom. - *British*

Builders bum - The exposure of the buttock cleavage of a man bending over in ill-fitting trousers - There was quite a lot of builders bum on show, when the man was bent over digging. - *British*

Chuff - The buttocks or anus - He said he wanted to take her up the chuff. - *British*

Crown jewels - Scrotum - The ball hit him in the crown jewels. - *British*

Derriere - Buttocks - He fell backwards onto his derriere. - *French*

Goolies - The male genitals and in particular the testicles - The ball smacked him at force in the goolies. - *British*

Hiney - Buttocks - She had a sore hiney. - *America*

Lunchbox - Scrotum - The ball hit him in the lunchbox. - *America*

Naughty bits - Genitalia - He touched her naughty bits. - *British*

Pins - Legs - She's got a lovely pair of pins. - *British*

Private parts - Genitalia - Show me your private parts? - *British*

Privates - Euphemism for the genitals - Show me your privates? - *British*

Pubes - Pubic hair - He had a pube stuck in his teeth. - *British*

Rear - Buttocks - She had a shapely rear. - *British*

Rear end - Buttocks - She had a shapely rear end. - *British*

Rude bits - Genitalia - He wanted to touch her rude bits! - *British*

Seat - Buttocks - She sat down hard on her seat. - *British*

Tackle - Scrotum - Watch me tackle! - *British*

Thatch - Pubic hair - He buried his head in her thatch . - *British*

Trouser department - Scrotum - He's big in the trouser department, apparently! - *British*

Unmentionables - Genitalia - She touched him on the unmentionables. - *British*

Wedding tackle - Scrotum - Watch my wedding tackle with that football! - *British*

Balcony - Female breasts - In some shops you can buy balcony bras for your breasts. - *America/British*

Bap - Female breasts - She's got a nice pair of baps! - *America/British*

Bazonga - Female breasts - What a nice pair of bazongas! - *America/British*

Bazoom - Female breasts - What a nice pair of bazooms! - *America/British*

Bee sting - Female breasts - Look at her small breasts, they are like bee stings! - *America/British*

Bewb - Female breasts - What a pair of bewbs? - *America/British*

Bitch tit - Female breasts - Look at her bitch tits. - *America/British*

Bittie - Female breasts - Give me some bittie? - *America/British*

Bolt-ons - Female breasts - She's got massive bolt-ons! - *America/British*

Boobage - Female breasts - Look at her boobage. - *America/British*

Boobies - Female breasts - She has gorgeous boobies. - *British*

Boobs - Female breasts - Her boobs bounced up and down as she ran along the beach. - *British*

Booby - Female breasts - Her booby fell out on stage and everyone laughed! - *America/British*

Breasticle - Female breasts - I love yor breasticles! - *America/British*

Bristols - A woman's breasts- cockney rhyming slang for Bristol bits which rhymes with tits - Nice Bristols! - *British*

Charleys - Female breasts - She's got a nice pair of charleys! - *America/British*

Charlies - Female breasts - She's got a nice pair of charlies! - *America/British*

Chest puppies - Female breasts - Look at her chest puppies bouncing! - *America/British*

Chesticles - Female breasts - Look at her chesticles. - *America/British*

Feeder - Female breasts - What a pair of feeders on her! - *America/British*

Fun bags - Female breasts - What a nice pair of fun bags! - *America/British*

Funbags - Female breasts - Give me a go on your funbags? - *British*

Gazonga - Female breasts - What a lovely pair of gazongas! - *America/British*

Gazongas - Female breasts - What a lovely pair of gazongas! - *America/British*

Gazunga - Female breasts - What a lovely looking gazunga! - *America/British*

Girls - Female breasts - Get the girls out! - *America/British*

Hanger - Female breasts - Her hangers hung low on her chest following breast feeding. - *America/British*

Headlights - Nipples - Nipples are sometimes called headlights, as they point towards you. - *America/British*

High-beams - Nipples - High-beams are another way to describe nipples. - *America/British*

Hooters - Female breasts - Hooters refers to a woman's breasts. - *British*

Jug - Female breasts - What a lovely pair of jugs! - *America/British*

Juggie - Female breasts - She has some juggie on her! - *America/British*

Juggy tits - Female breasts - She has lovely juggy tits. - *America/British*

Jugs - Female breasts - What a lovely pair of jugs! - *British*

Kahuna - Female breasts - Look at the kahuna in here! - *America/British*

Knockers - Female breasts - What a lovely pair of knockers! - *British*

Lady lumps - Female breasts - She had great lady lumps. - *America*

Lungs - Female breasts - She's got a good pair of lungs on her, hasn't she? - *America/British*

Body

Mammaries - Female breasts - Look at her mammaries! - *America/British*

Man boob - Male breasts, usually in overweight men - He has a pair of man boobs! - *America/British*

Melons - Female breasts - What a lovely pair of melons! - *British*

Mipple - Nipples - Sometimes men's nipples are called mipples. - *America/British*

Moob - Male breasts, usually in overweight men - Men can have moobs, these are man boobs. - *America/British*

Mosquito bites - Female breasts - If a woman's breasts are small they are sometimes referred to as mosquito bites. - *America/British*

Naa-naa - Female breasts - Naa-naa are breasts. - *America/British*

Naturals - Female breasts - The naturals are a woman's breasts. - *America/British*

Naughty pillow - Female breasts - Let me have a squidge of your naughty pillows? - *America/British*

Pair - Female breasts - She's got a nice looking pair! - *America/British*

Pokie - Nipples - Her pokies were erect and showed through her blouse. - *America/British*

Puffy - Nipples - Her puffies were visible through her sweater. - *America/British*

Puppies - Female breasts - She had a gorgeous pair of puppies! - *America/British*

Rack - Female breasts - Look at her rack, bloody gorgeous! - *America/British*

Sideboob - Female breasts - The sideboob is the part of the breast at the side of the body, which might be revealed wearing particular clothing. - *America/British*

Strawberry creams - Female breasts - He knocked me straight in my strawberry creams! - *America/British*

Sweater meat - Female breasts - The crude phrase 'sweater meat' refers to the breasts. - *America/British*

Sweater puppies - Female breasts - Look at her sweater puppies coming to attention. - *America/British*

T and A - Female breasts - What a nice pair of T and A she's got! - *America/British*

Tata - Female breasts - The phrase tata refers to the breasts. - *America/British*

Ta-ta - Female breasts - The phrase ta-ta refers to the breasts. - *America/British*

Tig old bitty - Female breasts - Tig old bitty' is a reference to breast feeding from a woman's breasts but now using them for sexual pleasure. - *America/British*

Tiggobitties - Female breasts - Tiggobitties refer to a woman's breasts. - *America/British*

Tittay - Female breasts - Tittay is a word referring to the female breasts. - *America/British*

Titties - Female breasts - She has a lovely pair of titties! - *British*

Titty - Female breasts - Titty is the/a female breast. - *America/British*

Tracts of land - Female breasts - The phrase 'tracts of land' refers to a woman's breasts. - *America/British*

Twins - Female breasts - Look at the size of her twins! - *British*

Twins, the - Female breasts - The twins are a woman's breasts. - *America/British*

Underboob - Female breasts - The underboob is the lower part of a woman's breast, especially if it is on show or revealed by clothing. - *America/British*

Yabo - Female breasts - Yabo are breasts. - *America/British*

French letter - Condom - Have you got any French letters in your pocket? - *British*

Harry Hill - Rhyming with:Pill (contraceptive) - Have you taken your Harry Hill today? - *cockney*

Johnny - Condom - sometimes 'rubber Johnny' - Have you got a rubber Johnny in your pocket? - *British*

Blow one's load - Ejaculation fluid/ semen - He needed to blow his load soon, or he thought he might just explode! - *British*

Bukkake - Related to orgasm - This word refers to a sexual act where several men ejaculate on another person at the same time. - *America/British*

Bust a load - Ejaculation fluid/ semen - He needed to bust his load soon, or he thought he might explode! - *British*

Jis - Semen - The bed covers were covered in jis - *British*

Jis/ jissom - Semen - The bed covers were covered in jissom - *British*

Jissom - Spunk- semen - The bed sheets were covered with jissom. - *British*

Jiz - Ejaculation fluid/ semen - The bed clothes were covered in jiz, after they had sex. - *British*

Jizm - Ejaculation fluid/ semen - The bed clothes were covered with jizm, after they had sex. - *British*

Shoot one's load - Ejaculation fluid/ semen - I feel really horny; I need to shoot my load! - *British*

Skeet - Related to orgasm - He was about to skeet. - *America/British*

Spunk - Semen, ejaculate or to have courage/ bravery - He spunked everywhere - *British*

A stiffie - An erection - I got a stiffie when I saw that woman down the pub. - *British*

Boner - Erect penis - That girl gave me a boner. - *America*

Bulge - Erect penis - He had a massive bulge in his pants. - *British*

Hard on - Fully erect penis - He had a hard on. - *British*

Hard-on - Male genitalia - David had a hard-on every time he saw the blond girl at the pub. - *America/British*

Kerry Katona - Rhymes with boner- a male erection - He had a Kerry Katona. - *cockney*

Lob on - Fully erect penis - He had a lob on. - *British*

Morning wood - Erect penis first thing in the morning - It was a bad case of morning wood! - *America*

Semi - Sexually aroused but not to full erection - I could only muster a semi. - *British*

Stiffie - Erection - Colin had a stiffie from watching pornography on his laptop. - *America/British*

Stiffy - Erection - Colin had a stiffy from watching pornography on his laptop. - *America/British*

Stonker - Erect penis - He had a massive stonker. - *British*

Woody - Erect penis - He has woody in his trousers. - *America*

A sewer snake to release - Defecate - I have a sewer snake to release, where's the toilet? - *British*

Abort a baby - Defecate - I need to abort a baby, where's the toilet? - *British*

Anaconda action - Defecate - I need some anaconda action, where's the toilet? - *British*

Anal leakage - Diarrhoea - He was embarrassed due to the anal leakage, soiling his trousers. - *America/British*

Arsefire - Defecate - I'm in need of an arsefire, where's the toilet? - *British*

Assquake - Diarrhoea - It was an assquake of huge proportions. - *America/British*

Back one out - Defecate - I need to back one out, where's the toilet? - *British*

Back-door trots, the - Diarrhoea - He had a case of the back-door trots! - *America/British*

Backing the big brown motorhome out of the garage - Defecate - I need to back the big brown motorhome out of the garage, where's the toilet? - *British*

Baiting the trap - Defecate - I need to bait the trap, where's the toilet? - *British*

Becoming the porcelain assassin - Defecate - I think I've become the porcelain assassin! - *British*

Blasting a dookie - Defecate - I need to blast a dookie, where's the toilet? - *British*

Blinking - Defecate - I need a good blink, where's the toilet? - *British*

Blow one out - also flatulence - Defecate - I need to blow one out, where's the toilet? - *British*

Blow the load - Defecate - I need to blow the load, where's the toilet? - *British*

Bm - Defecate - I need to bm, where's the toilet? - *British*

Bomb the porcelain sea - Defecate - I need to bomb the porcelain sea, where's the toilet? - *British*

Boo-boo - Defecate - I need to boo-boo! - *British*

Boom boom - Defecate - I need to boom boom! - *British*

Build a beaver dam - Defecate - I need to build a beaver dam, where's the toilet? - *British*

Building a log cabin - Defecate - I need to build a log cabin, where's the toilet? - *British*

Burn a mule - Defecate - I need to burn a mule, where's the toilet? - *British*

Caca - Defecate - I need to caca! - *British*

Call of doodey - Defecate - I feel the call of doody, where's the toilet? - *British*

Carpet bombing Afghanistan - Defecate - I feel like I have just carpet bombed Afghanistan! - *British*

Chocolate time! - Defecate - It's chocolate time, where's the toilet? - *British*

Colon blow - Diarrhoea - His colon was about to blow, so he needed to find a toilet quickly! - *America/British*

Create a custom extrusion - Defecate - I need to create a custom extrusion. - *British*

Crimp one off - Defecate - I need to crimp one off! - *British*

Cripping a crapple - Defecate - I have been crimping a crapple all morning! - *British*

Crowning - Defecate - I've got one crowning, where's the toilet? - *British*

Curling one off - Defecate - I need to curl one off, where's the toilet? - *British*

Cutting a monkey tail - Defecate - I need to cut the monkey's tail, where's the toilet? - *British*

Cutting rope - Defecate - I need to cut some rope, where's the toilet? - *British*

Deceiver of farts - Defecate - Oh, deceiver of farts, I need the toilet! - *British*

De-corking the borking - Defecate - Where's the toilet so I can be de-corking, the borking - *British*

Deucing - Defecate - I'm sorry I'm late, I have been deucing the toilet. - *British*

Dirty squirties - Defecate - I've got a bad case of the dirty squirties. - *British*

Doing brown - Defecate - I've been in the toilet doing some brown. - *British*

Doing some spring cleaning - Defecate - I've been in the toilet doing some spring cleaning. - *British*

Dominating - Defecate - I've been dominating the toilet. - *British*

Doodey (making/doing/having/taking a…) - Defecate - I've been making a doodey. - *British*

Doo-doo (making/doing/having/taking a…) - Defecate - I've been taking a doo-doo. - *British*

Dooey (making/doing/having/taking a…) - Defecate - I've been having a dooey. - *British*

Download a brownload - Defecate - I need to download a brownload. - *British*

Dr. Benjamin Fartlin - Defecate - I've been speaking to Dr. Benjamin Fartlin. - *British*

Drop a double deuce - Defecate - Don't go into the toilet for a bit, I've just dropped a double deuce! - *British*

Dropping a bomb - Defecate - I need to drop a bomb, where's the toilet? - *British*

Dropping a deuce - Defecate - I've been dropping a deuce in the toilet, sorry if it smells! - *British*

Dropping a dook - Defecate - I've been dropping a dook in the toilet, sorry if it smells! - *British*

Dropping a hoopsnake - Defecate - I've been dropping a hoopsnake in the toilet, sorry if it smells! - *British*

Dropping a jolst - Defecate - I've been dropping a jolst in the toilet, sorry if it smells! - *British*

Dropping a load - Defecate - I've been dropping a load in the toilet, sorry if it smells! - *British*

Dropping a loaf - Defecate - I've been dropping a loaf in the toilet, sorry if it smells! - *British*

Dropping a purtle - Defecate - I've been dropping a purtle in the toilet, sorry if it smells! - *British*

Dropping a sewer pickle - Defecate - I've been dropping a sewer pickle in the toilet, sorry if it smells! - *British*

Dropping a washburn - Defecate - I've been dropping a washburn in the toilet, sorry if it smells! - *British*

Dropping an otter (dropping a leith otter) - Defecate - I've been dropping an otter in the toilet, sorry if it smells! - *British*

Dropping anchor - Defecate - I've been dropping anchor in the toilet, sorry if it smells! - *British*

Dropping bass ("base" as in the opposite of treble, not the fish) - Defecate - I've been dropping bass in the toilet, sorry if it smells! - *British*

Dropping logs - Defecate - I've been dropping logs in the toilet, sorry if it smells! - *British*

Dropping some friends off at the pool - Defecate - I've been dropping some friends off at the pool, sorry if it smells! - *British*

Dropping the browns off at the super bowl - Defecate - I've been dropping the browns off at the super bowl, sorry if it smells! - *British*

Dropping the dangle - Defecate - I've been dropping the dangle, sorry if it smells! - *British*

Dropping the kids off at the pool - Defecate - I've been dropping the kids off at the pool, sorry if it smells! - *British*

Dropping the mexican boll weevil - Defecate - I've been dropping the Mexican boll weevil, sorry if it smells! - *British*

Dropping the weights - Defecate - I've been dropping the weights, sorry if it smells! - *British*

Dropping wax - Defecate - I've been in the toilet, dropping wax. - *British*

Faxing a shit to the toilet machine - Defecate - Sorry I am late, I have been faxing a shit to the toilet machine. - *British*

Feeding the toilet - Defecate - I've been feeding the toilet, sorry I am late. - *British*

Filing some papers - Defecate - I need to go and file some papers, be back in a bit. - *British*

Filling the bowl - Defecate - I've been filling the bowl all morning! - *British*

Fire away - Defecate - "Fire away," she said, "I don't mind the smell!" - *British*

Firing a rocket - Defecate - I've been in the toilet, firing a rocket. - *British*

Freeing me chocolate hostages - Defecate - I have been in the toilet, freeing me chocolate hostages. - *British*

Giving birth - Defecate - I need to go to the toilet and give birth! - *British*

Giving birth to the black eel - Defecate - I felt like I was giving birth to the black eel, this morning! - *British*

Giving birth to the spineless brownfish - Defecate - I feel like I am giving birth to the spineless brownfish, this morning! - *British*

Going boom boom - Defecate - I am going to boom boom in my pants, if we don't find a toilet soon! - *British*

Going poop - Defecate - If we don't find a toilet soon, I am going to poop in my pants! - *British*

Going to have a meeting with the governor - Defecate - I'm just going to have a meeting with the governor. - *British*

Going to have a talk with Mr. Hanky - Defecate - He needed to go and have a talk with Mr. Hanky. - *British*

Going to number two - Defecate - The little girl needed to go for a number two, but there was no toilet paper. - *British*

Going to the restitorial - Defecate - He was late going to the restitorial, as he had stomach ache. - *British*

Green apple nasties - Diarrhoea - He had a bad case of the green apple nasties, and needed to be close to a toilet! - *America/ British*

Green apple splatters, the - Diarrhoea - He had the green apple splatters, and felt really poorly with it too! - *America/British*

Green-apple quickstep - Diarrhoea - He was doing the green-appled quickstep to the toilet, all night, after eating something bad! - *America/British*

Growing a tail - Defecate - He was growing a tail, when the door went and a random man walked into the stalls. - *British*

Hanging a rat - Defecate - He was hanging a rat, when the call came to go to work. - *British*

Harry Plopper - Defecate - It was Harry Plopper in the toilet. - *British*

Havana omelette - Diarrhoea - He was making Havana omelettes, all day. - *America/ British*

Hershey squirts, the - Diarrhoea - He had the Hershey squirts. - *America/British*

Hungry hungry hippos - Defecate - He had a case of the hungry hungry hippos, and needed to play desperately. - *British*

Inaugurate Barack Obama to the White House - Defecate - He needed to inaugurate Barack Obama, to the White House. - *British*

Inserting a seal team - Defecate - They needed to insert a seal team, to evacuate his bowels. - *British*

Launching torpedoes - Defecate - He had been launching torpedoes, for about an hour, now. - *British*

Lay down some brown - Defecate - He needed to lay down some brown, urgently. - *British*

Laying a brick - Defecate - He was laying a brick, when someone knocked the bathroom door to come in. - *British*

Laying a brownie - Defecate - He needed to lay some brownies. - *British*

Laying a cable - Defecate - He was laying a cable, of considerable length. - *British*

Laying a hank - Defecate - He was laying a hank, when the doorbell went. - *British*

Laying a turd - Defecate - He was laying a turd, when his mobile phone rang. - *British*

Laying dumplings - Defecate - He had been laying dumplings, when his mum called him for breakfast. - *British*

Laying some wolf bait - Defecate - He was laying some wolf bait, when the telephone rang. - *British*

Lengthening the spine - Defecate - He was able to lengthen his spine this morning, and now felt more comfortable. - *British*

Letting loose - Defecate - He needed to let loose, in the loo. - *British*

Letting the dogs out - Defecate - He needed to let the dogs out soon, or there might be an accident! - *British*

Letting the toilet know who's boss - Defecate - I certainly let the toilet know who's boss, after that! - *British*

Liam Neeson - Defecate: a satisfying phrase to yell after a good bowel movement - James yelled, 'Liam Neeson', after going to the toilet to defecate! - *British*

Load your pants - Defecate - Oh, no, I've loaded my pants! - *British*

Loafin' - Defecate - I've been loafin' all day, today. - *British*

Logging - Defecate - I've been logging, all day, today! - *British*

Logging into the toilet and making a huge download - Defecate - I've been logging into the toilet, and making a huge download. - *British*

Logging out - Defecate - I'm off to do some logging out, see you later! - *British*

Lose some weight (also used in urination) - Defecate - I'm off to lose some weight! - *British*

Makin' bears - Defecate - I'm off makin' bears, see you later! - *British*

Making a tail - Defecate - He was making a tail in the toilet, when the telephone rang. - *British*

Making an appointment with Dr. John - Defecate - I need to make an appointment with Dr. John. - *British*

Making gravy - Defecate - I've been making gravy. - *British*

Making logs (or a log) - Defecate - I need to go and make some logs, in the toilet. - *British*

Making waves - Defecate - I need to go and make some waves, in the toilet. - *British*

Monopoly! - Defecate - I need to go and play monopoly. - *British*

Montezuma's revenge (traveller's diarrhoea) - Defecate - Since I have been on holiday, I have had a bad case of Montezuma's revenge. - *British*

Number 2 - Opening the bowels - I need a number two! - *British*

Number two - Defecate - I need a number two! - *British*

Pebble-dashing the porcelain - Defecate - I've been pebble dashing the porcelain all morning, must be something I have eaten. - *British*

Pinching (off) a loaf - Defecate - I was in the toilet pinching off a loaf, when the telephone rang. - *British*

Pinching a yam - Defecate - I was in the toilet pinching a yam, when the telephone rang - *British*

Piss out of (one's) ass - Diarrhoea - He had been pissing out of his ass, all day, after getting food poisoning from the prawns he had eaten. - *America/British*

Poo - Excrement - I need a poo, I'm off to the toilet. - *British*

Poohing machine - A jokey way of saying a baby who passes a lot of poo - Babies are nothing more than, poohing machines! - *British*

Poop - Excrement - I need to poop! - *British*

Poo-poo - Defecate - I need a poo-poo, mummy! - *British*

Poopy doo - Defecate - I need to poopy doo! - *British*

Poppin a gooky - Defecate - I need to pop a gooky! - *British*

Producing some output - Defecate - I've been producing some output overnight, and need to go to the toilet now. - *British*

Pull a few cones - Defecate - I need to pull a few cones, this morning. - *British*

Pump a clump of dump out of my rump - Defecate - Before I go to work, I need to pump a clump of dump, out of my rump! - *British*

Punching a growler - Defecate - I've been in the toilet punching a growler, sorry I'm late. - *British*

Punishing the porcelain - Defecate - I've been punishing the porcelain, all morning! - *British*

Punishing the toilet - Defecate - I've been punishing the toilet, all morning! - *British*

Put food in the dog's water - Defecate - He needed to put food into the dog's water, before leaving for work. - *British*

Releasing a depth charge - Defecate - He was about to sit down and release a depth charge, when the telephone rang - *British*

Releasing a dung bomb (from Harry Potter) - Defecate - He was about to sit down and release a dung bomb, when the telephone rang. - *British*

Releasing Meatloaf's daughter - Defecate - He was about to sit down and release Meatloaf's daughter, when the telephone rang. - *British*

Releasing the chocolate hostages - Defecate - He was about to sit down and release the chocolate hostages, when the telephone rang. - *British*

Releasing the hostages - Defecate - He was about to sit down and release the hostages, when the telephone rang. - *British*

Releasing the hounds - Defecate - He needed to release the hounds, soonest. - *British*

Releasing the kraken - Defecate - He needed to release the kraken, soonest. - *British*

Ride a pony and trap - Defecate - He needed a pony and trap, urgently. - *British*

Riding the centaur - Defecate - He was riding the centaur again, and it was making his anus sore. - *British*

Body

Ring of fire - Defecate - He had a ring of fire after eating a very spicy chilli, the night before! - *British*

Runs, the - Diarrhoea - He had a case of the runs, after eating a big bag of plums. - *America/British*

S.E. (sit and emit) - Defecate - I'm off to the toilet to S and E. - *British*

Sacrificing to the toilet/porcelain god - Defecate - He was sacrificing to the toilet/porcelain god, when his mum knocked the door to come in and clean her teeth. - *British*

Saturday morning special - Defecate - He was looking forward to his Saturday morning special, when he got up! - *British*

Scatter bombing - Defecate - It was a bad case of scatter bombing, and the toilet bowl was covered in pooh. - *British*

Sending a fax - Defecate - I need to send a fax, I'll be back in a bit. - *British*

Shed some ballast - Defecate - I've just been shelling some ballast, so I would not go in the toilet for a bit, if I was you! - *British*

Shits - Excrement - Sorry, I've got a bad dose of the shits, today. - *British*

Shitting bricks (houses or apartments as substitutes for higher quantity) - Defecate - I have been shitting bricks, all morning. - *British*

Showering the room with roses - Defecate - I have been showering the room with roses, sorry. - *British*

Shtounga - Defecate - Shtounga, my friends! - *British*

Slopping gruel in Oliver's bowl - Defecate - I have been slopping gruel into Oliver's bowl, this morning, not a pretty sight! - *British*

Spray-painting the porcelain - Defecate - I've been spray-painting the porcelain, all day, must have been something I ate! - *British*

Squirt juice - Defecate - I am full of squirt juice today, must be something I ate! - *British*

Squirts, the - Diarrhoea - He had the bottom squirts after he had drank too much concentrated orange juice. - *America/British*

Squits, the - Diarrhoea - He had the squits all day, after eating seafood at the restaurant the night before. - *America/British*

Stalling a brown sedan - Defecate - I was stalling a brown sedan, when you arrived. - *British*

Take a critical ambient to the lab - Defecate - I need to take a critical ambient to the lab. - *British*

Taking a brew - Defecate - I was taking a brew, and the door bell rang. - *British*

Taking a crap - Defecate - I was taking a crap, and my dad called me down for dinner. - *British*

Taking a dump - Defecate - I was taking a dump, when my telephone went. - *British*

Taking a Nixon - Defecate - She was taking a Nixon, when her mobile phone rang. - *British*

Taking a poo - Defecate - She was taking a poo, when the telephone rang. - *British*

Taking a Shatner - Defecate - He was taking a Shatner in the bathroom. - *British*

Taking a shit - Defecate - He was taking a shit in the back garden, how gross! - *British*

Taking a slam - Defecate - I need to take a slam. - *British*

Taking a Tarzan (crapping in the woods/forest) - Defecate - We were out for a walk and I needed to take a Tarzan. - *British*

Taking the mains offline and ejecting the warp coil - Defecate - I was taking the mains offline and ejecting the warp coil, when my little sister banged on the bathroom door, needing to go too! - *British*

Taking the morning curl - Defecate - I was taking the morning curl, when my dad walked into the bathroom! - *British*

Throwing up backwards - Defecate - I was throwing up backwards, when mum walked in! - *British*

Trots, the - Diarrhoea - He had a bad case of the trots. - *America/British*

Tuesday afternoons - Defecate - I need to go to the toilet, it's Tuesday afternoon. - *British*

Turtle time - Defecate - It's turtle time, watch out! - *British*

Uh-oh! - Defecate - Uh-oh...I need to go and change my underwear! - *British*

Uni - Defecate - I need to take a uni, excuse me a minute? - *British*

Unlikely traveller - Defecate - He had an unlikely traveller, and soiled himself. - *British*

Unload - Defecate - He needed to go to the toilet and unload. - *British*

Unloading a batch of cigars - Defecate - He had been in the toilet for ages, unloading a batch of cigars. - *British*

Upgrading my thetan level - Defecate - He had been in the toilet for ages, upgrading his thetan level. - *British*

Visiting Boston - Defecate - He needed to go and visit Boston, in the toilet. - *British*

Vote for president. - Defecate - He needed to go to the toilet and vote for president. - *British*

Whistle belly thumps - Diarrhoea - He had to keep running to the toilet, as he had whistle belly thumps. - *America/British*

Workin' the turd saw - Defecate - He had been workin' the turd saw, but still felt constipated. - *British*

Wrestling a leprechaun - Defecate - He needed to go to the toilet and wrestle a leprechaun! - *British*

Shiner - A black eye - He thumped the other man in the eye, resulting in a big shiner the next day. - *British*

Mug - Face - Look at his ugly mug. - *British*

Phiz - Face - You have a nice phiz. - *British*

Phizog - Face - Look at the phizog on that! - *British*

Bald man in a boat - Female genitalia - Some people crudely describe the female genitalia as a bald man in his boat. - *America/British*

Bearded clam - Female genitalia - I want to touch her bearded clam. - *America/British*

Bearded oyster - Female genitalia - I want to touch her bearded oyster. - *America/British*

Beef curtain - Female genitalia - Some people crudely describe the female genitalia-the labia-as beef curtains. - *America/British*

Beef flap - Female genitalia - Some people crudely describe the female genitalia-the labia- as beef flap. - *America/British*

Camel toe - Female genitalia - Oh, dear, that lady has a camel toe showing through her trousers! - *America/British*

Camel's foot - Female genitalia - Oh, dear, that lady has a camel's foot showing through her trousers! - *America/British*

Cha cha - Female genitalia - He touched my cha cha! - *America/British*

Chach - Female genitalia - He touched my chach. - *America/British*

Fat cat - Female genitalia - She really did have a fat cat! - *America/British*

Love taco - Female genitalia - The female genitalia has been described as a love taco. - *America/British*

Lunchmeat - Female genitalia - The female genitalia has been described as a lunchmeat. - *America/British*

Man in the boat - Female genitalia - Let me play with your man in the boat? - *America/British*

Meat curtains - Female genitalia - The phrase 'meat curtains' means the labia of the female genitalia. - *America/British*

Meat flap - Female genitalia - The meat flaps are the labia, of the female genitalia. - *America/British*

Moose knuckle - Female genitalia - A moose knuckle is the female genitalia. - *America/British*

Neden - Female genitalia - The word 'neden' refers to the female genitalia. - *America/British*

Piss flaps - Female genitalia - A crude phrase for the labia is, the piss flaps. - *America/British*

Twitchet - Female genitalia - Twitchet is another name for the female genitalia. - *America/British*

Body

Vertical smile - Female genitalia - The phrase 'vertical smile' is used by some to refer to the female genitalia. - *America/British*

Whisker biscuit - Female genitalia - Do you want a bite of my whisker biscuit? - *America/British*

Whispering eye - Female genitalia - The phrase 'whispering eye' refers to the female genitalia. - *America/British*

Nether regions - Genitals - The phrase 'nether regions' refers to a person's genitals. - *British*

Bonce - Head - On me bonce, Son! - *British*

Noggin' - Head - "I banged me noggin'," Doc! - *Australian*

Nut - Head - I hit me nut on the cupboard door. - *British*

Scone - Head - On me scone, kids! - *Australian*

Bald-headed yoghurt slinger - Male genitalia - Some people call the male genitalia, the bald-headed yoghurt slinger. - *America/British*

Ball sack - Male genitalia - The male testicles are sometimes referred to as the ball sack. - *America/British*

Bbc - Male genitalia - The male genitalia can be known as the bbc. - *America/British*

Bbd - Male genitalia - The male genitalia can be known as the bbd. - *America/British*

Big dick and the twins - Male genitalia - Roger wanted to let big dick and the twins out, but his wife wasn't interested tonight! - *America/British*

Boys - Male genitalia - Shall I get the boys out tonight? - *America/British*

Cack - Male genitalia - Some people call the male genitalia, the cack. - *America/British*

Coin purse - Male genitalia - He had a full coin purse! - *America/British*

Cojones - Male genitalia - Take a look at my cojones! - *America/British*

D&B - Male genitalia - Mind me D &B ! - *America/British*

D, the - Male genitalia - Watch the big D! - *America/British*

Down belows - Genitals - Doc, it's my down belows giving me trouble today. - *British*

Equipment - Male genitalia - Let me get my equipment out and see if I'm up for the job! - *America/British*

Garbage - Male genitalia - He has a right bit of garbage in his trousers! - *America/British*

General, two colonels - Male genitalia - The General and his two Colonels got some action last night! - *America/British*

Gonad - Male genitalia - The gonads are part of the male genitalia. - *America/British*

Hockey cocky - Male genitalia - Fancy a bit of hockey cocky? - *America/British*

Knap sack - Male genitalia - Would you like to put my knap sack on? - *America/British*

Nads - Male genitalia - Watch me nads! - *America/British*

Nards - Male genitalia - The nards are the male genitalia. - *America/British*

Package - Male genitalia - He looks like he has a good package in his trousers! - *America/British*

Packer - Male genitalia - He has a good packer! - *America/British*

Patz - Male genitalia - The word 'patz' refers to the male genitals. - *America/British*

Peen - Male genitalia - The word 'peen' refers to the male genitalia. - *America/British*

Ph.d - Male genitalia - The abbrevaition 'Ph.d' refers to the male genitalia. - *America/British*

Pop a chub - Penis erection - The phrase 'pop a chub' refers to having an erection. - *America/British*

Tripod - Male genitalia - The word 'tipod' refers to the three elements of the penis and testicles, the male genitalia - *America/British*

Tube steak - Male genitalia - 'The tube steak' is a crude phrase used to describe the male genitalia. - *America/British*

Twigs and berries - Male genitalia - The twig(s) and berries refers to the penis and testicles, the male genitalia. - *America/British*

Unit - Male genitalia - A unit is the male genitalia as a whole. - *America/British*

Body

Aunt Flo - Menstruation - I've got Aunt Flo staying with me this week. - *America/British*

Aunt Flo and Cousin Red - Menstruation - I've got Aunt Flo and Cousin Red, staying with me this week. - *America/British*

Cousin Red - Menstruation - I've got Cousin Red staying with me, this week. - *America/British*

Crimson wave - Menstruation - I'm on the crimson wave this week. - *America/British*

Delicate - Menstruation - I'm feeling a bit delicate this week. - *America/British*

Flow - Menstruation - I'm on the flow this week. - *America/British*

Get (one's) redwings - Menstruation - I've got my redwings this week. - *America/British*

Have the painters in - Menstruation - I have the painters in. - *America/British*

In her flowers - Menstruation - I'm in my flowers this week. - *America/British*

Late - Menstruation - I'm late...I haven't had my period yet this month. - *America/British*

On the rag - Menstruation - She's on the rag. - *America/British*

Red tide - Menstruation - She's on the red tide. - *America/British*

Ride the cotton pony - Menstruation - She's riding the cotton pony this week. - *America/British*

Sally - Menstruation - She's with Sally this week. - *America/British*

Shark week - Menstruation - It's shark week, if you know what I mean? - *America/British*

Surf the crimson wave - Menstruation - She's surfing the crimson wave. - *America/British*

That time of the month - Menstruation - It's that time of the month... - *America/British*

The curse - Menstruation - Jane had the curse so could not go swimming. - *British*

Women's trouble - Menstruation - She's having a bit of women's trouble! - *America/British*

Gob - Mouth - Shut your gob! - *British*

Laughing gear - Mouth - Get your laughing gear around that! - *British*

Mush - Face or mouth - I hit him in the mush. - *British*

Pie hole - Mouth - Shove that in your pie hole and shut up! - *British*

Bat in the cave - Mucus in the nose - The baby had a bat in the cave, from crying all night. - *British*

Blow snot bubbles - Mucus in the nose - The baby was blowing snot bubbles from his nose. - *British*

Blow snot rockets - Mucus in the nose - The baby blew snot rockets out of his nose. - *British*

Bogey - Mucus in the nose - The little girl had a bogey coming out of her nose. - *British*

Booger - Related to nasal mucus - The baby had a large booger, hanging out of his nose. - *America/British*

Boogey - Related to nasal mucus - The baby had a large boogey, hanging out of his nose. - *America/British*

Farmer's blow - Related to nasal mucus - Have a big farmer's blow, and try and rid yourself of all that mucus. - *America/British*

Greenie gremlins - Mucus in the nose - The children all had colds and were full of greenie gremlins! - *British*

Greenies - Mucus in the nose - She blew her greenies on to a handkerchief. - *British*

Hock a loogie - Related to nasal mucus - The man hocked up a huge loogie, and spat it out on to the floor. - *America/British*

Hook a loogie - Mucus in the nose - The little boy had his finger up his nose, trying to hook a loogie out. - *British*

Loagie - Related to nasal mucus - The man hocked up a huge loagie, and spat it out on to the floor. - *America/British*

Body

Body

Loogie - Mucus in the nose - The little boy had his finger up his nose, searching for a loogie. - *British*

Lugie - Related to nasal mucus - The man hocked a lugie, and spat it out on to the floor. - *America/British*

Nasal waste - Related to nasal mucus - He was full of nasal waste due to the bad cold he had. - *America/British*

Runny nose - Mucus in the nose - The children had runny nose, from the cold. - *British*

Snart - Mucus in the nose - Look at the snart running down her face! - *British*

Snot - Mucus in the nose - Look at the snot running down her face! - *British*

Snot monster - Mucus in the nose - The baby was so snotty, he could have been described as a snot monster! - *British*

Snot rocket - Related to nasal mucus - He blew a massive snot rocket. - *America/British*

Snotty - Mucus in the nose - Sorry I'm so snotty, I have a really bad cold. - *British*

Snough - Related to nasal mucus - He was full of snough. - *America/British*

Abs - Muscles - The athlete liked to show off his abs which he had cultivated by going to the gym. - *America/British*

Cuts - Muscles - He worked on his cuts at the gym, religiously. - *America/British*

Glute - Muscles - Look at his well formed glutes. - *America/British*

Guns - Muscles - It was a hot day so the man had his guns out. - *America/British*

Six pack - Muscles - Someone is said to have a six pack if they have well defined abdominal muscles that show. - *America/British*

Arm candy - An attractive sexy woman - I saw Dave down the pub, he had a bit of new arm candy. - *America/British*

Arse bandit - Term referring to a homosexual - Sam is an arse bandit. - *British*

Astronaut's wife - An attractive sexy woman - She was an astronaut's wife, so pretty. - *America/British*

Auntie - Homosexual - Well, you know he's an aunty, don't you? - *America/British*

Babe magnet - A sexually attractive person - Pete thinks he is a babe magnet but believe me, he is not! - *America*

Bad kitty - An attractive sexy woman - I bet she's a bad kitty! - *America/British*

Baldwin - A handsome or sexy man - He's a bit baldwin. - *America/British*

BBW - Stands for Big, Beautiful, Women - What a BBW! - *America/British*

Benjamin - An attractive sexy woman - What a Benjamin. - *America/British*

Booth babe - An attractive sexy woman - She was a booth babe. - *America/British*

Breezy - An attractive sexy woman - She was breezy, man. - *America/British*

Broad - Prostitute - She was a broad all her life. - *America/British*

Bum bandit - Homosexual - Joseph is a bum bandit. - *America/British*

Bum chum - Homosexual - Julian has got a new bum chum. - *America/British*

Bumder - Homosexual - He's such a bumder. - *America/British*

Bushpig - An unattractive woman - Harry's new girlfriend is a bushpig! - *America/British*

Butch - Homosexual - John's new boyfriend is really butch. - *America/British*

Butt hugger - Homosexual - He's a butt hugger. - *America/British*

Butter face - An unattractive woman - She was a butter face, sadly. - *America/British*

Butterface - An unattractive woman - She was a butterface, sadly. - *America/British*

Butterhead - An unattractive woman - She was a butterhead, sadly. - *America/British*

Call girl - Prostitute - She was a call girl all her life. - *America*

Carpet muncher - A lesbian - She's a carpet muncher. - *America*

Catcher - Homosexual - He's a catcher. - *America/British*

Chandelier - Rhyming slang- queer-gay/ homosexual - He's a chandelier. - *cockney*

Charva - A loose woman, a woman considered easy to have sex with - What a charva! - *British*

Charver - A loose woman, a woman considered easy to have sex with - She was such a charver. - *British*

Chaser - Homosexual - He's such a chaser. - *America/British*

Chick with a dick - A transsexual, with feminine features and with male genitals - He's a chick with a dick - *British*

Chicken hawk - Homosexual - He's a chicken hawk. - *America/British*

Chiquita banana - An attractive sexy woman - She was considered to be a chiquita banana by the local men. - *America/British*

Come out - To reveal ones sexual orientation (homosexual/lesbian/bisexual) - He came out last month to his friends and family. - *British*

Cougar - An attractive sexy woman - She was such a cougar, always after the younger men. - *America/British*

Crockadillapig - An unattractive woman - She was considered to be such a crockadillapig. - *America/British*

Cronk - An unattractive woman - She was such an old cronk. - *America/British*

Cub - Homosexual - He's a little cub. - *America/British*

Darren Day - Rhyming with : Gay/ homosexual - He's Darren Day. - *cockney*

Decent Rita - An attractive sexy woman - She's a decent Rita. - *America/British*

Dime - An attractive sexy woman - She's such a dime. - *America/British*

Dish - An attractive sexy woman - She's such a dish. - *America/British*

Dishy - A sexually attractive person - He's so dishy! - *British*

Doll - A good looking woman - She's such a doll. - *British*

Doris Day - Rhyming with: Gay/ homosexual - He's Doris Day. - *cockney*

Doubler - Enjoying penetration by two men at the same time. - She was a doubler, enjoying sex with two men at the same time. - *America/British*

Drag king - Homosexual - He's a drag king. - *America/British*

Dreamboat - A handsome or sexy man - He's such a dreamboat - *America/British*

Dyke - A lesbian - She's a dyke. - *British*

Easy - Prostitute or a promiscuous person who has a lot of sexual intercourse - She's considered to be easy. - *British*

Easy lay - Prostitute or sexually loose - She's considered to be an easy lay. - *British*

Escort - Prostitute or a person earning money by being a paid as a companion to events - He doesn't have a girlfriend so takes an escort to the party instead. - *British*

Faggot - Derogatory term for a homosexual - He's a faggot. - *British*

Fairy - A homosexual - He's such a fairy. - *British*

Fallen woman - Prostitute - She's a fallen woman, I'm afraid - *British*

Feedbag material - An attractive sexy woman - She was considered to be feedbag material. - *America/British*

Femme - Homosexual - He's a femme. - *America/British*

FILF - Father I'd Like to Fuck - He's such a FILF! - *America/British*

Filthy - Reference to sexual morals - They've got a filthy mind! - *British*

Fit - Sexually attractive - She's well fit! - *British*

Floozy - Prostitute - She was his floozy. - *British*

Fromage frais - Rhyming with: Gay/ homosexual - He's a fromage frais. - *cockney*

Gaylord - Homosexual - He's such a gaylord. - *America/British*

Gender bender - A person who explores different gender identities - He's such a gender bender - *British*

Body

Ghetto bird - An unattractive woman - She's such a ghetto bird. - *America/British*

GILF - Grandma I'd Like to Fuck: an attractive older woman - She's a very attractive woman for her age, such a GILF. - *America/British*

GLBT - Acronym - Gay, Lesbian, Bisexual and Transsexual - He's a member of GLBT. - *America/British*

Good sort - An attractive sexy woman - She's a good sort. - *America/British*

GQ - A handsome or sexy man - He's G and Q. - *America/British*

Grizzly chicken - An unattractive woman - She's such a grizzly chicken. - *America/British*

Harlot - Prostitute - She was a complete harlot - *British*

Harrison - A handsome or sexy man - He's harrison! - *America/British*

Hasbian - Homosexual - They're such a hasbian. - *America/British*

Heina - An attractive sexy woman - She was considered to be a heina. - *America/British*

Ho - Prostitute - She was a complete ho! - *America*

Hogbeast - An unattractive woman - What a hogbeast, she was! - *America/British*

Home and away - Rhyming with: Gay/ homosexual - He plays home and away. - *cockney*

Homo - Homosexual - He's a homo. - *America/British*

Ho-nasty - An unattractive woman - What an ho-nasty, she was! - *America/British*

Hoss - An unattractive woman - She was considered to be a complete hoss. - *America/British*

Hot ma' - An attractive sexy woman - She was considered to be a hot ma'. - *America/British*

Hunky - Masculine and attractive - He's a bit hunky. - *British*

Hunny - An attractive sexy woman - She was such a hunny! - *America/British*

In the closet - Homosexual - He's still in the closet. - *America/British*

Inspector Taggart - Rhyming with:Faggot- gay/ homosexual - He's such an Inspector Taggart. - *cockney*

Iron hoof - Rhyming with: Poof- gay/ homosexual - He's an iron hoof. - *cockney*

Jack the Ripper - Stripper - She works in a night club as a Jack the Ripper. - *cockney*

Jackpine savage - An unattractive woman - The men thought she was jackpine savage. - *America/British*

Jobby jabber - Homosexual - He's jobby jabber. - *America/British*

Julian Clairy - Rhymes with fairy- gay/ homosexual - He's so Julian Clairy. - *cockney*

Julian Ray - Gay/ homosexual - He's so Julian Ray. - *cockney*

Karena - An attractive sexy woman - She was considered to be a karena. - *America/British*

Knob jockey - Stupid or irritating person, or derogatory term to describe homosexual activity - He's such a knob jockey. - *British*

Ladies' man - A handsome or sexy man - He's such a ladies' man. - *America/British*

Lady of the night - Prostitute - She worked as a lady of the night. - *British*

Lech - Abbreviation of lecherous. To be lustful - He was such a lech. - *British*

Lemon - Homosexual - He's a lemon. - *America/British*

Leo Fender - Bender- gay/ homosexual - He's Leo Fender. - *cockney*

Lesbo - Lesbian - She's a lesbo. - *British*

Lez - Homosexual - She's a lez. - *America/British*

Lipstick lesbian - Homosexual, glamorous - She's such a lipstick lesbian. - *America/British*

Lolita - An attractive sexy woman - She was a Lolita. - *America/British*

Body

Long and flexy - Sexy - She so long and flexy! - *cockney*

Mami - An attractive sexy woman - She was a mami. - *America/British*

Manster - An unattractive woman - She was such a manster. - *America/British*

Mcdreamy - A handsome or sexy man - What a Mcdreamy! - *America/British*

MILF - An attractive sexy woman - Acronym (Mother I would like to fuck) - They boys said she was a MILF. - *America/British*

Minge muncher - Homosexual - She's a minge muncher. - *America/British*

Mona bushpig - An unattractive woman - She was considered to look like a mona bushpig. - *America/British*

Moose - A physically unattractive person - She's such a moose. - *British*

Mucky - Dirty, or sexually coarse - You mucky lad. - *British*

Mudpout - An unattractive woman - She's such a mudpout. - *America/British*

Munter - An ugly person - She's such a munter. - *British*

Nellie - Homosexual - Look at that right Nellie, over there. - *America/British*

Nelly - Homosexual - Look at that right nelly, over there. - *America/British*

Nympho - Prostitute or someone who is thought to be addicted to sex; a nymphomaniac - She loves sex so much, she's been called a nympho often! - *British*

Omega mu - An unattractive woman - She's not very attractive, such an omega mu. - *America/British*

P.Y.T. - An attractive sexy woman - acronym of pretty, young, thing - What a P.Y.T! - *America/British*

Pebbles - An attractive sexy woman - She's pebbles, isn't she? - *America/British*

Pervy - Perverted - She's so pervy. - *British*

Peter Puffer - Homosexual - Look at the Peter Puffer. - *America/British*

Piece of tail - Prostitute - Follow that piece of tail! - *America*

Pinup - An attractive woman who would look good on a poster (advert) - She was so beautiful, just like a pinup girl. - *British*

Power top - Homosexual - He's a power top. - *America/British*

Pretty boy - An effeminate male - Sam was such a pretty boy. - *British*

Prozzy - Prostitute - Such a prozzy! - *British*

Rasp - An attractive sexy woman - She's such a rasp. - *America/British*

Rub - An unattractive woman - What a rub! - *America/British*

Sea donkey - An unattractive woman - What a sea donkey! - *America/British*

Sea hag - An unattractive woman - What a sea hag! - *America/British*

Sex kitten - An attractive sexy woman - What a sex kitten! - *America/British*

Sexy mama - An attractive sexy woman - What a sexy mama! - *America/British*

Shirt lifter - Derogatory term for a homosexual - He's such a shirt lifter. - *British*

Skeezy ho - An unattractive woman - The girls thought she was such a skeezy ho for sleeping around. - *America/British*

Skins - An attractive woman - She skins, isn't she? - *Bristol*

Skirt - Derogatory term for a female - What a good looking piece of skirt. - *British*

Snack - A handsome or sexy man - I'd like him for a snack! - *America/British*

Street walker - Prostitute - She's been a street walker all her life. - *British*

Street worker - Prostitution, male or female - She works on the streets. - *British*

Strumpet - Prostitute - old fashioned phrase - What an absolute strumpet! - *British*

Susan Glenn - An attractive sexy woman - She's a bit Susan Glenn. - *America/British*

Swamp donkey - An unattractive woman - She's a bit of a swamp donkey - *America/British*

Tail - An attractive sexy woman - She's a good looking bit of tail. - *America/British*

Tart - A person perceived as sexually promiscuous - She's such a tart! - *British*

The town's bike - Derogatory term for a promiscuous woman - Everyone called her the town's bike! - *British*

Trannie - A transvestite - a man who wears female clothing, or a transexual - He's a trannie, you know? - *British*

Trim - An attractive sexy woman - She's pretty trim. - *America/British*

Troglodyte - An unattractive woman - She's such a troglodyte. - *America/British*

Twinkie - An attractive sexy woman - She's such a twinkie. - *America/British*

Two o'clock beauty queen - An unattractive woman - She's a two o' clock beauty queen. - *America/British*

Vamp - An attractive sexy woman - She looks like a vamp in that outfit. - *America/British*

Versatile - Homosexual - He's pretty versatile, if you know what I mean? - *America/British*

Whooty - An attractive sexy woman - What a whooty! - *America/British*

Whore - Prostitute - She's such a whore! - *British*

Wild - An attractive sexy woman - She's absolutely wild! - *America/British*

Woman of the streets - Prostitute - She's a woman of the streets. - *British*

Woofer - An unattractive woman - What a woofer! - *America/British*

Working girl - Prostitute - She's a working girl. - *British*

Xbox - An unattractive woman - She's a bit Xbox! - *America/British*

Yo yo knickers - A promiscuous person - I'd describe her as yo yo knickers, if you know what I mean? - *British*

Yummy mummy - An attractive young mother - Such a yummy mummy! - *British*

Innie - The navel - People often refer to their navel as an innie or an outie. - *America/British*

Outie - The navel protruding - A navel that sticks out and protrudes is referred to as an outie. - *America/British*

Conk - The head or the nose, or to strike them - You have a huge conk! - *British*

Hooter - Nose - He punched him right on the hooter. - *British*

Chunky - Overweight or obese - He's a bit chunky! - *America/British*

Cottage cheese - Overweight or obese - They're a bit cottage cheese, aren't they? - *America/British*

Dad bod - Overweight or obese - Gary's got such a dad bod these days! - *America/British*

Gock - Overweight or obese - Another word for obese is, gock. - *America/British*

Gothopotamus - Overweight or obese - Wow, look at the gothopotamus over there! - *America/British*

Gunt - Overweight or obese - What a gunt! - *America/British*

Gut scuff - Overweight or obese - What a gut scuff! - *America/British*

Hail damage - Overweight or obese - Watch the hail damage coming up the road. - *America/British*

Muffin top - Overweight or obese - A muffin top is a roll of fat over the top of the trouser waistband. - *America/British*

Obeast - Overweight or obese - He's obeast! - *America/British*

Pack of Frank's big-boned - Overweight or obese - The phrase, 'a pack of Frank's big boned' is used to refer to someone who is obese. - *America/British*

Pear-shaped - Overweight or obese - The lady had a pear shaped figure because she was overweight. - *America/British*

Body

Skinny fat - Overweight or obese - Look at that man he is pretty skinny fat. - *America/British*

Wisconsin skinny - Overweight or obese - Hey, look at that Wisconsin skinny over there. - *America/British*

100% all-beef thermometer - Male genitalia - He was a 100% all-beef thermometer! - *America/British*

Abd - Male genitalia - Let's have a look at your abd? - *America/British*

Acorn - Male genitalia - David had a small penis but it was an acorn that could grow! - *America/British*

Alabama black snake - Male genitalia - David had an Alabama black snake in his trousers, it was deadly! - *America/British*

Anaconda - Male genitalia - David had an anaconda lurking in his trousers. - *America/British*

Anal impaler - Male genitalia - Jo wondered if Dave was an anal impaler? - *America/British*

Ayers Rock - Rhyming with:Cock - He's got a big Ayers Rock! - *cockney*

Baby arm - Male genitalia - Simon's penis was as big as a baby's arm! - *America/British*

Baby maker - Male genitalia - Henry wanted to put his baby maker into his wife but she was not in the mood! - *America/British*

Baloney - Penis - Have you seen the size of his baloney? - *America*

Baloney pony - Penis - The penis is sometimes called the baloney pony. - *America/British*

Banana - Penis - Have you seen the size of his banana? - *British*

Beef bayonet - The penis - Have you seen the size of his beef bayonet? - *America/British*

Bell end - The end of the penis - I have a pain in my bell end. - *British*

Big Italian salami - Male genitalia - Roger has a big Italian salami! - *America/British*

Bits - Penis - John put your bits away. - *British*

Bobby dangler - Male genitalia - He's got a right big, bobby dangler! - *America/British*

Bologna pony - Male genitalia - Look at the size of his bologna pony! - *America/British*

Boom stick - Male genitalia - He has a large boom stick, I believe? - *America/British*

Bratwurst - Male genitalia - Look at the size of his bratwurst! - *America/British*

Broner - Male genitalia - I've been told I have got a big broner. - *America/British*

Chopper - Penis - He had the most huge chopper! - *British*

Chub - Male genitalia - I touched his chub! - *America/British*

Chubbie - Male genitalia - I touched his chubbie! - *America/British*

Chup - Male genitalia - I touched his chup! - *America/British*

Chut - Male genitalia - I touched his chut! - *America/British*

Cock - Penis - He has such a big cock, it's unbelievable! - *British*

Cock rocket - Male genitalia - Let me see your cock rocket! - *America/British*

D - Male genitalia - Have you had your D out recently? - *America/British*

D train - Male genitalia - Have you been on the D train recently? - *America/British*

Dangler - Male genitalia - Oh, look at the size of his dangler! - *America/British*

Dick smalls - Male genitalia - Watch Dick Smalls doesn't get caught in your zip! - *America/British*

Ding - Male genitalia - Ding dong! - *America/British*

Dingis - Male genitalia - Dingis in the house! - *America/British*

Dinker - Male genitalia - He's got such a small dinker. - *America/British*

Disco stick - Male genitalia - Do you want to touch my disco stick? - *America/British*

Doder - Male genitalia - He's got a big doder! - *America/British*

Doinker - Male genitalia - He's got a large doinker! - *America/British*

Domepiece - Male genitalia - Look at the size of his domepiece! - *America/British*

Dong - Penis - He had a huge dong. - *British*

Donger - Penis - He had a huge donger. - *British*

Donkey dick - Large penis - They called him 'donkey dick' due to the size of his penis! - *British*

Doodle - Penis - He had a huge doodle. - *Australian*

Dork - Male genitalia - He's such a dork! - *America/British*

German helmet - Top of the penis - His German helmet was sore. - *British*

Giggleberry - Male genitalia - Do you want to touch giggleberry? - *America/British*

Gut wrench - Male genitalia - Another phrase meaning penis is gut wrench. - *America/British*

Hampton - Rhyming slang for Hampton wick= prick (penis) Hampton rock= cock (penis) - How's your Hampton? - *British*

Helmet - The head of the penis - His helmet needed a wash. - *British*

Hooded - Male genitalia - The hooded snake needs some action. - *America/British*

Hotdog - Male genitalia - Fancy a lick of my hotdog? - *America/British*

Hung - Male genitalia - He is well hung. - *America/British*

Hung like a donkey - Large penis - He was hung like a donkey! - *British*

John Thomas - Penis - Look at my John Thomas, it's a bit sore on the end. - *British*

Johnson - Male genitalia - Look at my Johnson, it is a bit sore on the end. - *America/British*

Joystick - Male genitalia - Take hold of my joystick and hold on for the ride! - *America/British*

Kielbasa - Male genitalia - The penis has been called the kielbasa. - *America/British*

Kiwi - Male genitalia - A kiwi is a penis. - *America/British*

Knob - Penis - He has a big knob! - *British*

Knob end - Stupid or irritating person or the end of the penis - He is such a knob end! - *British*

Lady boner - Male genitalia - The penis has been crudely named, the lady boner, by some. - *America/British*

Length - Penis - He made sure he gave her a good length. - *British*

Lolly lick - Dick- penis - He let her have a go on his lolly lick. - *cockney*

Love muscle - Penis - She wanted a go on his love muscle. - *America*

Love shaft - Male genitalia - The penis has been known to be called, the love shaft. - *America/British*

Love stick - Male genitalia - The penis had been known to be called, the love stick. - *America/British*

Love truncheon - Penis - She wanted a go on his love truncheon. - *British*

Main vein - Male genitalia - Can I put my main vein into you tonight? - *America/British*

Man muscle - Male genitalia - The man muscle is the penis. - *America/British*

Manhood - Male genitalia - Don't be insulting my manhood! - *America/British*

Master of ceremonies - Male genitalia - He whipped his master of ceremonies out and it was fully hard. - *America/British*

Meat popsicle - Penis - A meat popsicle is a penis. - *America/British*

Meat thermometer - Penis - A meat thermometer is a penis. - *America/British*

Middle leg - Penis - He was hit in the middle leg. - *British*

Mr. Happy - Male genitalia - Mr. Happy is a man's penis. - *America/British*

Mr. Winky - Male genitalia - Mr. Winky is a man's penis. - *America/British*

Mr. Wobbly - Penis - Mr. Wobbly is a man's penis. - *Australian*

Mutton dagger - Penis - He whipped out his mutton dragger in readiness. - *British*

Needle dick - Penis - His penis was so small, such a needle dick! - *British*

Ol' one-eye - Male genitalia - He got ol' one-eye out and thought we would have sex! - *America/British*

Old fella - Penis - My old fella hasn't had any action for ages! - *Australian*

One-eyed monster - Penis - The one-eyed monster has been out of action for ages! - *America/British*

One-eyed snake - Penis - The one-eyed snake has been out of action for ages! - *America/British*

One-eyed trouser snake - Penis - The one-eyed trouser snake always gets me into trouble! - *America/British*

P - Penis - The letter P is used to denote the word penis. - *America/British*

Pecker - Penis - His pecker was up. - *British*

Peeper - Male genitalia - He has a peeper coming out. - *America/British*

Percy - Penis - I'm going to point Percy at the porcelain. - *British*

Peter - Penis - Peter is another name for penis. - *America/British*

Pickle - Penis - He's got a small pickle, hasn't he? - *America/British*

Pink tractor beam - Penis - The silly phrase 'pink tractor beam' is sometimes used to describe the penis. - *America/British*

Plum - Penis - The word 'plum' is sometimes used to describe the penis, perhaps because of the colour connotations? - *America/British*

Pocket rocket - Penis - Do you want to go on my pocket rocket? - *America/British*

Polaroid - Penis - Want a go on my polaroid? - *America/British*

Pole - Penis - Want a go on my pole? - *America/British*

Pork sword - Penis - Do you want to play with my pork sword? - *British*

Prick - Penis - He was such a prick. - *British*

Pud - Penis - The word pud refers to the penis. - *America/British*

Purple-headed soldier - Penis - The purple headed soldier was erect and ready for action! - *America/British*

Purple-headed warrior - Penis - The purple headed warrior was erect and ready for action! - *America/British*

Rod - Penis - Take a hold of my rod! - *America/British*

Russell the love muscle - Penis - Can we play with Russell, the love muscle? - *America/British*

Salami - Penis - Fancy a lick of my salami? - *America/British*

Sausage - Penis - He had a small sausage. - *British*

Schlong - Penis - He had a long schlong. - *America*

Schlort - Penis - The word 'schlort' means penis for some people. - *America/British*

Schmeckel - Penis - The word 'schmeckel' can mean the penis. - *America/British*

Schwartz - Penis - Look at my spicy schwartz! - *America/British*

Sconge - Penis - The word 'sconge' can be used to mean the penis. - *America/British*

Shlang - Penis - She ran her hand down his shlang. - *America*

Shlittle - Penis - The shlittle is a little penis. - *America/British*

Shlong - Penis - The penis can be called a shlong. - *America/British*

Shrinkage - Penis - The penis has shrinkage when it is cold, old or after sex. - *America/British*

Skin flute - Penis - The skin flute is a term used to describe the penis and it's width. - *America/British*

Steamin' semen roadway - Penis - The phrase 'steamin' semen roadway' refers to the penis and the act of sex. - *America/British*

Tadger - Penis - Watch me tadger! - *British*

Tallywhacker - Penis - A tallywhacker is a penis. - *America/British*

Body

Tent pole - Penis - His tent pole was erect in his trousers. - *America/British*

The one eyed monster - Penis - The one eyed monster stared up at her. - *British*

Thin stick - Small penis - He had a thin stick. - *America*

Thing - Penis - Do you want to cop a feel of my thing? - *America/British*

Third leg - Penis - Watch my third leg, boys! - *America/British*

Throbber - Penis - Can you feel my throbber between your legs? - *America/British*

Todger - Penis - He has a massive todger. - *British*

Tonsil tickler - Penis - The crude phrase 'tonsil tickler' refers to the penis during oral sex. - *America/British*

Tool - Penis - He has a massive tool. - *British*

Trouser meat - Penis - Trouser meat is the penis. - *America/British*

Trouser snake - Penis - Have you seen the size of his trouser snake? - *British*

Twig - Penis - The twig is the penis. - *America/British*

Walter - Female breasts - A Walter is another word for penis. - *America/British*

Wang - Penis - Look at his big wang. - *America/British*

Wanger - Penis - He has a huge wanger! - *America*

Wankie - Penis - Look at his wankie! - *America/British*

Weenie - Penis - He has a weenie weenie. - *America/British*

Well hung - Large penis - He's really well hung! - *British*

Whang - Penis - I've got a massive whang! - *America/British*

Whiskey dick - Penis - A whiskey dick is the penis. - *America/British*

Who who dilly - Penis - The phrase 'who who dilly' refers to the penis. - *America/British*

Wiener - Penis - Look at his little wiener! - *America/British*

Willie - Penis - Look at his big willie! - *America/British*

Willy - Penis - Percy had a big willy. - *British*

Winkle - Penis - He has a small winkle. - *British*

Winky - Penis - Look at his little winky! - *America/British*

Yam bag - Penis - The phrase 'yam bag' is another way to say penis. - *America/British*

Yoghurt slinger - Penis - The yoghurt slinger is a crude way to describe the penis. - *America/British*

Yoo-hoo - Penis - You-hoo is another phrase used to describe the penis. - *America/British*

Zubra - Penis - Zubra is another name used to refer to the penis. - *America/British*

Banus - The perineum - The perineum has been called the banus. - *America/British*

Choade - The perineum - What is a choade? - *America/British*

Choda - The perineum - What's a choda? - *America/British*

Gooch - The perineum - The gooch is another name for the perineum. - *America/British*

Grundel - The perineum - The grundel, is another word to describe the perineum. - *America/British*

Twitter - The perineum - The twitter refers to the perineum. - *America/British*

Franky Vaughan - Rhyming with:Porn - Let's watch a bit of Franky Vaughan? - *cockney*

Goldie Hawn - Rhyming with: Porn. Goldie Hawn is an American actress - Let's watch a bit of Goldie Hawn? - *cockney*

X rated - Lewd, obscene or pornographic - It's an X rated film. - *British*

Bun in the oven - Pregnant - She's got a bun in the oven. - *British*

Up the duff - Pregnant - She's up the duff with his baby! - *British*

Knocking shop - Brothel - There is a knocking shop at the end of the road. - *British*

Meat market - A nightclub where the majority of people go solely to find sexual partners - You're not going to that meat market, are you? - *British*

On the pull - Seeking a sexual partner - They were out on the pull. - *British*

Baby batter - Semen - We need some baby batter to make this baby. - *America/British*

Baby gravy - Semen - We need some baby gravy to make this baby. - *America/British*

Big O, the - Related to orgasm - She had never had the big O! - *America/British*

Blow (one's) load - Related to orgasm - He blew his load quickly, as he had not had sex for some time. - *America/British*

Blow (one's) wad - Related to orgasm - He blew his wad quickly, as he had not had sex for some time! - *America/British*

Bust (one's) nut - Related to orgasm - He bust his nuts quickly, as he had not had sex for a long time. - *America/British*

Bust a wad - Related to orgasm - He bust a wad last night! - *America/British*

Chocolate cum - Semen - He was covered in chocolate cum, after having sex with him. - *America/British*

Come - Point of orgasm in men and women - "Don't stop," said the woman, "I'm about to come!" - *British*

Cream of some young guy - Semen - I need the 'cream of some young guy,' if you know what I mean? - *America/British*

Creampie - Related to orgasm - He made me a creampie last night. - *America/British*

Cum - Point of orgasm in men and women - "Don't stop," said the woman, "I'm about to cum!" - *British*

Finish - Related to orgasm - He finished before her. - *America/British*

Get (one's) nut off - Related to orgasm - He often got his nuts off, looking at pornography. - *America/British*

Get off - Related to orgasm - He got off looking at pornography. - *America/British*

Ghost load - Related to orgasm - He produced a fair ghost load. - *America/British*

Jism - Semen - There was jism everywhere! - *America/British*

Jizz - Semen - There was jizz everywhere! - *America/British*

Jizzum - Semen - There was jizzum everywhere! - *America/British*

Man chowder - Semen - There was man chowder everywhere! - *America/British*

Man seed - Semen - He left a trail of man seed in the bed. - *America/British*

Nut butter - Semen - He left some nut butter behind on her leg. - *America/British*

Pearl necklace - Semen - He gave her a pearl necklace around her throat. - *America/British*

Pole milk - Semen - He left her some pole milk. - *America/British*

Protein shake - Semen - He gave her a big protein shake. - *America/British*

Schlong juice - Semen - He gave her some schlong juice. - *America/British*

Seed - Semen - The man has the seed... - *America/British*

Shoot (one's) load - Related to orgasm - He shot his load quickly. - *America/British*

Shoot (one's) wad - Related to orgasm - He shot is wad quickly. - *America/British*

Show (one's) o face - Related to orgasm - She showed him her O face. - *America/British*

Splooge - Semen - He left a trail of splooge. - *America/British*

Spluge - Related to orgasm - He spludged quickly. - *America/British*

Splurge - Related to orgasm - He splurdged as often as he could! - *America/British*

Spooge - Semen - He left a trail of spooge. - *America/British*

String of pearls - Semen - He shot a string of pearls across her. - *America/British*

Body

Body

Tattie water - Semen - He gave her a cup of tattie water. - *America/British*

Trouser gravy - Semen - He gave her some of his trouser gravy. - *America/British*

Two ball throat cream - Semen - He gave her a two ball throat cream. - *America/British*

Two pump chump - Related to orgasm - They came together, a two pump chump. - *America/British*

Two-ball compound - Semen - He gave him a two-ball compound. - *America/British*

Vinegar strokes - Closing stages of orgasm in a man - "Don't stop," said Bob, "I'm just on the vinegar strokes!" - *British*

A bit of how's your fathers - Sexual intercourse - Fancy a bit of how's your father tonight? - *British*

A bit of you know what - To have sexual intercourse - Come to bed for a bit of you know what! - *British*

A flasher - Someone who indecently exposes himself by showing his genitals to passerbys - When the children were walking home from school a flasher indecently exposed himself to them. - *British*

Ant and Decs - Rhyming with:Oral sex - Give me a bit of Ant and Decs? - *cockney*

B.J. - Blow job/oral sex - I got a B.J. off that girl in the pub, last night. - *British*

Be intimate with - To have sexual intercourse - I think they got intimate last night. - *British*

Bendy flex - Rhyming with:Sex - Did they have a bit of bendy flex, I wonder? - *cockney*

Bit o' luck - Fuck- sexual intercourse - I hope I have a bit o' luck tonight! - *cockney*

Blow job - Oral sex - I got a blow job from that girl in the pub, last night. - *British*

Blowy - Fellatio - I got a blowy off that girl in the pub, last night. - *British*

Bob on the knob - Fellatio - And then... she bobbed on my knob! - *British*

Boink - To have sexual intercourse - Jim and Kate boinked last night. - *British*

Bone - Sexual intercourse - I'd love to bone her! - *America*

Bugger - Various meanings: anal sex or a term of abuse when someone/ something is being difficult - Oh, bugger, she exclaimed, I've spilt milk everywhere - *British*

Bum nasties - Anal sex - Would you like to play bum nasties with me? - *America*

Butt fuck - Anal sex - Would you like to butt fuck? - *British*

Cattle truck - Fuck- sexual intercourse - They were going at it like a cattle truck. - *cockney*

Choke the chicken - To masturbate - I caught him choking the chicken! - *British*

Chubby chaser - Someone who finds overweight people attractive - She's such a chubby chaser, preferring to date obese men. - *British*

Come onto - To make sexual advances towards someone - He was coming onto her all night in the pub. - *British*

Deep throat - Fellatio - She gave him deep throat. - *British*

Do it - Sexual intercourse - I don't want to do it, until I am married. - *British*

Donald Trump - Rhyming with: Hump- sex - Have they Donald Trumped yet? - *cockney*

Dry hump - To give someone sexual pleasure to point of orgasm but with clothes on - We ended up just having a dry hump. - *British*

Finger - To give sexual pleasure by using fingers - Hawley fingered Miranda's clitoris to give her pleasure. - *British*

First base - Baseball allusion - kissing - It was their first date but they were already at first base. - *America*

Fist fuck - Using a fist to provide sexual pleasure - She let him fist fuck her. - *British*

82

Fool around - Sexual petting which may lead to full sexual intercourse, or may not - They were fooling around in the back of the car when the man knocked on the window. - *America*

Fornicate - Sexual intercourse - It is a sin to fornicate. - *British*

Frig - To masturbate - He likes to frig himself off whilst watching pornography. - *British*

Fuck - Sexual intercourse - Les desperately wanted to fuck Jill. - *British*

Fuck one's brains out - Sexual intercourse - Sarah and Tom were up all nigh fucking each other's brains out! - *British*

Fuzzy duck - Rhyming with: Fuck-sexual intercourse - Have you had a fuzzy duck yet? - *cockney*

Get a dicking - Sexual intercourse - She got a right dicking from him, apparently? - *British*

Get busy with - To have sexual intercourse - Sam and Samantha got busy behind the fence. - *British*

Get down and dirty - Sexual intercourse - Susan and Karim wanted to get down and dirty with each other. - *America*

Get intimate with - To have sexual intercourse - Zac and Brian wanted to get intimate with each other. - *British*

Get it on - To have sexual intercourse - Coby and Alice wanted to get it on with each other. - *British*

Get laid - To have sexual intercourse - It was ages since he'd gotten laid and he was very horny! *America*

Get lucky - To have sexual intercourse - He was hoping he might get lucky tonight! - *British*

Get nasty - Sexual intercourse - They wanted to get nasty with each other. - *America*

Get off with - To engage in sexual acts with someone - Dave got off with Sharon last night. - *British*

Get some ass - Sexual intercourse - He needed to get some ass. - *America*

Get some booty - Sexual intercourse - He needed to get some booty. - *America*

Get some pussy - Sexual intercourse - He needed to get some pussy. - *British*

Get your kit off - To remove clothes - Come on, get your kit off! - *British*

Get your leg over - To have sex - I got my leg over last night, for the first time in ages! - *British*

Give 'er the bone - Sexual intercourse - I gave 'er the bone last night. - *British*

Give head - Fellatio - I gave him head last night. - *British*

Glory hole - A hole in a wall through which people can watch or engage in sexual activities. Usually associated with homosexual activity and in public lavatories - I watched him masturbate through the glory hole. - *British*

Go all of the way - To have sexual intercourse - Have you ever been all of the way? - *British*

Go down on - Fellatio - She went down on him intending for him to ejaculate. - *British*

Golden shower - To urinate on a sexual partner - Have you ever had a golden shower? - *British*

Hand job - To masturbate another person - He gave him a hand job. - *British*

Hanky panky - Light hearted term for a sexual encounter - We'll have none of that hanky panky here, thank you! - *British*

Have a go at - Try to have sexual intercourse with a particular person - I'd like a go at that! - *British*

Have an affair - Be unfaithful to a partner, by having sexual relations with someone else - They've had an affair behind his back. - *British*

Have relations - Sexual intercourse - How recently have you had relations with her? - *British*

Have sex - Sexual intercourse - How recently have you had sex? - *British*

Body

Hit a home run - Baseball allusion- to have sexual intercourse - I hit a home run last night. - *America*

Hit skin - Sexual intercourse - How recently have you hit skin with her? - *America*

Holla - To make a sexual advance - Holla my way, guys. - *America*

Home run - Baseball allusion= full sexual intercourse - He was on a home run, now. - *America*

Knock boots - Sexual intercourse - They knocked boots on the grass in the park. - *America*

Liberty X - Sexual intercourse - I'd love a bit of liberty x with him! - *cockney*

Make babies - Sexual intercourse - Do you want to make babies with me? - *British*

Make love - Sexual intercourse - Would you like to make love with me? - *British*

Make woopie - Sexual intercourse - Would you like to make woopie, with me? - *America*

Monkey love - Sexual intercourse - Would you like a bit of monkey love? - *America*

Nob cheese - Smegma - His penis smelt of nob cheese. - *British*

Nookie/ nooky - Sexual intercourse - They were under the blanket having nooky when her dad caught them! - *British*

Perform the beast with two backs - Sexual intercourse - That night, they performed the beast with two backs! - *British*

Poke - Sexual intercourse - I poked him. - *British*

Pound the duck - Sexual intercourse - I pounded the duck last night. - *America*

Ravish - Sexual intercourse - I want to totally ravish you! - *British*

Root - Sexual intercourse - Fancy a root? - *Australian*

Rumpy pumpy - Jokey way to describe sexual intercourse - Fancy a bit of rumpy pumpy? - *British*

S and M - Sado Masochism - They were into S and M. - *British*

Screw - Sexual intercourse - Have you screwed him? - *British*

Seal the deal - Sexual intercourse - We sealed the deal last night. - *America*

Second base - Baseball allusion= heavy petting - We got to second base last night. - *America*

Sex someone up - Sexual intercourse - I want to sex you up! - *America*

Shagg - To have sex - I want to shagg her... - *British*

Slap and tickle - A fun way to refer to sexual acts, that may lead to full sexual intercourse - A bit of slap and tickle, does you good! - *British*

Sleep with - Sexual intercourse - Do you want to sleep with me? - *British*

Spank - Sexual intercourse - Do you want to spank me? - *America*

Take someone to bed - To have sexual intercourse - I'd like to take you to bed! - *British*

Third base - Baseball allusion= oral sex - They got to third base last night. - *America*

Threesome - Sexual acts performed between three partners - Have you ever had a threesome? - *British*

Titty fuck - Pushing the penis between the woman's breasts for sexual pleasure - He pleasured himself by giving her a titty fuck. - *British*

To be with - To have sexual intercourse - I've been with her. - *British*

To beast - To have sexual intercourse - He gave her a good beasting. - *America*

To bed - To have sexual intercourse - I've bedded her! - *British*

To cop a feel - To get with someone in a sexual way - Let me cop a feel of your breasts? - *British*

Body

84

To cop off with - To get with someone in a sexual way - I copped off with him last night. - *British*

To dip one's wick - To have sexual intercourse - I dipped my wick there once. - *British*

To engage in sexual relations - Sexual intercourse - They have even engaged in sexual relations - *British*

To get one's end away - To have sexual intercourse - I got my end away last night! - *British*

To go down on - To give someone oral sex - He went down on her to give her oral sex. - *British*

To have a jump - Sexual intercourse - We had a jump last night. - *British*

To hump - Sexual intercourse - He humped her on the floor! - *British*

Wank - Masturbation - He likes to wank whilst watching porn. - *British*

Fancy - To be sexually attracted to someone - Do you fancy me? - *British*

Call it a night - Related to sleeping - Let's call it a night? - *America/British*

Cat nap - Related to sleeping - I'm shattered, I need a cat nap! - *America/British*

Crash out - Related to sleeping - Jim crashed out after such a busy day. - *America/British*

Doze off - Related to sleeping - Oops, I must have dozed off then! - *America/British*

Get forty winks - Related to sleeping - I just need to get forty winks, then I'll be okay again. - *America/British*

Get some Zs - Related to sleeping - I need to get some Zs now. - *America/British*

Hit the sack - Related to sleeping - Let's hit the sack now? - *America/British*

Loaf - Related to sleeping - I need to rest my loaf now. - *America/British*

Passed out - Related to sleeping - As soon as my head hit the pillow, I passed out. - *America/British*

Saw wood - Related to sleeping - I'm so tired, I need to saw wood early tonight. - *America/British*

Shut-eye - Related to sleeping - I need a bit of shut-eye. - *America/British*

Winks - Related to sleeping - I need to get some winks in. - *America/British*

Crabs - Pubic lice - Dave had crabs and so had to go to the STI clinic to have them treated. - *British*

Kebab - Crabs- pubic lice - Dave had a dose of the kebabs and so had to go to the STI clinic to have them treated. - *cockney*

Beer gut - Overweight or obese - Joe has a beer gut as he drinks too much beer and it has made him fat. - *America/British*

Tummy - Stomach - My tummy hurts! - *British*

Frigging - An intensifier in a sentence- you ' idiot! considered a milder swear word than, say, 'fucking' - Figging hell , that was amazing! - *British*

Balls - Testicles - The balls are a man's testicles. - *British*

Blue balls - Male genitalia - He's got big blue balls. - *America/British*

Deez nutz - Male genitalia - Watch deez nutz! - *America/British*

Knackers - Vulgar term for testicles - I hit him in the knackers and he fell to the floor. - *British*

Nut sack - Male genitalia - Watch me nut sack! - *America/British*

Oooh me nuts - Testicles - Oooh, me nuts is a phrase used by men when they have been hit in the scrotum. - *British*

Sack - Testicles - The ball sack refers to the testicles. - *America/British*

Swamp nuts - Testicles - Swamp nuts are the testicles. - *America/British*

Aim Archie at the armitage - Urinate - I am just going to aim Archie at the Armitage, and urinate. - *British*

Body

Answer the call of nature (or nature's call) - Urinate - I need to answer the call of nature urgently. - *British*

Beating the piss out of the little guy - Urinate - I was beating the piss out of the little guy, in this gorgeous bathroom. - *British*

Blasting the beast - Urinate - I was blasting the beast, and I noticed that there was blood in my flow. - *British*

Bleeding the lizard - Urinate - I need to bleed the lizard, and go to the toilet. - *British*

Breaking the seal (specifically the first visit during a drinking session) - Urinate - Don't break the seal too soon, or you will be in the toilet half the night! - *British*

Change water on the goldfish - Urinate - I need to change the water on the goldfish, soon. - *British*

Coffee dump - Urinate - I need to take a coffee dump, urgently. - *British*

Cooling a tyre (American truck driver slang) - Urinate - I need to cool a tyre down! - *American*

Do a wee - Urinate - I need to do a wee, quickly, then I'll be ready. - *British*

Draining down the system - Urinate - I was draining down the system, when I noticed that there was a funny smell. - *British*

Draining the anaconda - Urinate - I need to drain the anaconda. - *British*

Draining the dragon - Urinate - I need to drain my dragon! - *British*

Draining the lizard - Urinate - I was draining the lizard and the urine sprayed all over the place! - *British*

Draining the main vein - Urinate - I was draining the main vein earlier, and noticed I had a lump on my penis. - *British*

Draining the one-eyed monster - Urinate - I was draining the one-eyed monster, sorry I am late. - *British*

Draining the radiator - Urinate - I was draining the radiator, sorry I am late. - *British*

Draining the sleepy weasel - Urinate - I was draining the sleepy weasel, sorry I am late. - *British*

Empty my tank - Urinate - I need to empty my tank now, can we stop please? - *British*

Flush my buffers - Urinate - I need to flush my buffers! - *British*

Freshen my snapple - Urinate - I need to freshen my snapple, before the meeting, please. - *British*

Go pee pee - Urinate - I need to go, pee pee. - *British*

Going for a waz - Going to urinate - I'm going for a waz, see you in a minute. - *British*

Going to the loo - Going to the toilet - I'm going to the loo, see you in a minute. - *British*

Going to the office - Urinate - I'm going to the office, be back in a bit. - *British*

Going to water my horse - Urinate - I'm just off to the toilet to water my horse. - *British*

Having a pee - Passing urine - I'm just having a pee, I won't be long. - *British*

Having a slash - Urinate - He was having a slash, when the fight broke out. - *British*

Having a wee - Passing urine - I'm just having a wee, I won't be long. - *British*

Hosing the porcelain - Urinate - He was hosing the porcelain, when he noticed he had a rip in his trousers! - *British*

Humping the cat loin - Urinate - I need to hump the cat loin! - *British*

Jimmy Riddle - Urinate - I desperately need a Jimmy Riddle. - *British*

Leak the lizard - Urinate - He needed to leak the lizard soon, or he might have an accident! - *British*

Let er' fly - Urinate - I need to let 'er fly! - *British*

Lift a leg - Urinate - "I need to lift a leg," said the man. - *British*

Lower the water level - Urinate - I need to lower the water level, soon. - *British*

Make one's bladder gladder - Urinate - I need to make my bladder gladder, by going to the toilet. - *British*

Number 1 - Passing urine - I'm just having a number one, I won't be long. - *British*

Number one - Urinate - I need to take a number one. - *British*

Parking my breakfast - Urinate - "I need to park my breakfast," said Kath. - *British*

Pass water - Urinate - "I need to pass water," said the retired lady. - *British*

Paying the water bill - Urinate - I am in need of paying the water bill, again. - *British*

Pee - Urinate - "I need to pee," said the woman. - *British*

Pee pee - Urinate - "I need a pee pee," said the child. - *British*

Piddle - Urinate - The cat piddled all over the carpet. - *British*

Pit stop - Urinate - Please could we have a pit stop, at the next service station? - *British*

Point Percy at the porcelain - Urinate - Do you need to point Percy, at the porcelain? - *British*

Point the pink pistol at the porcelain firing range - Urinate - Excuse me whilst I point the pink pistol at the porcelain firing range. - *British*

Pointing percy at the porcelain - Male passing urine - I need to point Percy at the porcelain. - *British*

Powder one's nose - Urinate - Excuse me, I need to powder my nose. - *British*

Punish the porcelain - Urinate - I need to punish the porcelain. - *British*

Putting out the fire - Urinate - I was putting out the fire in the toilet, sorry I am late. - *British*

Raining on the bowl - Urinate - I was stood raining on the bowl, when a woman walked into the toilet! - *British*

Refresh the body - Urinate - I need to refresh the body, do excuse me, for a moment. - *British*

Release the pressure - Urinate - I need to release the pressure, excuse me, for a minute. - *British*

Relieve yourself - Urinate - Mum, I need to relieve myself, where's the toilet? - *British*

See a man about a horse - Urinate - I'm off to see a man about a horse, I'll be back in a minute. - *British*

Shaking hands with the President - Urinate - Sorry I am late, I've been shaking hands with the President. - *British*

Shaking hands with the vicar - Urinate - Sorry I am late, I've been shaking hands with the vicar. - *British*

Shaking hands with the wife's best friend - Urinate - Sorry I am late, I've been shaking hands with the wife's best friend! - *British*

Shaking the dew off the lily - Urinate - I've been shaking the dew off the lily. - *British*

Soaking yourself - Urinate - I had an accident, and ended up soaking myself. - *British*

Splashing the pirate - Urinate - I've been splashing the pirate and I've made a mess, sorry. - *British*

Sprinkle - Urinate - I need to sprinkle! - *British*

Sprinkle my tinkle - Urinate - I need to sprinkle my tinkle, where is the bathroom? - *British*

Squeeze the lemon - Urinate - I need a squeeze of my lemon. - *British*

Squirt the dirt - Urinate - I need to squirt the dirt! - *British*

Steering Stanley to the stainless steel - Urinate - Where is the toilet so I can steer Stanley, to the stainless steel? - *British*

Syphon the python - Urinate - I need to syphon the python, where's the toilet? - *British*

Take a chinese singing lesson - Urinate - I'm in need of a Chinese singing lesson, where can I go? - *British*

Take a wicked "yes" - Urinate - Excuse me, I need to take a wicked "yes"! - *British*

Taking a leak - Male passing urine - I need to take a leak. - *British*

Body

Body

Taking a pee - Urinate - Excuse me, I'm taking a pee! - *British*

Taking a piss - Male passing urine - I need to take a piss. - *British*

Taking a piss - Urinate - Excuse me, I'm taking a piss! - *British*

Taking a slash - Urinate - Excuse me, I'm taking a slash! - *British*

Taking a squirt - Urinate - Excuse me, I'm taking a squirt! - *British*

Taking a whizz - Urinate - I need to take a whizz! - *British*

Taking or having a slash - Male passing urine - I need to take a slash. - *British*

Talking to grandma slowly - Urinate - I need to talk to grandma slowly, where is the bathroom? - *British*

Tapping a kidney - Urinate - I need to tap a kidney! - *British*

Tinkle - Urinating - I need to tinkle, where's the toilet? - *British*

To go and spend a penny - Urinate - I need to go and spend a penny, where is the toilet? - *British*

Training Thomas on the terracotta - Urinate - I've been training Thomas on the terracotta. - *British*

Troggle - Urinate - I need a troggle. - *British*

Twinkle - Urinate - I need to twinkle! - *British*

Visit the urination station - Urinate - I need to pay a visit to the urination station, where is the bathroom? - *British*

Visit Uncle Charley - Urinate - I need to visit Uncle Charley, where is the bathroom? - *British*

Void my bladder - Urinate - I need a void in my bladder, where is the toilet? - *British*

Walk my snake - Urinate - I need to walk my snake, desperately! - *British*

Wash my mongoose - Urinate - Where is the toilet? I need to wash my mongoose. - *British*

Water my weasel - Urinate - I need to water my weasel. - *British*

Watering the flowers (outdoor) - Urinate - I've been watering the flowers, sorry. - *British*

Write my name in the snow - Urinate - I need to write my name in the snow, do excuse me? - *British*

Write my name in the water - Urinate - I need to write my name in the water, do excuse me? - *British*

Axe wound - Vagina - Evie had never seen an axe wound before. - *America/British*

Badly wrapped kebab - Vagina - The vagina has been crudely described as a badly wrapped kebab. - *America/British*

Bang hole - Vagina - The vagina has been crudely called the bang hole, by some. - *America/British*

Bat cave - Vagina - He wanted to enter her bat cave! - *America/British*

Beav - Vagina - Jane's pants were so brief that her beav was on show! - *America/British*

Beaver - Slang for vagina - She was so drunk, she had her beaver out! - *British*

Birth cannon - Vagina - The vagina has been called the birth cannon, comparing it to firing out babies! - *America/British*

Blue waffle - Female genitalia - She's got a blue waffle. - *America/British*

Box - Slang for vagina - She had a nice box! - *British*

Buju - Female genitalia - He touched my buju. - *America/British*

Camel's toe - Female genitalia - Did you see the camel toe she had in those jeans? - *British*

Chocha - Female genitalia - I didn't like the look of her chocha! - *America/British*

Cho-cho - Female genitalia - I didn't like the look of her cho-cho! - *America/British*

Chonch - Female genitalia - I touched her chonch! - *America/British*

Clit - Clit is short for clitoris - Clit is a crude word meaning vagina. - *America/British*

Clown hole - Vagina - Clown hole is a crude way to describe a woman's vagina. - *America/British*

Clunge - Female genitalia - Look at her clunge on show! - *America/British*

Cock pocket - Vagina - A cock pocket is a crude way to describe a woman's vagina. - *America/British*

Cock socket - Vagina - Let me see your cock socket! - *America/British*

Cooch - Slang for vagina - She showed her cooch when her dress flapped up. - *America*

Coochie - Slang for vagina - She showed her coochie when her dress flapped up. - *America*

Cookie - Female genitalia - Who put the cookies in the cookie jar? - *America/British*

Coosie - Female genitalia - He touched her coosie. - *America/British*

Cooter - Slang for vagina - She showed her cooter when her dress flapped up. - *America*

Cuder - Vagina - Another crude name for the vagina is, the cuder. - *America/British*

Cunny - Female genitalia - Sometimes the vagina is called a cunny. - *America/British*

Cunt - Taboo word to describe vagina - In western cultures, the word cunt is a taboo word for a woman's vagina. - *British*

Cunt hole - Vagina - Sometimes the vagina is called a cunt hole but this is crude and deemed degrading. - *America/British*

Cut up - Vagina - Another derogatory way to describe women, would be to call their vaginas 'cut up'. - *America/British*

Fanny - Female genitalia - The ball hit her in the fanny. - *British*

Fish taco - Female genitalia - I had a bit of fish taco for my tea last night! - *America/British*

Front bottom - Vagina - Sometimes, when people are being polite, they call the vagina their front bottom. - *British*

Fuck hole - Vagina - Crudely, the vagina has been called the fuck hole. - *America/British*

Fur burger - Female genitalia - Do you fancy a bit of fur burger? - *America/British*

Fur pie - Vagina - Do you fancy a bit of fur pie? - *America/British*

Gap - Vagina - The vagina has been known as the gap between the legs. - *America/British*

Hair burger - Female genitalia - Fancy a hair burger? - *America/British*

Hair pie - Female genitalia - Fancy a hair pie? - *America/British*

Hairy axe wound -Vagina - The vagina has been crudly described as the, hairy axe wound. - *America/British*

Ham flap - Vagina - The vagina has been crudly described as, the ham flap. - *America/British*

Ham wallet - Vagina - The ham wallet is another crude way of referring to the vagina. - *America/British*

Hatchet wound - Vagina - Another way the vagina is described is as, the hachet wound. - *America/British*

Honey pot - Slang for vagina - He couldn't wait to get to her honey pot! - *British*

Hooded lady - Vagina - The hooded lady needs some action. - *America/British*

Hoo-hoo - Vagina - Do you want to touch my hoo -hoo? - *America/British*

Hot pocket - Vagina - She has one hot pocket! - *America/British*

Ill na-na - Vagina - Ill na-na is another way of referring to a woman's vagina. - *America/British*

Jute - Vagina - The vagina can be called jute. - *America/British*

Kitty - Female genitalia - Would you like to stroke my kitty? - *America/British*

Kooch - Vagina - A kooch is a vagina. - *America/British*

Kooter - Female genitalia - A kooter is a vagina. - *America/British*

Kuder - Vagina - A kuder is a vagina. - *America/British*

Lady garden - Vagina - Some women call their vaginas, their lady gardens. - *British*

Lip - Female genitalia - The vagina labia are known as lips. - *America/British*

Love box - Slang for vagina - He wanted to finger her love box. - *British*

Love cave - Vagina - Some people call the vagina a love cave. - *America/British*

Mangina - Female genitalia - Some people call the vagina, the mangina. - *America/British*

Meat wallet - Vagina - A meat wallet is a vagina. - *America/British*

Minge - Slang for vagina - He liked the idea of touching her minge. - *British*

Minnie - Vagina - Some people call their vaginas, minnies. - *British*

Mound - Slang for vagina - He liked the idea of touching her mound. - *British*

Muff - Slang for vagina - He liked the idea of touching her muff. - *British*

Muffin - Vagina - A muffin is a woman's vagina. - *America/British*

Na-na - Vagina - Na-na is a phrase for vagina. - *America/British*

Nappy dugout - Vagina - A nappy dugout is a crude phrase to mean vagina. - *America/British*

Ninja foot - Vaginaa - The phrase 'Ninja foot' refers to the vagina. - *America/British*

Nookie - Female genitalia - Fancy a bit of nookie later? - *America/British*

Nunny - Vagina - He touched my nunny! - *Jewish*

Open wound - Vagina - The phrase 'open wound' refers crudely to a woman's vagina. - *America/British*

Peach - Slang for vagina - He wanted to touch her peach. - *British*

Penny - Vagina - Some people call a woman's vagina, her penny. - *British*

Pink - Vagina - Some people simply call the vagina 'the pink'. - *America/British*

Pink canoe - Vagina - The pink canoe is the vagina for some people. - *America/British*

Pink taco - Vagina - The vagina has been compared to food when described as, a pink taco. - *America/British*

Pink velvet sausage wallet - Vagina - The silly phrase 'pink sausage pocket wallet' is sometimes used to describe the vagina. - *America/British*

Poo tang - Vagina - A poo tang is also a word to mean vagina. - *America/British*

Poon - Vagina - A poon is a vagina. - *America/British*

Poon tang pie - Vagina - Let's have a bit of poon tang pie? - *America/British*

Poonaner - Vagina - Poonaner is another, similar word, meaning vagina. - *America/British*

Poonani - Female genitalia - Poonani is a woman's vagina. - *America/British*

Poontang - Vagina - The poontang is yet another version, of the phrase, meaning vagina. - *America/British*

Poontank - Vagina - The poontank is another quirky word for vagina. - *America/British*

Pootang - Vagina - The phrase pootang refers to the woman's vagina. - *America/British*

Pooter - Vagina - The phrase pooter refers to the woman's vagina. - *America/British*

Pootie tang - Vagina - The phrase pootie tang refers to the woman's vagina. - *America/British*

Prison purse - Vagina - The 'prison purse' is a way to describe the vagina and carries connotations of illegal sex, such as rape or underage. - *America/British*

Promised land, the - Female genitalia - "Come to the promised land," said the girl. - *America/British*

Punanni - Vagina - Her punnani was warm and wet to the touch. - *America/British*

Body

Puntang - Slang for vagina - She had a nice puntang. - *America*

Puss - Vagina - Her puss was her vagina. - *America/British*

Pussy - Slang for vagina - He wanted her pussy. - *British*

Putang - Vagina - Her putang was warm and wet. - *America/British*

Pu-tang - Vagina - Her pu -tang was warm and wet. - *America/British*

Quiff - Vagina - The quiff is the vagina. - *America/British*

Quim - Vagina- possibly a play on the Welsh word for valley, cwm - He touched her quim. - *British*

Quivering mound of love pudding - Vagina - The quivering mound of love pudding is a way of describing the vagina, euphemistically. - *America/British*

Roast beef - Vagina - The crude phrase 'roast beef' refers to the labia of the vagina. - *America/British*

Roast beef curtains - Vagina - The crude phrase 'roast beef' curtains refers to the labia of the vagina. - *America/British*

Slit - Slang for vagina - He wanted to touch her slit. - *America*

Smush mitten - Vagina - The smush mitten is the vagina. - *America/British*

Snatch - Vulgar slang for a woman's genitalia - A crude term meaning vagina is to refer to it as, the snatch. - *British*

Snizz - Vagina - The snizz is the vagina. - *America/British*

Soggy box - Vagina - They had sex and so she had a soggy box from coming. - *America/British*

Sprained vagina - Vagina - They had sex so hard she sprained her vagina! - *America/British*

Tampon tunnel - Vagina - The crude phrase 'tampon tunnel' refers to the vagina. - *America/British*

Tunnel of love - Vagina - Let me in to your tunnel of love? - *America/British*

V - Vagina - V is short for vagina. - *America/British*

Vadge - Vagina - Some people call the vagina, a vadge. - *America/British*

Vag - Slang for vagina - She's had her vag waxed. - *British*

Vage - Vagina - Some people call the vagina, a vage. - *British*

Vagine - Vagina - Some people call the woman's vagina, a vagine. - *America/British*

Vagoo - Vagina - Some people call the woman's vagina, a vagoo. - *America/British*

Vajayjay - Vagina - Some people call the woman's vagina, a vajayjay. - *America/British*

Va-jay-jay - Slang for vagina - She's had her va-jay-jay waxed. - *America*

Vajizzle - Vagina - Some people call the vagina, a vajizzle. - *America/British*

Wizard sleeve - Vagina - After bearing children, some people crudely call the vagina 'a wizard sleeve' due to its slackness. - *America/British*

Woo - Vagina - Some people call the vagina, the woo. - *America/British*

Woogit - Vagina - Some people call the vagina, their woogit. - *America/British*

Wugget - Vagina - Some people call the vagina, their wugget. - *America/British*

Alan's psychedelic breakfast - Vomiting - Alan's psychedelic breakfast, made the odd appearance when he drank too much alcohol. - *British*

Baking a pavement pizza - Vomiting - He was baking a pavement pizza, when the police arrived. - *British*

Barfing - Vomiting - He had been known to barf after a good night! - *British*

Be the mother bird - Vomiting - He needed to be the mother bird, and find a toilet. - *British*

Bite the chobie - Vomiting - He needed to bite the chobie. - *British*

Body

Blow chunks - Vomiting - He was blowing chunks all morning. - *British*

Blowing beets/bile/breakfast/ chunks/donuts - Vomiting - He was blowing beets all morning. - *British*

Blue chip special - Vomiting - It was a case of the blue chip specials again! - *British*

Booting - Vomiting - He had been booting all day and thought that he must have eaten something bad. - *British*

Bow down before the porcelain god - Vomiting - He felt so sick he needed to bow down before the porcelain god, as soon as possible. - *British*

Bradding - Vomiting - He was bradding all day! - *British*

Bring it up for a vote - Vomiting - He needed to bring it up for a vote. - *British*

Bronx's nightmare - Vomiting - He was having a Bronx's nightmare! - *British*

Calling dinosaurs - Vomiting - He was always calling dinosaurs, after a big night out. - *British*

Calling huey - Vomiting - He was always calling Huey after a big night out! - *British*

Catch it on the rebound - Vomiting - He caught it on the rebound. - *British*

Cheektowaga scream - Vomiting - He needed to do a cheektowaga scream. - *British*

Cheese - Vomiting - He needed to bring up some cheese, after eating too much. - *British*

Chow - Vomiting - He chowed up, last night . - *British*

Chuck up - Vomiting - He chucked up everywhere, after drinking excessively all day. - *British*

Chuck wagon chowder - Vomiting - It was a bad case of chuck wagon chowder. - *British*

Chunder - Vomiting - He chundered everywhere! - *British*

Cook up a pavement pizza - Vomiting - He cooked up a right pavement pizza after the party! - *British*

Cry Ruth - Vomiting - She was known to cry Ruth, now and again. - *British*

Date porcelain patty - Vomiting - She had a date with porcelain patty after the party. - *British*

Driving the Buick to Europe - Vomiting - He was driving the Buick to Europe, all day. - *British*

Driving the porcelain (school) bus - Vomiting - She was driving the porcelain bus again; this morning sickness was driving her crazy! - *British*

Eat backwards - Vomiting - He found he was eating backwards, after consuming too much alcohol! - *British*

Feed the fish (when seasick) - Vomiting - I had to feed the fish when I was on the boat as I got terribly seasick. - *British*

Feed your young (like a mother bird regurgitates food for her chicks) - Vomiting - I had to feed my young, earlier. - *British*

Food escape! - Vomiting - Some food escaped into my throat, it was really unpleasant. - *British*

Going bologna - Vomiting - He was going all bologna, everywhere! - *British*

Have an out-of-stomach experience - Vomiting - I had an out-of-stomach experience, earlier. - *British*

Hiccup from hell - Vomiting - It was a hiccup from hell, I'm telling you! - *British*

Hock a furball - Vomiting - He had to hock a furball out, earlier! - *British*

Horking - Vomiting - He was horking everywhere, it was disgusting! - *British*

Hug the porcelain wishing well - Vomiting - He had to hug the porcelain wishing well! - *British*

Hurling - Vomiting - He was hurling, everywhere! - *British*

Hwarfing - Vomiting - He was hwarfing, everywhere! - *British*

Inverse gut - Vomiting - He had to inverse his guts this morning, as he felt so ill. - *British*

Jackson Pollock - Vomiting - He did a Jackson Pollock, all over the floor. - *British*

Jump shot - Vomiting - I had to jump shot my dinner, because I didn't feel very well. - *British*

Kiss the can - Vomiting - I had to kiss the can, last night. - *British*

Kneel before the porcelain throne - Vomiting - I had to kneel before the porcelain throne, this morning, after eating too much. - *British*

Lap lung butter - Vomiting - I had a lap lung butter, earlier. - *British*

Launch lunch - Vomiting - I launched my lunch, earlier. - *British*

Leaving lunch on the sidewalk - Vomiting - I left my lunch on the sidewalk! - *British*

Liquid laugh - Vomiting - I did a liquid laugh, earlier, and vomited. - *British*

Lose your lunch - Vomiting - I lost my lunch, earlier. - *British*

Make a crustless pizza - Vomiting - I made a crustless pizza in the toilet. - *British*

Make a hideous jiffy bag - Vomiting - I need to make a hideous jiffy bag. - *British*

Make an offering to the porcelain gods - Vomiting - I need to make an offering to the porcelain gods. - *British*

Make like mount St. Helens - Vomiting - I need to make like mount St. Helens. - *British*

McDonald's "special" - Vomiting - I need a McDonald's 'special'! - *British*

Munt - Vomiting - I need to munt. - *British*

New England clam chowder - Vomiting - It was a bad case of New England clam chowder. - *British*

Offer a sacrifice at the porcelain altar - Vomiting - I've had to offer a sacrifice at the porcelain altar. - *British*

Paint the sidewalk - Vomiting - He painted the sidewalk, bringing up his dinner. - *British*

Painting gastric graffiti - Vomiting - I've been painting gastric graffiti! - *British*

Park the tiger - Vomiting - Excuse me, I need to go and park my tiger. - *British*

Pay homage to the Irishman Huey O'Rourke - Vomiting - Sorry I'm late, I was paying homage to the Irishman, Huey O'Rourke. - *British*

Pop a gastric zit - Vomiting - I had to pop a gastric zit, earlier! - *British*

Pray to the porcelain god/goddess/princess - Vomiting - I was up all night, praying to the porcelain princess. - *British*

Pray/worship at the porcelain altar/temple - Vomiting - I was up praying all night, into the porcelain temple. - *British*

Protein spill - Vomiting - It was a bad case of protein spill, I am afraid. - *British*

Puking - Vomiting - I've been puking my guts up, all day. - *British*

Pulling the trigger (intentionally vomiting) - Vomiting - I had to pull the trigger and throw up, otherwise I would not have made it home. - *British*

Quease - Vomiting - I had to quease after dinner, I felt quite ill. - *British*

Ralphing - Vomiting - I was up all night, ralphing. - *British*

Regurgitate - Vomiting - I had to regurgitate my food, as I felt so sick. - *British*

Reverse-drink (from the thunder mug) - Vomiting - I had a reverse-drink from the thunder mug, in the toilets. - *British*

Revisit dinner - Vomiting - I was up all night, revisiting my dinner. - *British*

Ride the regurgitron - Vomiting - I had to ride the regurgitron, last night. - *British*

Rope pÅ elgen - Vomiting: Norwegian for "call the moose" - Rope pÅ elgen, I need to be sick. - *British*

Round trip meal ticket - Vomiting - It was definitely a round trip, meal ticket, situation! - *British*

Body

Scream at the ants - Vomiting - I had to scream at the ants, after drinking too much in the public house. - *British*

Shout at your shoes - Vomiting - I had to shout at my shoes after I drank too much beer. - *British*

Sing psychedelic praises to the depths of the china bowl - Vomiting - I had to sing psychedelic praises, to the depths of the china bowl, last night. - *British*

Snarf - Vomiting - I snarfed everywhere. - *British*

Soul coughing - Vomiting - I did a bit of soul coughing, earlier. - *British*

Spewing - Vomiting - I was spewing my guts up, all night. - *British*

Splatter house - Vomiting - I had a bad case of the splatter house! - *British*

Spraying McDonalds - Vomiting - I was so ill, it was like I was spraying McDonald's all over the pavement. - *British*

Talking on the porcelain telephone - Vomiting - I was talking on the porcelain telephone, all night, being violently ill. - *British*

Talking to god on the big white telephone - Vomiting - I was talking to god on the big white telephone, all night. - *British*

Talking to the weeds - Vomiting - She was bent over talking to the weeds, throwing up her lunch. - *British*

Technicolour yawn/yodel - Vomiting - She did a huge technicolour yawn, all over the pavement. - *British*

Throwing up - Vomiting - I was throwing up all over the place, for two days! - *British*

Thunder-chunder rainbow parfait - Vomiting - There was thunder-chunder, rainbow parfait, everywhere! - *British*

Toilet bowl toss - Vomiting - It was good case of, toilet bowl toss. - *British*

Tossing your cookies - Vomiting - I tossed my cookies back up earlier, not a pleasant sight! - *British*

Tossing your lunch - Vomiting - I tossed my lunch up earlier! - *British*

Turn your guts inside-out - Vomiting - I was so ill, it felt like I had turned my guts inside-out! - *British*

Un-eat - Vomiting - It was a case of un-eating everything, if you get my drift? - *British*

Upchuck - Vomiting - I was upchucking all day. - *British*

Vector-spew - Vomiting - It was a really bad case of vector-spew! - *British*

Vomiting - Vomiting - I was vomiting all night, last night. - *British*

Warhol wail - Vomiting - I was doing the Warhol wail, last night. - *British*

Waste good beer - Vomiting - Well, I was up all night wasting good beer, never again! - *British*

Whistling beef - Vomiting - I was whistling beef, all night, after I drank too much! - *British*

Yakking - Vomiting - I was up yakking, all of last night. - *British*

Yarfing - Vomiting - I yarfed last night, I drank too much wine. - *British*

Yawn for the hearing impaired - Vomiting - Jane made a yawn for the hearing impaired, after eating something that did not agree with her. - *British*

Yodelling to the porcelain megaphone - Vomiting - Justin was yodelling to the porcelain megaphone, all night. - *British*

Yorxing - Vomiting - Simon was yorxing, all over his new shoes! - *British*

A quick piece from the anus orchestra (in f minor) - Flatulence - Nigel had had a really strong curry, which gave him a quick piece from the anus orchestra! - *British*

Air poo - Flatulence - There's a smell of air poo drifting my way! - *British*

Airborne toxic event - Flatulence - Stand back, it's an airborne toxic event! - *British*

All-natural fumigation - Flatulence - It's a case of all-natural fumigation. - *British*

Anal music - Flatulence - He has been making anal music all day. - *British*

Anal thunder - Flatulence - It's a case of anal thunder. - *British*

Arsehole symphony - Flatulence - It's that arsehole symphony again. - *British*

Arse-music - Flatulence - He has been making arse-music, all day. - *British*

Arse-whistling - Flatulence - He has been arse-whistling, all day. - *British*

Backblast area all clear - Flatulence - Stand back from the backblast area, until all clear! - *British*

Backfire - Flatulence - He has been backfiring, all day. - *British*

Bake brownies (from South Park) - Flatulence - I need to bake some brownies. - *British*

Barking spiders - Flatulence - It was a case of the barking spiders, again! - *British*

Beef stew - Flatulence - It smells like beef stew. - *British*

Beef-cloud - Flatulence - What a beef-cloud, you've made! - *British*

Belch - To release gas through the mouth - Please, do not belch in my face, it is rude! - *British*

Biological backfire - Flatulence - There's a bad case of biological backfire coming your way, sorry! - *British*

Biological warfare - Flatulence - There's a bad case of biological warfare coming your way, sorry! - *British*

Blast off - Flatulence - I need to blast off! - *British*

Blow a big one - Flatulence - I need to blow a big one! - *British*

Blow one out - also defecation - Flatulence - I need to blow one out! - *British*

Blowing out the colon - Flatulence - That was a case of blowing out the colon! - *British*

Booty burp - Flatulence - I need to do a booty burp! - *British*

Bottom burp - Flatulence - Ha-ha, he just did a bottom burp! - *British*

Break wind - Flatulence - I need to break wind, apologies. - *British*

Breath of god - Flatulence - The smell was like the breath of god! - *British*

Brown cloud - Flatulence - Watch out, there's a brown cloud coming your way! - *British*

Browning your shorts - Flatulence - That probably browned your shorts! - *British*

Buckshot - Flatulence - The man made a loud sound with his buckshot. - *British*

Bum notes - Flatulence - What a bum note, that was! - *British*

Bum reports - Flatulence - And the bum reports, it will be windy! - *British*

Bunker blast - Flatulence - What a bunker blast that was? - *British*

Bunny - Flatulence - Apologies, I need to let a bunny out. - *British*

Burp - To release gas through the mouth - Please do not burp in my face, it is rude! - *British*

Bust arse - Flatulence - I need to bust arse, sorry. - *British*

Butt thunder - Flatulence - Oops, that was a bit of butt thunder ! - *British*

Chemical warfare - Flatulence - It's a case of chemical warfare, it's so bad! - *British*

Choke a donkey - Flatulence - That smell could choke a donkey! - *British*

Churning urn of burning funk - Flatulence - I have a churning urn of burning funk in my pants. - *British*

Corporal Fart sounds the trumpets for the arrival of General Kaka - Flatulence - That is the noise of Corporal Fart, sounding the trumpets for the arrival of General Kaka. - *British*

Crop dusting (while walking) - Flatulence - I need to do a bit of crop dusting. - *British*

Curry night - Flatulence - It's a bit of a curry night, sorry. - *British*

Diffusion - Flatulence - I'm suffering from diffusion, today. - *British*

Drop a bomb - Flatulence - I need to drop a bomb, sorry. - *British*

Drop one's guts (as in "who dropped their guts?") - Flatulence - I've literally dropped my guts, all day! - *British*

Dropping arse - Flatulence - I've been dropping arse, all day, and it stinks! - *British*

Dropping wolf bait - Flatulence - I've been dropping wolf bait, all day, and it stinks! - *British*

Erupting the anal volcano - Flatulence - The anal volcano is erupting, take cover! - *British*

Evacuating the second floor - Flatulence - They are evacuating the second floor, watch out! - *British*

Explosion between the legs - Flatulence - I have an explosion between the legs. - *British*

Explosion in my pants - Flatulence - I have an explosion in my pants. - *British*

Farting - Flatulence - I've been farting all day, must be the beans! - *British*

Feem - Flatulence - I need to feem. - *British*

Fire in the hole - Flatulence - There's a fire going on in my hole, sorry! - *British*

Firing the auxiliary rockets - Flatulence - I've been firing the auxiliary rockets, all day! - *British*

Flatulating - Flatulence - I've been flatualating, all day! - *British*

Floating an air biscuit - Flatulence - I'm just floating an air biscuit, sorry. - *British*

Freshing up the air - Flatulence - I'm just freshening up the air, no worries. - *British*

Gas leakage - Flatulence - There's a bit of gas leakage, over here! - *British*

Gaseous anal discharge (GAD) - Flatulence - There's a GAD coming your way. - *British*

Give birth to a brown baby ghost - Flatulence - I've given birth to a brown baby ghost, sorry. - *British*

Give up the funk - Flatulence - I've had to give up the funk, sorry. - *British*

Green cloud - Flatulence - There's a green cloud rising up over the sofa, sorry. - *British*

Grunt (as in "who grunted?") - Flatulence - What a smelly grunt! - *British*

Guff/guff an eggy - Flatulence - Sorry, I just guffed a really eggy one! - *British*

Honking for clearance - Flatulence - Ok, I am going to be honking for clearance in a minute. - *British*

Honking the butt horn - Flatulence - I need to honk my butt horn, sorry. - *British*

Killing the barking spiders (helps if you stomp) - Flatulence - To kill the barking spiders, it helps if you stomp! - *British*

Launch one off - Flatulence - I need to launch one off, stand back! - *British*

Launching a growler - Flatulence - I'm going to be launching a growler, stand back! - *British*

Let off a howler - Flatulence - Cor, I let off a howler earlier, you should have smelt it! - *British*

Let off a stinker - Flatulence - Cor, I let off a stinker earlier, you should have smelt it! - *British*

Let one go - Flatulence - I let one go, just as my girlfriend arrived! - *British*

Let one off - Flatulence - I let one off, just as my girlfriend arrived! - *British*

Let one rip - Flatulence - I let one rip, just as my girlfriend arrived! - *British*

Let Polly out of prison - Flatulence - Sorry, I let Polly out of prison, and it is a bit smelly. - *British*

Let slip the dog of war - Flatulence - Sorry, I let slip the dog of war, and it is a bit smelly. - *British*

Let the peach speak - Flatulence - I'm letting the peach speak, I'm afraid. - *British*

Letting the wookie win - Flatulence - I'm letting the wookie win, I'm afraid. - *British*

Lift off - Flatulence - We have lift off! - *British*

Light a bum cigar - Flatulence - I could light a bum cigar! - *British*

Like a knife - Flatulence - It cuts through the air, like a knife! - *British*

Meef - Flatulence - I need to meef. - *British*

Message from below - Flatulence - There's a message from below, brewing, sorry. - *British*

Missouri mud ducks - Flatulence - It was a bad case of Missouri mud ducks. - *British*

Mouse on a motorcycle - Flatulence - That is the sound of my mouse on his motorcycle! - *British*

Odour opera - Flatulence - It was a right odour opera. - *British*

Osmosis of the arse - Flatulence - It was a case of osmosis of the arse. - *British*

Parp - Flatulence - I need to parp, sorry. - *British*

Pass gas - Flatulence - I need to pass gas, apologies. - *British*

Pass wind - Flatulence - I need to pass wind, apologies. - *British*

Passing wind - To release gas through the anus- flatulence - Pat was used to passing wind quietly. - *British*

Poo dust - Flatulence - He had a bad case of poo dust brewing. - *British*

Pop off - To release gas through the anus - flatulence - Daisy was often popping off if she ate beans for her tea. - *British*

Pumping - Flatulence - He had been pumping gas, all night. - *British*

Rip arse - Flatulence - He had a bad case of rip arse. - *British*

Rip one - Flatulence - He let one rip, in front of the whole room of people! - *British*

Root de toot - Flatulence - I need to root the toot. - *British*

Shit symphony - Flatulence - He was playing the shit symphony, all night. - *British*

Silent, but deadly (SBD) - Flatulence - Oh, no, a silent but deadly, coming your way! - *British*

Silent, but violent (SBV) - Flatulence - Oh, no, a silent but violent, coming your way! - *British*

Speak to me, oh, toothless one - Flatulence - "Speak to me, oh, toothless one!" the man said to the toilet. - *British*

Step on a duck - Flatulence - I need to step on a duck. - *British*

Step on a frog - Flatulence - I need to step on a frog. - *British*

Taffing - Flatulence - She was taffing all night! - *British*

Taking the browns to the super bowl - Flatulence - She had been taking the browns to the super bowl, all night, after eating too many baked beans. - *British*

The lonely cry of an imprisoned poop - Flatulence - And then I heard the lonely cry of an imprisoned poop, and realised I needed the toilet! - *British*

Toot - Flatulence - I've been tooting all night since I ate my supper. - *British*

Tootle - Flatulence - I had a bad case of tootle, in my pants! - *British*

Trouser cough - Flatulence - I've got a trouser cough tonight, sorry about the smell. - *British*

Trouser trumpet - Flatulence - I've got a trouser trumpet tonight, sorry about the smell. - *British*

Trumping - Flatulence - I had the sprouts and now I've been trumping all night! - *British*

Under cloud - Flatulence - There is a bit of an under cloud drifting your way, sorry. - *British*

Underpants lion - Flatulence - I have an underpants lion, sorry about the noise. - *British*

Body

Vulcan butt breathing - Flatulence - The smell was so bad, it was like Vulcan butt breathing. - *British*

War cry - Flatulence - I let out a massive war cry, sorry about the smell. - *British*

Was that a mouse on a Harley? - Flatulence - Sorry, what was that noise, a mouse on a Harley? - *British*

Watch out for those barking spiders - Flatulence - I had to warn them to watch out for those barking spiders, I guessed they might stink! - *British*

Whicked whistlin' - Flatulence - He had a problem with whicked whistlin', as he had eaten too many green vegetables. - *British*

Woofie - Flatulence - Oops, a woofie just popped out! - *British*

Xenu speaks - Flatulence - Sorry about that, it was Xenu speaking! - *British*

Body

Body Idioms

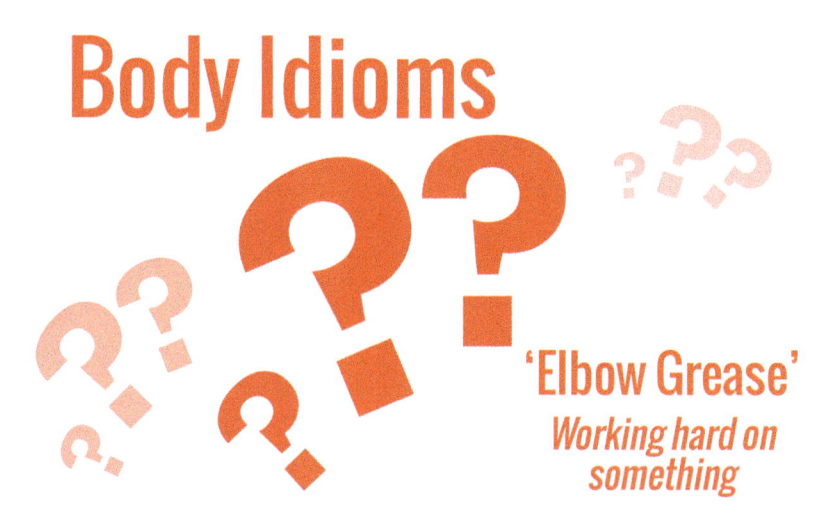

'Elbow Grease'
Working hard on something

A bundle of nerves - Very nervous - Whilst I was waiting for my interview I was a bundle of nerves. - *British*

A gut feeling - You sense that there is a problem, or something about a person or situation isn't right, but not sure why - Colin had a gut feeling that what he had been told was incorrect but he was not sure why. - *British*

A gut feeling/ reaction - An intuition - Debbie had a gut reaction telling her that she had failed her driving test. - *British*

A head start - An advantage over others - Because he was tall, Liam had a head start over other children when undertaking the high jump. - *British*

A heel - Generally used to describe a man who treats people badly and unfairly - Bill treated other people badly and unfairly and was often described as a heel. - *British*

A kick in the teeth - A set back, or feeling like you've been treated unfairly or poorly - Failing my exams was a real kick in the teeth and made me feel upset that I had performed so badly. - *British*

A kick in the teeth - A massive disappointment - Not being invited to the party was a massive kick in the teeth and I was very disappointed. - *British*

A knuckle sandwich - To be punched - When coming out of the pub on a Saturday night, there was often fighting with one person punching the other and giving them a knuckle sandwich. - *British*

A lot of nerve - Rude and arrogant - The girl had a lot of nerve to push into the queue in such a rude and arrogant way. - *British*

A lump in the throat - Feeling upset and on the verge of tears - The movie was so emotional it brought a lump to the throat. - *British*

A pain in the neck - A nuisance - Finlay thought Rufus was a pain in the neck because he was always making trouble. - *British*

A pat on the back - Congratulations or praise for a job well done - "Give yourself a pat on the back for a job well done," said the teacher to her pupils. - *British*

A shot in the arm - An action with a sudden and positive effect - Having new balls to play tennis was a shot in the arm, and instantly had a positive effect on play. - *British*

A shoulder to cry on - Someone who gives you time and sympathy when you are upset - My sister was always there as a shoulder to cry on during the troubled times. - *British*

A slap on the wrist - A telling off for making a mistake or doing something wrong (metaphorical) - My husband gave me a slap on the wrist for persistently getting the instructions wrong. - *British*

A slip of the tongue - When you say something by mistake - That was a bit of a slip of the tongue when I made a mistake by repeating the content of the report. - *British*

A thorn in ones' side - Being a constant irritation or annoyance to someone - Brendan was a thorn in Jane's side and just a constant irritation to her. - *British*

A weight off your shoulders - No longer need to worry about a situation as it is resolved - Passing her driving test was a real weight off Valerie's shoulders. - *British*

A yoke around someone's neck - A burden to carry - Taking out a huge mortgage on the house was like putting a yoke around your neck because of the time it would last. - *British*

Achilles heel - The fault or weakness in a person that could be their ultimate failing or downfall - The fact he was poor at mathematics was his Achilles heel and meant he would probably fail to get the job of accountant. - *British*

Aris - Arse- rectum - "Up your aris," said the man from London. - *cockney*

At each other's throats - Arguing a lot - The twins were constantly at each other's throats. - *British*

At first hand - Experience something yourself - Experiencing going up the Eiffel Tower, first hand, was amazing! - *British*

At the top of one's lungs - To shout really loudly - Daisy shouted out to Dexter at the top of her lungs. - *British*

Back against the wall - To be in a very difficult position personally - John's back is right up against the wall at the moment. - *British*

Back out - To fail to follow through with a plan or promise - She changed her mind about the marriage, and backed out of the wedding leaving him standing at the alter. - *British*

Back to back - Close together - I've read all the Harry Potter books back to back. - *British*

Bad blood - Ill feeling between people - There was bad blood between them since they were children. - *British*

Bare bones - Pared down version of something to the most important parts - They were running out of time on the project and needed to get down to the bare bones of it. - *British*

Behind someone's back - To talk (ill) about someone in secret without their knowledge or permission - She's always talking about him behind his back. - *British*

Belly up - Something's gone wrong. e.g. bankruptcy - It's all gone belly up! - *British*

Best foot forward - To do your very best - "Come on darling, best foot forward," said Dad. - *British*

Betty Boo - Pooh- excrement - I need a Betty Boo desperately. - *cockney*

Bite your tongue - Control yourself not to speak openly and truthfully to someone in order to protect feelings - "I'll have to bite my tongue in future," said Brendon. - *British*

Blood is thicker than water - Family members should be more important to each other than those outside of the family circle - Remember, blood is thicker than water, so be mindful of your family. - *British*

Blood runs cold - A state of fear - My blood ran cold as I realised someone was following me home. - *British*

Blood, sweat and tears - To put a lot of energy and commitment into something to make it a success - The project had taken a lot out of them, literally blood, sweat and tears to make it a success. - *British*

Body blow - Something causing damage - Failing her exams was like taking a body blow of extreme force. - *British*

Brain drain - The movement of qualified professional people who migrate from their own country to another to work where they can improve their economic standing - If we are not careful, this country will suffer from a brain drain, where all of the talented youngsters will go and work elsewhere. - *British*

Break one's neck - To work very hard on something, doing all you can to make it a success - "I've literally had to break my neck to get here on time today," said Susie. - *British*

Break your heart - Emotional pain following a relationship breakup - Everyone gets their heart broken at some point in life. - *British*

Breath down someone's neck - To scrutinise work, putting pressure on them - "My boss has been breathing down my neck for weeks now," said Emma. - *British*

Breath easy - Relax - Kick back and breathe easy, it's the weekend now. - *British*

Brixton riot - Diet - I've been on a Brixton riot, haven't I? - *cockney*

Bundle of nerves - Very nervous - I've been a bundle of nerves all day waiting to hear if I've been successful in my application. - *British*

Bust a gut - Try very hard to achieve something and be successful - I've had to bust a gut to get where I am today. - *British*

By heart - Learn by rote - When we were small we had to learn the alphabet by rote. - *British*

By the nape of one's neck - The back of the neck - The man grabbed me from behind, by the nape of my neck. - *British*

By the skin of your teeth - When you only just manage to do something - I passed my exams by the skin of my teeth. - *British*

By the sweat of one's brow - Hard work and effort to achieve something - I passed my exams by the sweat on my brow. - *British*

By word of mouth - Something becomes very well known due to lots of people talking to each other about it - I heard that the restaurant was good by word of mouth. - *British*

Caught red handed - Caught in the act of committing a 'crime' - The man was caught red handed, shoplifting beer. - *British*

Cheek by jowl - Side by side - They stood cheek by jowel at the graveside, their differences no longer important. - *British*

Chevy chase - Face - Take that look off your Chevy! - *cockney*

Chin up - Be brave over something and stay strong - "Chin up," said Mum, " you can always take your driving test again." - *British*

Close to the bone - Remarks made that are uncomfortable or embarrassing - "That joke about sex was a bit close to the bone," said Jenny to Jane at the comedy club. - *British*

Come to your senses - Act sensibly over a situation/ problem, perhaps after behaving irresponsibly or unwisely previously - "Oh, for goodness sake," she said, " when will you ever come to your senses and see the situation clearly?" - *British*

Contemplate one's navel - To spend an awful lot of time thinking about nothing much, when there are important things to be thought about/ considered - He spent most of his time lying in bed contemplating his own navel! - *British*

Cover one's back - To look after your self to protect from criticism and blame - "I don't trust him, I'd cover your back, if I were you," said Jeremy. - *British*

Cross fingers - Cross your fingers to give yourself immunity from the consequences of telling a lie - "Sorry I don't know anything about that officer," she said with her fingers crossed! - *British*

Curdle someone's blood - To frighten them - Being in that spooky house, curdles my blood. - *British*

Cut a fine figure of a (man/woman) - To look and dress well - Look at him in his new suit carving a fine figure of a man. - *British*

Cut off your nose to spite your face - React detrimentally to a situation - Be careful not to cut off your nose to spite your face. - *British*

Dairy lee - Wee- urinate - I need a dairy lee. - *cockney*

Dead from the neck up - Very stupid - He's so stupid, I think he is dead from the neck up! - *British*

Difficult to stomach - Inability to accept something or someone as thought unpleasant - The bloody scene of the car crash was difficult to stomach. - *British*

Dig your heels in - Be stubborn and resist or refuse to comply - "Be flexible on this deal, don't dig your heels in, it will achieve nothing," said Ambrose. - *British*

Do not breathe a word - A secret not to be told - "Please do not breathe a word of this to anyone, it's our secret," said the pervert. - *British*

Donald Trump - Dump- excrement - I need a Donald. - *cockney*

Don't move a muscle - Stay very still - "Don't move a muscle or the lion might bite you," said Mum. - *British*

Down to the bone - To the core - Let's get down to the bones of what really matters. - *British*

Drag your feet - Do something slowly as you don't want to do it - Julie didn't want to go to the Doctors so dragged her feet over making an appointment. - *British*

Drag your heels - Do something slowly as you don't want to do it - Julie didn't want to go to the Doctors so dragged her heels over making an appointment. - *British*

Dump something into someone's lap - To give someone else a problem to solve - Justin didn't want to deal with sorting out his mother's affairs so dumped it into Katie's lap. - *British*

Easy on the eye - Pleasant to look at - Catherine was very easy on the eye. - *British*

Eat your heart out - A jokey comment used to show off that you are better than another person, for example, I'm so good at singing now; eat your heart out Elvis! - Eat your heart out Elvis, my singing career is taking off now. - *British*

Elbow grease - Work hard on something - In order for the brass pot to come up shiny, the maid needed to put in a lot of elbow grease. - *British*

English lit - Shit- excrement - I need an English lit. - *cockney*

Eye lash - Slash- urinate - I need an eyelash. - *cockney*

Eye to eye - To share the same ideas and opinions on something - Les and Mike had never seen eye to eye over their politics. - *British*

Eyes are bigger than your stomach - Being greedy, taking more food than you can possibly eat - Caroline took way too much food from the buffet, proving her eyes were definitely bigger than her belly! - *British*

Eyes like a hawk - Simile comparing a hawk to someone who is very observant and sees everything that is going on around them - Grandad had eyes like a hawk, he knew exactly what was going on at all times. - *British*

Face to face - Meet someone in person - "I'd like to meet you face to face and get to know you better," said Mary. - *British*

False start - Fart- flatulence - Excuse me, it was a false start. - *cockney*

Fife and drum - Bum - bottom - As he walked past her, he slapped her on her fife and drum. "That's sexual harassment," she exclaimed. - *cockney*

Filter tips - Lips - She pressed her filter tips against his. - *cockney*

Flesh and blood - Family and relatives - "Don't be so unkind to your flesh and blood," said Mum. - *British*

Flex one's muscles - To do something that shows you have power or authority over others - "Did you see Jack flexing his muscles earlier, trying to persuade Teresa not to go out tonight." said Stuart. - *British*

Foot pump - Dump- excrement - I need a foot pump! - *cockney*

Force something down someone's throat - To act in an overbearing or aggressive manner - The salesman was trying hard to get the lady to buy his product, by forcing his ideas down her throat. - *British*

Forest Gump - Dump- excrement - I need a forest! - *cockney*

Gang and mob - Gob - spittle - He coughed up a horrible gang and mob. - *cockney*

Get if off your chest - Feeling the need to talk about something that has been bothering you - Jane was so upset she knew she had to talk to Jenny to get it all off her chest. - *British*

Get off on the wrong foot - To begin something badly or with a mistake - Marie was sorry they had gotten off on the wrong foot, the man seemed nice after all. - *British*

Get off someone's back - Stop nagging or criticising someone - "Get off my back," said Stu, "I'm fed up of you nagging me all of the time." - *British*

Get on someone's nerves - Irritate them - "That man is really getting on my nerves now," said June to her friend. - *British*

Get someone's back up - Annoy them - I think I've got Jodie's back up today because she isn't talking to me anymore. - *British*

Get something off your chest - Explain what has been bothering you - "I'm very worried about you and need to get this off my chest," said Sheila. - *British*

Get something out of your system - To be rid of a desire or need to do something/ own something or to get rid of a substance out of your body. e.g. drugs - I married young and now I want to go out and party, I need to get this out of my system. - *British*

Get the cold shoulder - Be ignored or rejected by someone - Jermaine has been giving me the cold shoulder for months and I have no idea what I have done to upset him. - *British*

Gird up one's loins - Motivate yourself to do something difficult - I don't like flying so will need to gird my loins to even get on the plane. - *British*

Give someone the shirt off your back - To be very generous - They are such a generous friend, they'd give you their shirt off their back if you needed it! - *British*

Give your right arm - Want something so badly, you will do anything to get it - I'd give my right arm to be famous. - *British*

Go for the jugular - To attack someone verbally knowing that you will do them severe harm by what you say - "Watch Tony in an argument, he goes straight for your jugular and always wins," said Doug. - *British*

Go over your head - To not pay attention to or understand something that was said - Good job Dexter wasn't listening to the conversation, it went right over his head. - *British*

Goosebumps - Bumpy skin when frightened or excited - That music is so eerie it gives me goosebumps. - *British*

Grab by the throat - Excitement/ fear or interest caused by creative performance or piece - That music is so eerie it grabs you by the throat. - *British*

Grease someone's palm - Bribe them - They'll help you out with a free delivery if you grease their palm with silver. - *British*

Green fingers - Good at gardening - Margaret and John are very good at gardening, they have such green fingers. - *British*

Green thumbs - Good at gardening - Margaret and John are very good at gardening, they have such green thumbs. - *British*

Hand over fist - Do something fast - He's losing money on the horses, hand over fist. - *British*

Hard to stomach - Unacceptable or unpleasant situation - The look of his injuries were hard to stomach. - *British*

Hard to swallow - Something you find hard to believe - The truth of his affairs was hard to swallow. - *British*

Hardly have time to breathe - Very busy - I'm so busy on this new project that I hardly have time to breathe! - *British*

Has the cat got your tongue? - Question asked if you are not contributing to talk/ conversation - The mother asked her son, " what's wrong with you, has the cat got your tongue?" - *British*

Body Idioms

Body Idioms

Have a chip on one's shoulder - Always getting into disagreements and conflicts with people over the same things - Jules had some issues growing up and now he has a right chip on his shoulder! - *British*

Have a finger in every pie - To be involved in a lot of different projects - Jonathan is quite a savvy business man, he has his fingers in lots of pies trying to make money. - *British*

Have a heart - Be kinder - "Have a heart," said Katie, "give the homeless man some money?" - *British*

Have a heart to heart - Have an open and honest talk with someone often about feelings - Emma and Jane needed to have a heart to heart to be honest about their feelings after their argument. - *British*

Have broad shoulders - The ability to be strong, work hard and take on criticisms given - Some people have broad shoulders and are able to take on the worries of the world. - *British*

Heartbroken - Sorrow, grief or disappointment - Fabian was absolutely heartbroken at the devastating news. - *British*

Heart-warming - Gladness or pleasure - This was heart-warming news, indeed. - *British*

Her indoors - Wife/ girlfriend - I'm not sure if I can come out to the pub, I'll have to ask her indoors. - *cockney*

Hit a raw nerve - Talk which upsets or embarrasses someone deeply - Dave mentioned the death of the child, hitting a raw nerve for the whole community. - *British*

Hold your head high - Be proud of yourself and your achievements - No matter what happens, hold your head high and be proud of yourself! - *British*

Horse and trap - Crap - excrement - I need a horse and trap! - *cockney*

In one breath - Spoken quickly without breathing - Emma was so excited about her wedding that she told everyone all about it in one breath! - *British*

In the same breath - At the same time - They were telling us all about their wedding plans and in the same breath started arguing! - *British*

Itchy feet - Used to express a feeling of unsettledness where someone wants to do something different or travel - Sam was bored at work and had itchy feet to travel the world. - *British*

It's in one's blood - Part of a person's genetic make up - The girl was good at riding horses because it is in her blood. - *British*

It's no skin off my nose - Implies you don't care about a situation or decision - It's no skin off my nose if they don't turn up to my party, I don't like them anyway! - *British*

It's written all over your face - The expression on someone's face, which reveals what they are feeling and thinking - "I know you've been unfaithful to me, it's written all over your face," said Maura. - *British*

Jack Dash - Slash - urinate - I need a Jack Dash. - *cockney*

Joined at the hip - A couple of people who do everything together and are inseparable - Justin and Jane are joined at the hip. - *British*

Jump down someone's throat - To become angry with someone very quickly and suddenly - He was so angry about the situation, he jumped straight down my throat without giving me the opportunity to explain. - *British*

Jump down your throat - Quick to react, strongly critical or berating - "You're making me so cross right now, I will jump right down your throat, if you're not careful," said the manager of the shop. - *British*

Keep your ear to the ground - Knowing the full facts and information about a situation - "Can I ask you to keep your ear to the ground to see if any houses come up for rent in that street?" said Bill - *British*

Keep your eye peeled - Watch carefully - "Keep your eyes peeled for cars, children, as we cross the road," said Granny. - *British*

Keep your eyes out for something or someone - Watch out for something/ someone - "Keep your eyes peeled out for lions, children, as we go around the safari park," said Mum. - *British*

Keep your nose clean - Stay out of trouble - "Keep your nose clean at school today, Tom," said Mum. - *British*

Keep your nose to the grindstone - Keep working hard - In order for this to be a success you need to keep your nose to the grindstone. - *British*

Lend someone a hand - Help someone - Maureen was really lovely, always lending a hand to help people. - *British*

Let your hair down - Enjoy yourself (perhaps for a change) - Tracey decided it was jolly time she let her hair down. - *British*

Look over one's shoulder - Be constantly worried and checking that something bad isn't happening - Melanie was so anxious about life she was constantly looking over her shoulder. - *British*

Lose face - A fall in status, regard or respect, due to making ill advised decisions - The project was a failure and all of the supporters lost face for believing it was such a good idea in the first place. - *British*

Lose your head - Publicly become very angry about something - He was so angry with the situation, he completely lost his head and shouted at the poor waiter. - *British*

Makes my blood boil - Very angry - Steph was so angry with the situation it was making her blood boil! - *British*

Makes my blood run cold - Frightened - Laura was so frightened her blood ran cold. - *British*

Makes my flesh crawl - A disgusting or unpleasant scenario that makes one frightened, scared or feel worried - Simone was so disgusted at the sight of the maggots squirming, it made her flesh crawl. - *British*

Many hands make light work - Working together as a team gets the job done quickly - If we all work together, we will get this job done quickly. After all, many hands make light work! - *British*

Nerves of steel - Very brave and confident; not fearful or nervous - The tightrope walker had nerves of steel to walk the thin rope between the buildings. - *British*

Off one's back - To stop someone bothering you - Lucy needed to get her boss off her back and stop harassing her. - *British*

Off one's chest - To talk to someone about your troubles or irritations - "I need to get this off my chest and tell you how annoyed I am." said Mickey. - *British*

Off the top of your/ my head - From memory - Off the top of my head, I think it is this way. - *British*

On (someone's) back - Criticising and pressuring someone - The manager was on his employees backs all day. - *British*

On (someone's) shoulders - Responsibility - The responsibility weighed heavily on Lynda's shoulders. - *British*

On your own head be it - If you ignore advice given you must take the consequences - "Go ahead and go to the rave but on your own head be it if something goes wrong," said Mum. - *British*

Out for blood - Looking to defeat someone or punish them due to anger or revenge - The gang roamed the streets, out for blood. - *British*

Out of breath - Difficulty in breathing - After the 10 kilometre run John was out of breath. - *British*

Out on one's arse - To be thrown out - Mary threw James out on his arse after she found out that he was cheating on her. - *British*

Out on your ear - To be thrown out - Mary threw James out on his ear after she found out that he was cheating on her. - *British*

Over my dead body - Care so passionately about preventing something from happening, you would metaphorically sacrifice your life to be sure it doesn't happen - "You and Harry can marry over my dead body, I just don't like him," shouted Dad. - *British*

Body Idioms

Body Idioms

Pick somebody's brains - To consult/ discuss with someone who has expertise or experience to improve your knowledge and understanding of a situation or topic - "I wonder if I may pick your brains over what you think about becoming vegan? " asked Angela. - *British*

Play it by ear - Don't plan ahead but, depending on the situation, do whatever seems right at the time - "Shall we play tonight by ear? I'm not sure yet, if I want to go." said Eileen. - *British*

Press the flesh - To shake hands - The gang members pressed flesh to seal the deal. - *British*

Pull someone's leg - Play a joke on someone that isn't true - "Sorry, I am only pulling your leg, it's just a joke," said Phillip. - *British*

Pull your finger out - Work harder - "Come on, mate, pull your finger out, we don't have all day!" said Grandad. - *British*

Put hairs on your chest - Something eaten or drunk is said to be good for you - "Drink this down, it'll put hairs on your chest!" said Pat. - *British*

Put one's shoulder to the wheel - To be very busy and hard at work - "Put your shoulder to the wheel, we need to get this finished today," said Maurice. - *British*

Put someone's nose out of joint - Upset someone - "I think I've put mum's nose out of joint by being so honest today," said Amy. - *British*

Put your back into it - To use a lot of physical energy to achieve something - "Come on, put your back into it, matey!" said my workmate. - *British*

Put your foot in it - Say something or do something wrong and make matters worse - "I think I've put my foot in it by being so honest today," said the chief. - *British*

Put your foot in your mouth - Say something or do something wrong and make matters worse - Shelia put her foot in her mouth by talking rudely in ear shot of her friend. - *British*

Rack your brains over something - Try hard to remember or think of a solution to something - I had to rack my brains to try and remember her name. - *British*

Raspberry tart - Fart- flatulence - Got a touch of the raspberry tarts. - *cockney*

Rub elbows with - To meet and mix with others - Once the young boy band became famous they were rubbing elbows with the rich and famous. - *British*

Run your eye over - Look over something quickly - "Can I please ask you to run your eye over this contract to check if I've made any errors?" asked the junior. - *British*

Save (someone's) neck/ skin - To save someone- danger: embarrassment or trouble - Katie saved her Dad's skin many a time. - *British*

Save one's breath - To stay silent as it's not worth saying anything - "Save your breath, I don't want to discuss it any further!" exclaimed Mum. - *British*

Say something under your breath - Speak softly on purpose so no one hears what you say - "No need to say that under your breath, I heard you anyway!" said Nigel. - *British*

See eye to eye - Totally agree with someone, share the same opinions - We may not see eye to eye over everything we discuss but we do agree on this. - *British*

Shoot yourself in the foot - You make a problem for yourself by doing something stupid or foolish- metaphorical problem with foot - I shot myself in the foot by declaring I didn't eat puddings, then a huge chocolate cake appeared and I couldn't ask for any, even though it looked delicious. - *British*

To be a butterfingers - Clumsy, and drops things - I'm such a butterfingers, I'm always dropping things! - *British*

To be a scatterbrain - Forgetful, disorganised and flighty - I'm such a scatterbrain, I'm always forgetting things! - *British*

To be all ears - Listen carefully and patiently, giving full attention - Dexter was all ears listening intently to the teacher's instructions. - *British*

To be all fingers and thumbs - Clumsy, and drops things - I'm all fingers and thumbs today, dropping things all over the place. - *British*

To be an old hand - Have a lot of experience - John was an old hand at making a nice breakfast. - *British*

To be caught red handed - To be caught doing something illegal or wrong - Chloe was caught red-handed stealing apples from the orchard. - *British*

To be down in the mouth - Sad or depressed - Emma was down in the mouth after not getting her promotion at work. - *British*

To be hand in glove - A very close relationship with someone - Cath and Emma are hand in glove over their plans to move away. - *British*

To be put out on your ear - To be thrown out or forced to leave somewhere, probably because you have done something wrong - The girl was thrown out on her ear for being so rude to her Father. - *British*

To be under the heel - Controlled by something or someone - Stuart was under the heel, controlled by his son. - *British*

To be up to your neck in something - To be in a very difficult situation - Andy was up to his neck in debt because of his gambling addiction. - *British*

To beat your breast/ chest - A public display of grief or guilt - The woman was so distraught at losing her daughter, she beat her chest with the grief. - *British*

To bite your tongue - Conscious decision to stop yourself from saying something that might upset another person - I've had to bite my tongue this week to not be honest about how I really feel. - *British*

To box someone's ears - To punish someone, used to be a physical beating around the ears - "Wait till I get you home, I'll box your ears, I will!" said Mum. - *British*

To brain someone - To hit them on the head - Did you hear that Dan Smith brained his best mate last night? - *British*

To break your back - To work very hard - I've broken my back working up the allotment this weekend! - *British*

To breathe down someone's neck - Annoy someone by watching and scrutinising everything they do - The manager was always breathing down their necks scrutinising their work. - *British*

To carry the weight of the world on your shoulders - To be very anxious - Tracey looked as if she was carrying the weight of the world on her shoulders. - *British*

To catch one's breath - The need to get breathing back to normal after exertion/ exercise - Give me a minute to catch my breath! - *British*

To chance your arm - Give something a go/ take a chance - I'm going to chance my arm and play the lottery this week. - *British*

To get cold feet - Change your mind over a decision because you are frightened - The groom had got cold feet and no longer wanted to get married. - *British*

To get in someone's hair - To be annoying - Catherine's persistent moaning got in everyone's hair! - *British*

To get it in the neck - To be told off for something you have done - Jeff was always getting it in the neck from his partner. - *British*

To get off someone's back - Stop nagging them and leave them to get on with it! - "Get off her back it's not her fault!" said Roger. - *British*

To get on someone's nerves - Be annoying - The bus driver was getting on everyone's nerves with his rendition of Elvis songs. - *British*

To get someone's back up - Annoy someone - The bus driver had got everyone's back up by being so rude to the passengers. - *British*

Body Idioms

To get something off of your chest - Tell someone something that you have been worrying over for sometime and now want to/feel able to share - I need to get it off my chest about the amount of work I have to do. - *British*

To get up someone's nose - To annoy someone - She get's right up my nose. - *British*

To give someone the elbow - To finish a love affair with someone - Dave had had enough of his wife's affairs and decided to give her the elbow. - *British*

To go in one ear and out of the other - Not/ cannot pay attention - Daisy found it hard to concentrate and so information often went in one ear and out the other. - *British*

To grate on someone - Irritate them - Dan's voice tended to grate on people, being high and nasal. - *British*

To hate someone's guts - Big hate - Kevin hated Jim's guts because of the way he had bullied him at school. - *British*

To have a big mouth - Be unable to be discreet or keep a confidence, often talk too much - Don't tell Maurice, he has a big mouth and won't be able to keep it a secret. - *British*

To have a bone to pick with somebody - A disagreement - Jenny had a bone to pick with her friend. - *British*

To have a brass neck - Extreme confidence - "Oh, the brass neck of that girl!" said Mum. - *British*

To have a free hand - Given the power to do what you like - Coralie was given a free hand on the project to hire and fire whoever she pleased. - *British*

To have a frog in your throat - Tickly cough or throaty speech - Eve got a frog in her throat every time she was nervous. - *British*

To have a hand in something - Have a part to play in something - Chris had a hand in ensuring the deadline for the book was met. - *British*

To have a head for heights - Confident of heights - I don't have a head for heights so wouldn't like to go up The Shard, in London. - *British*

To have a knees up - A party - "Let's have a knees up to celebrate," said the party girl. - *British*

To have egg on your face - Something that you have said or done has gone wrong and left you embarrassed and feeling stupid - Mike had egg on his face when his business failed. - *British*

To have eyes in the back of your head - Someone who intuitively knows what's going on even if they can't actually see it - You need eyes in the back of your head when you are looking after small children. - *British*

To have one's back to the wall - To be in a defensive position - I felt like I didn't have a choice and my back was up against the wall. - *British*

To have someone's blood on your hands - To be responsible for harming or the death of someone - After the fatal car crash, Candy knew that she would have to live with the blood on her hands for the rest of her life. - *British*

To have someone's hide - To punish someone - "I'll have your hide for being so naughty, Alfie! " shouted Mum. - *British*

To have the upper hand - Power and control - Ellie liked to feel that she had the upper hand in most situations. - *British*

To have your back to the wall - To be in a very difficult situation - Mal felt that her back was up against the wall, and she had a difficult decision to make. - *British*

To have your head in the clouds - A daydreamer - Daisy has her head in the clouds most of the time. - *British*

To hold one's breath - To stop breathing momentarily and wait for something to be revealed - As the curtain went up the crowd held their breath to see what lay behind. - *British*

To jump down one's throat - To react angrily to a situation or towards someone - David jumped down my throat this morning because I forgot to put sugar in his coffee! - *British*

To keep on your toes - Keep alert to a situation and everything going on - My twin babies certainly keep me on my toes. - *British*

To know something in one's bones - Intuition - I knew that I'd failed, in my bones. - *British*

To know where all of the bodies are buried - To know all the secrets and important information - I know where all of the bodies are buried, so watch out! - *British*

To not lift a finger - Lazy - They are so lazy! They never lift a finger to help me around the house. - *British*

To pick someone's brains - To talk a problem/topic over with someone in order to find a solution, or learn more about the topic - "Can I pick your brains about my business idea?" asked Maureen. - *British*

To play one's cards close to one's chest - To be very private and secretive in the way you conduct yourself - She's so quiet, always keeps her cards close to her chest so you don't know what she's thinking. - *British*

To point the finger - Identify and accuse someone as guilty - Fabien pointed the finger at Derrick after money went missing from the till. - *British*

To powder your nose - To go to the ladies or the toilet - "Excuse me, I'm off to powder my nose," said Lyndsey. - *British*

To pull one's weight - To do your share of something - Everyone working on this project must pull their weight for it to be a success. - *British*

To pull someone's leg - To joke or make fun of someone, often involves telling white lies which are then revealed as such - "Sorry if I upset you, I was only pulling your leg." apologised Algy. - *British*

To pull your hair out - Worry excessively about something/someone - I've been pulling my hair out worrying about that for weeks. - *British*

To put your back into something - To work very hard on something - "Put your back into it, otherwise we won't get this wall finished today," said Dad. - *British*

To put your feet up - To rest and relax - "Come in and put your feet up. I'll make us a nice cup of tea," said Rosie. - *British*

To put your foot in it - To say something that upsets someone or embarrasses them - "Sorry if I have put my foot in it, I thought you were married," said Sue. - *British*

To raise your eyebrows at something - An action which surprised or shocks others causing them to raise their eyebrows - Pat raised her eyebrows at the way that her children dealt with the situation. - *British*

To rap someone's knuckles - Tell someone off - Dexter had his knuckles rapped for not listening properly to the instructions. - *British*

To rip someone limb from limb - Behave in a very aggressive way - Les flung himself forward towards Gary, and if Tony hadn't intervened, he would have ripped him apart limb by limb. - *British*

To risk one's neck - To put oneself in a position of harm or danger to achieve something - Jackie risked her neck when she helped the refugees land safely. - *British*

To scratch someone's back - To do them a favour or help them out - I'll scratch your back, if you scratch mine, and help me finish this job. - *British*

To shoot from the hip - To speak directly and frankly - Simon shot straight from the hip as he told his family the news. - *British*

To show a bit of backbone - To show you are determined and strong - Paul had to show that he had a bit of backbone by being honest and come out to his family about his sexuality. - *British*

Body Idioms

109

To smell blood - To sense something intuitively with regards to danger or vulnerability - The girl could smell blood, and ran for her life. - *British*

To split one's sides (with laughter) - To laugh hard - That comedian is so funny, he makes me split my sides with laughter every time I see him do his act. - *British*

To talk the hind legs off a donkey - Talk a lot without a break - Katie could talk the hind legs off of a donkey. - *British*

To tan someone's hide - To beat someone - "I'll tan your hide for you, when we get home," said the Mother to her son on finding out about his naughty behaviour at school. - *British*

Tongue in cheek - Something meant as a joke, although can be said in a serious manner - Angela told Graham off but with her tongue firmly placed in the cheek. - *British*

Tongue tied - Describing the feeling when you feel awkward and unable to speak, possibly through embarrassment - Jonathan was so shy he became tongue tied around girls. - *British*

Warm-hearted - A kind and generous person - Emma is such a warm hearted person, she is always doing kind things for others. - *British*

Warts and all - To take into account all of the faults and disadvantages when weighing up a person or situation - Justin loves Jane, warts and all. - *British*

Wash your hands of something - You finish being involved in a project, either because you have lost faith in it or you disapprove of it - Andy washed his hands of the situation, being tired of hearing all of the lies. - *British*

Water off a duck's back - People who do not listen to advice or criticism, or get upset if in the wrong; they are impervious to it - You can say what you like to Susan, it's all just water off a duck's back. - *British*

Weak at the knees - Feeling such a strong emotion you literally feel unstable on your feet - When Andy saw Steph at the alter he went weak at the knees with love. - *British*

Wear your heart on your sleeve - Show your emotions openly - Jancy is a very sensitive person, she tends to wear her heart on her sleeve for all to see. - *British*

Wet behind the ears - Inexperienced - The new recruit was wet behind the ears and would need to learn how to cope quickly. - *British*

Wet one's whistle - To take a drink - "Coming to the pub to wet your whistle?" asked Doris. - *British*

With every breath - Repeatedly and continuously - I love that girl more with every breath I take. - *British*

With one hand tied behind one's back - To find something easy despite having a handicap - I could have completed that with one hand tied behind my back, it was so easy! - *British*

Words that stick in one's throat - A difficulty in talking due to high emotions felt - The Vicar tried to give the eulogy, but the words kept sticking in his throat, as it was so emotional. - *British*

Work your socks off - Work very hard - Lucy had to work her socks off to achieve her C grade in English. - *British*

Wring someone's neck - To be so angry with someone you wish them harm - I'm going to wring their necks when they get home! - *British*

Yellow bellied - A coward - He's such a yellow belly, always refusing to join in the daring stuff. - *British*

Young at heart - Someone who still feels and behaves in a younger way despite getting old in reality - Tony and Jan are in their 70s but they are so young at heart you would never guess. - *British*

Your /my heart isn't in it - You don't really want to do something anymore, you've lost interest and no longer feel the same about it - I'm sad to leave my job after all these years but my heart just isn't in it anymore. - *British*

Your hands are tied - You don't feel that you have the power or authority to change or resolve a situation - "I'd love to help you, but my hands are tied I am afraid, so it isn't possible," said the shop assistant. - *British*

Body Idioms

Your heart is in the right place - You have tried to do the right thing and help even if it doesn't work out - Kyle's heart was in the right place but he got things wrong a lot of the time. - *British*

To have a beer belly - An abdominal obesity causing a thickening waist and pot shaped stomach - Fred had a distinct beer belly as he liked beer a little too much! - *British*

To have a bun in the oven - Be pregnant - Kelly has another bun in the oven. She's due at Christmas. - *British*

To have a crick in one's neck - A painful cramp - I must have slept funny and have woken up with a terrible crick in my neck. - *British*

To huff and puff - To breath hard - I always end up huffing and puffing after climbing that hill. - *British*

To not have the stomach for something - To feel that something is wrong, unpleasant and to have no desire to do it - I don't have the stomach to watch television programmes about childbirth. - *British*

Twist and shout - Gout - I've got a touch of the twist and shout, Doc. - *cockney*

Watch and chain - Brain - I've got something wrong with my watch and chain! - *cockney*

Wrigley's gum - Bum - bottom - Got a problem with me Wrigley's gum, Doc. - *cockney*

Yogi bear - Hair - Off to get my yogi cut. - *cockney*

A muffin top - Roll of flesh visible above the waistband of item of clothing - It is amazing how many people today, because they are so overweight, have a muffin top roll around their waist. - *British*

Albert Hall - Balls- testicles - He was hit hard in the Albert Halls. - *cockney*

Alf Garnet - Hair - He'd lost all his Alf Garnet and so had to wear a toupee instead. - *cockney*

Alice bands - Hands - "Have you washed your Alice bands?" said the mum referring to her daughter's hands. - *cockney*

As broad as a barn door - Large person - He was as broad as a barn door, that man. - *British*

As smooth as a baby's bum/ bottom - Very smooth surface - The skin on Jenny's face was as smooth as a baby's bottom. - *British*

Baby-faced - To look youthful - Pat still looks so baby-faced. - *British*

Back and front - Rhyming slang for the taboo word, Cunt- vagina - Have you copped a feel of her back and front yet? - *cockney*

Back passage - Polite way of saying rectum - "It's my back passage, Doc," said the patient. - *British*

Back side - Posterior - "I fell and hurt my backside, Doc,"said grandad. - *British*

Bacon and eggs - Legs - Look at her bacon and eggs, all skinny and pink. - *cockney*

Bacon rind - Mind - I think I'm losing my bacon rind, sometimes. - *cockney*

Bad hair day - Everything seems to be going wrong today - Shelia was having a bad hair day again, she couldn't do a thing with it. - *British*

Bargain Hunt - Rhyming slang for the taboo word, Cunt - vagina - Have you touched her Bargain Hunt, yet? - *cockney*

Barnet fair - Hair - She's got a nice barnet. - *cockney*

Basil Brush - Thrush - She's got a touch of the Basil Brush. - *cockney*

Beating heart - Fart- flatulence - Oh, stop my beating heart! - *cockney*

Bell ringers - Fingers - Look at the chubbiness of her bell ringers. - *cockney*

Berkshire Hunt - Rhyming slang for the taboo word, Cunt - vagina - Have you touched her Berkshire Hunt, yet? - *cockney*

Bib and brace - Face - Mind my bib and brace with that! - *cockney*

Billy goat - Throat - It got stuck in my Billy goat. - *cockney*

Bird's nest - Chest - It's gone down on to my bird's nest. - *cockney*

Body Idioms

Blackpool rock - Cock- penis - Look at the size of his Blackpool rock! - *cockney*

Blade of grass - Arse- rectum - I've got a problem with me blade of grass, haven't I? - *cockney*

Bloody Mary - Hairy - Look at her Bloody Mary chin. - *cockney*

Blue blood - Royal, noble or aristocratic blood - They are like royalty, they've blue blood. - *British*

Boat race - Face - She's got a nice boat race. - *cockney*

Boiled beef and carrots - Claret- red wine- blood - She spilt boiled beef and carrots all over the floor. - *cockney*

Bottle and glass - Arse- rectum - It's my bottle and glass, Doc. - *cockney*

Bottle of beer - Ear - It's my bottle of beer, Doc. - *cockney*

Bottle of rum - Bum- bottom - It's my bottle of rum, Doc. - *cockney*

Bottomless pit - Shit- excrement - I need a bottomless pit. - *cockney*

Brainy - Considered clever - Susan is so brainy! - *British*

Brass bands - Hands - The lovers were strolling down by the river and holding brass bands. - *cockney*

Brighton sands - Hands - Look at the size of her Brighton sands. - *cockney*

Bristol and West - Chest - She's got a nice set of Bristol and Wests. - *cockney*

Cadbury's snack - Back - I've hurt my Cadbury's snack. - *cockney*

Cake hole - The mouth. i.e. shut your cake hole - Shut your cake hole, what do you know about it? - *British*

Camel's hump - Dump- excrement - I need a camel's hump! - *cockney*

Cankles - A mixture of calf and ankles, used to describe a fat woman's legs - Look at the cankles on her! - *British*

Cans - A lady's breasts - "She's got a nice set of cans," said Sharon. - *American*

Can't stomach - To dislike something or someone - "I hate fish, I just can't stomach it," said Jane. - *British*

Carpets and rugs - Jugs- breasts - Look at her carpet and rugs. - *cockney*

Chalk farm - Arm - I've hurt my chalk farm, Doc. - *cockney*

Chiselled - Muscly or well formed physically, strong facial features - The man had an handsome, chiselled face. - *British*

Clothes pegs - Legs - I doubt you'll find a good fitting pair of trousers for those clothes pegs! - *cockney*

Cobblers awls - Balls- testicles - Mind me cobblers awls! - *cockney*

Conan Doyle - Boil - She had a massive Conan Doyle on her nose! - *cockney*

Conk - Nose - She had a massive conk! - *British*

Corn on the cob - Knob- penis - Mind me corn on the cob! - *cockney*

Council gritter - Shitter- arsehole- rectum - He's got a problem with his council gritter! - *cockney*

Crack - Refers to the rectum - Her butt crack was sore. - *British*

Cream crackered - Knackers- testicles - Watch me cream crackers! - *cockney*

Crown - Head - As the woman's cervix dilated, the crown of the baby's head became visible. - *British*

Crown jewels - Tools- genitalia - Watch me crown jewels! - *cockney*

Crust (of bread) - Head - On me crust, son! - *cockney*

Davina McCall's - Balls- testicles - Watch me Davina McCall's! - *cockney*

Deaf and dumb - Bum- bottom - Look at the size of her deaf and dumb! - *cockney*

Derby Kelly - Belly- stomach - Look at the size of his Derby Kelly. - *cockney*

Down the drains - Brains - My down the drains are passed on from my Dad. - *cockney*

Dusty bin - Chin - Watch me dusty! - *cockney*

Elastic bands - Hands - Her elastic bands had swollen in the heat. - *cockney*

Fish and chips - Hips - Look at the size of his fish and chips! - *cockney*

Flowers and frolics - Bollocks- testicles - Watch me flowers! - *cockney*

Fred Astaire - Hair - I like the way you have coiffed your Fred Astaire. - *cockney*

Fruit and nuts - Guts/ intestines - He had dicky fruit and nuts. - *cockney*

George Best - Chest - He has a lovely tattoo on his George Best. - *cockney*

George Bush - Mush- mouth - The boy punched him in the George Bush. - *cockney*

George Michael - Menstrual cycle - I think it's that time of her George Michael. - *cockney*

German band - Hands - Relax your German bands so we can try these gloves on. - *cockney*

Get a lump in one's throat - Feel as if you are about to cry as you are emotionally moved by something - The music brought a lump to her throat. - *British*

Get butterflies in one's stomach - Be nervous about something - She was so nervous about her interview at the bank, she had butterflies in her stomach. - *British*

Gumble and runt - Rhyming slang for the taboo word, Cunt- vagina - He's such a rumble. - *cockney*

Hagen Daz - Arse - rectum - He has something stuck up his Hagen Daz! - *cockney*

Hammer and tack - Back - He's got a bad hammer and tack. - *cockney*

Horse and cart - Heart - My horse and cart was thumping in me chest. - *cockney*

Hydraulics - Bollocks- testicles - Watch me hydraulics! - *cockney*

I suppose - Nose - Watch me, I suppose! - *cockney*

Jackie Danny - Fanny- vagina - Have you touched her Jackie Danny yet? - *cockney*

Jackson Pollock's - Bollocks- testicles - The ball hit him right in the Jackson Pollock's. - *cockney*

Jacob's crackers - Knackers- testicles - The ball hit him right in the crackers! - *cockney*

Jam roll - Arsehole- rectum - He has a problem with his jam roll. - *cockney*

James Blunt - Rhyming slang for the taboo word, Cunt- vagina - She has a problem with her James Blunt. - *cockney*

Jazz bands - Hands - Look at her jazz bands. - *cockney*

Jelly tot - Spot - She had a massive jelly tot on the end of her nose. - *cockney*

Jeremy Hunt - Rhyming slang for the taboo word, Cunt- vagina - He whacked her in the Jeremy. - *cockney*

Jethro Tull - Skull - She whacked him on the back of the Jethro Tull. - *cockney*

Jimi Hendrix - Appendix - He had to have his Jimi Hendrix out. - *cockney*

Joe Hart - Fart- flatulence - He's got a bad case of the Joe Harts. - *cockney*

Kate Nash - Gash- vagina - She's got a lovely Kate Nash. - *cockney*

Keith Vaz - Wazz- urinate - I need a Keith Vaz. - *cockney*

Khyber Pass - Arse - rectum - He hurt his Khyber Pass by falling off the chair. - *cockney*

King Lear - Ear - He hurt his King Lear. - *cockney*

Kingdom come - Bum- bottom - He's got a problem with his kingdom come. - *cockney*

Kisser - The mouth - The ball smacked him in the kisser. - *British*

Lager and lime - Spine - He hurt his lager and lime falling off the chair. - *cockney*

Life and death - Breath - She let out her last life and death before sinking under the water. - *cockney*

Loaf (of bread) - Head - Use your loaf, boy! - *cockney*

Melody lingers - Fingers - She trapped her melody lingers in the car door and squashed them. - *cockney*

Body Idioms

Mince pies - Eyes - Use your mince pies and you'll see them in the distance, nan. - *cockney*

Mods and rockers - Knockers- a woman's breasts - Look at her mods and rockers! - *cockney*

Myleene Klass - Arse- rectum - He's got a problem with his Myleene Klass. - *cockney*

Newington butts - Guts - He's got poorly Newington butts. - *cockney*

Niagara Falls - Balls- testicles - He's been hit in the Niagara Falls. - *cockney*

Noggin - Head - Watch my noggin. - *British*

Nuts - The testicles - Watch me nuts! - *British*

Oliver Hardy - Lardy- obese - What an Oliver Hardy! - *cockney*

Pea shooter - Hooter- nose - He had a boil on the end of his pea shooter. - *cockney*

Pin (pegs) - Legs - Look at her lovely pins. - *cockney*

Plates of meat - Feet - Look at her huge plates of meat. - *cockney*

Pony and trap - Crap- excrement - I need a pony and trap. - *cockney*

Rabbit hutch - Crutch - Watch me rabbit hutch! - *cockney*

Sage and onion - Bunion - She has got a huge sage and onion on her foot. - *cockney*

Screaming Lord Sutch - Crutch - He was hit by the ball in his screaming Lord Sutch. - *cockney*

Shop front - Rhyming slang for the taboo word, Cunt- vagina - Mind her shop front. - *cockney*

Shoulder to shoulder - Stand united with others, side by side in a common cause - The soldiers stood shoulder to shoulder on the front line. - *British*

Skin and bones - Someone who is vastly underweight/ thin - Jane had lost so much weight in the last couple of months, she was all skin and bone. - *British*

Spanish archer - Elbow- pun on El Bow - I've got a problem with my Spanish archer, Doc. - *cockney*

Spanish onion - Bunion - I've got a problem with my Spanish onion, doc. - *cockney*

Struggle and grunt - Rhyming slang for the taboo word, Cunt- vagina - She had an itchy struggle and grunt. - *cockney*

Calf length - Items of attire that finish at the calves - Her skirt was calf length. - *British*

Breathe one's last - To die - Sadly, Frieda breathed her last yesterday and died. - *British*

Brown bread - Dead - He's brown bread, I'm afraid. - *cockney*

A bone of contention - A controversial topic that causes arguments - The class could not agree on the topic and several themes were a real bone of contention with most students. - *British*

Blood on the carpet - A disagreement - "Oh, goodness, there'll be blood on the carpet now," said Granny. - *British*

Raspberry ripple - Cripple- disabled person - They've even got facilities for raspberry ripples. - *cockney*

A breath of fresh air - New ideas and energy, a different perspective - The new teacher brought new ideas and energy to the classroom and saw things from a different perspective. - *British*

A list as long as your arm - A very long list - Joanne gave me a list as long as my arm to complete before I next came to work. - *British*

On the other hand - Setting out of an argument with two contrasting ideas/ opinions - I like ice cream but on the other hand I also like lollies. - *British*

Shove something down someone's throat - To force someone to listen to your point of view and agree with you - That political party are notorious for shoving their policies down your throat. - *British*

Sight for sore eyes - When you are glad to see them or they look beautiful in an outfit - Well, don't you look lovely, a real sight for sore eyes! - *British*

Skeleton in the closet - Secrets that you don't want revealed - Susan had a skeleton in her closet that she hoped would never be found out. - *British*

Skeleton in the closet/ cupboard - Hiding secrets from the past - Susan had a skeleton in her closet that she hoped would never be found out. - *British*

Skin deep - No deep meaning behind something - Her compliments were only skin deep, she really didn't mean what she said, at all. - *British*

Slipped my mind - Forgot - "Oh, sorry, that date slipped my mind!" said Belinda. - *British*

Slit one's own throat - To do something that is certain to end in disaster - Oh, let me slit my throat now, it's bound to end badly! - *British*

Smell the blood - The desire to cause someone further pain or hurt - James could smell the blood, and hoped Joe would be at the party so he could confront him. - *British*

Soaked to the skin - Very wet clothes - Joanne got caught in the downpour of rain and was soaked to the skin. - *British*

Straight from the shoulder - Open and honest talk - "I'm going to tell you this straight from the shoulder as I want to be honest with you." said Tracey. - *British*

Strike a raw nerve - Upset someone by talking about a subject that bothers them - I think I struck a raw nerve when I told Dave that he needed to sort himself out. - *British*

Strong arm - Use threats and or violence to get what you want - "I've strong arms, you know, so don't upset me!" said Justin. - *British*

The gift of the gab - A natural ability to talk confidently and persuasively which people can find entertaining - John has the gift of the gab and could sell ice to Eskimos! - *British*

The hair of the dog - An alcoholic beverage taken to supposedly cure a hangover - I have such a bad hangover from drinking too much alcohol last night, I need the hair of the dog! - *British*

The tip of your tongue - The feeling one gets when one cannot recall information but you know you know it - Oh, I just can't remember...it's on the tip of my tongue! - *British*

Thick skinned - Someone who does not seem to care what others think of or say about them - Mary had such a thick skin, she didn't care what she said or to whom. - *British*

Thin-skinned - Easily upset - Violet was so thin-skinned, she got upset very easily by what people said to her. - *British*

Throw one's weight around - Be bossy and controlling, perhaps even physically abusive - Keith liked to throw his weight around at work. - *British*

Time to catch one's breath - Time to relax after being very busy - This is the first time today I've had a chance to catch my breath! - *British*

To be a bighead - Boastful and conceited - He's always so big headed! - *British*

To be all brawn and no brain - Physically strong but intellectually weak - He was a handsome looking man but, sadly, all brawn and no brain. - *British*

To be head and shoulders above something/ someone - Think you are/ you are better or more superior than - To think you are better or more superior than others, or to actually be better at something than others. - *British*

To be long in the tooth - Too old for something - I'm too long in the tooth for disco dancing now. - *British*

To be near the knuckle - A joke that might be near to being offensive, as it covers a taboo subject such as sex, death or gender - That joke was a bit near the knuckle. - *British*

To beat your brains out - To spend a lot of time thinking and worrying over a problem - I've been beating my brains out all week, trying to think how to solve this. - *British*

To bottom out - Reach its lowest point - The market economy has bottomed out. - *British*

To carry one's weight - To play your part in something - Everyone must carry their weight for this project to be successful. - *British*

To cost an arm and a leg - Very expensive - "I don't shop there, it costs and arm and a leg to buy anything!" said Mike. - *British*

To cross someone's mind - Think about something or someone - It crossed my mind today that we haven't seen each other for ages. - *British*

To cut one's own throat - To do something very likely to cause an instant problem or one in the near future - I think I've cut my own throat by telling the truth. - *British*

To cut something to the bone - To pare something right down, cut back extensively - The resources in the NHS have been cut to the bone. - *British*

To drag your feet - Go deliberately slowly in making a decision - I'm going to drag my feet on this one, I don't want to make a hasty decision. - *British*

To face up to something - To accept a difficult situation - Tomasina had to face up to the fact that she had flat feet. - *British*

To feel something in your bones - To sense something intuitively - I felt the change in the atmosphere in my bones, I knew it would result in a fight. - *British*

To flesh something out - To add detail to - The proposal needed to have more detail added, it needed to be fleshed out in order to be successfully received. - *British*

To get your teeth into something - To get very involved in something - I'm loving this research, lots of detail to get my teeth into. - *British*

To give someone a leg up - To help someone get on in life - Kay liked to help people and often gave youngsters a leg up where she could. - *British*

To go belly up - Ruined something or made a mistake and its all gone wrong - The project went belly up and they lost all of their money. - *British*

To put hairs on your chest - To eat or drink something of benefit to your body/ to make you stronger - "Fancy this black pudding? It'll put hairs on your chest!" laughed Andy. - *British*

To put your finger on something - Solve a mystery - I think I've put my finger on the reason that I don't like peas. - *British*

To ram something down one's throat - To force someone to listen and accept something against their will - "Stop ramming that idea down my throat, I'm sick of hearing about it." grumbled Ruth. - *British*

A kink in one's neck - Cramp and pain - After doing gymnastics I had a real kink in my neck which was very painful. - *British*

Ace of spades - Aids - He's drawn the ace of spades and only has months to live now. - *cockney*

All behind - Blind - She was all behind, sadly. - *cockney*

Chilled to the bone - Very cold - After standing in the cold rain for an hour waiting for the bus to come, they were chilled to the bone. - *British*

Corned beef - Deaf - He's a bit corned beef! - *cockney*

Cupid's dart - Fart- flatulence - I've been struck by cupid's dart tonight! - *cockney*

Dibs and dabs - Crabs- a sexually transmitted disease - After sleeping with Joan, Jack had a bad case of the dibs and dabs. - *cockney*

Have a frog in one's throat - A croaky voice - The teacher had been talking all day resulting in a frog in her throat that was hard to clear. - *British*

Hong Kong Phooey - Fluey - I feel a bit Hong Kong Phooey. - *cockney*

In and out - Gout - He's got a bad case of in and out! - *cockney*

Mutt and Jeff - Deaf - He's a bit mutt and Jeff. - *cockney*

Mutton - Deaf - He's a bit mutton. - *cockney*

Break a leg - Wish someone luck, especially used as a saying before a performance in the theatre - Good luck everyone, break a leg! - *British*

Down at heel - Run down and shabby - After the recession, the shop was down at heel. - *British*

Draw blood - To be wounded and bleed - The cat bite drew blood on Jane's hand. - *British*

Elbow room - Enough space to move around - The seats in the theatre were so close together, there was hardly any elbow room. - *British*

Eye-catching - Very attractive - The way the colours had been mixed in the painting was very eye-catching. - *British*

Fall into my/ your lap - To have a gift of a situation without looking for it - "I feel this project fell into our laps, somewhat," said the director. - *British*

Feel the pinch - Finding it difficult to live comfortably on the income you have - They were struggling to pay their bills, and felt the pinch. - *British*

Find your feet - Adjusting to new circumstances- place or situation - I've just started a new job and am still finding my feet. - *British*

Get under someone's skin - Irritating - The sound of that dripping tap is really getting under my skin now! - *British*

Have your hands full - Be very busy with something - "I'm sorry I can't babysit for you tomorrow but I already have my hands full looking after my own children," said Lauren. - *British*

Head and shoulders above the rest - To be superior - The last candidate for the job was a head and shoulders above the rest of them. - *British*

Heads will roll - People who are to lose their jobs or be made to take responsibility for making mistakes - "Heads will roll for this," said the Queen. - *British*

In cold blood - Without any emotion. Also related to murdering someone without giving them a chance to defend themselves - The man was murdered in cold blood. - *British*

In the blink of an eye - Very quickly - The day passed in the blink of an eye. - *British*

In the flesh - In person - I met them in the flesh once and it was quite disappointing! - *British*

Jump out of one's skin - Be very frightened or surprised - That loud noise made me jump right out of my skin. - *British*

Jump out of your skin - Fear induced, suddenly shocked by something - Did that loud noise make you jump right out of your skin? It did me! - *British*

Keep an eye on something or someone - Watch them/ it very closely - I'll need to keep an eye on that situation. - *British*

Keep body and soul together - To survive - I'll need to keep my body and soul together to survive this. - *British*

Keep your feet on the ground - Stay realistic - Keep your feet well and truly on the ground, despite finding fame. - *British*

Keep your fingers crossed - Cross your fingers to give yourself good luck or best outcomes - Keep your fingers crossed that we win the league this year. - *British*

Keith Cheggers - Preggers- pregnant - She's Keith Cheggers. - *cockney*

Like a millstone round one's neck - A burden - The mortgage was like a millstone around their necks. - *British*

Like getting blood out of a stone - Very difficult to achieve or get something - Getting Kevin to come and fix the bathroom was like getting blood out of a stone. - *British*

More than meets the eye - A situation that is more complicated, or interesting than first realised - There's more to this situation than meets the eye. - *British*

Music to your ears - You are told exactly what you wanted to hear - "Oh, thanks," said Angela, "that's music to my ears". - *British*

My hands are tied - To have no other options - "I'm sorry," said the bank manager, "my hands are tied so I cannot help you." - *British*

My heart bleeds - Used to imply you do not care - Oh, my heart bleeds for you! - *British*

Neck and neck - Competitors are level; running side by side - The horses ran the whole race course neck and neck. - *British*

Body Idioms

New blood - New people brought into a situation - "We need new blood in this team, now," said the manager, "if we are to go on and win." - *British*

No sweat - No problem - "Thanks for helping out," said the woman. "No sweat," said the man, "I was here working today anyway." - *British*

On your last legs - Close to dying, breaking or simply wearing out - The washing machine was on its last legs and likely to break down any day. - *British*

One's last breath - To die - The dog took it's last breath on Tuesday and will be buried early next week. - *British*

Pay through the nose - To pay more than the usual price for something - "Don't go to the high street for your essential shopping, you end up paying through the nose for some things it's so expensive!" exclaimed Ivor. - *British*

Stick out like a sore thumb - Not the same as everyone around you. Easily noticed and obvious - Melissa stuck out like a sore thumb, being the only one not wearing black for the funeral. - *British*

Stick to one's ribs - Food related-filling meal that bans hunger - That pie is sticking to my ribs, I'm so full! - *British*

Sweat it out - Wait patiently - "You're going to have to sweat it out," said the police officer to the prisoner. - *British*

Take it on the chin - Take the blame, stay strong and not complain - I'm going to have to take that on the chin, aren't I? - *British*

Teething problems - Having problems during the initial stages of something - Pat was having teething problems with her new computer. - *British*

The cold shoulder - To deliberately ignore someone - Pam gave Julie the cold shoulder when she found out she had been lying to her. - *British*

The long arm of the law - The police - Watch out, here comes the long arm of the law! - *British*

The naked eye - To see something without the use of a microscope or lens - Tonight you can see Pluto with the naked eye. - *British*

The shirt off someone's back - To take the last thing a person has- can be metaphorical - Katie is so generous, she would give you the shirt off her back! - *British*

The upper hand - Advantage or power over others - Justin had the upper hand in the tennis match against Jim. - *British*

To not believe your ears - Not believe what you have heard - I couldn't believe my ears when they announced the winner and it was me! - *British*

To stab someone in the back - To be unkind about someone when they are not there - Cody stabbed Mike in the back by betraying his lack of a valid passport to the authorities. - *British*

To stick in the throat - A displeasing idea that is difficult to accept - Saying sorry stuck in my throat, as I really don't like the woman. - *British*

To stick one's neck out - To do something dangerous or risky to help someone out - Kandy stuck her neck out by employing the man without a reference but her instinct told her to trust him anyway. - *British*

To stick your neck out - Take a chance on someone or something despite what others tell you - The police officer stuck his neck out and released the boy without charge. - *British*

To stretch your legs - Move around after a period of inactivity - Joan was glad to get up out of her chair and stretch her legs which had seized up from sitting down for so long. - *British*

To stuff your face - Eat an awful lot - The buffet was extensive and so it was very tempting to stuff your face with lots of treats. - *British*

To sweat blood - To be anxious and tense - Alison was so nervous whilst she waited for her exam results, it felt like she was sweating blood. - *British*

To take someone's breath away - To cause someone to become out of breath or overwhelmed by beauty, awe or grandeur - When Justin saw Jane for the first time, it took his breath away! - *British*

To the bone - To the core - Their money was pared right down to the bone now. - *British*

To turn your back on someone - To stop being friends with someone and being involved in their life - Tracey would never turn her back on Phillip, no matter what happened between them. - *British*

To twist someone's arm - Metaphorically- use powers of persuasion to get someone to do what you want them to - John tried to twist Justin's arm and persuade him to have another pint of beer. - *British*

To warm the cockles of your heart - A tale or sight that makes you feel happy as it shows people can be kind and empathetic towards one another - There was a lovely story on the news last night that warmed the cockles of your heart! - *British*

To waste one's breath - To feel that your opinion is not heeded - I'm not going to say another word, it's just a waste of my breath! - *British*

To win by a nose - To win by a very small margin - The election was won by a nose. - *British*

Toe the line - Abide by the rules - All of the party members were expected to toe the line, or leave. - *British*

Too rich for someone's blood - Expensive - These expensive chocolates are too rich for my blood. - *British*

Turn a blind eye - Ignore something or a situation you know is wrong - The policeman turned a blind eye to the car parked on double yellow lines. - *British*

Turn one's back on someone or something - To give up and abandon someone, perhaps when they need help - Job turned his back on his Dad when her found out that he was a thief. - *British*

Turn one's stomach - To make someone distressed or feel nauseous - The sight of the butchered animal turned my stomach. - *British*

Turn your nose up at something - To not like something because you think it isn't good enough for you - Daisy turned her nose up at the cabbage on her plate. - *British*

Twiddle your thumbs - Have nothing useful to do, be bored - Margaret was so bored she sat twiddling her thumbs all day. - *British*

Up in arms - Annoyed about something as you think it is unjust or wrong - The men were up in arms about the lack of health and safety measures applied in the mines. - *British*

Up to one's ears in something - To have a lot to do - "Sorry I can't meet you for coffee, I'm up to my ears in dirty laundry today," said Annie. - *British*

Up to one's eyeballs in something - To have a lot to do or to have a lot of something, like debt for example - David was up to his eyeballs in debt since losing his job. - *British*

Up to one's neck in something - To have a lot of something, work or debt etc. - Melanie was up to her neck in debt since losing her promotion at work. - *British*

Up to your eyeballs - A big problem or issue that is overwhelming - I'm up to my eyeballs in ironing today. - *British*

Up to your neck - A big problem or issue that is overwhelming - I'm up to my neck in debt, at the moment. - *British*

Vent one's spleen - Speak in an open, opinionated, and often rude and aggressive way about what has upset you - I was so angry about the situation that I ended up venting my spleen to anyone that would listen. - *British*

Vent your spleen - Express your frustration and anger - When you're very angry you can end up venting your spleen at people to make yourself feel better. - *British*

Body Idioms

Vote with your feet - To show your opinion of something through positive action - The men were so angry about the lack of health and safety measures in the mine, that they ended up voting with their feet and walking out. - *British*

Wait with bated breath - To wait anxiously and nervously for news or an answer - Steph waited for the postman with baited breath. - *British*

You scratch my back and I'll scratch yours - If you do me a favour, I will do one back for you - Jan said, " if you scratch my back, I'll scratch yours," to the woman she was doing business with. - *British*

Your/ my heart goes out to you - Empathy for someone - "I'm so sorry for the loss of your father, he was a lovely man and my heart goes out to you and your family," said Aaron. - *British*

A white knuckle ride - A scary ride which makes you hang on tight - Going down the white knuckle ride at the funfair was very scary. - *British*

Back breaking - Heavy manual work - Building that wall in the garden was back breaking work. - *British*

Crime

'Rap Sheet'
List of previous convictions

Billy - Amphetamines - I got caught carrying some billy. - *British*

Clock - A scale used to measure illegal drugs during dealing - When the police raided the house, they found his clock. - *British*

Drop - Drugs - Larry has got the drop. - *British*

Jag - Drug or drinking binge - Nicky was on the jag. - *America*

To jack up - Inject an illegal drug - Harry went to the toilet to jack up. - *British*

Collar - Arrested by the police - Aaron got collared by the police for that fight last night. - *British*

Nail - Arrested by the police - Mickey got nailed by the cops. - *British*

Rolled - Arrested by the police - Ellis got rolled by the cops. - *British*

To have your collar felt - Arrested by the police - When Nick saw the police car, he knew he was going to have his collar felt. - *British*

Aid and abet - To assist in a criminal activity - Martha would always aid and abet Joan, to commit criminal offences! - *British*

Backhander - A bribe - The corrupt official gave the judge a back hander. - *British*

Bum beef - False accusations - They held Pete overnight in the cells, but it was just bum beef. - *America*

Bung - A payment or a bribe - The official was dodgy and he offered the judge a bung. - *British*

On the fiddle - To cheat or defraud - Alan is on the fiddle, he doesn't declare all of his income. - *British*

On the take - Corrupt police officer or member of an organisation who is taking money, illegal pay, or bribes to assist criminal activity - That official is well dodgy, I reckon he is on the take. - *British*

Take the rap - Take the blame - I'm not going to take the rap for this on my own! - *British*

Hot wire - To start a car without keys - Dylan and Dave went out to hot wire a car. - *British*

Joyride - To steal a car and ride around in it - Ray and Danny went off for a joy ride. - *British*

Ram raid - To use a vehicle to drive through a shop front in order to break in - Jay stole a car and used it to ram raid the local shop. - *British*

Cop a plea - To plead guilty to a lesser charge hoping to avoid a more serious charge - Doug copped a plea so that he could get a lighter sentence. - *British*

Crime

Get away with murder - Taking no responsibility for the crime/ or not guilty of committing a crime - He got away with murder! - *British*

Get off easy - Not proven guilty of a crime - Delvin got off, easy. - *British*

Get off with it - Not guilty of a crime - They nicked Dev, but he got off with it. - *British*

Inky smudge - Judge - Nancy goes to court tomorrow to face the inky smudge. - *cockney*

Skate - Not proven guilty of a crime - Kenny managed to skate, he was lucky. - *British*

Walk - Not guilty of a crime - They let Jim walk, he was lucky to avoid prison for what he had done. - *British*

Worm out of it - To avoid blame for a misdeed - They arrested Toby, but he managed to worm out of it. - *British*

Dodgy (deal) - Something risky or dangerous or outside of the law - Danny knew it was a dodgy deal, but he couldn't resist it. - *British*

Duck and dive - Skive- non attendance at work or school on purpose to have added leisure time - Joe loves to duck and dive! - *cockney*

Job - A crime - Keith and Dave went out to do a job. - *British*

Lemon and lime - Crime - Joe got caught for that lemon and lime. - *cockney*

Snide - Fake or illicit - All the things Sammy sells are snide. - *British*

To moon - To expose one's backside to people - Tyson decided to moon at people, outside the pub. - *British*

Bad- ass - Criminal - I wouldn't mess with him, he is a bad ass! - *America*

Bad guy - Criminal - I wouldn't trust him, he is a bad guy. - *America*

Bent as a nine bob note - Extremely dishonest or corrupt- this type of money-9 bob note- never existed so therefore it would have been counterfeit and dishonest to try to use it - That guy is not to be trusted, he is as bent as a nine bob note. - *British*

Bobby Dylan - Villain - Rich is a proper Bobby Dylan! - *cockney*

Bovver boy - Old fashioned term for a youth seeking and causing trouble - Pete was a bovver boy. - *British*

Clark Kent - Bent- either homosexual or unlawful - Rich is Clark Kent. - *cockney*

Con/ex-con - Convict - Sam is a con. - *British*

Coyote - Criminal - Rich is a coyote. - *America*

Crew - Criminal - Wayne is part of a tough crew. - *British*

Crim - Criminal - Roy is a crim. - *British*

Criminole - Criminal - Jose is a criminole. - *America*

Crook - A criminal - Dan is a crook. - *British*

Fish - Criminal - Colin is a fish. - *America*

Gang banger - Criminal - Lew is a gang banger. - *America*

Gangsta - Gangster - Peter is a gangsta. - *British*

Gangstar - Criminal - Jerry is a gangstar. - *British*

Get away with it - Taking no responsibility for the crime/ or not guilty of committing a crime - They nicked Ian for his part in the brawl, but he got away with it! - *British*

Got previous - Has previous criminal record - Bazzer is dodgy, he has got previous. - *British*

Gutter punk - Criminal - Calvin is a gutter punk. - *America*

Home boy - Criminal - Roberto is a home boy. - *America*

Joe Rook - Crook- criminal - Dan is Joe Rook. - *cockney*

Lag - A convict - Mitch is a lag. - *British*

Loc - A criminal - Larry is a loc. - *America/ British*

Mack Daddy - Criminal - Mat is the Mack Daddy. - *America*

Mobster - Criminal - Sam is a mobster. - *America*

Perp - Short for perpetrator - Darren was the perp. - *British*

Person of interest - Criminal - Alan is a person of interest. - *British*

Porkies - Lies- cockney rhyming slang for pork pies - Dougal has been telling porkies, again. - *British*

Rap sheet - List of previous convictions - Davina has a long rap sheet. - *America*

Rat - Criminal - Paulo is a rat. - *America*

Rude boy - A streetwise male - Nick is a rude boy. - *British*

Scum - Criminal - Paul was scum. - *British*

Tag - Police tag placed on the ankle, used to monitor a criminal's movements - He is on tag. - *British*

Thug - Criminal - He is such a thug! - *British*

Wanksta - Criminal - What a wanksta! - *America*

Wise guy - Criminal - Nick is a wise guy. - *America*

Yak - Criminal - Stevo is a yak. - *America*

(he/ she/ they've) Done one - Run away from a crime or someone - I don't where he's gone, he smashed the window and now he's done one! - *British*

Blag - To rob or commit a robbery - Rich was done for blagging the local shop. - *British*

Cabbage - To steal - Rich was on the cabbage, again. - *British*

Cough - To own up to a crime or give information on a crime - Jim decided to cough, he knew there was no other way out. - *British*

Do one - Run away - Quick, we need to do one, before the police arrive. - *British*

Done up like a kipper - Beaten up, or framed for a crime not committed, or caught by the police - Martyn was done up like a kipper by the other gang members. - *British*

Ducking and diving - To evade the authorities - Barry is always ducking and diving. - *British*

Fall off the back of a lorry - Goods that have been acquired through illegal means - All the stuff Yaz sells, has fallen of the back of a lorry! - *British*

Fit up - Framed for something - It was a fit up, Ken had not even been there when the robbery happened. - *British*

Flasher - Someone who exposes themselves (genitals) in public - Samuel was a flasher. - *British*

Kite - To fraudulently use stolen or dud cheques - Alex was an expert with a kite. He had ripped off so many people, before he was finally arrested. - *British*

Pinch - To steal - Luke pinched the wallet. - *British*

Scarper - To run away in suspicious circumstances - The cops arrived so we had to scarper. - *British*

Screwed over - To be conned - Jo got screwed over by Ray. - *British*

Sicko - A perverted person - Mick is a total sicko. - *British*

To do a bunk - To run away in suspicious circumstances - The cops arrived, so we had to do a bunk. - *British*

To glass someone - To attack and hurt someone using a broken glass, usually about the face or head - Alison got glassed. - *British*

To mug - To rob or commit a robbery or swindle - Stuart was looking for someone to mug. - *British*

Duke of Kent - Bent- either homosexual or unlawful - Ryland is a bit Duke of Kent. - *cockney*

Fifty cent - Bent- either homosexual or unlawful - Ethan is fifty cent. - *cockney*

G - A person considered to be a gangster - Cam is a G! - *British*

Stiff - A dead body - When the police arrived, they found three stiffs. - *British*

Hustler - Someone who tricks others out of their money - Mike was a hustler. - *British*

A racket - Dishonest or illegal activity, often run by a gang - The drug dealers were running a right racket, and making lots of money from selling drugs. - *British*

Ball - An 8th of an ounce of an illegal drug, or to sell crack cocaine - He was caught carrying a ball. - *British*

Cooker - A person who makes methamphetamines - Yasmeen is a cooker. - *British*

Deal - To sell illegal drugs - Rob deals, to make a bit extra money. - *British*

Dealer - To sell illegal drugs - Ray is a dealer. - *British*

Dope peddlar - To sell illegal drugs - He is a dope peddlar. - *British*

Dummy man - Person who sells fake drugs - Steven is a dummy man. - *British*

Hook up - A person met who sells you drugs - Owen is a hook up. - *America*

Hustle - A person selling illegal drugs - Baz was the local hustle. - *America*

Mad hatter - A person selling illegal drugs - Dev is a mad hatter. - *British*

Potrepreneur - A person who makes a whole business out of growing and selling marijuana - Lee is a potrepreneur. - *British*

Sampson - Generic code name for someone who sells drugs - If you want anything, go and ask Sampson, he's in the corner. - *British*

Snotter - A person selling illegal drugs - Tim is a snotter. - *British*

Trap - A place where drugs are sold - Everyone knew where the local trap was. - *British*

Monkey - Drug addiction - Danny has still got his monkey. - *America*

Mule - A person who earns money by transporting drugs illegally from country to country - Ellie is a drugs mule. - *British*

Dabs - Fingerprints - Sam had his dabs, all over the car. - *British*

Has beef - Grudge - Peter has beef with Johnny. - *British*

Manor - An area owned by a gang - I wouldn't go that way, that's Simon's manor! - *British*

Mob - Group of criminals - Gary's mob, are the meanest in town. - *America*

Turf - Area belonging to a gang - I would not go home that way, that is their turf! - *British*

Yardie - A member of a Jamaican gang - Lee Roy was a yardie. - *British*

Carrying - Carry a gun - Don't mess with Pete, he is always carrying! - *British*

Drive by - To shoot a gun at someone whilst in a moving vehicle - Keith was shot in a drive by. - *America*

Lead poisoning - This phrase is used in reference to acts of physical violence - You are going to get lead poisoning if you mess with me; I will shoot you! - *America/ British*

Pack heat - Carry a gun - Justin doesn't mess around, he will probably be packing heat. - *British*

Piece - A gun - Mo carries a piece. - *British*

Pump full of lead - This phrase is used in reference to acts of physical violence - Stuart will pump you full of lead. - *America/British*

To blow someone's brains out - To shoot someone in the head - Timmy was ready to blow someone's brains out. - *British*

Tooled up - Carrying a weapon - Sim was tooled up and ready for a fight. - *British*

Darbies - Handcuffs - They put Declan in the darbies. - *British*

Blabbermouth - Someone who cannot keep a secret, a gossip or a police informant - Rich is a blabber mouth. - *British*

Canary - Police informant- he sang like a canary! - Keith is a canary. - *British*

Grass - Police informant - Ray is a grass. - *British*

Grass in the park - Nark- a police informer - Alvin is a grass in the park. - *cockney*

Nose - Police informant - Melvin is a nose. - *British*

Crime

Rat on - To inform the police about a crime - Arge is not to be trusted, he will rat on you! - *British*

Snitch - A police informant - That boy is a snitch! - *British*

Snitcher - A police informer - That girl is a snitcher! - *British*

Squeal - To reveal information - I would not tell Tommy anything, he is likely to squeal. - *British*

Squealer - Police informant - Kev is a squealer. - *British*

To finger - Inform on someone to the police - Kenny decided to finger the rest of the gang. - *British*

To rat on someone - To give information to the police about a crime/ criminal - Kelly decided to rat on the rest of the gang. - *British*

Troll - To harass someone via the internet - Raimondo loved to troll people on the internet. - *British*

I'm gonna slice you up - To threaten with violence - Paul said," 'I'm gonna slice you up." - *British*

Jack the lad - A man who is a rogue - Les is a bit of a Jack the lad. - *British*

Charlie Chester - Child molester - paedophile - Robbie is a Charlie Chester. - *cockney*

Cousin Kyle - Paedophile - Phil is a cousin Kyle. - *cockney*

Dodge and swerve - Pervert - Steve is a dodge and swerve. - *cockney*

Fiddle with someone - To sexually molest - Antonio got arrested for fiddling with the kid next door. - *British*

Kiddie fiddler - A paedophile - Sven is a kiddie fiddler. - *British*

Nonce - A paedophile - Wayne is a nonce. - *British*

Paedo - Abbreviation of paedophile - Stevie is a paedophile. - *British*

Mugshot - A photograph of a suspected criminal taken whilst in police custody as part of the booking in procedures - They had captured Kevin's mugshot on CCTV. - *British*

Aggro - This phrase is used in reference to acts of physical violence - I don't know why she keeps giving me aggro, when I have done nothing to provoke her. - *America/British*

Back of my hand - To slap someone - "You will get the back of my hand, if you carry on like that." said Dad. - *British*

Ball up - This phrase is used in reference to acts of physical violence - The gang was looking for a ball up. - *America/British*

Ballistic therapy - This phrase is used in reference to acts of physical violence - I'm going to give you some ballistic therapy. - *America/British*

Bang out - This phrase is used in reference to acts of physical violence - I will bang you out, if you carry on like that. - *America/British*

Beat (one's) ass - This phrase is used in reference to acts of physical violence - I'm going to beat your ass! - *America/British*

Beat down - This phrase is used in reference to acts of physical violence - Tiger got beat down by some other gang. - *America/British*

Beat the hell out of - This phrase is used in reference to acts of physical violence - She beat the hell out of Les, did you see it? - *America/British*

Beat the shit out of - This phrase is used in reference to acts of physical violence - Oh, goodness, dad beat the shit out of Justin last night. - *America/British*

Bitch slap - A type of physical fighting between two women or men who slap rather than punch. - Katy got bitch slapped by Jane, in the pub. - *British*

Bottled - A type of physical fighting between two women or men who slap rather than punch. - Kim got bottled by Karen last night. - *British*

Brain - This phrase is used in reference to acts of physical violence - Kalvin will brain you, if you give him any trouble. - *America/British*

Bust a cap - This phrase is used in reference to acts of physical violence - Adrian will bust a cap in your ass, if you confront him. - *America/British*

Bust up - This phrase is used in reference to acts of physical violence - Ahmed and Yameen had a bust up. - *America/British*

Bust your ass - To beat up and seriously injure someone - Rich will bust your ass, if you argue with him. - *America*

Catch the fair one - This phrase is used in reference to acts of physical violence - You will catch a fair one, if you keep annoying me, like that. - *America/British*

Chelsea smile - A knife slash from the corner of the mouth and across the cheek. (Used by gangs to mark their enemies) - Sam gave Kenneth a Chelsea grin. - *British*

Chib - To slash someone with a knife - Stevie got chibbed. - *British*

Chin - To use the force of the head and chin to inflict injuries on another - Doug will chin you if you annoy him like that! - *British*

Cruising for a bruising - Looking to get into a fight - Kenneth, you are cruising for a bruising. - *America*

Deck - To knock someone to the floor - Stu will deck you, if you talk to his missus. - *British*

Do some damage - To beat up and seriously injure someone - Jonathan will do some damage, if you annoy him. - *British*

Do someone over - To beat up and seriously injure someone - Ken was looking to do some one over. - *British*

Drill - This phrase is used in reference to acts of physical violence - Keith got drilled. - *America/British*

Dustup - This phrase is used in reference to acts of physical violence - Oliver and John had a dust up. - *America/British*

Fill in - To beat up and seriously injure someone - He is going to fill you in when he finds out you scratched his car! - *British*

Fist of fives - This phrase is used in reference to acts of physical violence - You are going to get a fist of fives, if you are not careful! - *America/British*

Floored - To knock someone over - Andy was floored by Declan at the pub last night. - *British*

Front - This phrase is used in reference to acts of physical violence - Joe fronted up to Paul; that was a mistake! - *America/British*

GBH - Grievous bodily harm - Kev was charged with GBH. - *British*

Get banked on - This phrase is used in reference to acts of physical violence - You are going to get banked on for that! - *America/British*

Get crunk with - This phrase is used in reference to acts of physical violence - Caf is going to get crunk with you, now. - *America/British*

Get medieval - This phrase is used in reference to acts of physical violence - If you are not careful, Karen will get all medieval on you! - *America/British*

Give a thumper - This phrase is used in reference to acts of physical violence - Greg will give you a thumper. - *America/British*

Glassed - To use a whole or broken glass to inflict wounds on another - Kenneth got glassed last night. - *British*

Go for the jugular - To attack someone - Steve always goes for the jugular! - *British*

Go for the throat - To attack someone - David will go for the throat, if you annoy him. - *British*

Go postal - This phrase is used in reference to acts of physical violence - Dex will go postal when he finds out! - *America/British*

Gouge your eyes out - To beat up and seriously injure someone - I'm going to gouge your eyes out! - *British*

Happy slap - A violent prank, where one person slaps another without warning - Caron tried to happy slap me, that was a mistake! - *British*

Crime

Head-butt - To beat up and seriously injure someone - Kim tried to head-butt me, that was a big mistake! - *British*

I'm gonna cave your head in - To threaten with violence - Pete said, "I'm going to cave your head in!" - *British*

I'm gonna do you over - To threaten with violence - Kenneth said, "I'm gonna do you over!" - *British*

I'm gonna fuck you up - To threaten with violence - Doug said, "I'm gonna fuck you up!" - *British*

I'm gonna kick your head in - To threaten with violence - Kenneth said, "I'm gonna kick your head in!" - *British*

I'm gonna mash you up - To threaten with violence - Rick said, "I'm gonna mash you up." to Pauline, on finding out she was cheating on him. - *British*

I'm gonna mess you up - To threaten with violence - "Stevie, I'm gonna mess you up, real good." said Dan - *British*

I'm gonna stove your head in - To threaten with violence - Dave said, "I'm gonna stove your head in". - *British*

I'm gonna tear you up - To threaten with violence - Keith said, "I'm gonna tear you up". - *British*

Kick (one's) ass - This phrase is used in reference to acts of physical violence - Peter will kick your ass! - *America/British*

Kicking - To beat up and seriously injure someone - Dave will give you a kicking, if you don't go along with the plan! - *British*

Kneecap - Used as a punishment to cripple someone by hitting or shooting their knees - Stefan will kneecap you, if you don't do as he says. - *British*

Knock out - This phrase is used in reference to acts of physical violence - Do you want me to knock you out? - *America/British*

Knocked about - To be beaten up - Chris was knocked about as a child. - *British*

Knuckle dusters - Metal rings on the fingers that are used in fights to inflict more damage - Kev was wearing knuckle dusters on his hands. - *British*

KO'd - To beat up and seriously injure someone. Abbreviation of knocked out - Louis was KO'd by lee. - *British*

Lamp - This phrase is used in reference to acts of physical violence - I'm gonna lamp you, if you don't stop giving me grief! - *America/British*

Lashed - Whipped - Mary was lashed as a warning. - *British*

Mess up - This phrase is used in reference to acts of physical violence - I'm going to mess you up! - *America/British*

Nutted - To beat up and seriously injure another by using one's head as the weapon - Ahmed got nutted by Ollie. - *British*

Offer someone out - To challenge to a fight - David offered Mo out, that was a mistake! - *British*

Open a can of whoop ass - This phrase is used in reference to acts of physical violence - Ahmed opened a can of whoop ass on Jo. - *America/British*

Panned in - Beaten up - Ann got panned in by Tony. - *British*

Paste - To beat someone up - Peter will paste you, if you annoy him. - *British*

Pasting - A beating - Isaac got a right pasting off Carmel. - *British*

Pop a cap - This phrase is used in reference to acts of physical violence - Phillip was ready to pop a cap. - *America/British*

Pulverise - To beat up and seriously injure someone - Lewis got pulverised by Stephen. - *British*

Pummel - To beat up and seriously injure someone - Wiggy got pummelled by Pete. - *British*

Roll - This phrase is used in reference to acts of physical violence - Emma and Stu had a roll. - *America/British*

Crime

Rough up - This phrase is used in reference to acts of physical violence - Greg got roughed up by Alexandra. - *America/British*

Scrap - To fight - Davina and Pete had a scrap. - *British*

Send to the farm - This phrase is used in reference to acts of physical violence - I'm going send you to the farm. - *America/British*

Shown the light - To beat up and seriously injure someone - Bert got shown the light by Barry. - *British*

Skullfuck - This phrase is used in reference to acts of physical violence - I'm going to skullfuck you! - *America/British*

Slap - To hit someone - Percy gave John a slap. - *British*

Slashed up - To beat up and seriously injure someone - Keith got slashed up in the fight. - *British*

Slug - This phrase is used in reference to acts of physical violence - Yasmeen and Jose slugged it out. - *America/British*

Sock - This phrase is used in reference to acts of physical violence - Cameron socked Bill, right on the jaw. - *America/British*

Spark out - To hit someone and knock them out - Pedro hit John and sparked him out. - *British*

Squeeze the light out of - To beat up and seriously injure someone - Peter squeezed the light out of Ken. - *British*

Step - This phrase is used in reference to acts of physical violence - Do you wanna step? - *America/British*

Stick - This phrase is used in reference to acts of physical violence - usually knife crime - I'm going to stick you! - *America/British*

Stick one on - To beat up and seriously injure someone - Lewis tried to stick one on me. - *British*

Stick the boot in - To kick someone - Pete will stick the boot in, if you fall down. - *British*

Stick the nut on - To beat up and seriously injure someone using your head (nut) - David will stick the nut on you, if you annoy him. - *British*

Stove in - To damage - Jeremy was stoved in by Doug. - *British*

Stuck the nut on - To beat up and seriously injure someone using one's head - Alex stuck the nut on Andy. - *British*

Sucker-punch - This phrase is used in reference to acts of physical violence - Angelo got caught by a sucker-punch. - *America/British*

Take a pop - To verbally or physically assault someone - Do you wanna take a pop at me? - *British*

Take down - This phrase is used in reference to acts of physical violence - I'm going to take you down. - *America/British*

Take it outside - This phrase is used in reference to acts of physical violence - Do you want to take it outside? - *America/British*

Take someone out - To beat up and seriously injure someone - Joe got taken out by Penny. - *British*

Throttle - This phrase is used in reference to acts of physical violence - Karen tried to throttle Bill. - *America/British*

Throw hands - This phrase is used in reference to acts of physical violence - Sam and Justin were going to throw hands. - *America/British*

Thump - This phrase is used in reference to acts of physical violence - Dave got thumped. - *America/British*

Wail on - This phrase is used in reference to acts of physical violence - Gary was wailing on Lew. - *America/British*

Want a piece of - This phrase is used in reference to acts of physical violence - Do you want a piece of me? - *America/British*

Whack - To hit - Pete whacked John over the head. - *British*

Whoop - To beat up and seriously injure someone - Katie got whooped! - *America*

Whoop (one's) ass - This phrase is used in reference to acts of physical violence - I'm going to whoop your ass! - *America/British*

Whup - This phrase is used in reference to acts of physical violence - James got whupped! *America/British*

Woop - To beat up and seriously injure someone - Adam got wooped! *America*

Wupp - To beat up and seriously injure someone - Jim got wupped! *America*

Back up - Call for further police assistance - We need back up here, as soon as possible. - *British*

Bang to rights - Caught in the act of committing a 'crime' - Les was caught speeding, and the police had him bang to rights! - *British*

Bizzie(s) - Police- Liverpool - Look out here come the bizzies. - *British*

Blue - Police - Look out, here comes the blues. - *British*

Bobbies - Police - Look out here come the bobbies. - *British*

Bobby (on the beat) - Police - Dave was just an ordinary bobby on the beat. - *British*

Bottle and stopper - Copper-policeman - Look out, here comes a bottle and stopper. - *cockney*

Boys in blue - Police officer - Look out, here come the boys in blue. - *British*

Brass - Police officer - Here comes the brass. - *British*

Cop - Police - Call the cops! - *British*

Cop shop - Police station - They took Ken down the cop shop. - *British*

Copper - Policeman - Where's a copper, when you need one? - *British*

Cozzers - Cops- police - Call the cozzers. - *cockney*

Dibble - A police officer - Here comes dibble! - *British*

Down the cop shop - Police station - They took Frank down the cop shop. - *British*

Downtown - Police station - They took Kate downtown. - *America*

Feds - Police officer - Call the feds! - *America*

Filth - The police force - Look out, here comes the filth. - *British*

Fishing rod - P.C. plod- a policeman - Look out here comes a fishing rod. - *cockney*

Five O - Police - Call the Five O. - *British*

Fuzz - Police officer - Look out here comes the fuzz. - *British*

Gavver - Police officer - Justin is a gavver. - *British*

Grass hopper - Copper- policeman - Look out, here comes a grass hopper. - *cockney*

Hog - Police officer - Look out, here comes a hog. - *America*

Jam sandwich - Police car - Look out, here comes a jam sandwich. - *British*

Jo Hoppers - Copper- policeman - Call the Jo Hoppers. - *cockney*

John Hop - Cop - police - Here comes a John Hop. - *cockney*

Johnny law - Police officer - Look out, here comes Johnny law. - *British*

Mounties - Mounted police officers on horses - The mounties were on patrol in town, last night. - *America*

Panda car - Police car - Look out, here comes a panda car. - *British*

Plod - Police officer - Here comes plod. - *British*

Rozzer - Police - Here comes a rozzer. - *British*

Rozzers - Police officers - Look out here come the rozzers, run! - *British*

Sleuth - Detective police officers - The sleuths were called in to investigate. - *British*

The Filth - Derogatory term for the police - Look out, here comes the filth. - *British*

The Fuzz - The police - Look out here come the fuzz. - *British*

Crime

The old bill - The police - Somebody call the old bill. - *British*

Bang up - Send to prison - They are going to bang you up this time, Lynda! - *British*

Banged up - Jail - Stephen got banged up for GBH. - *British*

Behind bars - Jail - I was behind bars for two years. - *British*

Bird - Used to describe time spent in prison - I've done bird before. - *British*

Bird lime - Time - prison sentence - Rich did bird lime last year. - *cockney*

Boom and mizzen - Prison - Rich spent a year down the boom and mizzen. - *cockney*

Can - Jail/ prison - Rich got sent to the can for shoplifting. - *America*

Clink - Prison - Justin got sent to the clink. - *British*

Cockney rhyme - Time- prison sentence - Dave did cockney rhyme, for his part in the robbery. - *cockney*

Digeridoo - Screw- prison warders - Dave was a really mean digeridoo. - *cockney*

Ding wing - Prison psychiatric ward - They sent Kyle to the ding wing. - *America*

Do time - Prison - Luke is doing time. - *British*

Doing bird - Jail - Steven is doing bird. - *British*

Doing time - To spend time in prison - Andrew is doing time. - *British*

Done time - To have spent time in prison - Pam has done time, before. - *British*

Ginger ale - Jail - He's gone to ginger ale. - *cockney*

In the clink - Prison - He is in the clink. - *British*

Inside - Prison - Kerry has spent most of his life inside. - *British*

Kitchen sink - Clink- prison - They sent him to the kitchen sink. - *cockney*

Klink - Prison - Louis was sent down the clink. - *British*

Lifer - Someone serving life in imprisonment - Toby was a lifer. - *British*

Pen - Prison - Rich got sent to the pen. - *America*

Porridge - Time spent in jail - Alvin had done a lot of porridge. - *British*

Screws - Police officer/ prison officer - The screws are really mean around here. - *British*

Slammer - Jail/ prison - They sent Paul to the slammer. - *America*

Stretch - A time spent in prison - Pops was given a long stretch. - *British*

Time - A prison sentence - Stevo served time for GBH. - *British*

To go down - To go to prison - Rick knew he was going to go down for the robbery. - *British*

Beggar boy's arse - Brass- prostitute - Richard was looking for a beggar boy's arse to sleep with. - *cockney*

Forty four - Whore- prostitute - Sally was a forty four. - *cockney*

Kerb crawler - A person who drives slowly up to, and by, prostitutes in order to procure their services - Baz was a kerb crawler. - *British*

Madam - Manager of a brothel - Sally is a madam. - *British*

On the game - Working as a prostitute - Jen is on the game. - *British*

Perform a trick - Prostitute - Sal performed a trick behind the pub. - *British*

Punter - A person who visits a prostitute - Andrea took the punter behind the pub and had sex with him. - *British*

Slag - Worthless or insignificant person or a promiscuous woman - Katie is a slag. - *British*

Trick - A prostitutes client, or sexual act performed by the prostitute on the client - Sammy was waiting for her next trick. - *British*

Paki-bashing - Unprovoked attacks on Pakistanis living in Britain. (Racially motivated) - Carl got arrested for Paki-bashing. - *British*

Crime

Bust - Police raid - There was a drugs bust down the road last night. - *British*

See a man about a dog - A non committal euphemism used to avoid revealing your true plans - Lewis went to the pub, to see a man about a dog. - *British*

Cottage - Public lavatory - Mike was caught in a cottage with his trousers down! - *British*

Cottaging - Homosexual activity in a public lavatory - Sammy was arrested for cottaging. - *British*

Jailbait - A sexually attractive person who is under the age of consent - Debby is cute, but be careful as she is jailbait too. - *British*

Kip - Irish for brothel - Patrick went to the kip. - *Ireland*

Apple bobbing - Robbing - Stealing - The women in the shop were apple bobbing, and stealing from handbags. - *cockney*

Fence - Someone who deals in stolen property - Alan is a fence. - *British*

Five finger discount - To gain item for free by means of shoplifting - Wing went into Marks and Spencers, and got himself a five finger discount. - *British*

Half inch - Pinch - Steal - Louis went to town. To half inch a few valuables. - *cockney*

Half-inch - Rhyming slang for pinch, meaning to steal - Alan went to town, to half-inch a few valuables. - *British*

Lift - To steal - Richard went to town to lift a few things. - *British*

Nab - To take something without permission - Margi nabbed some clothes from the shopping centre. - *British*

Nick - To take something without permission - Paul nicked some new trainers. - *British*

On the rob - Stealing - Nick is on the rob. - *British*

Pilfer - To steal - Michael went out to pilfer a few valuables. - *British*

Skank - To steal - Lesley went to town to skank a few valuables. - *British*

Swag - Illicit goods - Davey hid the swag at his girlfriend's house. - *British*

Tea leaf - Thief - Mickey was a tea leaf. - *British*

Whip - To steal - Karim went into town to whip a few valuables. - *British*

Hooky - Illegal, often used in reference to stolen goods - All the things Dave sells, are hooky. - *British*

Hot - Recently stolen goods - Caroline was trying to sell the phone quick, it was hot. - *British*

Knock off - Stolen goods - That phone is a knock off, I wouldn't buy it if I were you. - *British*

Loot - Money or goods from ill gotten gains - Derek hid the loot in his garage. - *British*

Go straight - To renounce a life of crime - Jimmy decided it was time to go straight. - *British*

Doing the Dutch - Committing suicide - James is planning on doing the Dutch, he is really depressed. - *America*

Barney - An argument or confrontation - John got into a barney down the pub. - *British*

Barney Rubble - Rhyming slang for trouble - Paul got himself into a bit of Barney Rubble. - *British*

Mark - A suitable victim for a con or swindle - The gang had put a mark on Seb. - *British*

A good hiding - To beat up and seriously injure someone - The rival gangs were determined to give one another a good hiding, and were always looking for a fight. - *British*

A.A.B. - Assault and battery - The criminal was charged with a crime of A.A.B., for assaulting and battering the stranger. - *America*

A.B.H. - Actual bodily harm charge - John got charge with A.B.H., after that fight in the pub last night. - *British*

Acid attack - A vicious assault where acid is thrown at a person, potentially leading to disfiguring facial injuries - The girl had severe facial disfigurement, which had been caused by an acid attack. - *British*

Crime

Argy-bargy - An argument or confrontation - There was a lot of argy-bargy going on, with no-one agreeing. - *British*

Bash you/ them - Hit - I will bash you, if you don't shut up! - *British*

Bottle - Attack with a broken bottle, usually around the face or head, or to lose one's nerve in a situation and 'bottle it' - John got bottled. - *British*

Bovver boots - Heavy boots, often with steel toecaps worn by 'bovver boys' and used for kicking people in fights - Pete kicked him in the head with his bovver boots. - *British*

Brawl (brawling) - Fight - There was a brawl down the pub last night. - *British*

Break someone's balls - Punish - Pete will break your balls, if you step out of line! - *America*

Bust someone's balls - Punish - Pete will bust your balls if you disagree with him. - *America*

Clobber - To hit - Pete will clobber you, if you disagree with him. - *British*

Concrete boots - To drown someone by weighing them down - Lewis will put you in concrete boots, if you confront him. - *British*

Concrete overcoat - To drown someone by weighing them down - You will end up in a concrete overcoat, if you mess with Pedro! - *British*

Crucify - Severely punish - Ali will crucify you, if you confront him. - *British*

Cut you up - Attack with knife - Barry will cut you up, if you mess with him. - *British*

Derry and Tom - Bomb - I heard a massive explosion; I think it was a Derry and Tom. - *cockney*

Do in - Kill - Richard will do you in, if you fight with him. - *British*

Do someone's kneecaps - Punish - Tony will do your kneecaps, if you double cross him. - *British*

Done in - Beaten up - Kerry was done in, by that gang. - *British*

Done over - To beat up and seriously injure someone - Ian got done over by that gang. - *British*

Doner kebab - Stab - You will be a doner kebab, if you cross Den! - *cockney*

G.B.H. - Grievous bodily harm charge - Julian got nicked for G.B.H. - *British*

Handbags - A harmless fight between two women, often described as 'handbags at dawn' with the allusion to duelling - The fight was ridiculous, it was just handbags, really. - *British*

Jump - Pounce out on - The gang jumped Penny outside the pub. - *British*

Scrapping - Fight - Paulo was arrested for scrapping, last night. - *British*

Shaft - To con someone - He was always trying to shaft the company. - *British*

Shank - To stab with a knife - Bazzer will shank you, if you try to fight him. - *British*

Shiv - Knife blade/ razor - Raheem is always carrying a shiv. - *America*

Snuff movie - A film recording of an actual murder - Stevie showed me a snuff movie, it was disgusting. - *British*

Stick with a blade - Attack with a knife - Phillip will stick you with a blade, if you confront him. - *British*

Stick you up - Attack with a knife - Larry will stick you up, if you fight him. - *British*

Tar and feather - Punish - He will tar and feather you, if you confront him. - *British*

To bottle someone - To attack and hurt someone using a broken bottle, usually about the face or head - Laura got bottled. - *British*

Twat - To hit something/ someone hard - Herb will twat you, if you confront him. - *British*

Waste - Kill - Robbie will waste you, if you try to confront him. - *America*

You are done for - To threaten with violence - Art, you are done for! - *British*

Crime

Drugs

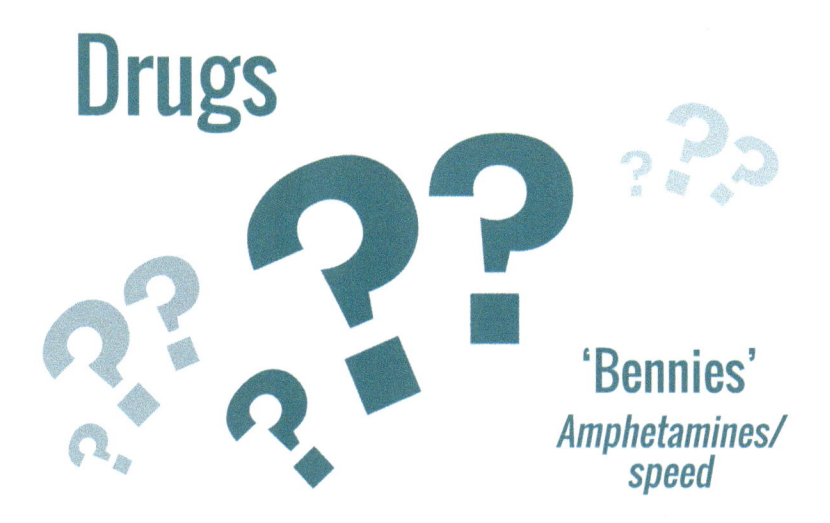

'Bennies'
Amphetamines/ speed

Bake-out - The act of doing drugs and its effect on you - Kate has gone to bake-out. - *America/British*

Blown - Heavily under the influence of drugs - Fabia is blown after taking too many drugs. - *America/British*

Blown out - Heavily under the influence of drugs - Carole is blown out on drugs. - *America/British*

Bow and arra - Para (paranoid) - Deetleef is off his head, and is feeling a bit bow and arra. - *cockney*

Burned - Heavily under the influence of drugs - Holly is burned after a night on drugs. - *America/British*

Burned out - A drugs user, someone who is dependent on drugs - Stephanie is burned out by drugs. - *America/British*

Burner - A drugs user, someone who is dependent on drugs - Jess is a burner. - *America/British*

Burnout - A drugs user, someone who is dependent on drugs - Cathy is a burnout. - *America/British*

Candy flip - Heavily under the influence of drugs - Karim went candy flip. - *America/British*

Cane it - The act of doing drugs and its effect on you - Sue loves to cane it. - *America/British*

Chill pill - Any drug used to alleviate stress, or commonly used figuratively i.e. take a chill pill (relax) - John you need to take a chill pill. - *British*

Comedown - A depressive episode in the aftermath of a bout of drugs taking - Mike is on a comedown after a heavy weekend. - *British*

Cooked - Heavily under the influence of drugs - Dave is cooked! - *America/British*

Ding dong - Rhyming slang for bong-apparatus used for smoking drugs - Ken, pass me the ding dong? - *cockney*

Dirp - The act of doing drugs and its effect on you - Becky is dirp. - *America/British*

Do a line - The act of doing drugs and its effect on you - Let's do a line? - *America/British*

Doctored - The act of doing drugs and its effect on you - Dave is doctored! - *America/British*

Donnie Darko - Sparko- unconscious/ out of it on drink and/ or drugs - Phil passed out, he is Donnie Darko! - *cockney*

Dose - The act of doing drugs and its effect on you - Pansy took a massive dose. - *America/British*

Faced out - Heavily under the influence of drugs - I am faced out. - *America/British*

Drugs

Fire it up - The act of doing drugs and its effect on you - Fire it up Edgar, lets get high! - *America/British*

Foopy - Heavily under the influence of drugs - Marina is foopy. - *America/British*

Fur rugs - Drugs - Got any fur rugs? - *cockney*

Geeked - Heavily under the influence of drugs - Kriss is totally geeked. - *America/British*

Get a fix - The act of doing drugs and its effect on you - I need to get a fix. - *America/British*

Get blazed - The act of doing drugs and its effect on you - I want to get blazed. - *America/British*

Get geeked - The act of doing drugs and its effect on you - I want to get geeked. - *America/British*

Get high - The act of doing drugs and its effect on you - Let's get high? - *America/British*

Get right - The act of doing drugs and its effect on you - Let's get right? - *America/British*

Get slizzard - The act of doing drugs and its effect on you - Let's get slizzard? - *America/British*

Get wrecked - To get intoxicated on drink or drugs - Let's get wrecked? - *British*

Go up to bat - The act of doing drugs and its effect on you - It's my turn to go up to bat, now. - *America/British*

Gouch - Heavily under the influence of drugs - Mary is gouch. - *America/British*

Gowed up - Heavily under the influence of drugs - Devon is gowed up. - *America/British*

Gurning - Involuntary facial movements due to use of MDMA - Edward is so high, he is gurning! - *British*

Hit the pipe - The act of doing drugs and its effect on you - Let's hit the pipe? - *America/British*

Hop-head - A drugs user, someone who is dependent on drugs - Maisie is a hophead. - *America/British*

Hubbly bubbly - A water pipe used to smoke marijuana - Nick uses a hubbly bubbly to smoke dope. - *British*

Jack up - To inject drugs - Liv went to the bathroom, to jack up. - *British*

Load a fat one - The act of doing drugs and its effect on you - Let's load a fat one? - *America/British*

Main line - The act of doing drugs and its effect on you - Let's go main line? - *America/British*

Mainlining - Refers to solution injected into bloodstream - James is mainlining, again. - *America/British*

Mong - To relax. Can refer to drug takers - Olivia is a mong. - *British*

Peyote - Refers to mescaline - I was so high after taking peyote, I fell down the stairs. - *America/British*

Poke smot - The act of doing drugs and its effect on you - Let's go and poke smot? - *America/British*

Powder (one's) nose - The act of doing drugs and its effect on you - Rocky went to powder his nose. - *America/British*

Ride the white horse - The act of doing drugs and its effect on you - Reg likes to ride the white horse. - *America/British*

See Mr. H - The act of doing drugs and its effect on you - Phil went to see Mr. H. - *America/British*

Sesh - Abbreviation of session- a prolonged period of time, usually used in reference to drinking or drug taking - We had a massive sesh last night. - *British*

Session - The act of doing drugs and its effect on you - Let's go for a session? - *America/British*

Slip a Mickey - The act of doing drugs and its effect on you - Let's go and slip a mickey? - *America/British*

Smoke up - The act of doing drugs and its effect on you - Let's go for a smoke up? - *America/British*

Spark - The act of doing drugs and its effect on you - Let's go for a spark? - *America/British*

Spark it up - The act of doing drugs and its effect on you - Are you going to spark it up? - *America/British*

Spike up - The act of doing drugs and its effect on you - Will went to the bathroom to spike up. - *America/British*

Tab - Abbreviation of tablet. Used in drugs culture - Pete took a tab. - *British*

Torch up - The act of doing drugs and its effect on you - Ollie went to the toilet, to torch up. - *America/British*

Tranq - The act of doing drugs and its effect on you - I was totally tranq. - *America/British*

Trip balls - The act of doing drugs and its effect on you - I'm going to trip balls, when I get my drugs. - *America/British*

Cough medicine - Refers to contains alcohol - Kirsty is on the cough medicine, again! - *America/British*

Bennies - Refers to amphetamines/speed - Karl is on bennies. - *America/British*

Billy whizz - Amphetamines - Candy is high on billy whizz. - *British*

Black beauties - Refers to amphetamine/speed - Nobby took some black beauties. - *America/British*

Co-pilots - Refers to amphetamines/speed - Gary bought some co -pilots from the dealer. - *America/British*

Crank - Refers to amphetamines - Mark is on crank, now. - *America/British*

Dexies - Refers to amphetamines/speed - John is on dexies. - *America/British*

Eye openers - Refers to amphetamines/speed - Yasmin is on eye openers. - *America/British*

Lid poppers - Refers to amphetamines/speed - Margy took some lid poppers. - *America/British*

Meth - Refers to amphetamines/speed - Alistair is hooked on meth. - *America/British*

Pep-pill - Refers to caffeine or amphetamines/speed - Sam took a pep-pill and then regretted it. - *America/British*

Speed - Refers to amphetamines - Have you got any speed? - *America/British*

Speed freak - A person addicted to amphetamines, or can mean a person who likes to drive very fast - Jack is a speed freak. - *British*

Speeding - High on amphetamines - Jed is speeding. - *British*

Uppers - Refers to amphetamines - I bought some uppers. - *America/British*

Ups - Refers to amphetamines - I bought some ups. - *America/British*

Wake-ups - Refers to amphetamines/speed - Andy took some wake-ups. - *America/British*

Barbs - An abbreviation of barbiturates - Karim is hooked on barbs. - *America/British*

Bluebirds - Refers to barbiturates - Jermaine is on bluebirds. - *America/British*

Blues - Refers to barbiturates - Yasmeen has taken some blues. - *America/British*

Downers - Refers to barbiturates - Ally is hooked on downers. - *America/British*

Goofball - Refers to barbiturates - Did you know that Ken is on goofball? - *America/British*

Sleepers - Barbiturate drugs - Britt is on sleepers. - *British*

Tooties - Refers to barbiturates - Nigel got some tooties. - *America/British*

Yellow-jackets - Refers to barbiturates - I've taken some yellow-jackets. - *America/British*

Liquid incense - Refers to butyl nitrite - We took some liquid incense. - *America/British*

Bob Hope - Dope- cannabis - Wanda bought some Bob Hope. - *cockney*

Cancer stick - Cigarette - Tosh smoked a cancer stick. - *British*

Cancer sticks - Refers to tobacco - Cassie bought some cancer sticks. - *America/British*

Cigs - Refers to tobacco - Jamie, have you got any cigs? - *America/British*

Andy Parley - Rhyming slang for Charlie - cocaine - The man offered me some Andy Parley, but I told him I did not do cocaine. - *cockney*

Drugs

Base - Refers to cocaine free base - Ahmed has taken base. - *America/British*

Blow - Refers to cocaine - Ken bought some blow. - *America/British*

Bob Marley - Charlie- cocaine - Joe bought some Bob Marley. - *cockney*

C - Refers to cocaine - Chloe bought some C. - *America/British*

Chang - Cocaine - Steven bought some chang. - *America*

Charlie - Refers to cocaine - Tonya did some charlie. - *America/British*

Ching - Cocaine - Jenny has got some ching. - *British*

Chisel - Cocaine - Mel has got some chisel. - *British*

Coke - Refers to cocaine - Sadly, I found out that, Simon is on coke. - *America/British*

Coked up - To be high on cocaine - Chloe is coked up! - *British*

Controlled - Cocaine - Laura got some controlled, if you fancy it? - *British*

Crack - Refers to cocaine free base - Kieron is on crack. - *America/British*

Crack cocaine - Free base cocaine - Sadly, Karl is on crack cocaine. - *British*

Crack head - A person addicted to free base cocaine - Karen is a crack head. - *British*

Crystal - Cocaine - Absalom took some crystal, and now feels high. - *America*

Devil's dandruff - Refers to cocaine - Jerry took some Devil's dandruff, earlier. - *America/British*

Flake - Refers to cocaine - Have you got any flake? - *America/British*

Freebase - Cocaine - Lucy bought some free base. - *British*

French fries - Refers to crack cocaine - Have you got any French fries? - *America/British*

Gak - Cocaine - Loo loo loves a bit of gak. - *British*

Happy dust - Cocaine - I want to get some happy dust. - *British*

Joy powder - Cocaine - Phil got some joy powder from his dealer. - *British*

Line - A quantity of cocaine laid out and cut into a line, prior to snorting - We did a few lines. - *British*

Magistrate mate - An eighth of cocaine - Jo has got some magistrate mate. - *cockney*

Marching powder - Refers to cocaine - Let's get some marching powder? - *America/British*

Nose candy - Cocaine - He is on the nose candy. - *British*

On crack - To be high on crack cocaine - Claire is on crack. - *British*

Pearl-flake - Refers to cocaine - We did some pearl-flake last night. - *America/British*

Peruvian marching powder - Refers to cocaine - Let's get some Peruvian marching powder? - *America/British*

Posh - Cocaine - I brought some posh to the party. - *British*

Ready rock - Refers to crack cocaine - Rudy bought some ready rock. - *America/British*

Snort - To inhale drugs through the nose. e.g. cocaine - Toby went for a snort in the bathroom. - *British*

Snorting - Refers to sniffing - We were all snorting coke. - *America/British*

Snow - Cocaine - Let's get some snow. - *British*

Speedball - Refers to combination of cocaine with heroin - He overdosed on a speedball. - *America/British*

Stardust - Cocaine - He was on stardust. - *British*

Sugar - Cocaine - Have you got any sugar? - *British*

White horse - Cocaine - Fiona is on the white horse. - *British*

White lady - Cocaine - I've brought a white lady to the party, if anyone is interested? - *British*

Dynamite - Refers to combination of cocaine with heroin - Carole is on dynamite. - *America/British*

Garden gate - An eighth of cocaine - I've got a garden gate with me. - *cockney*

A-bomb - Refers to combination of marijuana with heroin - Julian overdosed after taking an, A-bomb. - *America/British*

Whiz-bang - Refers to combination of cocaine with heroin, or cocaine with morphine - He overdosed on some whiz-bang. - *America/British*

Schoolboy - Refers to codeine - Have you got any schoolboy? - *America/British*

Acid house - A form of dance music usually associated with drugs use - Stu loves to dance to acid house music. - *British*

Rave - Dance event usually associated with the drug ecstasy - We went to a rave at the weekend. - *British*

Raving - To go to a rave - We went raving last night. - *British*

Skanky - Dirty, some reference to marijuana pipe - Pass the skanky? - *British*

Pusher - A person who earns money by selling illegal drugs - Dec got some drugs from a pusher in the pub. - *America/British*

Shotter - A person who earns money by selling illegal drugs - Michael got his gear, from a shotter in town. - *America/British*

Sorted - Refers to acquiring drugs. i.e. sorted for e's and whizz - We are sorted for the party this weekend. - *British*

Spannered - Intoxicated on drink or drugs - I was spannered after taking too many drugs. - *British*

Bag bitch - A drug user, someone who is dependent on drugs - She is a bag bitch! - *America/British*

Baghead - A heroin addict - Lucy is a bag head. - *British*

Baked - Heavily under the influence of drugs - Caroline was baked after taking too many drugs. - *America/British*

Boof - A drugs user, someone who is dependent on drugs - Caf is a boof. - *America/British*

Chronic lag - A drugs user, someone who is dependent on drugs - Jack is a chronic lag. - *America/British*

Coke whore - A drugs user, someone who is dependent on drugs - Jerry is a coke whore! - *America/British*

Crank whore - A drugs user, someone who is dependent on drugs - Roger is a crank whore! - *America/British*

Dope fiend - A drugs user, someone who is dependent on drugs - Mick is a dope fiend. - *America/British*

Dope head - A drug addict - Julia is a dope head. - *British*

Dope monger - A drugs user, someone who is dependent on drugs - Colin is a dope monger. - *America/British*

Dope peddler - A person who earns money by selling illegal drugs - Xena is a dope peddler. - *America/British*

Dope whore - A drugs user, someone who is dependent on drugs - Tim is a dope whore! - *America/British*

Doper - A drugs user, someone who is dependent on drugs - Pearl is a doper. - *America/British*

Druggie - A drugs user, someone who is dependent on drugs - Betty is a druggie. - *America/British*

Geek monster - A drugs user, someone who is dependent on drugs - Solomon is a geek monster. - *America/British*

Hooked - A drugs user, someone who is dependent on drugs - Alison is hooked on heroin. - *America/British*

Junkie - A drug addict - Danny is a junkie. - *British*

Junky - A drug addict - Stacey is a junky. - *British*

Kisses and hugs - Drugs - Aaron, did you bring the kisses and hugs? - *cockney*

Perma-fried - A drugs user, someone who is dependent on drugs - Val is perma-fried. - *America/British*

Pill popper - A drugs user, someone who is dependent on drugs - Jane is a pill popper. - *America/British*

Psychonaut - A drugs user, someone who is dependent on drugs - Jojo is a psychonaut; he takes too many drugs. - *America/British*

Drugs

Toker - A drugs user, someone who is dependent on drugs - I am a toker. - *America/British*

Tweaker - A drugs user, someone who is dependent on drugs - Felix is a tweaker. - *America/British*

Tweeker - A drugs user, someone who is dependent on drugs - He is a tweeker. - *America/British*

User - A drugs user, someone who is dependent on drugs - John is a heavy user. - *America/British*

Viper - A drugs user, someone who is dependent on drugs - I used to be a viper. - *America/British*

Burgers - Refers to ecstasy - Toni ate some burgers. - *America/British*

Disco biscuit - Ecstasy tablet as used in the rave scene - Stu took a disco biscuit. - *British*

Disco biscuits - Refers to ecstasy - Justine loves disco biscuits! - *America/British*

Doves - Refers to ecstasy - The man took some doves. - *America/British*

E bomb - MDMA (ecstasy) a party drug used to increase energy that results in a feeling of euphoria - Darren took the E bomb last night. - *America/British*

Eccies - Refers to ecstasy - Have you got any eccies? - *America/British*

Echoes - Refers to ecstasy - Have you got any echoes? - *America/British*

Ecky - MDMA (ecstasy) - Have you got any ecky? - *British*

Ecstasy - Refers to MDA MDE MDMA MMDA - Miranda is on ecstasy. - *America/British*

Es - Ecstasy tablets as used in the rave scene - Koleen bought some e's. - *British*

Fantasy - Refers to ecstasy - I am on fantasy. - *America/British*

Hug drug - Refers to ecstasy - Ian's on the hug drug. - *America/British*

Littles - Ecstasy tablets, as used in the rave scene - Hannah is on littles. - *British*

Pill head - A frequent user of ecstasy - Fred is a pill head. - *British*

Pill it - To take ecstasy - Let's pill it? - *British*

Pilled up - High on ecstasy - Kirsty was totally pilled up last night. - *British*

X - MDMA (ecstasy) a party drug used to increase energy that results in a feeling of euphoria - He took some X. - *America/British*

XTC - MDMA ecstasy tablets - He took some XTC. - *British*

Kick the habit - To give up drugs - I just can't seem to kick the habit! - *British*

Rattling - Suffering the effects of withdrawal from drugs - Dave is in a bad state. He is rattling because he is trying to give up drugs. - *British*

Scooby snacks - Food eaten when high on drugs, to satisfy cravings - I'm starving, I need to go and get some scooby snacks. - *America*

Tramlines - The scars created by repeated injection of drugs - Have you seen the tramlines on Pat's arm? - *British*

Forget-me-pill - Refers to FLUNITRAZEPAM - Mandy took a forget-me-pill. - *America/British*

Get roached - Refers to be under the influence of FLUNITRAZEPAM - Let's get roached? - *America/British*

Rohypnol - Refers to FLUNITRAZEPAM the date rape drug - I think my drink was spiked with rohypnol. - *America/British*

Blotter - Hallucinogens; drugs that cause hallucinations - Andy took a blotter. - *America/British*

Electric koolaid - Hallucinogens; drugs that cause hallucinations - Lee has been drinking the old electric koolaid, again! - *America/British*

Jenkem - Hallucinogens; drugs that cause hallucinations - Simon loves jenkems. - *America/British*

Liquid sunshine - Hallucinogens; drugs that cause hallucinations - Let's get some liquid sunshine? - *America/British*

Mushies - Magic mushrooms - a hallucinogenic drug - We took some mushies. - *British*

Mushrooms - Hallucinogens; drugs that cause hallucinations - Let's get some mushrooms? - *America/British*

Shrooms - Refers to psilocybin a hallucinogenic drug - We were on shrooms, when it happened. - *America/British*

Soap bar - Refers to hashish - Have you got any soap bar? - *America/British*

Squidgy black - Hashish - Susie bought some squidgy black. - *British*

Big H - Heroin - Jan is hooked on the Big H. - *America*

Black tar - Refers to heroin - Jake bought some black tar. - *America/British*

Candy - Heroin - Ahmed has got some candy. - *British*

Chase the dragon - To inhale heroin through a tube by burning it over aluminium foil - Kyle loves to chase the dragon. - *British*

Chasing the dragon - Refers to smoking - Karen is chasing the dragon. - *America/British*

China white - Refers to heroin - Matt took some china white. - *America/British*

Crap - Heroin - Lynn bought some crap from the dealer. - *British*

Donald Duck (ing) - Clucking- craving more heroine - Lynda is suffering with withdraw, she is Donald Duck(ing), badly. - *cockney*

Doojee - Heroin - Trish is on doojee. - *British*

Dust - Refers to heroin - Carmel has some dust. - *America/British*

Fix - A dose of drugs typically heroin - I need a fix! - *British*

Flea powder - Heroin - He bought some flea powder from the dealer. - *British*

H - Heroin - Rob is on H again. - *British*

Horse - Refers to heroin - Now, he's doing horse. - *America/British*

Mexican mud - Refers to heroin - Where did you buy that Mexican mud? - *America/British*

Mojo - Heroin - I need to get some mojo. - *British*

On heroin - To be high on heroin - Dave is on heroin. - *British*

Scag - Heroin - Maureen went to score some scag. - *British*

Shit - Refers to heroin - Deryn went out to get his shit. - *America/British*

Shoot up - To inject drugs. typically heroin - Robert went out to shoot up. - *British*

Skag - Heroin - Len is on skag. - *British*

Skaghead - Heroin addict - Gordon is a skaghead. - *British*

Smack head - A heroin addict - He is a smack head. - *British*

Smacked - Heavily under the influence of drugs - Darcy is totally smacked. - *America/British*

Strung out - Negative effects of withdrawal from heroin - Chris is really strung out, he is trying to come off the drugs. - *British*

White stuff - Heroin - Mo is on the white stuff. - *British*

Amped-out - Heavily under the influence of drugs - The girls in the night club were amped out, and heavily under the influence of cannabis. - *America/British*

Blunted - Heavily under the influence of drugs - Ken is blunted on drugs. - *America/British*

Caned - Intoxicated - Kirsty is caned. - *British*

Caramelized - Heavily under the influence of drugs - Leslie is caramelized. - *America/British*

Charged - High on drugs - Yasmeen is charged. - *British*

Chonged - To be intoxicated - Elsie is chonged. - *British*

Destroyed - Highly intoxicated - Guy is destroyed! - *British*

Doped up - Heavily under the influence of drugs - Amanda is all doped up. - *America/British*

Flame-broiled - Heavily under the influence of drugs - Caz is flame-broiled. - *America/British*

Fried - Heavily under the influence of drugs - I am fried! - *America/British*

Jib - Heavily under the influence of drugs - Lewis is jibbed. - *America/British*

K-hole - Heavily under the influence of drugs - John is k-holed. - *America/British*

Krunked - Heavily under the influence of drugs - I'm totally krunked! - *America/British*

Lit up - Heavily under the influence of drugs - Liz was totally lit up. - *America/British*

Loved up - High on drugs - I'm loved up. - *British*

Mong out - To be high on drugs and unable to converse or move - Annie was so high, she just monged out. - *British*

Mortalled - Intoxicated - Catherine was mortalled. - *British*

Nod out - To lapse into a drug induced stupor - He frequently nods out. - *British*

Nodder - Heavily under the influence of drugs - Gareth is a nodder. - *America/British*

Off (one's) tits - Heavily under the influence of drugs - Bill was off his tits on drugs. - *America/British*

Off his head - Someone affected by drugs - Bert was off his head last night. - *British*

Off it - High on drugs - I've taken three tabs, I'm off my head. - *British*

Off my/ their face - Someone affected by drugs - I'm off my face on acid. - *British*

Off one's box - To be intoxicated by drink or drugs - I'm off my box on heroin. - *British*

Off one's nut - To be intoxicated by drink or drugs - Cameron is off his nut! - *British*

Off one's tree - To be intoxicated by drink or drugs - I'm off my tree on acid. - *British*

Off the planet - Someone affected by drugs - Kevin was off the planet on crack. - *British*

Pied - Heavily under the influence of drugs - Katie was pied last night. - *America/British*

Pill face - Heavily under the influence of drugs - Evan is a pill face. - *America/British*

Roll balls - Heavily under the influence of drugs - We were rolling balls last night. - *America/British*

Ruined - Intoxicated - We got ruined yesterday. - *British*

Shot away - Intoxicated on drugs - Candice is completely shot away. - *British*

Skied - Heavily under the influence of drugs - Kev was skied last night. - *America/British*

Smacked up - High on heroin - I was smacked up, yesterday. - *British*

Smoked - Extremely intoxicated either with drink/ and or drugs (marijuana) - We were smoked, after a heavy session doing drink and drugs. - *America*

Splifficated - Extremely high - He was splifficated. - *America*

Spun - Extremely inebriated or/ and under the influence of meta amphetamines - He was totally spun. - *America*

Spun out - Affected by drugs, marijuana - I spun out after taking too many drugs. - *British*

Stuck - Heavily under the influence of drugs - Mark was totally stuck. - *America/British*

Tall - Heavily under the influence of drugs - I was tall last night. - *America/British*

Thizz - Heavily under the influence of drugs - Trish is thizz. - *America/British*

Trashed - Intoxicated - I was trashed last night. - *America/British*

Trolleyed - Intoxicated - Les is totally trolleyed! - *British*

Trousered - Intoxicated - I was trousered last night. - *British*

Drugs

Twatted - Intoxicated on drink and drugs - Kieron is completely twatted. - *British*

Twisted - Intoxicated - I got twisted last night. - *America*

Well gone - Intoxicated on drink or drugs - Emma is well gone. - *British*

Whacked - Affected by drugs, marijuana - I was whacked, last night. - *Australian*

Wig - Heavily under the influence of drugs - Eleanor was wigged last night. - *America/British*

Yippered up - Heavily under the influence of drugs - John was yippered up. - *America/British*

Zonked out - Heavily under the influence of drugs - Jane was zonked out. - *America/British*

Gook - Refers to HYDROXYBUTYRATE - I took some gook. - *America/British*

Liquid-E - Refers to HYDROXYBUTYRATE - Wayne is on liquid-e. - *America/British*

Liquid-G - Refers to HYDROXYBUTYRATE - Norris is on liquid-g. - *America/British*

Liquid-X - Refers to HYDROXYBUTYRATE - Matthew is on liquid-x. - *America/British*

Glue - Refers to inhalant - Keith's on the glue. - *America/British*

Solvent - Refers to inhalant - Paul uses solvents. He is a glue sniffer. - *America/British*

Transmission fluid - Refers to inhalant - Paul is on transmission fluid. - *America/British*

K - Refers to ketamine - Let's do some k. - *America/British*

Ket - Refers to ketamine - Let's get some ket. - *America/British*

Special k - Ketamine - Yasmin bought some special k. - *British*

Vitamin K - Refers to ketamine - Have you got any vitamin k? - *America/British*

Acid - The psychedelic drug, LSD - The man was high on acid, and was threatening to throw himself off the building. - *British*

Acid freak - A drugs user, someone who is dependent on drugs - The drug user was described as an acid freak, as he was dependent on drugs. - *America/British*

Acid head - A person who uses the hallucinogenic drug LSD - Joe is an acid head. - *British*

Blotter acid - Refers to LSD - Jeff is on blotter acid. - *America/British*

Blotters - Refers to LSD - Tookie took some blotters. - *America/British*

Dots - Refers to LSD - I bought some dots. - *America/British*

Instant zen - LSD - I took a tab, it was instant zen. - *British*

Micro dots - LSD - We took some micro dots. - *British*

On acid - To be high on LSD - Mandy is on acid. - *British*

Tabs - Refers to LSD - Have you got any tabs? - *America/British*

Trips - Refers to LSD - Have you got any trips? - *America/British*

Windowpane - Refers to LSD or ecstasy tablets - Have you got any windowpane? - *America/British*

Acapulco gold - Marijuana - "Would you like some Acapulco gold?" said the dealer, reaching for the marijuana. - *America*

African bush weed - Marijuana - He was smoking African bush weed, which he had obtained from a drug dealer. - *British*

Bhang - Refers to marijuana - Maureen is high on bhang. - *America/British*

Bifta - A cigarette typically containing marijuana - Colin rolled a bifta. - *British*

Bifter - A marijuana cigarette - Tony rolled a fat bifter. - *British*

Blunt - Marijuana - Nargis rolled a blunt. - *America/British*

Cali - Marijuana - Izzie is smoking cali. - *America/British*

Drugs

141

Cheeba - Marijuana - Nabib has got some cheeba. - *America/British*

Chiba - Marijuana - Nargis has got some chiba. - *America/British*

Chronic - Marijuana - Pete is on the chronic. - *America/British*

Cigga-weed - Marijuana - Ann smoked some cigga-weed. - *America/British*

Cigweed - Marijuana - Lisa smoked some cigweed. - *America/British*

Colitas - Marijuana - Eileen has got some colitas. - *America/British*

Colombian - Refers to marijuana - Doug bought some Colombian from the dealer. - *America/British*

Combustible herbage - Marijuana - Livvie bought some combustible herbage from the dealer last night. - *America/British*

Crippy - Marijuana - Jan bought some crippy. - *America/British*

Dirt weed - Marijuana - Susie is on the dirt weed! - *America/British*

Ditch weed - Marijuana - Tracey smoked some ditch weed. - *America/British*

Doob - Marijuana - Have you got any doob? - *America/British*

Doober - Marijuana - Let's roll a doober? - *America/British*

Dough - Refers to marijuana - Penny bought some dough from a dealer. - *America/British*

Draw - Marijuana - Bert bought some draw. - *British*

Dube - Marijuana - Xavier has some dube. - *America/British*

Dutchie - Marijuana - I've got some dutchie, wanna share? - *America/British*

Fatty boom blatty - Marijuana - Have you got any fatty boom blatty? - *America/British*

Gange - Marijuana - I've brought some gange with me. - *America/British*

Ganja - Refers to marijuana - I bought some ganja. - *America/British*

Gear - Drugs. usually marijuana - Let's get some gear? - *British*

Get a build on - To roll a joint, typically a cigarette containing marijuana - Let's get a build on? - *British*

Giggle stick - Marijuana - I love a bit of giggle stick! - *America/British*

Glass of water - A quarter of cannabis - I bought a glass of water. - *cockney*

Green - Marijuana - Have you got any green? - *British*

Green bud - Marijuana - Randy's got some green bud. - *America/British*

Happy feed - Weed- cannabis - I need some happy feed. - *cockney*

Harry monk - Skunk- cannabis - I've got some harry monk. - *cockney*

Hash - Abbreviation of hashish (a form of marijuana) - Hide my hash? - *British*

Hashish - Refers to marijuana - Got any hashish? - *America/British*

Henry the Eighth - An eighth of cannabis - I brought Henry the Eighth to the party. - *cockney*

Herbal refreshment - Marijuana - I need some herbal refreshment. - *America/British*

Hippie lettuce - Marijuana - Have you got any hippie lettuce? - *America*

Home-grown - Refers to marijuana - I've got some home-grown. - *America/British*

Hot knives - A method of burning cannabis and exhaling the fumes - We did hot knives in the kitchen. - *British*

Hot rocks - A smouldering piece of marijuana that falls from a joint - Hot rocks can burn holes in your clothes, so be careful. - *British*

Indian - Refers to marijuana - Matt has bought some Indian for us. - *America/British*

Indica - Refers to marijuana - I have some indica. - *America/British*

Indo - Marijuana - I have some indo to share. - *America/British*

Drugs

J - Abbreviation of joint (marijuana) - Pass the J this way, man. - *British*

Jamaican - Refers to marijuana - I've got some Jamaican. - *America/British*

Jay - Abbreviation of joint (marijuana) - I'm going to roll a jay. - *British*

Jive - Refers to marijuana - I have some jive. - *America/British*

Keef - Marijuana - I have some keef, do you fancy a smoke? - *America/British*

Kief - Marijuana - I bought some kief. - *America/British*

Killer weed - Refers to combination of marijuana with PCP - Tiffany is smoking killer weed. - *America/British*

Laugh and joke - Smoke - Let's have a laugh and joke? - *cockney*

Left-handed cigarette - Marijuana - Jo-jo rolled a left-handed cigarette. - *America/British*

Limbo - Marijuana - Richard bought some limbo. - *America/British*

Mary Jane - Refers to marijuana - Have you got any Mary Jane? - *America/British*

Maui-wowie - Refers to marijuana - Let's get some maui-wowie? - *America/British*

Mexican - Refers to marijuana - I bought some Mexican. - *America/British*

Mexican dirt weed - Marijuana - Willy had some Mexican dirt weed. - *America/British*

Mota - Marijuana - I got some mota. - *America/British*

Mr. J - Marijuana - I bought Mr. J to the party. - *America/British*

Nib - Marijuana - Pete bought some nib. - *America/British*

Northern lights - Marijuana - Sandy's got some northern lights. - *British*

Number - Cannabis cigarette - Let's roll a number? - *British*

O.J. - Refers to combination of marijuana with opium - Graham is on O.J. - *America/British*

Onion - Marijuana - Have you got any onion? - *America/British*

Pot head - Marijuana user - They were all total pot heads. - *British*

Red leb - Marijuana - I bought some red leb. - *British*

Reefer - A cannabis joint - We smoked a reefer in the park. - *British*

Reggie - Marijuana - Have you got any Reggie? - *America/British*

Reggs - Marijuana - Have you got reggs? - *America/British*

Schwag - Marijuana - Have you got any schwag? - *America/British*

Shake - Marijuana - Have you got any shake? - *America/British*

Shwag - Marijuana - Let's get some shwag? - *America/British*

Sinse - Refers to marijuana - Let's get some sinse? - *America/British*

Sinsemelia - Marijuana - I've got some sinsemelia. - *British*

Skater - Marijuana - Have you got any skater? - *America/British*

Skin up - To roll a cannabis joint - Mo went outside to skin up. - *British*

Skunk - An extremely potent form of marijuana - Eddie was smoking skunk at the party. - *British*

Skunk weed - Marijuana - Dwayne likes skunk weed. - *America/British*

Smoke dope - The act of doing drugs and its effect on you - I like to smoke dope. - *America/British*

Smoke pot - The act of doing drugs and its effect on you - I don't like to smoke pot. - *America/British*

Spliff - A marijuana cigarette - He rolled a spliff. - *British*

Spliffy - Marijuana - Pass me the spliffy? - *America/British*

Sticky icky icky - Marijuana - Have you got any sticky icky icky? - *America/British*

Stiva - Refers to marijuana - Have you got any stiva? - *America/British*

Strap up - To roll a cannabis joint - Dominic went to the bathroom to strap up. - *British*

Drugs

Super skunk - Marijuana - Abe is smoking super skunk. - *British*

Supergrass - Refers to combination of marijuana with PCP - Do you want any supergrass? - *America/British*

Tex Mex - Marijuana smuggled into America from Mexico - I got hold of some Tex Mex. - *America*

Thai stick - Marijuana - He gave me some Thai sticks. - *British*

Toke up - The act of doing drugs and its effect on you - Frankie went to the bathroom to toke up. - *America/British*

Toking - Refers to the act of inhaling marijuana - We were toking all day. - *America/British*

Treats - Marijuana - Have you got any treats? - *America/British*

Tweed - Marijuana - Have you got any tweed? - *America/British*

Wacky backy - Cannabis or marijuana - He is on the wacky backy. - *British*

Wacky tobaccy - Marijuana - Have you got any wacky tobaccy? - *America/British*

Whifty - Marijuana - Have you got a whifty? - *America/British*

Wired to the ground - Affected by drugs, marijuana - I was wired to the ground, last night. - *Australian*

Woolies - Marijuana - Have you got any woolies? - *America/British*

Zombie - Marijuana - Have you got any zombie? - *America/British*

Zoot - Marijuana cigarette - Pass me that zoot? - *British*

Love drug - Refers to MDMA - I'm on the love drug. - *America/British*

Henry - Derived from King Henry the Eighth, refers to a measurement an eighth of an ounce of marijuana - I bought a Henry. - *British*

Teenth - A measurement of a 16th of an ounce, commonly used in reference to marijuana - Tasha bought a teenth from the guy down the pub. - *British*

Leg of lamb - Gram - An amount of drugs - Kandy bought a leg of lamb. - *cockney*

M - Refers to morphine - Nan takes M, to relieve pain. - *America/British*

Morf - Refers to morphine - I acquired some morf. - *America/British*

Blue-bottle - Refers to nitrous oxide - Candice is on the blue-bottle. - *America/British*

Laughing gas - Refers to nitrous oxide - Vinnie is on the laughing gas. - *America/British*

Whippitts - Refers to nitrous oxide - We were doing whippitts, last night. - *America/British*

Bobby - Opiates or drug that is derived from opium - Rachel got some bobby. - *America/British*

Brown - Opiates or drug that is derived from opium - Womad is on brown. - *America/British*

Schmeck - Opiates or drug that is derived from opium - Laura bought some schmeck. - *America/British*

Angel dust - Refers to PCP - Rob is off his head on angel dust! - *America/British*

PCP - Refers to phencyclidine - Lou bought some PCP. - *America/British*

Peace pill - Refers to PCP - Caz took a peace pill. - *America/British*

Poppers - A stimulant drug used on the gay scene - He was off his head on poppers. - *British*

Magic mushrooms - Refers to psilocybin - We took some magic mushrooms. - *America/British*

Jellies - Tranquilizer drugs such as TEMAZEPAM - Nicole is on jellies. - *British*

Downer - Tranquillisers - I took a downer. - *British*

Tranks - Tranquillisers - I bought some tranks. - *British*

Drugs

General

'Mither'
To fuss

By accident - Not on purpose - I deleted my essay by accident. - *British*

Check it out - Take a look - There is a brilliant play on in town, you should check it out. - *British*

Come a cropper - To fall over - I was half way up a ladder when I came a cropper. - *British*

Cop a load of that - Look at - Dude, cop a load of that woman over there! - *British*

Cut and run - To leave quickly - I need to cut and run. - *British*

Done and dusted - Finished - Finally the report was done and dusted. - *British*

Down on ones luck - Unlucky - It hasn't been a good year for me, I'm really down on my luck. - *British*

From strength to strength - An improving situation - I feel much better, I'm going from strength to strength. - *British*

Gander - To peruse - I had a gander at the shops in town. - *British*

Gawp - To stare - He was stood there, just gawping at the ladies on the dance floor! - *British*

Gone to pot - Ruined - This hospital has gone to pot! - *British*

Gone to the dogs - Ruined - The town has gone to the dogs. - *British*

Little by little - To gradually develop or improve - I'm getting better, little by little. - *America/British*

Make tracks - To start a journey - I don't want to be late, I better make tracks. - *British*

Make yourself scarce - Go away - The boss is angry with you, you better make yourself scarce. - *British*

Mosey - To look around - Let's have a mosey around town. - *British*

Muck in - To help someone - My sister needed help moving house, so she asked the whole family to muck in. - *British*

Off like a shot - To leave quickly - When the bill arrived, Vaughan was off like a shot! - *British*

Peg it - To run - Quick, peg it, the police are coming! - *British*

Pipped at the post - To be narrowly defeated - I nearly beat Justin at snooker, but he just pipped me at the post. - *British*

Prang - Accident - I had a prang in my new car. - *British*

Scram - To run a way - If the police come, we will scram. - *British*

Shipshape and bristol fashion - Organised - We need to tidy up to make this place, ship shape and Bristol fashion. - *America/British*

145

Shoot off - To leave - I need to shoot off now, or I will be late for work. - *British*

Take a chill pill - Relax - Hey, calm down, you need to take a chill pill! - *British*

Take it easy - Relax - On the weekend, I like to take it easy. - *British*

Take the load off your feet - Sit down - If you are tired, you should take a load off. - *British*

Take/ have a gander - Old fashioned phrase for have a look - I like to have a gander at the shops. - *British*

To nick off - To leave - Darren said he is going to nick off early from work today. - *Australian*

To take a 'butcher's' - Rhyming slang for look. Butcher's hook= look - Take a butchers at my new car. - *British*

Affirmative - In other words -yes - "That will be in the affirmative," said Mel, when agreeing to cut the hedge. - *America*

Against the grain - In opposition - I find that goes against the grain and therefore I shall oppose it. - *British*

Ageest - Interpreted as - astonished - I was absolutely ageest that he would even suggest such a thing! - *Devon*

Agree to disagree - To accept another has a different viewpoint to yourself - Although I did not agree with Kate, I accepted I would have to agree to disagree. - *British*

Bolloxed - Drunk - They were all totally bolloxed after drinking all afternoon! - *Ireland*

Largurr - Lager beer - Robert had a pint of largurr. - *Bristol*

Messy - A party or social gathering that gets out of hand, usually with reference to drink or drugs - I drank a whole bottle of vodka, it got very messy! - *British*

Piss artist - A drunken person - Someone who loves to drink is a piss artist. - *British*

Piss head - An alcoholic - Colin is a piss head. - *British*

Piss it up against a wall - To waste one's money on alcohol - Simon spent all his wages on booze, he just pissed it all up against the wall. - *British*

Shedded - Intoxicated - April is shedded. - *British*

Shit faced - Intoxicated - He got shit faced on cheap lager. - *British*

A cappella - Meaning 'in chapel style', from the Italian word for: sung without instrumental accompaniment - The choir sang a cappella, without any backing instruments to accompany them. - *British*

A deux - From the French word for: involving two people - Janet and I went to the restaurant "a deux" and it was good to just be the two of us. - *British*

A fortiori - Meaning 'from a stronger argument' from the Latin word for: more conclusively - After much discussion the team decided to go with my proposal, as it was a fortiori. - *British*

A huis clos - Meaning 'with closed doors'. From the French word for: in private - The meeting was held in private behind closed doors or was 'a huis clos' in the french language. - *British*

A posteriori - Meaning 'from what comes after', from the Latin word for: based on reasoning from known facts or past events, rather than on assumptions or predictions - The diagnosis was based on a posteriori knowledge. - *British*

A priori - Meaning 'from what is before', from the Latin word for: based on deduction rather than experience - The diagnosis was determined a priori. - *British*

Ab initio - From the Latin word for: from the beginning - The roots of an illness need to be traced back ab initio. - *British*

Ad hoc - Meaning 'to this', from the Latin word for: made or done for a particular purpose - The new system was designed ad hoc, and this was going to be a big problem! - *British*

Ad infinitum - Meaning 'to infinity'. From the Latin word for: endlessly; forever - The rain seemed to go on ad infinitum and didn't seem to stop all day. - *British*

Ad interim - From the Latin word for: for the meantime - Until a new manager is employed, Richard will step up ad interim. - *British*

Ad nauseam - Meaning 'to sickness'. From the Latin word for: to a tiresomely excessive degree - The reading went on ad nauseam, it was excessive and tiring. - *British*

Agent provocateur - Meaning 'provocative agent', from the French word for: a person who tempts a suspected criminal to commit a crime so that they can be caught and convicted - The boss suspected that someone was stealing so he set some traps and acted as an agent provocateur. - *British*

Al dente - Of food cooked so as to be still firm when bitten, meaning 'to the tooth' in Latin - Like the Italians, I prefer my pasta al dente after cooking. - *British*

Alfresco - Meaning 'in the fresh', from the Italian word for: in the open air - We are having a barbeque al fresco, if the sun comes out! - *British*

Annus mirabilis - From the Latin word for: a remarkable or auspicious year - This year has been our annus mirablis and we have had a really good year. - *British*

Au fait - Meaning 'to the point', from the French word for: having a good or detailed knowledge - I wasn't au fait with the new computer system, and struggled to even log on. - *British*

Au naturel - From the French word for: in the most simple or natural way - It is more healthy to eat au naturel, rather than have lots of processed foods. - *British*

Carpe diem - Seize the day!' Latin word meaning: make the most of the present time - It is important to make the most of your opportunities, Carpe Diem! - *British*

Carte blanche - Meaning 'blank paper', from the French word for: complete freedom to act as one wishes - The new management had carte blanche to change all of the existing operations. - *British*

Cognoscenti - People who know: people who are well informed about something - The cognoscenti, had been predicting that the company would be solid for some time. - *British*

Compos mentis - From the Latin word for: sane; in full control of mind - Derek is still compos mentis, but he has lot of mobility issues as he has gotten older and more frail. - *British*

Coup d'État - Meaning 'blow of state', from the French word for: a sudden violent seizure of power - The government were very weak and there were rumours of a coup d'État. - *British*

Coup de grâce - Meaning 'stroke of grace', from the French word for: a blow by which a mortally wounded person or thing is mercifully killed - Nancy was in the latter stages of terminal cancer and she was in so much pain that we all prayed for a coup de grâce. - *British*

De facto - From the Latin word for: in fact, whether by right or not - After the sudden death of his father, the young boy became the de facto leader of his family. - *British*

De jure - Meaning 'of law', from the Latin word for: rightful; by right - After the divorce, assets were split equally de jure. - *British*

De profundis - Meaning 'from the depths', from the Latin word for: expressing deepest feelings - The bereaved husband spoke de profundis at his wife's funeral. - *British*

De rigueur - Meaning 'of strictness', from the French word for: obligatory; required by etiquette or current fashion; thorough - It was vital that all the men in the office wore a suit; this was the de rigueur. - *British*

Déjà vu - Meaning 'already seen', from the French word for: the sense of having experienced the present situation before - I just had déjà vu, I'm sure I have been here before! - *British*

Doppelgänger - Meaning 'double-goer', from the German word for: an apparition or double of a living person (lookalikie) - I'm sure I just saw you getting on a bus. Maybe you have a doppelgänger! - *British*

General

Double entendre - From the French word for: 'double understanding' : a word or phrase with two possible interpretations - Pete is very sleazy, he is always making comments that have double entendres. - *British*

En masse - Meaning 'in a mass', from the French word for: all together - The workers were not happy with the new contract so they decided to walk out en mass. - *British*

Enfant terrible - Meaning 'terrible child', from the French word for: a person whose behaviour is unconventional or controversial - The rock star had a very wild daughter, she was an enfant terrible. - *British*

Esprit de corps - Meaning 'spirit of body', from the French word for: a feeling of pride and loyalty uniting the members of a group - The staff has a great esprit de corps and were determined to succeed. - *British*

Ex gratia - From the Latin word 'of payment'. Given as a favour rather than because of any legal obligation meaning 'from favour' - The company provided their service ex gratia. - *British*

Fait accompli - Meaning 'accomplished fact', from the French word for: a thing that has been done or decided and cannot now be altered - The decision to close the factory had already been finalised, it was a fait accompli. - *British*

Faux pas - Meaning 'false step', from the French word for: an embarrassing blunder or indiscretion - I made a faux pas when I asked the lady when the baby was due and she wasn't even pregnant! - *British*

Femme fatale - Meaning 'disastrous woman', from the French word for: a seductive woman - The new secretary at work is a femme fatale. - *British*

Haute couture - Meaning 'high dressmaking', from the French word for: the designing and making of clothes by leading fashion houses - The new boss was very extravagant, she only dressed in haute coutre. - *British*

Haute cuisine - Meaning 'high cookery', from the French word for: high-quality cooking - The lunch was delicious, it was haute cuisine. - *British*

In absentia - Meaning 'in absence', from the Latin word for: while not present - The boss was away on holiday so we had to make the decision in absentia. - *British*

In extremis - From the Latin word for: in an extremely difficult situation; at the point of death - The accident had been very serious and the old man was now in extremis. - *British*

In situ - From the Latin word for: in the original or appropriate position - Normal service should be resumed now we have a manager in situ. - *British*

Ipso facto - From the Latin word for: by that very fact or act - I missed the bus, ipso facto, I will be late for work. - *British*

Je ne sais quoi - Meaning 'I do not know what', from the French word for: a quality that is hard to describe - The new secretary had a certain, je ne sais quoi. - *British*

Joie de vivre - Meaning 'joy of living', From the french word for: exuberant enjoyment of life - The old man was very frail but he still had a joie de vivre. - *British*

Laissez-faire - Meaning 'allow to do', from the French word for: a non-interventionist policy - The new teacher had a very laissez -faire attitude towards her teaching. - *British*

Locum tenens - Meaning 'one holding a place', from the Latin word for: a temporary deputy or stand-in - The doctor was on holiday so a locum tenens was brought in. - *British*

Magnum opus - Meaning 'great work', from the Latin word for: the most important work of an artist, writer, etc. - The final writings from Freud are considered to be his magnum opus. - *British*

Mea culpa - Meaning 'by my fault', from the Latin word for: an acknowledgement that something is one's fault - The surgeon is unlikely to concede mea culpa. - *British*

Ménage à trois - Meaning 'household of three', from the French word for: an arrangement in which a married couple and the lover of one of them live together - Pete has a ménage à trois with Sally and Debbie. - *British*

Modus operandi - Meaning 'way of operating', from the Latin word for: a way of doing something - The new boss is very strict, his modus operandi is to rule by fear. - *British*

Nil desperandum - From the Latin word for: do not despair - Nil desperandum, help is on its way. - *British*

Non sequitur - Meaning 'it does not follow', from the Latin word for: a conclusion or statement that does not logically follow from the previous statement - To suggest that poverty leads to crime is a non sequitur. - *British*

Nouveau riche - Meaning 'new rich', from the French word for: people who have recently become rich and who display their wealth ostentatiously - The property developer was part of the noveau riche, he was always bragging about how rich he had become. - *British*

Par excellence - Meaning 'by excellence', from the French word for: better or more than all others of the same kind - The meal was par excellence. - *British*

Per annum - From the Latin word for: each year - The salary was fifty thousand pounds per annum. - *British*

Per capita - Meaning 'by heads', from the Latin word for: for each person - The average salary had increased by one thousand pounds per capita. - *British*

Per se - From the Latin word for: by or in itself or themselves - Just because he has a criminal conviction, it doesn't mean that he is guilty of another crime per se. - *British*

Persona non grata - From the Latin word for: a person who is not welcome somewhere - Margy got banned from the shop, she is now a persona non grata. - *British*

Pièce de résistance - Meaning 'means of resistance' from the French word for: the most important or impressive item - The meal was delicious and the pudding was the pièce de résistance. - *British*

Prima facie - Meaning 'at first face', from the Latin word for: accepted as so until proved otherwise - You have to believe prima facie that Keith is telling the truth. - *British*

Pro rata - Meaning 'according to the rate', from the Latin word for: proportional - The salary was fifty thousand pounds pro rata. - *British*

Quid pro quo - Meaning 'something for something', from the Latin word for: a favour or advantage given in return for something - The company provided their service quid pro quo. - *British*

Raison d'Etre - Meaning 'reason for being', from the French word for: the most important reason for someone or some thing's existence - Paul was an alcoholic, his whole raison d'Etre was to get drunk. - *British*

Sangfroid - Meaning 'cold blood', from the French word for: the ability to stay calm in difficult circumstances - Neil showed great sangfroid when dealing with the angry customer. - *British*

Terra firma - Meaning 'firm land', from the Latin word for: dry land; the ground - Judy did not like travelling by airplane, she was glad to be back on terra firma. - *British*

Tête-á-tête - Meaning 'head-to-head', from the French word for: a private conversation - Richard and the boss had a tête-á-tête today to discuss his misgivings about the company. - *British*

Tour de force - Meaning 'feat of strength', from the French word for: a thing accomplished with great skill - The way the new boss transformed the company was a tour de force. - *British*

Zeitgeist - Meaning 'time spirit', from the German word for: the characteristic spirit or mood of a particular historical period - The current zeitgeist is to turn away from others, which has led to a growing distrust of outsiders and authorities. - *British*

General

General

A dose of one's own medicine - To be given the same treatment as you gave to others- not medical. e.g., she was unkind to me so I was unkind back to her! - Mary was given a dose of her own medicine when she was treated so unkindly by her colleagues. - *British*

A law unto oneself - Independent or rebellious - The teenager was a law unto himself, and would not obey instructions from his teacher. - *America/British*

Ace up your sleeve - Keep a winning tactic in reserve - The runner kept one ace up his sleeve, and knew he would use it to win, if necessary. - *British*

Agging - Egging on, encourage - He was agging me on all the time to ask her out. - *Devon*

All mouth and no trousers - All talk and no action - often in a sexual context - Wayne was all mouth and no trousers, always bragging about his prowess in the bedroom. - *British*

All piss and wind - All talk and no action - "You are all piss and wind, with lots of talk but no action," commented Phillip. - *British*

Allock - Dawdle - When he was bored he would allock behind everyone else. - *Yorkshire*

An eye opener - Something that happens that enables you to see the truth or a situation in reality and more clearly - Marie's behaviour was a real eye opener, when she displayed another side to her character by dancing on the tables! - *British*

Arse about face - Back to front - The reason the remote control won't work is that Jim put the batteries in arse about face! - *British*

Arse around - Waste time or mess around - I was bored in school, so I used to just arse around. - *British*

Arse over tit - Fall over head over heels - I slipped getting out of the shower, and fell arse over tit. - *British*

Backed into a corner - A difficult situation - I hate my boss, but I can't afford to leave my job, I feel backed into a corner. - *British*

Backs to wall - To be trapped in a situation where fighting is the only option - We were in serious debt, so it was backs to the wall. - *British*

Badger to death - Keep nagging on and on about something until the other person cannot stand it anymore, and gives in to you! - My child wanted an Xbox, so he badgered me to death all the way up to Christmas. - *British*

Bail out - To escape from a situation - I had to bail out of the job, I couldn't stand working there any more. - *America*

Banging your head against a wall - Frustration that a situation cannot be resolved - I've been trying to get John to tidy up, but it's like banging your head against a brick wall. - *British*

Beck and call - To take orders from another - The new boss is really strict, he has me at his beck and call. - *British*

Below the belt - Underhand - It was below the belt when Stan kept the deposit and moved out of the flat. - *British*

Berserk - Very angry - I went berserk when she took my last cigarette. - *British*

Bite the hand that feeds you - To betray someone who is important to your own welfare - He is always arguing with the boss, but he really shouldn't bite the hand that feeds him. - *British*

Bite your hand off - To eagerly agree to a proposal - If you offer me that job, I will bite your hand off. - *British*

Body blow - A setback that is upsetting or damaging - It was a body blow when I found out my girlfriend had cheated on me. - *British*

Bolt - Synonym for run - I saw the police coming so I decided to bolt. - *Ireland*

Bolt from the blue - A surprising event - When my girlfriend cheated on me, it was a bolt from the blue. - *British*

Bother - Intimidate and threaten - Stop bothering that elderly couple! - *America*

Bugger about or around - Fool about and/ or waste time - Do you always have to bugger about? - *British*

Bumped into - Met someone by chance - I bumped into Sally down the town the other day. - *Bristol*

Bunk (off) - Truant from school or work - Emma liked to bunk off school. - *British*

Bunk off - To intentionally avoid a scheduled event usually school or work - He decided to bunk off work so he could watch the football. - *British*

Burn the candle at both ends - To miss sleep due to over activity - I had to be up early for work but I didn't want to miss the party, so I decided to burn the candle at both ends. - *British*

Bury your head in the sand - To ignore a problem - He knew we didn't have the money for the rent, but he just buried his head in the sand anyway. - *British*

By the skin of my teeth - To narrowly avoid a negative outcome - I avoided a parking ticket by the skin of my teeth. - *British*

C word - The C word refers to the taboo word of 'cunt' and is used offensively - He was extremely rude to the traffic warden, calling her the C word. - *America/British*

Call for back up - To ask others to assist you in a difficult situation - I was struggling to cook the meal for eight people, so I had to ask for back up. - *British*

Can't be arsed - When you cannot be bothered to do something - I can't be arsed to cook dinner tonight, let's get a takeaway? - *British*

Can't see beyond the end of your nose - Selfish, or narrow minded - He never considers anyone else's feelings because he can't see beyond the end of his nose. - *British*

Carry on - Verbally insulting another - There was a right carry on down the pub last night. - *America/British*

Catch flies - To have your mouth open in a gormless facial expression - Dave was so shocked, it looked like he was catching flies! - *British*

Chop and change - To change plans repeatedly - The doctor keeps chopping and changing my medicine. - *British*

Chuck a wobbly - A tantrum/ got angry - I will chuck a wobbly if they stop my medication. - *British*

Chucking out time - Closing time at the pub - There was a fight outside the pub, at chucking out time. - *British*

Cloak and dagger - To act in an underhand or deceitful manner - When they were restructuring the company, it was so cloak and dagger; no one knew whether their job was safe, or not. - *British*

Cold shoulder - To ignore someone - My girlfriend was giving me the cold shoulder. - *America/British*

Cook the books - To make false claims in writing, generally fraudulent and for financial gain - We weren't going to meet our performance targets, so we were told to cook the books. - *British*

Cool your jets! - Calm down! - You need to cool your jets, or there will be a fight! - *America*

Crack the whip - Metaphorical phrase used to show how hard a person has had to work - The new boss cracked the whip. - *British*

Creature of habit - Habitual. Doing the same things over and over without change - He won't stop smoking; he is a creature of habit! - *America/British*

Curry favour - To behave in a sycophantic manner in order to gain rewards - Simone is trying to curry favour with the new boss. - *British*

Cut your own throat - To defeat yourself - I cut my own throat when I admitted I hadn't done the reports that the boss wanted. - *British*

Devil and the deep blue sea - To be in a situation where all choices appear to be bad ones - I couldn't afford to kick James out because I needed his share of the rent, so I was stuck between the devil and the deep blue sea. - *British*

Do one's nut - Annoy - She is doing my nut in! - *British*

Don't throw the baby out with bath water - Don't make rash decisions - Aaron was going to quit his job after arguing with the boss, but I said not to ' throw the baby out with the bath water.' - *British*

General

Earwigging - To eavesdrop. To listen to another person's conversation without permission - I asked the man to stop earwigging on my conversations. - *British*

Economical with the truth - To conceal lies and present only favourable information - There were bound to be cutbacks due to the recession, but the bosses were economical with the truth, nevertheless. - *British*

End of your rope - End of your tether or to run out of patience - I was at the end of my rope with her rude behaviour. - *America*

Extract the Michael - To tease - He decided to extract the Michael out of the new boss! - *British*

Fly on the wall - To quietly observe events - There was a lot of gossip in the office, I decided to act like a fly on the wall so I could listen in. - *British*

Fobbed off - To have your complaints discounted and disregarded, leaving you unsatisfied and frustrated - I wanted the doctor to investigate my back problems, but I was fobbed off with painkillers. - *British*

Free for all - A situation where there are no rules - It's impossible to get an appointment, it's just a free for all. - *America/ British*

Give a wide berth - Avoid a potentially dangerous situation - If I was you, I would give Pete a wide berth, he is trouble! - *British*

Give it a shot - To have a go - If you want to change careers, you need to give it a shot. - *British*

Give your right arm - Willing to do anything to obtain a desired item - I would give my right arm to be famous. - *British*

Go different ways - To separate - Me and my partner decided to go different ways. - *America/British*

Go to pieces - To lose form - I go to pieces when under pressure. - *America/British*

Hard boiled - Crazy - The young woman was described as hard boiled, because she acted in a crazy way. - *America/British*

Harden one's heart - To follow a chosen course with determination - I've hardened my heart, I'm determined to move out before Christmas. - *America/British*

Heart and soul - To fully engage in an activity - I put heart and soul into completing the project. - *America/British*

Hell broke loose - Everything got out of hand and went a bit crazy; people might also get angry - There was an argument outside the pub, and all hell broke loose! - *British*

Hold a gun to your head - To be forced into a undesirable course of action - I didn't want to stay late, but the boss held a gun to my head. - *British*

Horsing around - To be silly and mess about - The kids were horsing around in the playground, playing hop scotch. - *America*

Kick into the long grass - To delay a decision indefinitely - I asked about promotion last year, but my boss seems to have kicked it into the long grass. - *British*

Kick into touch - To give up on a certain course of action - This project doesn't seem to be working, maybe we should kick it into touch. - *British*

Knee jerk reaction - To act instinctively, without thinking - I lashed out when that guy was insulting me, it was a knee jerk reaction. - *British*

Knees up - A lively party - We had a great knees up last night. - *British*

Knock it off - Stop it - You have been nagging me all day, I wish you would just knock it off. - *British*

Knocks spots off - To outdo - You are good at dancing but Jane could knock spots off all of you! - *British*

Knuckle under - To collapse under pressure - If things get too stressful, I might knuckle under. - *America/British*

Laiking - Playing - The children were laiking in the garden. - *Yorkshire*

Lash - To urinate or to go out drinking excessive alcohol - We went out on the lash last night. - *British*

General

Lay into - The act of verbally insulting another - Paul is so untidy, I will lay into him for that. - *America/British*

Leave it out! - Stop it - Kev stop being rude, just leave it out will you? - *British*

Let bygones be bygones - To forget another's past wrongdoings - I think we should forgive each other; let bygones be bygones. - *British*

Life is too short - Implies that certain activities are a waste of time - Life is too short to worry about what other people might think of you. - *British*

Like a bull in a china shop - Very clumsy person - Roger is so clumsy, he is like a bull in a china shop! - *British*

Mickey taking - To ridicule - Sandra is always mickey taking, it gets annoying. - *British*

Mischief - To cause bodily harm to another - If you keep annoying me, I will do you a mischief! - *America*

Mither - To fuss - My mum always mithers me. - *British*

Mooch - To do something in a leisurely fashion - I had the afternoon free so I just mooched around town. - *British*

Mooch about - Wander aimlessly - I like to mooch about the shops. - *British*

Muck about - Waste time or mess around - Ben likes to muck about. - *British*

Mugged off - To be disrespected by someone - James is so rude, yesterday he totally mugged me off. - *British*

Nauped - To hit - Ken nauped him right in the head. - *Yorkshire*

O.T.T. - Abbreviation of the phrase over the top, which means the extreme - When Joe has a drink he is O.T.T. - *British*

On one - To be absorbed by something - You can't talk to him when he's on one! - *British*

On the cadge - Begging - She is always on the cadge for cigarettes. - *British*

Out of all proportion - Over exaggerated - Simon got angry, his reaction was out of all proportion. - *America/British*

Out of order - To speak out of turn or to act unfairly - Dave was angry, the way he spoke to you was out of order. - *British*

Over the top - Extreme - Jim got angry but his reaction was over the top. - *British*

Pack it in - Stop it - Gramps was annoying me so I told him to pack it in. - *British*

Paddy - A temper tantrum - The man had a paddy when he missed the football match. - *British*

Paint the town red - Go out with the intention of having a good time and getting drunk - Let's go and paint the town red. - *British*

Panties in a wad - In other words -knickers in a twist- to get annoyed - Dex got his panties in a wad when he missed the football match. - *America*

Pass the buck - To evade responsibility - Jim kept trying to pass the buck, not wanting to admit we were lost. - *British*

Piss about - To mess around - Stop pissing around! - *British*

Piss arse - To mess around - Stop piss arsing around! - *British*

Play silly beggars - To mess around - Ken likes to play silly beggars. - *British*

Pot calling the kettle black - Hypocritical - When he said I drink too much, I said, well, that's the pot calling the kettle black! - *America/British*

Pour it on thick - To exaggerate a problem in order to gain sympathy - He was looking for sympathy, he was really pouring it on thick. - *British*

Power behind the throne - Someone who controls a situation from behind the scenes - He is the power behind the throne. - *America/British*

Rag - To tease or annoy someone - I like to rag him, sometimes. - *British*

Razzle - To go on a pleasurable spree - Me and Jo went out on the razzle. - *British*

Rib - To tease or annoy someone - Ali likes to rib people. - *British*

Ride roughshod - To ignore feelings of others and behave selfishly - Sholto rides roughshod over other people's feelings. - *America/British*

General

153

Rod of iron - To dominate others through intimidation - The boss rules with a rod of iron. - *America/British*

Rough with the smooth - To accept difficulties - You have to learn to take the rough with the smooth. - *America/British*

Safe as houses - Reliable - Maureen is as safe as houses. - *British*

Sarkey - Sarcastic - She is very sarkey, isn't she? - *America*

Scive - To avoid responsibilities - He likes to scive. - *British*

Screwed - To be in a hopeless situation - We are screwed. - *British*

Shit on someone - To betray - Be careful, John is likely to shit on someone. - *British*

Shot myself in the foot - A plan that goes wrong - I shot myself in the foot, when I turned up late for the job interview. - *British*

Sick to death - Extremely disgusted by something or someone - I'm sick to death with her attitude! - *British*

Skivvy - A derogatory term for someone who performs menial tasks - Debbie treats me like a skivvy. - *British*

Snaps one's fingers - To demand immediate action from others - You have to jump when the boss snaps her fingers. - *America/British*

Spaced out - In a dreamy state - Becky is spaced out, again! - *British*

Stitch up - To betray someone - It was a stitch up, they had let me down, again! - *British*

Straight up - Honestly - I didn't believe him, but he said, straight up. - *British*

Street cred - Reputation - He has no street cred, at all. - *British*

Take the Michael - To tease or annoy someone - Sometimes, I like to take the Michael out of people. - *British*

Take the Mickey - To tease or annoy someone - Sometimes, I take the Mickey out of people. - *British*

Take the piss - To tease or annoy someone - Sometimes, I take the piss out of people. - *British*

Take the piss (out of) - To mock - He always takes the piss out of me! - *British*

Test the waters - To perform a trial/ to measure something - I'm not sure if I want to live with my girlfriend, maybe I should stay for the weekend to test the waters. - *British*

The buck stops here - To accept responsibility - He knew it was his fault so he said, "fair enough the buck stops here." - *British*

Time after time - Repeatedly - He has been told to be punctual, time after time! - *America/British*

To chuck a mental - Get very angry - He chucked a mental when he got a parking fine. - *Australian*

To go against the grain - To do the opposite of what is expected - Sometimes Doug can be rebellious, he likes to go against the grain. - *British*

To go mental - Get very angry - If you annoy Dave, he is likely to go mental. - *British*

To go spare - To become very angry or enraged at someone - Ken is likely to go spare, if you take his cigarettes. - *British*

To stab someone in the back - To betray someone - I wouldn't trust that man, he is likely to stab you in the back. - *British*

To take the Mick - To make fun of someone - She likes to take the Mick. - *British*

To take the Mickey - To tease/ mock - She likes to take the Mickey. - *British*

Two time - To cheat on someone - My partner two timed me. - *British*

Up him/ her self - Over confident, full of self importance - Karen is really up herself! - *British*

Up shit creek - In trouble - Eric spent the rent money, now we are really up shit creek! - *British*

Up shit creek without a paddle - A vulgar way of saying: you are in a difficult situation and can see no way to make it better - Jim spent the rent money, now we are really up shit creek, without a paddle. - *British*

General

154

Wallop - To hit - I gave him a wallop. - *Bristol*

Wanna - To want to - Do you wanna go to the shops? - *British*

Whinge - To complain - Pete likes to whinge about his job. - *British*

Whinging - Moaning - Stop whinging, please! - *British*

Whopper - To tell a lie - Ian told an absolute whopper. - *British*

Wind up - Make fun of someone and/ or deliberately make them cross, frustrated or angry - He likes to wind me up. - *British*

Wind up merchant - Someone who persistently teases or plays pranks on others - Lois is a wind up merchant. - *British*

Wing it - To improvise - Joe didn't know what do, so as usual, he decided to wing it. - *British*

Your/ my goose is cooked - In trouble now - Peter, your goose is cooked, the boss knows you've been skiving! - *British*

A word in your shell like - To whisper in someone's ear - "Can I have a word in your shell like?" said Brian, referring to Claudia's ear. - *British*

Belly - Stomach - I have a pain in my belly. - *America*

Boss eyed - Cross eyed- eyes are turned in towards each other - She was so drunk, she went boss eyed. - *British*

Bum - Buttocks or anus or both. (not considered very rude) - I have a pain in my bum. - *British*

Butt - Posterior - I have a pain in my butt. - *America*

Cake-hole - Mouth - I told Liam to shut his cake-hole, when he was being rude to me. - *Ireland*

Claret - Blood - I fell over and hit my head, there was a lot of claret on the floor. - *British*

Gob/gobbed - This phrase means spit/spat from the mouth (at someone or something) - The filthy man, gobbed on the floor. - *Bristol*

Kisser - Slang for mouth - I punched him straight in the kisser! - *America*

Lap - Knees creating an area when sitting down - The child was tired and fell asleep on his mother's lap. - *America*

Meat and two veg - A traditional dinner with meat and vegetables, or euphemistic reference to the male genitalia - My pants fell down, revealing my meat and two veg. It was all very embarrassing! - *British*

Moobs - Male boobs - Des is so fat, he has moobs! - *British*

Tush - Posterior - I have a pain in my tush. - *America*

Zit - Spot or a pimple - Godfrey gets lots of zits. - *America/British*

A duff - Broken or a waste of money - The toy that Dexter received for his birthday was a duff, and was broken inside. - *British*

Completely shot - To describe something as broken and beyond repair - My car is completely shot, I will have to buy a new one. - *British*

Duff - Defective - That DVD was duff. - *America*

It is shot - Broken - This car, will never pass the MOT, it is shot. - *British*

Knackered - Broken or worn out - I had to throw out my trainers, they were completely knackered. - *British*

On the blink - Broken - My car is on the blink again. - *British*

Packed in - Broken - My TV packed in last night. - *British*

Median - Central reservation - The car swerved across the road and over the median. - *America*

Monkey wrench - A tool called a spanner - I need to fix the car, have you seen my monkey wrench? - *America*

Motoring - To do something with speed - I had to get there quickly, so I was really motoring. - *British*

Petrol head - A motoring enthusiast - Ian loved cars, he was a real petrol head. - *British*

Ride - A lift in your car - "Will you give me a ride to Sally's house?" asked Jill. - *American*

General

Tarhead - Someone who enjoys and is involved in tar based hobbies like motor racing - "Rick is a tarhead," said Louis. - *American*

Chain smoking - To smoke a lot of cigarettes one after another - I was so stressed before the operation, I was chain smoking. - *British*

Darts - Cigarettes - I can't give up the darts. - *Australian*

Dog end - What is left from a used cigarette - Wayne had left the room in a terrible state, there were empty beer cans and dog ends all over the floor! - *British*

Fag - Slang word for cigarette - I don't want to give up the fags. - *Ireland*

Smokes like a chimney - Cigarettes - Amber smokes like a chimney. - *British*

Smokes like a train - Cigarettes - Coralie smokes like a train. - *British*

Spark up - To light a cigarette - Sam sparked up a fag. - *British*

Cool - Very good - "That girl is so cool!" said Dad. - *American*

Dope - Very good - "That band are dope!" said Will.i.am. - *American*

My child - A term of endearment for anything that is loved - That band are my child. - *British*

Peak - Amazing - That song is peak. - *British*

Sick - Amazing - That video is sick. - *British*

Swag - Indicates something is good - That bike is swag. - *British*

That is sick - Can mean bad but nowadays means good - That car is sick. - *British*

Well bad - Good - That skateboard is well bad. - *British*

Brotox - Men getting botox - Ryan went to have some brotox. - *American*

Bang out of order - Completely wrong or unacceptable - I was so angry when Liam mugged that old lady, it was bang out of order. - *British*

Be in hot water - In trouble - Emma, you are going to be in hot water if you are late for work again. - *British*

Fair cop - To be caught out doing something wrong - Les was always late, so when the boss caught him, it was a fair cop. - *British*

Tax - To borrow something without returning it, or to steal - She loves to tax my cigarettes. - *British*

The game is up - The end of an activity, generally used when wrongdoings have been discovered - The game is up, Carol, we know you are a cheat! - *British*

A slingshot - A woman's brassiere (bra) - "Are you wearing a slingshot?" said my friend, referring to my bra! - *Australian*

Adrian Mole - Rhyming slang for dole- social benefits; job seekers allowance - Tim is on the Adrian Mole. - *cockney*

Cacks - Underwear - I went to the shops to buy some new cacks. - *Bristol*

Cans - Headphones - I got a new pair of cans for Christmas. - *America*

Dummy - Pacifier for a baby - Where's the baby's dummy? - *Ireland*

Emo - Was a type of music that adolescent youngsters could relate to; it is associated with wearing black and a particular style of dress, often self harm and being very pale skinned - He is such an emo. - *British*

Gangsta - Both black rap music and a cool/ tough type of person who listens to it - "Shane is gangsta," said Darrius. - *American*

Hand to mouth - To live in poverty - It was difficult growing up, we lived hand to mouth. - *British*

Inside out - The wrong way round - I got dressed in a hurry, and I put my jumper on inside out! - *British*

Journal - A diary - Don't read my journal, it is private. - *America*

Lackey band - Elastic band - I used a lackey band to tie my hair back. - *Bristol*

Lacy - Frilly, delicate and intricate material - I bought a dress, it was all lacy. - *America*

Mosh - To dance in a violent punk fashion - I like to mosh at gigs. - *British*

Old hat - Old fashioned, hackneyed - No, I don't wear those clothes anymore, they are old hat now. - *British*

Pew - A type of bench/ chair, often related to churches - Pull up a pew? - *British*

Prezzie - A present - Emma Jane bought me a lovely birthday prezzie. - *British*

Rock and roll - Rhyming slang for dole- job seekers allowance - Coleen is on the rock and roll. - *cockney*

Snazzy - Smart or stylish - Hills has a snazzy new jacket. - *British*

Tag - Signature of a graffiti artist - Did you see my tag in the toilet? - *British*

Undies - Underwear - Do I need to remove my undies? - *British*

Way out - Unusual - That music is way out. - *British*

Zany - Unusual or bizarre - John is zany. - *British*

A brush with death - A close encounter with death or dying - Fanny was so ill, she had a brush with death before she recovered. - *British*

Belly up - Dead - The old lady fell gravely ill, and went belly up last night. - *America*

Flamed - To have taken everything way too seriously - "I got a bit flamed then!" said Martha. - *American*

To be spitting feathers - To be really mad/ angry - I'm so angry about getting a parking ticket, I'm literally spitting feathers! - *British*

Number two - Euphemism for defecate - I need to use the toilet for a number two. - *British*

....one's head off - Loud or excessive behaviour - I laughed my head off. - *British*

A bee in your/ my bonnet - To be upset about something - I was so upset about what happened, I had a real bee in my bonnet. - *British*

A shoulder to cry on - A person who is there in a time of emotional need - When I was upset, Carina was a shoulder to cry on. - *British*

A skeleton in the closet - A secret that you wish to keep hidden - The fact that I had a child out of wedlock was a bit of a skeleton in my closet, and something I wished to keep secret. - *British*

A taste of your own medicine - To be given the same treatment as you gave to others- not medical. e.g., she was unkind to me so I was unkind back to her! - I gave Miranda a taste of her own medicine, and was as unkind to her, as she had been to me! - *British*

Abide - Referring to the word suffer - "I cannot abide that man," said the nurse. - *Yorkshire*

All at sea - Unsure, shaky or lost - The little boy was all at sea when he did not have his mother close to him. - *British*

Big let down - A disappointment - I didn't enjoy that film, it was a big let down. - *British*

Bone dry - Completely dry - Please can I get a glass of water? I'm bone dry. - *British*

Butterflies - To signify anxiousness; a fluttering in the stomach - I get butterflies when I think about the operation. - *Australian*

Cotton mouth - A dry mouth - I am so thirsty, I have a cotton mouth. - *Australian*

Dingy - Horrible - The hotel room was dingy. - *British*

Get a kick out of it - Enjoy and get a buzz from doing something - I get a kick out of driving fast. - *British*

Gordon Bennett - An expression of surprise - Gordon Bennett, I didn't know it was your birthday. - *British*

General

Grot/ grotty - Dirty/ nasty - The house was a bit grotty. - *British*

Have mixed feelings about - To be unsure about how you feel about something - I have mixed feelings about David; he can be fun, but he is also really irresponsible. - *British*

In the pit of your stomach - Deep inside - I knew she wasn't right for me, I felt it in the pit of my stomach. - *British*

Laff - Laugh - It was so funny, we had a real laff. - *Bristol*

Like a kid in a sweetshop - Very happy - There were so many beautiful women at the nightclub, I was like a kid in a sweet shop. - *British*

Manky - Dirty/ filthy - The house was disgusting, everything was manky. - *British*

Minging - Disgusting - That hotel room was minging. - *British*

Peckish - Hungry - He was peckish so he bought a sandwich. - *British*

Piss one's self - To laugh - Sam is so funny, you will piss yourself laughing. - *British*

Poxy - Rubbish, poor quality - The food at the hotel was poxy. - *British*

Rank - Disgusting - The food at the hotel was rank. - *British*

Reasty - Rancid - That meal was reasty. - *Yorkshire*

Reek - To smell - This place reeks, open a window! - *Yorkshire*

Rough - Unpleasant or unsavoury - The food was rough. - *British*

Sorry - Inadequate or pathetic - That was a sorry excuse for a party! - *America*

Stone the crows - An exclamation of surprise - When Joe won the lottery, he was amazed, saying:" stone the crows, I can't believe it!" - *British*

To get the hump - To get in a mood over something - Julian is likely to get the hump, if you take his cigarettes. - *British*

Waterworks - Crying/ tears - Emma brought on the waterworks. - *British*

Yuck - An exclamation of disgust - Yuck, that fish has gone off. - *British*

Yucky - A description of an unpleasant or disgusting item - That food was yucky. - *British*

Aluminium foil - Tinfoil - I will wrap the turkey in aluminium foil when I cook it at Christmas. - *America*

Bursting at the seams - Full up (after eating) - I can't eat any more, I'm bursting at the seams! - *America/British*

Hangry - A word sandwich of the words: hungry and angry, to show you are both - I am hangry. - *British*

Nosh - Food - I love a good nosh up. - *British*

Nosh up - A feast - We had a massive nosh up at the local restaurant. - *British*

Scoff - To eat rapidly, implies greediness - Who scoffed all the biscuits? - *British*

Scran - Food - The scran at the hotel was excellent. - *British*

Stuffed - To be full of food - He had eaten too much, he was stuffed! - *British*

Veggie - Vegetarian - Shelia is a veggie. - *British*

Flutter - To gamble - JJ likes a flutter on the football results. - *British*

Punt - To gamble, wager or take a chance - Dan took a punt on a second hand car. - *British*

Planking - A game involving stretching and stiffening your body to allow you to lay balanced prostrate often across something such as a car bonnet - "I hurt my back when we were planking," said my friend. - *American*

Joe Bloggs - A generic term used to describe the average man in the street, unremarkable - Joe Bloggs would not have a clue what that means! - *British*

Man or woman in the street - A member of the general public - If you want to know the public opinion, ask the man in the street. - *America/British*

Tom, Dick and Harry - Used to indicate the general mass population - Katie isn't fussy, she will talk to any Tom, Dick or Harry! - *British*

General

A dial like a bosted boot - Defined as to look miserable - Isabelle had a "dial like a bosted boot" and she looked extremely miserable. - *midlands*

A face as long as Livery Street - To look miserable - Christopher had a face as long as Livery Street , and was very miserable at the prospect of going out in the rain. - *midlands*

Aar kid - Defined as our kid, which generally means younger brother, or family member - "Can aar kid come too?" said Benjamin, referring to his little brother. - *midlands*

Aboot - This means -about - "I really don't know what this is aboot," said the doctor to the physiotherapist. - *Scotland*

Ackers - Money - The banker had plenty of ackers and was very rich. - *midlands*

Addick - Defined as haddock - I do like a nice piece of addick with my chips! - *midlands*

A-doors - The outside - "I am going a-doors to play," said the child to his mother. - *Jamaican*

Aeriawl - A particular region - I live in the Bristol aeriawl. - *Bristol*

Aff - Off - "Clear aff," said the old man, telling me to go away. - *Scotland*

Affpast - Half past the hour - I will see you at affpast six for a drink. - *midlands*

Aft rawl - After all, taking everything into account - Aft rawl, when I had taken everything into account, that is the conclusion I came to. - *Bristol*

Agany - In standard English this would mean agony - I was in agany because it really hurt. - *Jamaican*

Agin - Against - I am agin doing that because I don't think it is a good thing to do. - *Scotland*

Ain - To own - "I ain that," said Charles, referring to his bike. - *Scotland*

Ales Owen - Defined as Halesowen - "I'm off to Ales Owen this afternoon," said Bob. - *Midlands*

All fruits ripe - Everything is going well - All fruits are ripe with the business, which is going very well at the moment. - *Jamaican*

Alley boy - An alibi- evidence or excuse to show that you were elsewhere when a crime was committed - "Do you have an alley boy to prove where you were?" said the police sergeant to the criminal. - *midlands*

Alloy - friend - "He is my alloy," said Christine, when referring to her friend. - *midlands*

Allus - Always - "We allus go here together,"said Bridget. - *Yorkshire*

Alms ouse - Nonsense - "That's a load of alms 'ouse and you are speaking nonsense," said Barry. - *Jamaican*

Almunsbree - Almondsbury: a place just outside of Bristol - I am going to Almunsbree for the day, to visit my friend. - *Bristol*

Am bag - Handbag - We were dancing around our 'am bags, which we'd put on the floor. - *Bristol*

Amaze-balls - Good and positive - The TV judge described the act as being amaze-balls and was very positive about it. - *America/British*

Amblance - Ambulance - "Quick. send for an amblance to take her to hospital," said Dad. - *Bristol*

Americawl - America - "I am going to Americawl for my holidays," boasted Tim. - *Bristol*

Amt - Have not - "I amt got it," said Boris, when asked about the missing watch. - *Bristol*

An - And - "An' then we went to school," said the little boy. - *Scotland*

Ancient Greek - Reek- smell - There was a bit of an ancient Greek in the basement. - *Cockney*

Anda - Under - "It is anda the sofa," said Marigold. - *Jamaican*

Andswuff - Handsworth: an urban area in Birmingham, diverse population and a high crime rate - I live in Andswuff. - *Midlands*

Andy McNab - Cab - Can you order an Andy McNab, to get us home after our night out? - *Cockney*

An'e - Haven't you - "An'e got any food for me? " said Bill. - *Bristol*

General

Anekka Rice - Price - Before I buy, I will need to know the Anekka Rice, please. - *Cockney*

Ank - To go fast - " 'ank it up a bit and try to go faster," said Arthur. - *Bristol*

Ankle biter - Small child - "What's that ankle biter doing under the table?" asked Percy. - *Australian*

Anneye - Question: haven't I? - "Got to go to me mum's house now, anneye." said Jilly. - *Bristol*

Annum - Hanham, An urban area of Bristol - "I'm going to Annam, today, for a bus ride." said May. - *Bristol*

Annus - Haven't we - "We have enough to do, annus, without him playing up ." said Dad. - *Bristol*

Ansah - Answer - He never gives me an ansah, when I asks him a question! - *Jamaican*

Ansum - Handsome - "He is very ansum, that young man." said Mary. - *Bristol*

Ant - Has not - He ant got it. - *Bristol*

Ant chew erred? - Haven't you heard? - "Ant chew erred? He's been suspended for misconduct!" said Greg. - *Bristol*

Antenna - Aerial - "You will need an antenna for your TV." said Byron. - *America*

Anthea Turner - Earner - Selling drugs can be an Anthea Turner and you can make loads of money. - *Cockney*

Antiseptic cream - Germoline - "You will need to put an antiseptic cream on that abrasion," said my mother. - *America*

Any road up - Anyway - "Any road up, that is what I think." said Andy. - *Midlands*

Anyroadup - Anyhow - "Anyroadup, that's the way I am going." said Bert. - *Midlands*

A-OK - Good and positive - "Yes, I am A-OK," said Martin, feeling very positive about life. - *America/British*

Apartment - Flat - I was hoping to get a mortgage so that I could buy an apartment on the waterside. - *America*

Apeth - A halfpenny worth of sweets - "When I was a boy we would buy an 'appeth of sweets'," said the old man. - *Yorkshire*

Apple and pears - Stairs - "Off you go, up the apple and pears to bed," said my mother. - *Cockney*

Apple pie - Sky - "Look up at the apple pie and you might see an aeroplane." said my dad. - *Cockney*

Apurt - Sullen - The little girl had an apurt face and was not happy! - *Devon*

Ar - Or - "It could be this ar that." said the man. - *Jamaican*

Arbun Edge - Harborne Hedge - "We are going to Arbun Edge for the day." said mum. - *Midlands*

Areddi - Already - "I alreddi told you all I know," said the teenager. - *Jamaican*

Arf soaked - Stupid - He is always arf soaked and never seems to understand what he is told to do. - *Midlands*

Arffa - Half - "Could I have an arffa, please?" said the man, to the barman. - *Midlands*

Arg - Argue - "Why do you always arg about everything?" said my mum. - *Devon*

Aringe/arinj - An orange - "Could I have an aringe drink?" said the young Jamaican boy. - *Jamaican*

Ark - Listen - " 'ark to what I am saying to you!" said Mum. - *Midlands*

Backyard - Garden - I was gardening in the backyard. - *America*

Bangers and mash - Rhyming slang for cash - Lau doesn't have any bangers and mash. - *cockney*

Batty - Bottom/ buttocks - I hurt my batty when I fell over. - *Jamaican*

Batty boy - An homosexual male - Nigel is a batty boy. - *Jamaican*

Becks and Posh - Rhyming slang for dosh - money - Danny doesn't have any Becks and Posh. - *cockney*

Bees and honey - Rhyming slang for money - Katie doesn't have any bees and honey. - *cockney*

Benny hills - Pills - I need some more Benny Hills. - *cockney*

Bint - A slag/ a promiscuous woman - Sally is a right bint. - *midlands*

Bling bling - Flashy diamond jewellery - Beyoncé wears lots of bling bling. - *Jamaican*

Blob on - A woman's time of menstruation - She has got the blob on. - *Yorkshire*

Bloke - Gentleman - He is such a strange bloke. - *midlands*

Bob on - Exactly right - That meal was bob on. - *midlands*

Bunsen burner - Earner - Dave's new job is a real bunsen burner. - *cockney*

Cack-handed - Clumsy (or can mean left handed) - Emma is so cack-handed, she breaks everything. - *midlands*

Cadger - A borrower - Dave is always asking to borrow things, he's such a cadger. - *Yorkshire*

Canny - Careful - I try to be canny with money. - *Scotland*

Canting - Synonym for talking - We were canting late into the night. - *midlands*

Captain Cook - Rhyming slang for: look - Have a Captain Cook, at that new car. - *Cockney*

Deaf it - To forget it! - I'm not going to give up smoking, deaf it. - *Midlands*

Diaper - American word for a baby's nappy - I need to change my baby's diaper. - *America*

Dibby dibby - Bad quality - The food was dibby dibby. - *Jamaican*

Got a cob on - Moody - The manager got a cob on when he had to work late. - *midlands*

Greet - To weep/ cry - The baby was greeting because it needed feeding. - *Scotland*

Grizzling - Crying - The little girl was grizzling because she had fallen over. - *midlands*

Gumption - Common sense or motivation - Pedro has no gumption, he is so daft! - *Yorkshire*

Gurt - Great/large or can mean good - I had a gurt meal last night. - *Bristol*

Gurt lush - Very nice - The hotel was gurt lush. - *Bristol*

Im - Him or her - Go and ask 'Im. - *Jamaican*

Inchew - Aren't you - "Inchew going to do the washing up?" said Gran. - *Bristol*

Injin - Found under the bonnet of a car, the engine - My new car has got a massive injin. - *midlands*

Innit - Isn't it - Its nice here, innit? - *Bristol*

Inntit - Abbreviation of isn't it - Its hot today, inntit? - *Northern*

Innum - Are you - Innum going to the beach today? - *Bristol*

Insane bonkers - Mad - He wasn't making any sense, he was insane bonkers! - *America*

Int - Isn't or am not - There int no point complaining! - *Bristol*

Intae - Into - I'm going intae town. - *Scotland*

Irie - Nice/ right/ cool - I love this place it's irie. - *Jamaican*

Irrint - It is not - There irrint any good looking women here. - *Midlands*

Ither - Other - I don't like Sammy, I like the ither one. - *Scotland*

Jah - God - I believe Jah will protect me. - *Jamaican*

Jaloused - Suspected - He looked so guilty, I jaloused him. - *Yorkshire*

Jamdung - Jamaica - I'm from the Caribbean, I was born in Jamdung. - *Jamaican*

Jammin' - Dancing - The music was really good; it got me jammin'. - *Jamaican*

Jasper - Wasp - I got stung by a giant jasper, it was so painful. - *midlands*

Jawanna - Do you want to… - Jawanna go to town? - *Midlands*

Jaysus! - Jesus - Jaysus! I didn't expect to see you here. - *Ireland*

Jeerme? - Did you hear me? - I was talking to you, jeerme? - *Bristol*

Jeezan or jeezan peas - Surprise or amazement - Jeezan, that was a shock! - *Jamaican*

General

Jellied eel - Rhyming slang for: deal - I have bought a new car. I drove a hard bargain and in the end, I got a jellied eel. - *Cockney*

Jings! - Expression of exclamation such as, gosh - Jings, I didn't expect that! - *Scotland*

Jook - To prod/ pierce/ stick to poke to stab - I jooked him with my knife. - *Jamaican*

Jubee - A nice girl - She was so sexy, a real jubee. - *Jamaican*

Juicy - Derogatory word for pretty - She was so juicy. - *Ireland*

Kayliyed - Intoxicated through drugs or alcohol - I got so drunk last night, I was totally kayliyed. - *midlands*

Keks - Trousers - I bought a new pair of keks last week. - *Yorkshire*

Ken - Know - It is beyond my ken to understand algebra. - *Scotland*

Kill mi dead - I would rather die - Kill mi dead, if I ever become grumpy. - *Jamaican*

Kinave - Can I have? - Kinave a cup of tea? - *Bristol*

Kinnoy - Question starter, 'Can I?' - Kinnoy I have a cup of tea? - *Midlands*

Labba labba - Gossip - People always talk about my business, labba labba! - *Jamaican*

Labba mout - A loose mouthed person who gossips - Ed is a labba mout, always talking about my business. - *Jamaican*

Labrish - Idle chat - We relaxed in the evening and chatted labrish. - *Jamaican*

Laddie - Boy - The young laddie was eight years old. - *Scotland*

Laldy - Thrashing - The boy was naughty, so his father gave him a laldy. - *Scotland*

Lang - Long - The journey took three hours because the road was so lang. - *Scotland*

Lard'ed - Thick - It was a thick fog, proper lard'ed. - *midlands*

Larpom - Toilet - I needed to go to the toilet, the larpom. - *midlands*

Lassie - Girl - The lassie was only ten years old. - *Scotland*

Laters - Short for: see you later - I'm got to go now, laters. - *Bristol*

Latin - Searching - I lost my keys, I spent hours latin for them. - *Yorkshire*

Latta - Later - I won't do my homework now, I will do it latta. - *Jamaican*

Lav - Short for: I will have - What do you want to drink? Lav a whiskey please, he replied. - *Bristol*

Lawd - Lord (God) - Praise the lawd for small mercies. - *Jamaican*

Lawp - Leap - It was a giant lawp for mankind. - *Yorkshire*

Leebim/leebem - Leave him - If he carries on being selfish, I will have to leebim. - *Bristol*

Leggo - Let it go, out of control - I danced all night, I really leggo of my inhibitions! - *Jamaican*

Len - Lend - Ali, will you len me a tenner? - *Jamaican*

Liad - A liar - Pedro doesn't tell the truth, he is a liad. - *Jamaican*

Lick - To hit - He was angry and he licked me. - *Jamaican*

Licky licky - Fawning - Jennifer is always fawning over the boss, licky licky. - *Jamaican*

Likkle - Little - A likkle boy went to the playground. - *Jamaican*

Liltin - Light-hearted - We teased each other playfully, we were only liltin. - *Yorkshire*

Link up - Hook up/ meet - I like you, we should link up sometime? - *Jamaican*

Looks like a sack of potatoes - Unattractive - He was very unfit, he looked like a sack of potatoes. - *midlands*

Lug - To pull - I had to lug the suitcase up the hill. - *Yorkshire*

Macky - Very big - The meal was huge. the steak was macky. - *Bristol*

Madda - A mother - My madda took care of me when I was sick. - *Jamaican*

Mampie - A derogatory term used to describe a fat person - He was mampie and needed to go on a diet. - *Jamaican*

Marnin - Morning - The sun rose early in the marnin. - *Bristol*

Maungy - Spoilt - I left the food out in the sun, now it has gone maungy. - *Yorkshire*

Mawday - Mouldy - I have a leaky roof so the bathroom wall is mawdy. - *Bristol*

Mawga - Meagre or skinny - We didn't have much to eat when I was a kid, I was so mawga. - *Jamaican*

Mawks - Maggots - The meat was rotten, it was covered in mawks. - *Yorkshire*

Mawning - Morning - I got up early in the mawning. - *Jamaican*

Mazen - Bristolian dialect for, amazing - I got a brand new car, it is mazen. - *Bristol*

Me - My, Bristolian dialect - Where's me hat? - *Bristol*

Meech - To play truant for work or school - Kyle is such a meech, he hasn't been to school for weeks. - *Devon*

Mek - To make - I'm hungry, I'm going to mek a sandwich. - *Jamaican*

Mekhace/mikhace - To make haste or to hurry up - We will be late unless you mekhace. - *Jamaican*

Mell - Meddle - Why do you always mell in my affairs? - *Yorkshire*

Memba - To remember - I memba when I was young. - *Jamaican*

Member - Used instead of remember in Bristolian dialect - I member when I was young. - *Bristol*

Mentaller - Crazy - Darren is a mentaller. - *Ireland*

Merrit - Married - We got merrit last September. - *Scotland*

Messages - Groceries - I need to go the shops to get some messages. - *Ireland*

Mi - My or mine - Where's mi hat? - *Jamaican*

Midden - Rubbish heap - I need to tidy the garden, it's just a huge midden. - *Scotland*

Middlin - Moderate - The weather is not great today, it's middlin. - *Yorkshire*

Milling - Fighting - The kids are always milling. - *Ireland*

Mind - Added to end of sentences to encourage the listener to take heed - You have to go careful when crossing the road, mind. - *Bristol*

Miskin - A dustbin - Put that rubbish in the miskin. - *Midlands*

Misses - Wife or partner - The misses doesn't like me going down the pub. - *Midlands*

Mo - More - I'm still hungry can I have some mo? - *Jamaican*

Mo' time - See you later - I've got to go, mo' time. - *Jamaican*

Moff - Good and positive - I had a great time, it was moff there. - *America/British*

Moi - French- belonging to me - Where's moi hat? - *Midlands*

Moikrawev - Microwave - I'm hungry, I'm going to warm up my dinner in the moikrawev. - *Midlands*

Moither - Harass - That group of lads always moither me. - *Yorkshire*

Mom - American spelling of mum, short for mother - It is my mom's birthday next week. - *midlands*

Mon - Man - He was a very tall mon. - *Jamaican*

Money - Good and positive - That song is money. - *America/British*

Montel - A man who is a playboy - Roy is such a Montel. - *Jamaican*

Mooth - Mouth - I punched him in the mooth. - *Scotland*

Morkins - Someone stupid - Ian is a morkins. - *midlands*

Mortified - Embarrassed - I tripped over in front of everyone, I was mortified. - *Ireland*

Mouldy - Rotten - The bread was old and had gone all mouldy. - *Ireland*

Mout-a-massy - A gossip - They were all talking about me, mout-a-massy. - *Jamaican*

Mowta - An automobile/ car - My new car is a really classy mowta. - *midlands*

Mr. Mention - A ladies man (a man who likes women a lot) - Cal is a Mr. Mention. - *Jamaican*

Mucka - A good friend - He is my mucka. - *midlands*

Mud up - Confusing - I don't understand; mud up! - *Jamaican*

Mullock - A mess - Tidy up, your room is a mullock! - *Yorkshire*

Muss muss - Ugly or not up to standard - Sue is muss muss. - *Jamaican*

Nawse - Someone who makes you feel sick/ nauseous - He is disgusting and nawse. - *Midlands*

Nebbersin - Phonetic dialect for, never seen - I nebbersin a shark around here! - *Bristol*

Odds - Loose change - I don't have much money on me, just odds. - *Ireland*

Ole lady - Derogatory way of describing your mother - My ole lady is a great cook. - *Ireland*

Ole man - Father - My ole man was very strict. - *Ireland*

On the doss - To truant - He was on the doss from school. - *Ireland*

Perishing - Freezing cold - It is perishing outside today. - *Ireland*

Picky picky - Fickle and fussy - Todd is a fussy eater, picky picky. - *Jamaican*

Pictures - The movies - I went to the pictures last night and saw a great film. - *Ireland*

Podging - To jump the queue - Louis was impatient so he started podging. - *midlands*

Puck - To slap - I gave Camila a puck for being cheeky. - *Ireland*

Reef - To beat up - I'm going to reef you, in a minute. - *Ireland*

Riling - Fidgeting - Steve, will you stop riling? - *midlands*

Runs - Diarrhoea - I've got a sore belly, I've had the runs for two days now! - *Ireland*

Sap - A wimp or wuss - Alison is a sap. - *Ireland*

Scrubba - A prostitute - She is a scrubba. - *midlands*

Slash - A crude term to urinate - Peter needed a slash. - *midlands*

Snog - To kiss passionately - People snog when they are in love. - *Ireland*

Sound - Nice or good - The new house is sound. - *Ireland*

Squittering - To talk in an uninteresting manner - Nan was squittering on as usual! - *midlands*

Star - A friend - Jane is a star! - *Jamaican*

The local - A public house (pub) close to home - John loves it down the local. - *Ireland*

Traper - A slut/ promiscuous woman - She is a traper. - *Devon*

Wee - A small amount - Let's have a wee drink on the way home from work? - *Scotland*

Ace in the pack - The best in a group - Boris was the ace in the pack and was the best at everything! - *British*

Aced it - Perform a task perfectly - Christopher performed the task so perfectly, he knew he had aced it. - *British*

Active - Good and positively organised/ managed - The running group was very active and had a very positive feel to it. - *America/British*

Ain't no thing but a chicken wing - Good and positive - "That car ain't nothing but a chicken wing," said George, "and I love it." - *America/British*

All good - Good and positive - Jeremiah felt that all was good with the world when he heard he had passed his exams. - *America/British*

Alrighty - Good and positive - Alrighty, I will get to that and start the plan straight away. - *America/British*

Awesomity - To be very awesome - "That band are awesomity!" said Julia. - *American*

General

Bait - Good - That girl is bait. - *British*

Bang on - Good and positive - That party was bang on. - *America/British*

Bee's knees, the - Good and positive - Roberto is confident with the ladies, he thinks he is the bee's knees! - *America/British*

Best thing since sliced bread, the - Good and positive - Joe is confident with the ladies, he thinks he is the best thing since sliced bread. - *America/British*

Big up - To promote something with confidence - Jim likes to big up his job. - *British*

Big yourself up - To promote yourself or to brag - You are good at cooking, you should big yourself up. - *British*

Blow your own trumpet - To promote yourself - He likes to blow his own trumpet, that one! - *British*

Bomb, the - Good and positive - That nightclub is the bomb. - *America/British*

Brill - Good and positive - The hotel was brill. - *America/British*

Brownie points - Metaphorical points received for doing good or kind works - I will get brownie points if I tidy the shed. - *British*

Cat's whiskers - The best - That new car is the cat's whiskers. - *British*

Champion - The best - That meal was champion. - *British*

Come up trumps - To get a positive result - I feel much better now, everything has come up trumps. - *British*

Cooking on gas - Performing well - I managed to hit all my monthly targets within a week, I was cooking on gas. - *British*

Corker or corking - Someone or something outstanding - My new car is a corker. - *British*

Cracker - Someone or something outstanding - That film was a cracker. - *British*

Cracking - Good - That meal was cracking. - *British*

Dench - Good - That new song is dench. - *British*

Dog's bollocks - Especially good, sometimes just abbreviated to 'the dog's' - My new car is the dog's bollocks. - *British*

Dog's bollocks, the - Good and positive - That new band are the dog's bollocks. - *America/British*

Golden - Good and positive - The hotel was golden. - *America/British*

Hunky dory - Good - Everything is hunky dory. - *British*

Ideal - To express satisfaction - We won the match, and now we are in an ideal position to win the league. - *Bristol*

Immense - Good and positive - That was really fun, it was immense. - *America/British*

Jammed - Good and positive - It's all going great; everything is just jammed, right now. - *America/British*

Jesus made (it) - Good and positive - It's so good here, Jesus made it. - *America/British*

Jinky - Good and positive - I love it here, it is jinky. - *America/British*

Jolly good - Good and positive - I'm having a jolly good time! - *America/British*

Kewl - Good and positive - That rock band are so kewl. - *America/British*

Kickass - Good and positive - That rock band are totally kickass. - *America/British*

Knock into a cocked hat - To perform perfectly - You did so well, you knocked it into a cocked hat. - *America/British*

Kushti - Good - The hotel was excellent, proper kushti. - *British*

Kushty - Good - My new flat is kushty. - *British*

Legendary - Good and positive - The hotel is great, the staff are legendary. - *America/British*

Mean - Good and positive - The food was mean. - *America/British*

Monster - The best - That team are monster. - *British*

Numero uno - The best. The boss - When playing snooker, John is always numero uno. - *British*

Off da hook - Good and positive - That movie is off da hook. - *America/British*

Off the chain - Good and positive - That movie is off the chain. - *America/British*

Off the chart - Excellent - That movie is off the chart. - *British*

Okie dokie - Good and positive - He asked me to drive him to the shop so I said, okie dokie. - *America/British*

On fire - Enthusiastic - That band set me on fire. - *British*

Out of sight - Good and positive - That movie was out of sight. - *America/British*

Out of this world - Unusual or exceptional - That movie was out of this world. - *America/British*

Peachy - Good and positive - The holiday was peachy. - *America/British*

Phat - Excellent - That is a phat tune. - *British*

Phatness - Good and positive - That song has got major phatness. - *America/British*

Phenom - Good and positive - That show was phenom. - *America/British*

Pimp tight - Good and positive - That car is pimp tight. - *America/British*

Pimping - Good and positive - That club is pimping. - *America/British*

Popping fresh - Good and positive - That beat is popping fresh. - *America/British*

Prime - Good and positive - The food was prime. - *America/British*

Pro - Professional - John is a pro snooker player. - *British*

Proper job - Good - The hotel was a proper job. - *Bristol*

Pukka - Excellent - The hotel was pukka. - *British*

Rancid - Unpleasant and stale, off! - The food at the hotel was rancid. - *America/British*

Result - A successful outcome - He won ten pounds on the lottery, result! - *British*

Ridiculous - Good and positive - That restaurant is ridiculous. - *America/British*

Rocking - Good and positive - This hotel is rocking. - *America/British*

Rock-solid - Good and positive - John is rock-solid. - *America/British*

Rude - Good and positive - The music was rude. - *America/British*

Safe - Good - Joan is safe. - *British*

Savage - Good and positive - The band playing are savage. - *America/British*

Shit hot - Excellent - The hotel was shit hot. - *British*

Sic - Good and positive - That song is sic. - *America/British*

Sicc - Good and positive - That song is sicc. - *America/British*

Smashing - Good and positive - This hotel is smashing. - *America/British*

Smooth - Good and positive - This place is smooth. - *America/British*

Smoove - Good and positive - This place is smoove. - *America/British*

Stonking - Good - The party was stonking. - *British*

Superfly - Good and positive - Will.I. Am is superfly. - *America/British*

The bee's knees - Excellent - The hotel was the bee's knees. - *British*

The mutt's nuts - Something that is really good - That hotel was the mutt's nuts. - *British*

Tickety boo - Good - I'm feeling tickety boo. - *British*

Tickety-boo - Good and positive - I'm feeling tickety-boo - *America/British*

Tidy - Neat, in order, or can mean good - My new car is really tidy. - *British*

Tits, the - Good and positive - That car is the tits! - *America/British*

To die for - Good and positive - That pudding is to die for. - *America/British*

Top hole - Enthusiastic - Dad said he felt, top hole! - *British*

Tope - Very good - "That car is tope!" said Jensen. - *American*

Vibe - Abbreviation of vibrations, used to describe a good or bad atmosphere - The restaurant had a good vibe. - *British*

All right me luvver - How are you? - "All right, me luvver? I hope you's well?" said Albert. - *Bristol*

Alright me luvver - How are you? - "Alright, me luvver?" said the man from Bristol, when asking how I was feeling. - *Bristol*

Catch you later - Goodbye - I've got to go, catch you later? - *America*

Hiya - Hello - Hiya love, how are you today? - *British*

How are you doing? - Question asked at the beginning of a conversation as a greeting - How are you doing, love? - *America*

How are you going? - Question asked at the beginning of a conversation as a greeting - How are you going, Steve? - *Australian*

How are you? - Question asked at the beginning of a conversation as a greeting - How are you, Pete? - *British*

How be on? - How are you? - How be on, Kate? - *Bristol*

How goes it - Hello - How goes it, Justin? - *British*

Howdy - Hello - Howdy, partner! - *British*

How's it hanging? - A greeting used predominantly by males, where hanging refers to the male genitals - How's it hanging, Jim? - *British*

How's tricks - A greeting - How's tricks, Zane? - *British*

Me old mucker - Friend - How are you, me old mucker? - *British*

Wass up? - How are you? - Wass up, John? - *British*

What's up? - What's wrong? or, how are you? - What's up, Kev? - *British*

As fit as a fiddle - Healthy - I feel great, I'm as fit as a fiddle! - *British*

Band Aid - Plaster - I've cut my finger, do you have a band aid? - *America*

Clapped out - Broken or worn out - I'm so unfit, my body is completely clapped out. - *British*

Darren Gough - Cough - I have a bit of a Darren Gough. - *cockney*

Look like death - Visibly looking very ill - The man was so unwell, he looked like death. - *British*

Pale as a ghost - Very pale, perhaps due to illness or shock - She felt ill and looked as pale as a ghost. - *British*

Queer - To feel strange - I ate some dodgy food and began to feel queer quickly. - *British*

Scrage - To scratch yourself and break the skin - Tom scraged his leg when he fell over. - *Bristol*

Throw up - Vomit - I think I'm going to throw up, where's the toilet? - *British*

To be in good/bad nick - Health - Vikram looks after himself, he is in good nick. - *British*

To draw a blank about - Inability to remember or find any information on something - I can't remember the accident, I just draw a blank. - *British*

A brain wave - An idea - Whilst I was sitting quietly, a real brainwave came to me and I had a great idea for our holiday. - *British*

A fly in the ointment - Something that spoils an idea - The rain poured down and was a real fly in the ointment, to the idea of a picnic. - *British*

A foot in the door - To seize an opportunity - Belinda thought that if she could only get one foot in the door, she could become a popstar. - *British*

And pigs might fly - Something that is impossible - "And pigs might fly," said my mother, when I told her I was going to pass my exams. - *British*

As broad as it is long - Equal - John and Pete argued about which route to take, but actually it was as broad as it is long. - *America/ British*

Back to front - Something that is in the wrong order - Dexter put his shoes on back to front! - *British*

Back to the drawing board - To form a new plan - I wanted to become a teacher, however I quickly realised it wasn't for me, so now it's back to the drawing board! - *British*

Beggar belief - Unbelievable - It beggars belief that he still has a job, after the way he has behaved! - *British*

Beyond the pale - Unbelievable - When Catherine took my cigarettes it was beyond the pale. - *America/British*

Bloody minded - Determined to pursue an idea in the face of objections - We all told Yameen not to fight with Pete, but he was being bloody minded. - *America/British*

Cotton on - To suddenly understand something - It took me a while to cotton on, but, then I realised I needed to get medical help. - *British*

Cut your nose off to spite your face - To stubbornly stick to a counterproductive course of action - By refusing to apologise, Tony was cutting his own nose off to spite his face. - *British*

Don't count your chickens before they have hatched - Do not believe something is true until it is a reality - I know the scan says I'm all clear, but I won't count my chickens before they are hatched. - *British*

Figure out - Come to realise an idea or solution to a problem - I figured out a way to save some money. - *America*

Hair brained - Stupid - He comes up with some pretty hair brained ideas, doesn't he? - *British*

Have a change of heart - Change your mind over something - I was going to move out but I had a change of heart. - *British*

Have second thoughts - Have some doubts about something that may lead to a change of mind - I was going to move out but now I am having second thoughts. - *British*

Ideawl - An idea - "That's a great ideawl," said Bob. - *Bristol*

Jump on the bandwagon - To mindlessly follow the ideas of others - As soon as David Beckham got a new haircut, everyone else jumped on the bandwagon. - *British*

Nitty gritty - The finer details of a topic - We agree in principle, but let's look at the nitty gritty. - *British*

P.C. - Abbreviation of 'politically correct' - Grandad is very old fashioned, some of the things he says aren't P.C. - *British*

Penny dropped - To suddenly realise something - The penny dropped and I finally realised we were lost! - *British*

Pissed on your bonfire - To thwart someone's plans - The boss didn't like my idea, that really pissed on my bonfire! - *British*

Scupper - To thwart someone's plans - The boss didn't like my idea, so scuppered my plans. - *British*

Spot on - Exactly right - Dan was spot on, when he said we were lost! - *British*

The long, short and the tall - The essence of an idea - The long, short and tall was that, we were lost. - *America/British*

Thin end of the wedge - The first in a series of progressively unpleasant ideas - The boss asked us to make savings to the budget, but that was just the thin end of the wedge; the next week, he announced redundancies! - *America/British*

To flog a dead horse - To continue talking or trying to find a solution to something when it is unsolvable - I tried to start my car for ten minutes, but it was like flogging a dead horse. - *British*

Use your loaf - Think about - You have to use your loaf, if you want to get a good deal. - *British*

Murder - A bad situation or a death by another - The traffic was terrible, the whole journey was murder. - *British*

Roller coaster - An uncomfortable journey - The car ride was a bit of a roller coaster. - *America/British*

Round the houses - To take an indirect route - We got lost, and ended up going around the houses. - *British*

Step by step - To gradually develop or improve - Don't rush, you will get there if you go step by step. - *America/British*

Up sticks - To move location - Dad decided to up sticks and emigrate to Australia! - *British*

Aarsh - Harsh - "That's a bit aarsh!" said Kevin, when describing the referee's yellow card shown for a foul. - *Bristol*

Above board - Legitimate, decent or fair - "I think you will find it is all above board and legitimate," said the police officer. - *British*

Accidentally on purpose - A mistake that you secretly tried to make - "You did that accidentally on purpose," said Robert, " and always intended to!" - *British*

Ackrut/ackrutlee - Accurate - "Your sums were ackrut and you added up well," said the teacher to the student. - *Bristol*

Bone up - To study - I need to bone up for my exam on Monday. - *America*

Bone up on - To learn something - You need to bone up on your anatomy before the test. - *British*

Brush up on - To learn something - I need to brush up on my anatomy before the test. - *British*

Catch on - To learn something - If you explain it to me, I will soon catch on. - *British*

Gen up - To gather information - I need to gen up for my next exam. - *British*

Know one's onions - To know one's subject - Adrian is really good at maths. He can answer any question, he really knows his onions. - *British*

Know the ropes - To be experienced in a certain matter - If you want to know how to do it, ask John, he really knows the ropes. - *British*

Nous - Common sense - You need to have a bit of nous to do well here. - *British*

Savvy - Well informed - John is savvy. - *British*

Suss out - To gather information - Dave went off to suss out where to park the car. - *British*

A drop in the ocean - A small insignificant amount - The money raised was only a drop in the ocean, compared with the overall amount that would be needed. - *British*

Coming thick and fast - Under continuous pressure - People were coming thick and fast into the A and E Department. - *America/British*

Drop in the ocean - A small amount - It's not a huge project, it's a drop in the ocean. - *America/British*

In spades - A large amount - He is so charming, he has charisma in spades. - *British*

Jar - A pint glass/ measure - I went to the pub last night and had a few jars. - *Ireland*

Piddly - Small - My new flat is piddly, I don't have enough room for all my belongings. - *British*

Pint sized - Small - Caf is short, she is pint sized! - *British*

Shed load - A large amount - Josie drank a shed load of booze. - *British*

Shitload - A large amount - My new car cost a shitload. - *British*

Tad - A little bit - Greg was a tad late for work. - *British*

Tiddler - Small - My brother's son is only three years old, he is still a tiddler. - *British*

Supersize - A huge over sized portion of something or someone - "I'm going to go supersize at McDonald's," said Chris. - *American*

Screw loose - Mentally unsound - They have a screw loose! - *America/British*

Balls up - To mess something up - I burnt your birthday cake. Sorry, what a balls up! - *British*

Clanger - To make a mistake - I dropped a clanger when I forgot my girlfriend's birthday. - *British*

Cockup - A mess up or blunder - Sandy made a cockup when he lost the house keys. - *British*

Fluff - To make a mistake - I had the opportunity to get promoted, but I fluffed my lines. - *British*

Goof up - A mistake - I forget to pay my road tax, what a goof up! - *America*

Muck up - To make a mistake - Sorry about my mistake, I muck up when I am nervous. - *British*

169

Put your foot in it - To make a silly mistake, or say something in error and embarrass yourself- not medical - "Sorry," she said, "I didn't mean to put my foot in it!" - *British*

Schoolboy error - To make a mistake that was easy to avoid - Putting diesel in my petrol engine was such a school boy error! - *British*

The wrong end of the stick - To be misled - I'm afraid she got the wrong end of the stick. - *British*

A grand - Thousand pounds - I paid a grand for the car and the garage confirmed it was worth a thousand pounds. - *British*

A nicker - Pounds sterling - Most items cost you a nicker at the pound shop. - *British*

A rip off - Too expensive - The cost of the replacement windows was a right rip off, and far too expensive! - *British*

A shot in the dark - To take a risk or to speculate without knowledge - Setting up a business in such troubled times was a shot in the dark, and very uncertain in terms of success. - *British*

Add up - In other words -total - "When you have finished shopping, I will add it all up and let you know the total," said the assistant. - *America*

Astronomical - Suggesting something is very expensive - The hotel was nice, but the prices were astronomical. - *British*

Back payment - A payment in lieu of previous services - I got a back payment for all the overtime I had been doing. - *British*

Boracic - To have no money, broke - I am completely boracic. - *British*

Bring home the bacon - To earn money - I have to do overtime if I want to bring home the bacon. - *British*

Broke - Without money, often referred to as 'stony broke' or just 'stony' - I am broke. - *British*

Coin it - To make lots of money - When I qualify as a doctor I will be coining it. - *British*

Cost a bomb - Very expensive - The treatment for my medical condition will cost a bomb. - *British*

Cost an arm and a leg - Expensive - My new medicine costs an arm and a leg. - *British*

Cough up - To pay for something - I will need to cough up, if I want to have the operation done more quickly. - *British*

Fiver - Five pounds - My new T shirt only cost a fiver. - *British*

Fork out - To have to pay out money for something with some reluctance or frustration - I had to fork out a fortune to get my car fixed. - *British*

Ker-ching - Money - I got a huge tax rebate, ker-ching! - *British*

Lolly - Money - That new car is expensive, it will cost a lot of lolly. - *America*

Minted - Extremely wealthy - John is very wealthy, he is absolutely minted. - *British*

Money for old rope. - Money that is easily earned - It was such an easy job, it was money for old rope. - *British*

Nest egg - Financial savings - I started saving up when I was young. I have quite a nice little nest egg now. - *British*

On the never never - Borrow money that you are unable to repay - I got my car on the never never. - *British*

On the scrounge - To borrow - They are always on the scrounge. - *British*

Packet - Large sum of money - Les earns a packet. - *British*

Ponce - Someone who manipulates another for money - He is always poncing cigarettes off of me. - *British*

Potless - Lacking money - I had spent all my money, I was potless. - *British*

Quids in - To make a profit - I sold my old car and now I am quids in. - *British*

Readies - Cash that is available to spend - Louis asked to borrow some money, because he didn't have any readies of his own. - *British*

Shell out - To pay for an item - I had to shell out a fortune on my new car. - *British*

Skint - Broke/ lack of money - I couldn't afford the rent, I was totally skint. - *Yorkshire*

Strapped - Lacking in ideas or money - He couldn't pay the rent, he was strapped for cash this month. - *British*

Stump up - To pay for an item - I had to stump up five hundred pounds to MOT my car. - *British*

To make a bomb - Make a lot of money - Kyle reckons if he sells his car, he is going to make a bomb. - *British*

Wonga - Money - Caf had loads of wonga. - *British*

A birdbrain - Someone scatty - Maisie was a real birdbrain she was so scatty. - *British*

A bunch of numpties - A group of idiots - The young people behaved liked a group of numpties, and were called idiots for vandalising the play park. - *British*

A dosser - A person who does nothing of any value in society - The unemployed, homeless person, was described as a dosser by passers by. - *British*

A Jerry - A German or German soldier - The English soldier was approached by a Jerry; a German soldier, in the Second World War. - *British*

A right Billy - Someone with no friends - Poor Graham was a right Billy and had no friends to play with. - *British*

A rose between two thorns - To stand out from the crowd, to be the prettiest - Belinda deliberately stood next to two of the least attractive girls in the class so that she looked like a rose between two thorns! - *British*

A sandwich short of a picnic - Lacking intellect - The teacher described the boy as someone who lacked intellect, and a sandwich short of a picnic! - *British*

A Shelia - A woman - Australian men usually refer to women as Sheilas. - *Australian*

Arsehole - Anus, or derogatory term for someone - James is an arsehole. - *British*

Arsewipe - A general insult - Kim is an arsewipe. - *America/British*

Beaten with an ugly stick - An unattractive person - Tony was a funny looking chap, it looked like he had been beaten with the ugly stick. - *British*

Better half - A person's life partner - I'm not sure if we can make that appointment, I need to ask my better half. - *British*

Bird-brain - Describes someone of low intelligence - Larry is a bird-brain. - *America/British*

Black leg - A person who betrays others - You cant trust Keith, he is a black leg. - *America/British*

Blonde - Someone deemed of low intelligence by others/ derogatory and insulting - Jane is a typical blonde! - *America/British*

Bludger - Lazy person - That man is a bludger, he won't help anyone. - *Australian*

Bollock - The act of verbally insulting another/ reprimand - The boss will bollock you if you are late again. - *America/British*

Bonehead - Someone deemed of low intelligence by others - Des is a bonehead. - *America/British*

Boob - Describes someone of low intelligence - Derrick is a total boob, sometimes. - *America/British*

Bottom feeder - A general insult - What a bottom feeder! - *America/British*

Bozo - Describes someone of low intelligence - You are a bozo! - *America/British*

Brasser - Prostitute - Naomi is a brasser. - *Ireland*

Bust (one's) chops - To verbally insult - The boss is always busting my chops. - *America/British*

Busted - Ugly - That girl is busted. - *British*

Butt-head - A general insult - John is a butt-head. - *America/British*

Butt-munch - Someone deemed of low intelligence by others - That man is a butt-munch. - *America/British*

Carrot cruncher - A derogatory term for a person who lives in the countryside - I grew up in the countryside, people used to call me a carrot cruncher. - *British*

Carving knife - Rhyming slang for: wife - I will have to tell the carving knife that we will be back late from the pub. - *cockney*

Chancer - Someone dodgy - I wouldn't trust Keith, he is a chancer. - *Ireland*

Chinky - Derogatory term for the Chinese takeaway - I got a takeaway from the chinky. - *British*

Chippy - Fish and chip shop or a skilled carpenter - I went down the chippy for my dinner. - *British*

Codger - An elderly person - The hospital is full of old codgers. - *British*

Coffin dodger - An elderly person - The lady in the next ward is a real coffin dodger. - *British*

Creep - A general insult - That guy is a creep. - *America/British*

Cretin - A general insult - Adam is a cretin. - *America/British*

Crinkly - Old person - There are so many crinklies in this ward. - *British*

Cut of your jib - Refers to the way a person presents themselves - I like the cut of your jib. - *British*

Dim - Lacking intellect - Ellie is very dim. - *British*

Dimp - Stupid - What a dimp! - *America/British*

Dipstick - Someone of low intelligence, a bit of an airhead - Kev is a dipstick. - *America/British*

Ditzy - Air head/ silly/ disorganised - Sally is ditzy. - *British*

Div - Slang term for idiot - John is a div. - *British*

Dog - A derogatory term for a woman - His new girlfriend is a real dog! - *British*

Doosh - A general insult - Andy is a doosh. - *America/British*

Dosser - Derogatory term for a homeless person; or someone sleeping rough; or someone who does not work - Yameen is a total dosser. - *British*

Douche - A general insult - Leo, you douche! - *America/British*

Douche bag - A general insult - Ahmed, you are a douche bag. - *America/British*

Down and out - A homeless person - The down and out was begging outside the office again today. - *British*

Duffer - Silly person - Don't be a duffer! - *Australian*

Dufus - Silly person - You are a dufus! - *British*

Dumbass - Someone of low intelligence - What a dumbass! - *America/British*

Eejit - Idiot - Kate is an eejit. - *Ireland*

Gaffer - The boss - The new gaffer is very strict. - *British*

Geezer - Informal term for a man, sometimes with some swagger and, perhaps, a petty criminal - Phil is a geezer. - *British*

Get - A git, someone incompetent and annoying - Bill is a get. - *British*

Gimmer - An elderly person - Jenny is a gimmer. - *British*

Gippo - Derogatory word for a gypsy traveller - I bought a TV off a gippo. - *British*

Gobshite - Taboo word to describe a stupid or despicable person - What an absolute gobshite! - *British*

Greycation - Having your grandparents come on holiday with you - "This year, we had a greycation," said Jane. - *American*

Hooray Henry - Derogatory term for someone from the upper classes - I don't like the new boss, he is a Hooray Henry! - *British*

Iceman - A person with nerves of steel - "Dave is so calm, he is the iceman," said Bluey. - *American*

Jack Joner - Rhyming slang for: loner - He doesn't mix with other people, he's such a Jack Joner. - *cockney*

Jack Jones - Rhyming slang for alone - Why don't you talk to anyone else? You are always on your Jack Jones. - *cockney*

Jack off - A general insult - He was annoying me so I told him to jack off. - *America/British*

Jackass - A general insult - That guy is such a stupid jackass. - *America/British*

Jan - A tramp - He is a jan, he has slept rough on the streets for years and years. - *Bristol*

Jerk - Stupid or dummy - Colin is such a jerk! - *America*

Jerk off - A general insult - Sandy is such a jerk off! - *America/British*

Jerk wad - A general insult - Simon is a jerk wad! - *America/British*

Jerk-ass - A general insult - Pete is such a jerk-ass! - *America/British*

Jerk-face - A general insult - Mani is a total jerk-face! - *America/British*

Jerk-nut - Someone deemed of low intelligence by others - Sholto is a jerk-nut. - *America/British*

Jessie - A derogatory term to describe an effeminate man who might be afraid or weak - Sam is a Jessie. - *Scotland*

Jet lag - Rhyming slang for: fag, a derogatory word used to describe homosexuals - He fancies men, he is a jet lag. - *cockney*

Joan on - This phrase describes the act of verbally insulting another - He annoyed me, so I'm going to joan on him later. - *America/British*

Jork - A general insult - Don't be a jork! - *America/British*

Jug head - Someone deemed of low intelligence by others - Keith isn't very bright, he is a jug head. - *America/British*

Kawaii - Cute, adorable - That little dog is kawaii. - *British*

Knobhead - Stupid or irritating person - He is a knobhead. - *British*

Knuckle dragger - Someone deemed of low intelligence by others - What a knuckle dragger! - *America/British*

Knucklehead - Someone deemed of low intelligence by others - What a knucklehead! - *America/British*

Knuckle-nuts - Someone deemed of low intelligence by others - Stu is a knuckle-nuts. - *America/British*

Kutta - A general insult - Dan is a kutta. - *America/British*

Lad - Man - The young lad was good at football. - *British*

Lady - Woman - She was a beautiful lady. - *British*

Lame-ass - A general insult - Julian is a lame-ass. - *America/British*

Lame-o - A general insult - Jake is a lame-o. - *America/British*

Lass - Woman - The woman was a beautiful young lass. - *British*

Leebo - A general insult - Tyrone is a leebo. - *America/British*

Lencho - A general insult - Dave is a lencho. - *America/British*

Llama - A general insult - Mark is a llama. - *America/British*

Louse - A general insult - What a louse! - *America/British*

Lunkhead - Someone deemed of low intelligence by others - He is so stupid, he is a lunkhead. - *America/British*

Mare - Derogatory term for a woman - Simon's new girlfriend is a mare. - *British*

Melon - Someone deemed of low intelligence by others - Katie is a melon. - *America/British*

Melvin - A general insult - Margaret is a Melvin. - *America/British*

Mimbo - Someone deemed of low intelligence by others - Lewis is a mimbo. - *America/British*

Minger - Derogatory phrase for an unattractive person - Lily is a minger. - *British*

Missus - Wife or long term partner - The missus is a great cook. - *British*

Mo Fo - Someone deemed of low intelligence by others - Brian is a Mo Fo! - *America/British*

Moggy - Cat - We own an old moggy called, Jess. - *British*

General

Mole - A general insult - Matthew is a mole. - *America/British*

Moll - A general insult - Richard is a moll. - *America/British*

Momo - Someone deemed of low intelligence by others - Dick is a momo. - *America/British*

Mongrel - Ugly person - Cathy is a mongrel. - *British*

Moony - Foolish - Ali is moony. - *British*

Moron - Someone deemed of low intelligence by others - Daniel is a moron. - *America/British*

Mothafucka - Very offensive phrase used as a general insult - He is such a mothafucka! - *America/British*

Mother fucker - Offensive phrase used as a general insult/ swearing - He is such a mother fucker! - *America/British*

Mother trucker - A play on words from 'mother fucker'. A general insult - He is such a mother trucker! - *America/British*

Mouth breather - Someeone deemed of low intelligence by others - Jill is a mouth breather. - *America/British*

Muggins - To refer to oneself as being put upon - Everyone else went to the pub, whilst muggins here stayed behind to do the washing up. - *British*

Mule head - Someone deemed of low intelligence by others - Sam is a mule head. - *America/British*

Munta - An ugly person - Andrew is a munta. - *British*

Munta/ munter - An ugly person - Ian is munter. - *British*

Mushroom - Someone of low intelligence - Laura is a mushroom. - *America/British*

My little woman - Derogatory term to describe a wife - I love my little woman. - *British*

Nancy - A person lacking aggression - Lee doesn't like fighting, he is a nancy boy. - *America/British*

Need a check up from the neck up - Someone deemed of low intelligence by others - Dewy is stupid, he needs a check from the neck up. - *America/British*

Nimrod - Someone deemed of low intelligence by others - Mark is a nimrod. - *America/British*

Nincompoop - Someone deemed of low intelligence by others - What a nimcompoop! - *America/British*

Ninny - Idiot - Sam is a ninny. - *Yorkshire*

Nipper - Young person or child - The nipper was only four years old. - *British*

Nitwit - Someone deemed of low intelligence by others - Ken is a nitwit. - *America/British*

No oil painting - Unattractive - She is no oil painting. - *British*

Nob - Person of high social standing or the head of an organisation - Paul is a nob. - *British*

Not a rocket scientist - Lacking intellect - Catherine is not a rocket scientist. - *British*

Not the sharpest tool in the tool box! - Lacking intellect - Alison is not the sharpest tool in the tool box. - *British*

Nugget - A general insult - Simi is a nugget. - *America/British*

Numb nut - Someone deemed of low intelligence by others - Cathy is a numb nut. - *America/British*

Numb-nuts - Someone deemed of low intelligence by others - Gill is a numb-nuts. - *America/British*

Numbskull - Someone deemed of low intelligence by others - Nick is a numbskull. - *America/British*

Nummah - Someone deemed of low intelligence by others - Yameen is nummah. - *America/British*

Numpt - Someone deemed of low intelligence by others - Cliff is a numpt. - *America/British*

Numptie - Someone deemed of low intelligence by others - Candy is a numptie. - *America/British*

Numpty - Incompetent and stupid person but often used with affection - Phillip is a numpty. - *British*

Oik - Derogatory term for someone of low social standing - Dwayne is an oik! - *British*

Old bag - Derogatory term for an elderly lady - That woman is such an old bag. - *British*

Old boiler - Unattractive woman - She was horrible, what an old boiler. - *British*

Old boot - Derogatory term for an elderly lady - She was an old boot. - *British*

Old fart - Derogatory term for an old aged person - The old fart was driving so slowly. - *British*

Old lady - Derogatory way to describe your mother, wife or girlfriend - My old lady doesn't like me going down the pub all day. - *British*

Other half - Life partner - I've lived with my other half for seventeen years now. - *British*

Oxygen thief - A general insult - Les is an oxygen thief. - *America/British*

Pain in the arse - Something that is annoying - You are a pain in the arse! - *British*

Pen pusher - Demeaning phrase for an office worker - Tony was bored with his job, he was a pen pusher. - *British*

Pencil pusher - Demeaning phrase for an office worker - Phillip hated his job, he was a pencil pusher. - *British*

Penis-face - A general insult - What a penis-face! *America/British*

Pickle fucker - A general insult - Cameron is a pickle fucker. - *America/British*

Piece of shit - An insult - Fabien is a piece of shit! - *British*

Pikey - Derogatory term to describe travellers or gypsies - Darren is a pikey. - *British*

Pill - A general insult - James is a pill. - *America/British*

Pillock - A stupid person - Jay is a pillock. - *British*

Pinhead - Someone deemed of low intelligence by others - Bo is a pinhead. - *America/British*

Piss taker - A person who teases or annoys others - Stephanie is a piss taker. - *British*

Piss-ant - A general insult - Kyle is a piss-ant. - *America/British*

Pisshead - A general insult - Rich is a pisshead. - *America/British*

Pizza face - Derogatory way to describe someone with acne - That girl is a total pizza face. - *British*

Plonker - A stupid person - Keith is a plonker. - *British*

Poophead - A general insult - Dexter is a poophead. - *America/British*

Posser - A stirrer, someone who gossips and makes trouble for others - What a posser! - *Yorkshire*

Pram face - A teenage mother - Sally is a pram face. - *British*

Prannock - Someone deemed of low intelligence by others - She is a right prannock. - *America/British*

Prole - Someone deemed of low intelligence by others - He is a prole. - *America/British*

Psycho-bitch - A general insult - Miranda is a psycho-bitch. - *America/British*

Pud whacker - A general insult - He is a pud whacker. - *America/British*

Pud-whack - Someone deemed of low intelligence by others - He is a pud-whack. - *America/British*

Punk - A person who doesn't follow conventions - Anton is a punk. - *British*

Quayle - Someone deemed of low intelligence by others - He is a quayle. - *America/British*

Queaf - A general insult - Dan is a queaf. - *America/British*

Queef - A general insult - Eddie is a queef. - *America/British*

Raw prawn - Implies innocence - John is a raw prawn. - *Australian*

General

Reject - A general insult - Jo is a reject. - *America/British*

Retaardvark - Someone deemed of low intelligence by others - Les is a retaardvark. - *America/British*

Riff-raff - Snobby or jokey way to imply the other people present are of a lower class than you, or 'rough' - Doug doesn't like to mix with the riff-raff! - *British*

R-tard - Someone deemed of low intelligence - Angel is an r-tard. - *America/British*

Sack of shit - A general insult - You look like a sack of shit. - *America/British*

Scally - A hooligan youth - Gary is a bit of a scally! - *Liverpool*

Scatter brained - A bit stupid or low in intellect - John is a scatter brain. - *British*

Schmuck - A general insult - That man is a schmuck! - *America/British*

Scrote - Term of verbal abuse, refers to male scrotum - Kyle is a scrote. - *British*

Scrubber - A 'common' woman of low social standing - Her new girlfriend is a right scrubber. - *Ireland*

Scruff - Unkempt person - Joe is a scruff. - *British*

Scum of the earth - A general insult - Wez is the scum of the earth. - *America/British*

Scutler - A promiscuous girl - She is a scutler. - *Bristol*

Shitface - A general insult - Dave is a shitface. - *America/British*

Shithead - A general insult - Tobe's is a shithead. - *America/British*

Shmuck - A general insult - Joseph is a shmuck. - *America/British*

Sick fuck - A phrase incorporating swear words: general insult - He is such a sick fuck. - *America/British*

Skiver - Someone who consistently avoids responsibilities - Karen is a skiver. - *British*

Slack-jaw - Someone of low intelligence - Dwayne is a slack-jaw. - *America/British*

Slap head - A bald man - Roger is a slap head. - *British*

Sleaze ball - A general insult - Andy is a sleaze ball. - *America/British*

Slime ball - A general insult - Matt is a slime ball. - *America/British*

Slub - A general insult - He is a slub. - *America/British*

Smoll - Cute, adorable - That puppy is so smoll. - *British*

So-and-so - A general insult - Kirsty is a so-and-so! - *America/British*

Sod - Annoying person - Tim is a sod. - *British*

Son of a gun - A general insult - What a son of a gun! - *America/British*

Sons of bitches - A general insult - Those guys are sons of bitches. - *America/British*

Sprog - A small child - John has a sprog called Katie. - *British*

Sprogg - Child - Katie is a sprogg. - *British*

Stoopid - Someone of low intelligence - Harry is stoopid. - *America/British*

Swede - This phrase describes someone of low intelligence - Ian is a swede. - *America/British*

The lights are on but no one's home - A bit stupid or low in intellect - What a fool; the lights are on but no one's home! - *British*

The old man - Husband (older) or father - The old man is a great father. - *British*

Thing ma bob - Generic name for an item whose name escapes memory - Have you seen my thing ma bob? - *British*

Thingy ma jig - Generic name for an item whose name escapes memory - Have you seen my thingy ma jig? - *British*

Toff - Posh person - Guy is a toff. - *British*

Tosser - Mild form of verbal abuse - Pete, you are a tosser! - *British*

Tramp - Homeless person - The tramp had been sleeping rough for about a year. - *British*

Turd - A general insult - John is a turd. - *America/British*

Twit - A general insult - Colin is a twit. - *America/British*

Uncle fucker - A general insult - Karim is an uncle fucker. - *America/British*

Wack - Bad, worthless - Will is wack. - *British*

Wally - Silly person - Chelsea is a wally. - *British*

Wassock - A general insult - Dave is a wassock. - *America/British*

Waste of space - Useless - Roberto is a waste of space! - *British*

Wrinkly - Old person - Nanny is a bit of a wrinkly. - *British*

Yob - Rude, noisy and aggressive youth - When Dave gets drunk, he can be a bit of a yob! - *British*

Yobbo - Rude, noisy and aggressive youth - Wayne is a yobbo! - *Australian*

Harlot - Prostitute - She was a complete harlot. - *British*

All to cock - Gone wrong - The plan to go on holiday had gone all to cock, when the airlines went on strike. - *British*

Ball ache - A difficult task - The rush hour traffic is a real ball ache. - *British*

Bane of my life - A recurring serious problem - My car keeps breaking down, it is the bane of my life! - *British*

Bodge - To make a poor job of something - I tried to do the decorating myself but I made a right bodge job of it. - *British*

Dog's dinner - To make a mess of something - I made a real dog's dinner out of that report. - *British*

Down the drain - Everything has gone wrong - The whole project went down the drain. - *British*

Down the pan - A wasted opportunity - I had a chance for promotion but it all went down the pan. - *British*

Drop a bollock - To make a mistake - I dropped a bollock when I forgot to pay my road tax. - *British*

Fall short - Inadequate - I'm worried I might fall short of the standards needed to pass the course. - *America/British*

Fly in the ointment - Something that spoils a good plan - I was happy with my new car until I discovered it needed a new gearbox, that was a fly in the ointment. - *British*

Hanging by a thread - A critical situation which may go wrong at any moment - The business deal was hanging by a thread. - *British*

Lousy - Awful - The food at the hotel was lousy. - *British*

Lumbered - To be burdened with a demanding task - I got lumbered with the worst job. - *British*

Nothing to shout about - Not good - The hotel was nothing to shout about. - *America/British*

Pear shaped - Gone wrong - The holiday was a total disaster, everything went pear shaped. - *British*

Pete Tong - Gone wrong - The holiday was a disaster, everything went Pete Tong. - *British*

That's not much cop - Not much good - My new car is not much cop. - *British*

A place for everything - Organised - Margaret was really well organised and had a place for everything in her study. - *America/British*

A wild goose chase - Being misled or engaging in a pointless activity - The secretary had been sent on a wild goose chase looking for something which did not exist. - *British*

All over the place - Disorganised - Bernard is all over the place, and very disorganised. - *America/British*

All over the shop - Disorganised and chaotic - Brenda was all over the shop, and very disorganised and chaotic in her approach. - *British*

Get your act together - Be organised and well behaved - If you want to pass the course, you need to get your act together. - *British*

General

A few cans short of a six pack - Someone deemed of low intelligence by others - The teacher described the student of low intelligence as being, a few cans short of a six pack. - *America/British*

Cooped up - To be in a confined space for an extended period of time - I will be glad when I can leave hospital, I am sick of being cooped up in here. - *British*

Dosshouse - Cheap boarding house; or derogatory term to express frustration at the state of the home if it is untidy and dirty - Scot treats this place like a dosshouse! - *British*

Emergency Room - Casualty/Accident and Emergency Department in a hospital - I was badly injured, so they took me to the Emergency Room. - *America*

Gaff - A house/ home - I moved into my new gaff last week. - *British*

Jam packed - Full to capacity - The pub was crammed full of people; it was jam packed. - *British*

Packed out - Full or crowded - The night club was packed out. - *British*

Sofa surfing - The act of moving from one friend's house to another due to having no home of your own - I haven't had my own flat for a while now, I've been sofa surfing for the last three months. - *British*

Tip - A rubbish dump - I'm going to take all my recycling down the tip. - *British*

A tattle-tale - In other words - a grass or a police informer - He was known in the gang as a tattle-tale, as he was always informing the police of their plans. - *America*

Old bill - The police - If you carry on harassing me, I will call the old bill. - *British*

Knock up - To get someone pregnant - Sally is pregnant, I think it was me who knocked her up. - *America*

Keep it under your hat - Do not reveal information - I'm throwing a party for my wife, but keep it under your hat as it is a secret. - *British*

Keep schtum - Keep information to yourself - You better keep schtum or else you will get me in trouble. - *British*

Keep your beak out - Don't be nosey into other people's business - He is so nosey, I wish he would keep his beak out of my business! - *British*

Keep your cards close to your chest - To withhold information - Toby doesn't share his feelings, he likes to keep his cards close to his chest. - *British*

Let the cat out of the bag - Reveal a secret - I didn't realise it was a secret, sorry, I think I might have let the cat out of the bag, then! - *British*

Mum's the word - Keep secret - I'm throwing a surprise party, mum's the word. - *British*

Nosy parker - A person who is overly interested in another's private life - She is such a nosy parker, she's always interested in my private affairs. - *British*

On the Q.T. - Secretly - On the Q.T. I know who is going to get the job. - *British*

Put your cards on the table - To reveal information - You need to be honest and put your cards on the table. - *British*

Tip off - To reveal information - Ian gave me a tip off, the boss was on the warpath. - *British*

By hand - Without machinery - These boots were made by hand. - *British*

Blood is thicker than water - Family ties are more important than other relationships - Me and my brother don't always get on, but blood is thicker than water. - *British*

Chip off the old block - When a younger member of the family either looks or behaves like a parent - Steve is just like his dad, he is a chip off the old block! - *British*

Cut the knot - To separate - We decided to cut the knot last night. - *America/British*

Following - Viewing particular people's posts on social communication media sites such as Twitter. Interested in their ideas and opinions - I am following Justin Bieber. - *Global*

Frenemy - Someone who is considered your friend but is also antagonistic towards you at times - Salky is my frenemy. - *American*

General

Hook up with - Meet someone or have sexual relations with someone - I went to the cafe to hook up with Sally. - *America/British*

Making out - To kiss another in a sexual manner - John was making out with Marge on the sofa. - *America*

Mucker - A mate/ friend - Lee is me old mucker. - *British*

To friend and unfriend - Adding or removing people to your friend list on social media websites - I had to unfriend Paul, he was annoying me. - *America/British*

Come down like a ton of bricks - Discipline or reprimand - The boss will come down like a ton of bricks, if you are late to the office again. - *America/British*

Ticking off - To be reprimanded - The boss gave Victor a stern ticking off for being late. - *British*

A fate worse than death - A terrible fate - Peter thought to climb a mountain would be a fate worse than death for him, as he was likely to fail. - *British*

A hiding to nothing - A waste of time - Trying to win the lottery is a hiding to nothing, with no chance of a win. - *British*

A horse of a different colour - Something that is markedly different - When describing chalk and cheese you might say they are horses of a different colour . - *British*

A leopard can't change it's spots - A persons character is fixed and cannot be hidden for long - "A leopard cannot change his spots", said William, when referring to the way that Anne always did things the same way, regardless of whether she was right or wrong. - *British*

A load of bollocks - An exclamation of disbelief or displeasure - Fred said, "that's is a load of bollocks", when Douglas said that England would win the world cup. - *British*

A piece of cake - Easy - Jumping six foot was a piece of cake for the most athletic boys in the class. - *British*

A spread - A buffet provided for a special occasion - Christine had offered to put on a spread in the form of a buffet to celebrate Liam's birthday. - *British*

A wolf in sheep's clothing - Someone in disguise pretending to be nice but they are not - Harry discovered that Jim was a wolf in sheep's clothing, always pretending to be someone he was not. - *British*

Abandon all hope, all ye who enter here - A light hearted phrase suggesting doom - So you have just joined our company? Abandon all hope, all ye who enter here! - *British*

Absence makes the heart grow fonder - To miss someone when they are away from you - I haven't seen Sally for three weeks now. Absence makes the heart grow fonder - *British*

Ad lib - To improvise - The presentation was a bit dull, so I decided to ad lib. - *British*

Adam's apple - The Adam's apple, or laryngeal prominence is a protrusion near the throat formed by thyroid cartilage surrounding the larynx - I fell over and hurt my Adam's apple. - *British*

Add insult to injury - A situation where suffering is compounded - I didn't get promoted and to add insult to injury they promoted Dave. He is the worst person in the department. - *British*

Albatross round one's neck - A nagging burden - We moved to a bigger house last year but the mortgage is an albatross around my neck. - *British*

All and sundry - Everyone - The manager was very indiscreet and he was discussing my condition to all and sundry. - *British*

All good things come to an end - Acknowledgement of the fleeting nature of happiness - I used to love playing football before my injury. I suppose all good things must come to an end. - *British*

All in a day's work - Acknowledgement of the duties you undertake - Today I had to support a student who was grieving. All in a day's work for a teacher. - *British*

All over bar the shouting - Finished, not worth pursuing anymore - The game was all over bar the shouting, and not worth pursuing any more. - *British*

General

179

General

All singing, all dancing - Used to describe something that possesses a multitude of useful functions - I got a new all singing, all dancing phone yesterday, it is brilliant. - *British*

All that glitters is not gold - Realisation that superficial appearances do not always match internal qualities - I thought Sally was beautiful, but she turned out to be horrible. All that glitters is not gold. - *British*

All things to all men - Describes the attempt to please everyone - Dave is a very indecisive manager, he tries too hard to be all things to all men. - *British*

Alpha *and* Omega - Bible quote, which describes something as all encompassing - Pete is so arrogant, he thinks he is the Alpha *and* Omega. - *British*

An elephant never forgets - To have a good memory, particularly for the misdeeds of others - I accepted Harry's apology, but an elephant never forgets. - *British*

An eye for an eye - To seek revenge - I believe in an eye for an eye, so if someone is rude to me, I will be rude back. - *British*

Anything for a quiet life - An attitude of acceptance and submission to the will of others in order to avoid conflict - Ralph does all the cooking and housework, anything for a quiet life. - *British*

Apple of one's eye - The object of love or desire - Pete will do anything for Susan, she is the apple of his eye. - *British*

Armed to the teeth - To be fully equipped. Originally related to warfare but can be used in an everyday context - The gang are so scary, they are armed to the teeth. - *British*

Artful Dodger - Used to describe someone as crafty or sly, as in the novel Oliver by Charles Dickens - I wouldn't trust Paul, he is a right artful dodger. - *British*

As luck would have it - Favoured by fortune - I missed the bus, but as luck would have it, Ali was driving past me so he took me home. - *British*

As night follows day - Certain - Jack will lose his job if he keeps coming in late; I'm as sure, as night follows day. - *America/British*

As the crow flies - Used to describe the direct distance between two places - It is only a few miles from here as the crow flies, but it takes a long time because the roads aren't straight. - *British*

At a loose end - To have free time and be unsure how to fill it - I was at a loose end so I decided to call Sally. - *British*

At death's door - To be in a critical condition - Chloe was very ill, she was at death's door. - *British*

At full blast - The maximum amount - I turned the heating up full blast because it was so cold. - *British*

At sixes and sevens - To be confused or disorganised - I didn't expect to be made redundant, I'm at sixes and sevens at the moment. - *British*

At the drop of a hat - Immediately - The boss is very demanding, he expects things to be done at the drop of a hat. - *British*

At the eleventh hour - Something that occurs at the end - I thought I was going to sell my house but the buyers pulled out at the eleventh hour - *British*

Back of beyond - Far away from civilisation - Helen lived on a remote farm, in the back of beyond. - *British*

Back to square one - To have to start again - I was getting out of debt, then the electricity bill arrived, and now I'm back to square one. - *British*

Bad books - A metaphorical book that accounts for people's bad deeds - Richard is in my bad books because he didn't do the washing up. - *British*

Ball is in one's court - To have the initiative or power - I said sorry to Jill for missing her birthday. The ball is in her court now. - *British*

Ballpark figure - A rough estimate of costs - To complete the project on time won't be cheap. I was quoted a ball park figure of ten thousand pounds. - *British*

Be all and end all - A description of the importance of a situation - I wanted to go to a really prestigious university in London, but Bristol Uni was also good and it was closer. In the end I realised that location wasn't the be all and end all. - *British*

Beat a hasty retreat - To quickly withdraw from a hazardous situation - There was a big fight outside the pub, so I decided to beat a hasty retreat. - *British*

Beat about the bush - To talk in an unspecific manner without getting to the key idea - If you don't want to go to the cinema, stop beating around the bush and just tell me! - *British*

Beaver away - To work hard - I will have to beaver away all weekend to get the project completed on time. - *British*

Bed of roses - A positive situation. No bed of roses would be a negative situation - Sally and Keith looked happy but their relationship is no bed of roses. - *British*

Been there, done that - To have experience in a certain area - I have already had chicken pox, been there and done that! - *British*

Best bib and tucker - To dress in a very smart fashion - I wore my best bib and tucker to the interview. - *British*

Best laid plans of mice and men. - An acknowledgement that sometimes things do not go according to plan - We were all set to move house, when the buyer suddenly changed his mind. The best laid plan of mice and men. - *British*

Between the devil and the deep blue sea - To be faced with a difficult dilemma - My job is very badly paid but I don't have the time or money to retrain. - *British*

Between you, me and the gatepost - Used to signify that information is confidential - Between you, me and the gatepost, I don't like my boss. - *British*

Beware of Greeks bearing gifts - This phrase indicates distrust - Debbie received a bunch of flowers from Paul after he had cheated on her. I told her to beware of Greeks bearing gifts. - *British*

Bits and bobs - Miscellaneous trivial items - I always put my keys in the top drawer with all the other bits and bobs. - *British*

Blaze a trail - To act in an independent and innovative way, that others may be inspired to follow - Bob Dylan blazed a trail by writing anti-war protest songs. - *British*

Blaze of glory - To act with valour even when facing inevitable defeat - Even though Gary had terminal cancer, he was determined to enjoy his last months of life. He lived life to the full and went out with a blaze of glory. - *British*

Blimey - Exclamation of shock or surprise - Blimey, I didn't know it was your birthday. - *British*

Blow hot and cold - To act in an unpredictable manner. To change between positive and negative feelings quickly - I never know how Julie really feels, she blows hot and cold. - *British*

Blue Chip - A Blue Chip is a nationally recognized, well-established and financially sound company - Harry worked for a Blue Chip company in the city. - *British*

Blue rinse brigade - A light hearted phrase used to describe a group of old ladies (blue rinse being hair dye) - Look out here comes the blue rinse brigade! - *British*

Bob's your uncle - A humorous saying meaning that a situation has been resolved as expected - I just changed the battery and it worked straight away, Bob's your uncle! - *British*

Bog off - Go away - Bog off, I'm not in the mood to talk to you! - *British*

Bog standard - Average - The food at the restaurant was bog standard. - *British*

Booby prize - A patronising award for coming last in a competition - Kevin got the booby prize for his awful attempt at karaoke. - *British*

Boot is on the other foot - A change of fortune - Pete used to pick on Dave at school. Now Dave is the boss where Pete works, so the boot is on the other foot. - *British*

General

Bore to death - So boring the other person feels like committing suicide, or turning to stone - I thought he was going to bore me to death when he was talking about football. - *British*

Born again Christian - The convert to Christianity later in life - Ron became a born again Christian after his wife died. - *British*

Born with a silver spoon - To be from a wealthy family - Sarah was born with a silver spoon in her mouth; she's really posh! - *British*

Bottom line - The final conclusion - The bottom line is that I need to earn more money. - *British*

Bottomless pit - Used to express that something is never ending - The project was costing a fortune, it was a bottomless pit. - *British*

Brand new - A recently purchased and unused item - Do you like my new car, it's brand new. - *British*

Brand spanking new - A recently purchased and unused item - Do you like my new car, it's brand spanking new! - *British*

Break the bank - An expensive or risky purchase - I will need to break the bank to get that new car. - *British*

Bring to heel - To correct someone, or gain control over their behaviour - As a manager you will need to bring all the staff to heel, because they currently have a lot of bad habits. - *British*

Buck the system - To act in a rebellious manner - Derek thought he could buck the system and not pay tax. - *British*

Buck the trend - To act in a rebellious manner - Derek thought he could buck the system and not pay tax. - *British*

Bugger all - Nothing - Jane got me bugger all for my birthday. - *British*

Bugger off - Go away - Bugger off, please! - *British*

Bull dust - Untrue - He reckons he could have been a professional footballer, but that is bull dust! - *Australian*

Bum steer - Misled - The instructions told me to turn left at the first roundabout, but that was a bum steer. - *Australian*

By a long chalk - Far away from reaching a target - Joan never fully recovered from her illness. She just was not her former self; not by a long chalk. - *British*

By and large - In general or overall - By and large the neighbours are very friendly. - *British*

By hook or by crook - To achieve something by whatever means are necessary - I will get that job by hook or by crook. - *British*

By the book - To follow instructions exactly - I like to do things by the book. - *British*

Call one's bluff - To challenge someone to prove their claims - Fiona said that if she didn't get a pay rise, she was going to leave her job. The boss called her bluff. - *British*

Cast aspersions - To make unsubstantiated claims about someone - The people in the office were casting aspersions about Michael's sexual orientation. - *British*

Cast the first stone - To be the first to use aggression in an argument or situation - It wasn't all Terry's fault, I think Daniel cast the first stone. - *British*

Chalk and cheese - Used to suggest that two things have no similarities - Bob and Rob are like chalk and cheese. - *British*

Charity begins at home - Used to suggest that people should look after their own interests before helping others - I don't agree with spending money on overseas aid. Charity begins at home. - *British*

Cheap at half the price - Inexpensive - I got a new car for three thousand pounds. It was cheap at half the price. - *British*

Chicken's come home to roost - The final outcome of your actions - Harold had been cheating on Matilda for years, now his chickens have come home to roost because she has kicked him out. - *British*

Chief cook and bottle washer - To have a lot of menial responsibilities - Whenever Alex is around, I end up being the chief cook and bottle washer! - *British*

Chocolate fireguard - Something which is of no use - This medicine is as much good as a chocolate fireguard! - *British*

Chocolate teapot - Something which is of no use - This medicine is as much good as a chocolate teapot! - *British*

Clapped out - Broken or not working properly - I need a new car, this one is clapped out. - *British*

Clean as a whistle - Very clean - I just had my car washed, it is as clean as a whistle. - *British*

Clean bill of health - To be medically healthy - The nurse gave me a clean bill of health in my annual check up. - *British*

Clean slate - An empty space. A fresh start - After the old boss left we have a clean slate and we can start again. - *British*

Cleanliness is next to godliness - This phrase emphasises the importance of hygiene - You really need to tidy up your room, cleanliness is next to godliness. - *British*

Coast is clear - It is safe to continue your activities because the danger has passed - The coast is clear, you can stop hiding from the boss now! - *British*

Cold comfort - A minor consolation - I broke my neck in the car accident. It was a cold comfort when the other driver admitted full responsibility. - *British*

Come up to scratch - To meet a target - I failed my driving test, I didn't quite come up to scratch. - *British*

Come up trumps - To experience good fortune - I got a new job last week, everything had suddenly come up trumps. - *British*

Cook one's goose - To be in peril - The boss will cook your goose if you are late again. - *British*

Covers a multitude of sins - Describes how a superficial element can hide bad things - I painted over the damp patches, it covered a multitude of sins. - *British*

Crikey! - An exclamation of surprise - Crikey, I'm late for work. - *America*

Cross the Rubicon - To do something that inevitably commits one to following a certain course of action - When Paul finally admitted his affair, he crossed the Rubicon. He knew his life would never be the same again. - *British*

Cry all the way to the bank - Tolerate conflict and bad feeling, in order to achieve financial gain - The property developer didn't care that the villagers hated him, he was crying all the way to the bank. - *British*

Cry wolf - To pretend to have a problem - Frankie cried wolf because she didn't want to go to school. - *British*

Curry favour - To ingratiate yourself with others in order to achieve a personal goal - Hakan wanted to get promoted so he was trying to curry favour with the other team members. - *British*

Curtains - Used to signify the end of something - I thought it was curtains for me, after that accident. - *British*

Cut and dried - Certain - Sam was going to get the sack, it was cut and dried. - *America/British*

Cut and dried - A firm conclusion - Dave and Kim had split up for good, it was cut and dried. - *British*

Cut to the quick - Painful - It really cut to the quick when Don said I was no good with the women. - *British*

Dab hand - To have skills in a certain area - I am a dab hand at painting. - *British*

Damn with faint praise - To evaluate negatively whilst appearing to do the opposite - I painted my mum a portrait for her birthday and she damned it with faint praise when she thanked me by saying she liked the frame! - *British*

David and Goliath - Expresses the difference in strength of two people - Pete beat up Steve, it was like David and Goliath. - *British*

Davy Jones' Locker - To die - Ron is in Davy Jones' Locker. - *British*

General

Daylight robbery - To express dismay at the price of something - The cost of my medicine is absolute daylight robbery! - *British*

Days are numbered - To be near the end of life, or something - I don't think Sue and Guy will stay together for much longer, their days are numbered. - *British*

Dead as a dodo - To be broken, finished or dead - My TV broke last night, it is as dead as a dodo. - *British*

Dead cert - A certainty - It's a dead cert that I will be back to work on Monday. - *British*

Dead in the water - To be broken, finished or dead - The project was a total failure, it is dead in the water. - *British*

Dead ringer - To bear a resemblance to another person - Elton is a dead ringer for Elvis. - *British*

Dead to the world - To be sound asleep - It was hard to wake my daughter up for school this morning, she was dead to the world. - *British*

Deffo - Abbreviation of definitely - I asked Joe if he was going to the pub after work and he said, deffo! - *British*

Dicey - Risky - That operation sounds dicey. - *British*

Discretion is the better part of valour - The importance of keeping things confidential - The boss ensured me that our meeting was confidential. Discretion is the better part of valour. - *British*

Diss - To disrespect someone - Don't diss me! - *America*

Doddle - An easy task - My new car is a doddle to drive. - *British*

Dodgy - Risky - That operation sounds dodgy. - *British*

Dog's body - A slave or someone that runs lots of general errands for you - Sometimes I feel like I am treated like a dog's body around here. - *British*

Dog's life - Describes things as relaxing or pleasant - It's a dog's life for Yuri, he doesn't have to work because his parents are rich. - *British*

Don't go there - Used to imply that the current topic is not up for discussion - I asked Steve about his parents, he said, don't go there! - *British*

Dot the I's and cross the T's - To finalise an agreement - I will be moving house next week, I just need to dot the I's and cross the T's. - *British*

Double whammy - Two painful events that occur in the same time period - I lost my job and then my girlfriend left me. It was a double whammy. - *British*

Doubting Thomas - Used to describe a cynical or sceptical person - Aaron is so sceptical of any of my plans, he is a doubting Thomas. - *British*

Draw the line - A firm boundary or a non negotiable point - I didn't mind working late during the week but I draw the line at working on the weekend. - *British*

Draw the short straw - To be selected for an undesirable task - I drew the short straw and had to do the washing up. - *British*

Dutch courage - To feel more confident as a result of drinking alcohol - I needed a bit of Dutch courage before I asked out Lindsay on a date. - *British*

D'ya get me ? - Do you understand? - I really want this job, d'ya get, me? - *British*

Dyed in the wool - A fixed quality - He is so unreliable, it's dyed in the wool. - *America/ British*

Eagle eyed - To have a good eye for detail or to spot something that is out of place, or wrong - The boss is eagled eyed, he will spot any little mistakes that you make. - *British*

Ear to the ground - To listen carefully or to analyse in detail, in order to predict what might happen - I kept my ear to the ground, so I knew that the company would make redundancies. - *British*

Eat humble pie - To apologise or perform a penance for wrongdoings - I had to eat humble pie after coming home late from the pub and waking up my girlfriend. - *British*

General

Eat my hat - Used to express doubt. e.g. if you win the X factor, I will eat my hat! - If you win the X Factor, I will eat my hat! - *British*

Eat out of someone hand - To unquestioningly follow another - She had the boss eating out of her hand. - *British*

Elephant in the room - The elephant refers to an awkward or embarrassing problem that is not being addressed/ discussed - I hadn't got the promotion, Susie had got it instead, so nobody wanted to mention the elephant in the room. - *British*

Enter the lion's den - To face a hostile reception - The staff were angry about up coming redundancies. The manager knew at the next staff meeting he would have to enter the lion's den. - *British*

Every cloud has a silver lining - To find the positive in a bad situation - I lost my job but at least now I can look for one that I actually enjoy. So every cloud has a silver lining. - *British*

Everyone has their cross to bear - We all have problems - Sarah, you are not the only one who is feeling stressed, we all have a cross to bear. - *British*

Face the firing squad - To be confronted for your wrongdoings - He was late for work again, so now he would have to face the firing squad! - *British*

Face the music - To be judged for your actions - He was late again, now he would have to face the music! - *British*

Fair and square - A mutually satisfactory agreement - We split the bill equally, so it was all fair and square. - *British*

Fall foul of - To get in trouble - I fell foul with the police for speeding. - *British*

Fall guy - Someone who takes the blame for another person's wrongdoings - When the company failed to make a profit, they looked for a fall guy, and decided to sack me! - *British*

Fall on deaf ears - A message that is ignored - I tried to tell the boss I couldn't work late, but that fell on deaf ears. - *British*

Fall on stony ground - An environment that is not beneficial for growth - I tried to keep my business going during the recession, but all my ideas fell on stony ground. - *British*

Family jewels - Valuable items - When Keith robbed the house, he took the family jewels. - *British*

Famous last words - Used to imply that events will not live up to expectations - Karen promised to finish the report by Friday, famous last words! - *British*

Far cry from - Not up to standard - The food in the hotel was a far cry from what I expected. - *British*

Fat chance - Referring to something that in reality is never going to happen - Fat chance I will ever get promoted! - *British*

Fate worse than death - Something that seems worse than dying - Continuing to work here would be a fate worse than death! - *British*

Feather in one's cap - To gain recognition for good deeds - It was a feather in my cap when the project became successful. - *America/British*

Feather one's nest - To act in a self interested manner - The new salesman isn't a team player, he is only interested in feathering his own nest. - *British*

Few and far between - Rare - It's hard to find a good house for sale in my price range, they are few and far between. - *British*

Fiddle while Rome burns - To waste time or to ignore the most important task - The company needed to make cutbacks but the boss was more interested in decorating the shop. He was fiddling while Rome burns. - *British*

Field day - To have an enjoyable time - When the boss was away we had a field day, we didn't get much work done but we had a good laugh. - *British*

Filthy Lucre - Money - I need to get my hands on some filthy lucre. - *British*

Fingers crossed - A superstitious action meant to bring good luck - I might get promoted, fingers crossed. - *British*

Flavour of the month - To be the preferred choice of a fickle person - Uma was flavour of the month at work, but I am sure the boss will change his mind. - *British*

Flog a dead horse - To waste time by asking for the impossible - Getting the teenager to tidy up, was like flogging a dead horse. - *British*

Fly by night - Used to describe an unreliable or devious person - The builders we employed were fly by night and did not complete the job. - *British*

Fly in the face of fashion - To do the opposite of conventional wisdom - Steve always does his own thing, he isn't afraid to fly in the face of fashion. - *British*

Fools rush in where angels fear to tread - Used to describe an impulsive person - I wouldn't have bought the house for that price, but fools rush in where angels fear to tread. - *British*

Foot loose and fancy free - To have the freedom to do as you please - Irene is footloose and fancy free since she left Brian. - *British*

Foot the bill - To pay the financial costs - Someone broke the wing mirror on my car, then drove off, leaving me to foot the bill. - *British*

For the high jump - To be in trouble - Fanny is for the high jump when the boss catches up with her. - *British*

Foregone conclusion - Inevitable - It was a foregone conclusion that Jenny and Ken would get back together. - *British*

Forlorn hope - Impossible - It was a forlorn hope that I would get promoted. - *British*

Fresh as a daisy - To be healthy and invigorated - Oliver was fresh as a daisy after his afternoon nap. - *British*

From pillar to post - To go on a long complicated journey, and sometimes to feel metaphorically pushed around - My complaint was passed from pillar to post but was never resolved. - *British*

From the horse's mouth - Information received from a first hand source - The boss said there will be redundancies, I heard it from the horse's mouth. - *British*

From the sublime to the ridiculous - Describes how things can change from positive to negative in a short space of time - I was head of the department, now I am unemployed, things have gone from the sublime to the ridiculous. - *British*

Fuck off - Go away - Lew, fuck off! - *British*

Full Monty - Naked or all of the way - Harry was so drunk he tried to do the Full Monty in the pub. - *British*

Full of beans - Happy or healthy - Janice was full of beans on her birthday. - *British*

Gash - Rubbish - That hotel was gash. - *British*

Get a life - Phrase used to admonish someone for wasting their own time - That man is always down the pub, he needs to get a life! - *British*

Get down to brass tacks - The essence of an idea - The meeting was so long and boring, I wish we could just get down to the brass tacks. - *British*

Get down to the nitty gritty - The essence of an idea - The meeting was so long and boring, I wish we could just get down to the nitty gritty. - *British*

Get one's back up - To react angrily - When Debbie lies to me, it really gets my back up. - *British*

Get one's gander up - To react angrily - Seeing the child shouted at in the supermarket, really got my gander up! - *British*

Get the bit between your teeth - To work in a determined manner - I had to finish the project by Friday so I had to get the bit between my teeth. - *British*

Gild the lily - To apply unnecessary decoration - There's no point gilding the lily, we won't sell the house for any more money if we redecorate it. - *British*

Gilt edged - Valuable - The football player signed a new gilt edged contract. - *British*

Gird one's loins - To protect yourself from harm - You need to gird your loins because Pete is angry with you. - *British*

Given no quarter - To show no mercy - The boss was very strict. Deadlines had to be met and we were given no quarter. - *British*

Go AWOL - To go missing - Karen was expected to work today but she has gone AWOL. - *British*

Go Dutch - To share the costs - We always go Dutch when we pay for a meal. - *British*

Go for broke - To put in maximum effort or to take a big risk - I will need to go for broke if I want to finish the project by Friday. - *British*

Go haywire - Chaotic - The computer has gone haywire. - *British*

Go out on a limb - To take a risk - I'm going to go out on a limb and offer the job to Kate. - *British*

Good books - To perceive someone in a positive way - Jack is in my good books because he did his homework. - *British*

Good innings - To live for a long time - Nan has had a good innings she is 101 years old now! - *British*

Good Samaritan - A kind person - Joseph is a good Samaritan, he is always helping his elderly neighbours. - *British*

Grasp the nettle - To engage in a undesirable but important task - Nobody wanted to deal with the customer's complaint, so I decided to grasp the nettle. - *British*

Grass is always greener on the other side - People often envy others, when in reality their lives are no better than our own - Carol was envious when she saw Jill's holidays photos. She didn't realise that the holiday was actually a disaster. - *British*

Grass roots - Political term related to current trends in public opinion, held by loyal supporters of a political party - The grass roots were furious about the way the party was being run. - *British*

Gravy train - Money that is acquired with little effort - The new owners treated the business like a gravy train. - *British*

Great unwashed - The general public, particularly the lower classes - The great unwashed have little knowledge of politics. - *British*

Green with envy - To be envious - George was green with envy when he saw Ian's new car. - *British*

Gung ho - To act in a fearless or careless manner - Derek was gung ho about his meeting with the new boss. - *British*

Hail from - Place of birth or where you currently live - Alex hails from Yorkshire. - *British*

Hair raising - A terrifying or exhilarating experience - That rollercoaster ride was a hair raising experience. - *British*

Hard up - To have no money - Betty was very hard up and was struggling to pay the rent. - *British*

Haul over the coals - To have your actions scrutinised and to be reprimanded by someone - The new boss hauled Steve over the coals. - *British*

Have one's work cut out - To face a challenging task - I will have my work cut out, if I want to finish this project by Friday. - *British*

He who pays the piper, calls the tune - Those with money also have power - The business spent a great deal of money on its public image. He who pays the piper calls the tune. - *British*

Head on a platter - To punish someone - The boss will have your head on a platter if you are late again. - *British*

Heard it from the horse's mouth - Information received from a first hand source - The boss told me there were going to be some redundancies, I heard it from the horse's mouth. - *British*

Hide one's light under a bushel - To keep your talents hidden - Jim was very good at singing but he had always hid his light under a bushel. - *British*

High jinks - Light hearted boisterous fun - Steve and Rich were wrestling in the office, but it was only high jinks. - *British*

Hit and run - A road traffic accident where the driver does not stop to report the event - Ursula is in hospital after getting ran over by a car, it was a hit and run. - *British*

Hit for six - To be extremely shaken by an event - Martha was hit for six when Eric died. - *British*

Hocus pocus - Magic, superstition or nonsense - Deirdre was reading her horoscope in the newspaper, but I don't believe in that hocus pocus. - *British*

Hoi polloi - The common people - Bertie hated having to mix with the hoi polloi. - *British*

Hoist by one's own petard - To cause your own misfortune - Jeff was hoist by his own petard when he was caught trying to sell stolen goods at the market. - *British*

Hold the fort - To take responsibility - The boss was in a meeting and he asked me to hold the fort. - *British*

Hold the purse stings - To be in control of the finances - I'm not sure how much money we have in our joint account, my wife holds the purse strings. - *British*

Holier than thou - To claim moral superiority - William is so judgemental, he believes he is holier than thou. - *British*

Holy grail - A metaphor for a desired outcome that is almost impossible to achieve - Preventing the aging process was the holy grail of modern medicine. - *British*

Home straight - To be close to completing a task - We only needed to do one more report and then we were finished for the weekend; we were on the home straight. - *British*

Hope springs eternal - Optimism - I'm not sure if I will get promoted, but hope springs eternal. - *British*

How the other half live - To express envy for another's lifestyle - Joan has just got back from her holiday and she is already booking her next one. How the other half live! - *British*

If the cap fits, then wear it - Accept what you are - I'm really interested in computers, so I think I will retrain for a career in IT. If the cap fits then wear it. - *British*

Iffy - Uncertain - The weather is a bit iffy today, I think it might rain later. - *British*

Ill gotten gains - Rewards for immoral or illegal activities - Paul was a drug dealer and he made a fortune from his ill gotten gains. - *British*

I'm buggered if.. - Expressed to show annoyance or frustration at having to complete something - I'm buggered if I'm giving them any more money. - *British*

In a nutshell - The essence of an idea - There are loads of reasons why I don't like my job but in a nutshell it is stressful, poorly paid and boring. - *British*

In a pickle - To be confused - The old lady got in a pickle when trying to send an email. - *British*

In fine fettle - To feel healthy - I saw Ernie yesterday, he was in fine fettle. - *British*

In the lap of the gods - To accept that a desired outcome is beyond your control - I did everything I could to get promoted, it's up to the board to make a decision now. It is in the lap of the gods. - *British*

In the pipeline - A plan for the future - The company had some exciting ideas in the pipeline. - *British*

In your dreams - An expression of disbelief - He said he could get any woman, so I said, in your dreams! - *British*

Innit - Isn't it - It's too hot today, innit? - *British*

Is the Pope Catholic? - Ironic question used if something is obvious - John asked if I wanted a free iPad, I said, is the Pope a Catholic? - *British*

It ain't over till the fat lady sings - Don't give up yet, see what happens - We were losing the match at half time, but it ain't over till the fat lady sings! - *British*

It beggars belief - Unbelievable - He was caught drink driving with no licence, and yet he only got a caution. It beggars belief! - *British*

It is in the bag - To be confident of victory - I did brilliantly at the interview, I know this job is in the bag. - *British*

General

It will be a cold day in hell when... - Show strong defiance in a situation - I hate that woman, it will be a cold day in Hell when I apologise to her! - *British*

It's a slippery slope - A course of action which will potentially end badly - It's really difficult getting out of debt. It's a slippery slope. - *British*

It's all done and dusted - Completely finished - I split up with my girlfriend last week, it's all done and dusted now. - *British*

It's all downhill from here - Things are not going well and will probably just get worse still - I found my first grey hair last week, it's all downhill from here! - *British*

It's all Greek to me - To be confused - I can't understand the instruction manual, it is all Greek to me. - *British*

It's all over bar the shouting - Finished; not worth pursuing anymore - We are winning by seven goals, it's all over, bar the shouting. - *British*

It's all to cock - Something that is completely wrong - The whole thing is falling to pieces; it's all to cock. - *British*

It's in the bag - Certain - We are winning by seven goals, it's in the bag! - *British*

It's not over till the fat lady sings - Don't give up yet - Even though it looks like I won't get promoted, it's not over until the fat lady sings. - *British*

It's not rocket science - Easy enough to understand - It's easy to use the internet, it's not exactly rocket science! - *British*

Ivory tower - A place where you are protected from the realities of life - The boss has no idea how hard we work, he just sits in his ivory tower. - *British*

Jack it in - To give up - I'm fed up with this job. It is so boring, I think I'm going to jack it in. - *British*

Jammer - Somebody who is very lucky - He is so lucky! Yesterday, he found a twenty pound note; he is such a jammer. - *Bristol*

Jammy - Lucky - I passed the test without revising, I am so jammy! - *British*

Jammy dodger - Lucky - I passed the test, I'm such a jammy dodger! - *British*

Jekyll and Hyde - To have two sides to your personality; one that's 'good' and one that's not! - Jarrod is a Jekyll and Hyde character, one minute he is happy, the next he is angry. - *British*

Jog on - Go away - That guy was being annoying so I told him to jog on! - *British*

Jump on the bandwagon - To follow the actions of others - I was the first person to suggest we modernise the company, now everyone is jumping on the bandwagon. - *British*

Jump the gun - To act hastily - I jumped the gun when I said Gary was a useless salesman. He has actually turned out to be quite good. - *British*

Jury is still out - It is too soon to predict an event - We haven't decided where to go on holiday yet; the jury is still out. - *British*

Just what the doctor ordered - Exactly what is needed or wanted in a situation- not necessarily medical - I was tired, but this holiday has rejuvenated me, it was just what the doctor ordered! - *British*

Keep me posted - Keep me informed - Keep me posted about any issues you have. - *British*

Keep mum - To retain confidential information - We are arranging an office party for Hannah's birthday, but keep mum, ok? - *British*

Keep one's powder dry - To hold back from an argument for tactical reasons - I decided to keep my powder dry and wait for a better moment to confront the boss. - *British*

Keep the wolf from the door - The need to do any task in order to avoid poverty - I hate my job but I have to do something to keep the wolf from the door. - *British*

Keep up with the Joneses - Social competition between peers or neighbours - Clark got a new car last week. Now I really have to upgrade mine if I want to keep up with the Joneses. - *British*

General

189

Keep your hair on - An instruction used to try to calm someone down - I know you are angry but keep your hair on. - *British*

Keep your pecker up - To stay positive - It is a pity that you didn't get promoted Jon, but keep your pecker up and I'm sure there will be other opportunities. - *British*

Keep your shirt on - Keep calm - Keep your shirt on Dave, there is no need to get angry. - *British*

Kill the goose that lays the golden egg - Self destructive act - I really regret selling my business, I feel like I killed the goose that lays the golden egg. - *British*

Kiss of death - An action or relationship that has failed - When my partner cheated on me, it was the kiss of death for our relationship. - *British*

Knight in shining armour - A heroic character or a good looking man - Sally is always waiting for a knight in shining armour to rescue her. - *British*

Knock it on the head - To give up - I decided to stop smoking, it's no good for me so I am going to knock it on the head. - *British*

Labour of love - A time consuming/ expensive but rewarding hobby - I rebuilt a classic car from scratch. It took three years and cost a lot of money, but it was a true labour of love. - *British*

Lamb to the slaughter - To be innocent and unaware of forthcoming events - The gang ambushed me in an alleyway; I was like a lamb to the slaughter! - *British*

Lame duck - A person who lacks authority - The new boss is a lame duck. - *British*

Land of nod - Sleep - I'm so tired, I'm off to the land of nod. - *British*

Last ditch effort - A final attempt - We made a last ditch effort to save our marriage. - *British*

Laughing stock - A fool - When I fell over, it was hilarious; I was a laughing stock! - *America/British*

Law of the jungle - Survival of the fittest - It was tough growing up in the inner city. To survive you had to follow the law of the jungle. - *British*

Lead a merry dance - To make others do your bidding - My boss is so demanding, he leads us all on a merry dance. - *America/British*

Lead up the garden path - To mislead someone - He is a conman, he led us up the garden path. - *British*

League of their own - Better than another - I'm good at football, but John is in a league of his own. - *America/British*

Leave no stone unturned - To try every possible solution - There must be a way to save the company from bankruptcy. We will leave no stone unturned. - *British*

Lecky - Electricity - I haven't got enough money to pay the lecky bill. - *British*

Lectric - Electricity - I need to pay the lectric bill. - *Bristol*

Left in the lurch - To be let down by someone - I was meant to be going to the cinema with Philippa but she has left me in the lurch. - *British*

Life of Riley - An easy life - Freddy doesn't need to work because his parents are so rich. He lives the life of Riley. - *British*

Like a cat on hot bricks - Restless - The toddler had so much energy, he was like a cat on hot bricks. - *British*

Like a fish out of water - Feeling like you don't belong in a situation - I felt really uncomfortable around all those posh people; I was like a fish out of water. - *British*

Like a house on fire - To enjoy each other's company - Sarah and Rich got on like a house on fire. - *British*

Like a rose between two thorns - To stand out from the crowd; to be the prettiest - The beautiful woman stood out from the crowd. She was like a rose between two thorns. - *British*

Like billio - Very fast - I had to go like billio to finish the project in time. - *British*

Like it or lump it - An ultimatum - I don't care how you feel about it, like it or lump it! - *British*

Lily livered - Cowardly - Yohan is so lily livered. - *British*

Lion's share - The majority - Ken worked with Rob. Ken did the lion's share of the work. - *British*

Lip service - To verbally agree to something whilst never intending to fulfil the agreement - The boss paid lip service to staff pay rises. - *British*

Lock, stock and barrel - Everything - When I emigrated I had to sell everything, lock, stock and barrel. - *America/British*

Long shot - A speculative or extremely hopeful gamble - I knew it was a long shot but I decided to apply for the job. - *British*

Loose cannon - An unpredictable person who doesn't follow the rules - It was risky inviting Paul to the business meeting; he was a bit of a loose cannon. - *British*

Lose one's bottle - To back out of an event, due to fear of failure - I was going to ask Diane out but I lost my bottle. - *British*

Make a clean breast of it - To make a fresh start - I'm going to emigrate and make a clean breast of it. - *British*

Make a hash of - To make a mistake - I made a hash of my exams. - *British*

Make a mountain out of a molehill - To inflate the importance of a situation - John is very stressed and is over reacting, he makes a mountain out of a molehill! - *British*

Make do and mend - To repair things to prolong their usefulness and to save money - My mum always used to darn our socks. "Make do and mend" she said. - *British*

Make ends meet - To work within a tight budget - It was to make ends meet, we had no spare cash. - *British*

Make no bones about - To be uncompromising and unconcerned about hurting people's feelings - Adam made no bones about telling Susie she was rubbish at her job. - *British*

Make one's blood boil - To get angry - When George was drunk, it made my blood boil. - *British*

Make the grade - To achieve a certain standard - I will need to work hard if I am going to make the grade. - *British*

Matter of life or death - An issue of such urgency, to the point that it feels as if it is a matter of living or dying - Please help me, this a matter of life or death. - *British*

Mend fences - To make an effort at restoring a positive relationship with someone - Guy and Mabel had fallen out, but Guy was determined to mend fences. - *British*

Method in the madness - The underlying logic behind a seemingly chaotic action - I had no idea why Gary took a detour when driving us to work, but he said there was method in the madness because there was roadworks in town. - *British*

Mickey Mouse - Shoddy, second rate - I got a cheap iPhone from the market, but it was Mickey Mouse. - *British*

Midas touch - The ability to make a success out of any endeavour - Sri had the Midas touch when it came to business. - *British*

Mind one's p's and q's - To speak in a polite and considered manner - When the boss is around, you have to mind your p's and q's. - *British*

Miss the boat - An opportunity that was not taken - I could have been a professional footballer but I got injured and I've missed the boat now. - *British*

Mug's game - An activity that is unproductive - There's no point trying to please her, it's a mug's game. - *British*

Mumbo jumbo - Nonsense - I couldn't understand the doctor, he was talking mumbo jumbo. - *British*

My bad - A mistake - I didn't realise it was your birthday today, my bad. - *British*

My lips are sealed - To keep a secret - I won't tell anyone that you have a crush on Derek, my lips are sealed. - *British*

Naff - Poor quality, rubbish - John wears really naff clothes. - *British*

Naff off - Go away - Naff off, Jim! - *British*

Nail your colours to the mast - To express your opinions publicly - There was a lot of office politics so I was careful not to nail my colours to the mast. - *British*

Near the knuckle - A risky or dangerous situation - We went rock climbing, it was good fun, but it was near the knuckle at one point. - *British*

Neck and neck - Equal - The race was so close, it was hard to pick a winner, they were neck and neck most of the way. - *America/ British*

Needle in a haystack - Something that is hidden and impossible to find - I had lost my keys in the park but it was like looking for a needle in a haystack. - *British*

Nest egg - Financial savings - I hope to have a nice nest egg when I retire. - *British*

Never in a month of Sundays - Something that is impossible - I won't ever say sorry to him, never in a month of Sundays! - *British*

No bed of roses - An unpleasant situation - My marriage was no bed of roses. - *America/British*

No great shakes - Not any good - My new car is no great shakes. - *British*

No great shakes - Used to describe something that is unimpressive - The food at the hotel was no great shakes. - *British*

No kidding - Telling the truth - I'm going to emigrate, no kidding. - *British*

No rhyme or reason - No obvious pattern, lacking in logic - I couldn't understand the management's decision there seemed to be no rhyme or reason to it. - *British*

No worries - Not a problem - He asked me to drive him to the shop so I said, no worries. - *British*

Not a sausage - Nothing - I asked Joanne what she got for Christmas and she said, not a sausage! - *British*

Not cricket - To deviate from the rules - Freddy never paid his taxes, it was just not cricket. - *British*

Not my cup of tea - Not to my taste - I don't like rap music, it's not my cup of tea. - *British*

Not the foggiest - Unsure - I haven't got the foggiest idea where I left my keys. - *British*

Nothing to write home about - Average - The hotel was nothing to write home about. - *British*

Nowt - Nothing - I've got nowt in the bank at the moment. - *British*

Old boy network - Refers to the rich upper classes and the way they monopolise positions of power - It was obvious they would give the job to Tobias, he was part of the old boys network. - *British*

Olive branch - A metaphor for peace - Karen offered Susie an olive branch. - *British*

Omg - Oh my god! A declarative phrase to add emphasis to what you are saying - Omg, I didn't realise it was your birthday today. - *British*

On a hiding to nothing - To be in a situation where you cannot succeed - I will never get this job done in time, I'm on a hiding to nothing. - *British*

On a mission - Seeking a good time - Me and the boys are going to town, we are on a mission. - *British*

On a shoe string - To achieve something on a very small budget - The department was run on a shoe string. - *British*

On a wing and a prayer - To hope for the best - I don't hold out much hope, it's more of a wing and a prayer. - *British*

On a wing and a prayer - An act of blind faith - I applied for the job on a wing and a prayer. - *British*

On cloud 9 - Very happy - I'm on cloud 9 since I got my new car. - *British*

On cloud nine - To be ecstatic - I'm on cloud nine since I got promoted. - *British*

On it's last legs - An item which is close to breaking - My car is so old now, it's on its last legs. - *British*

On one's high horse - To express moral indignation - Diane was on her high horse because I forgot to do the washing up. - *British*

General

On one's todd - To be alone - I was on my todd all weekend, it was so boring. - *British*

On pain of death - Something you have to do which is so important that if you don't do it you might be euphemistically 'killed' - I have to get this report done, on pain of death. - *British*

On tap - Easy to obtain - The night club was great, there were women on tap. - *British*

On tenterhooks - An anxious wait - I was on tenterhooks, waiting to hear if I had got into university. - *British*

On the back foot - To retreat - The way they spoke to me, put me on the back foot. - *British*

On the ball - To be focused and in control - Irene is on the ball when it comes to the finances. - *British*

On the cards - An anticipated outcome - Redundancies were on the cards. - *British*

On the grapevine - Gossip - On the grapevine, there was talk of redundancies. - *British*

On the up - An improving situation - Things are on the up since I had the operation. - *British*

On your bike - Go away or hurry up - He was annoying me so I told him to get on his bike. - *British*

On your head be it - To place responsibility onto another person - If you decide to take that money, then on your head be it. - *British*

Once in a blue moon - A rare event - We only go out once in a blue moon. - *British*

One and the same - Equal - It doesn't matter if you turn left or right here, it's one and the same. - *America/British*

One in a million - Exceptional - John is one in a million! - *America/British*

Open Pandora's box - To create chaos - I wouldn't study the business accounts too closely. It's like opening Pandora's box. - *British*

Out for the count - To be knocked out or just asleep - I was so tired, I was out for the count last night. - *British*

Out of the ark - Ancient or out of date - The computer system at work is rubbish, it is out of the ark! - *British*

Out of the blue - A surprise situation - I didn't expect to lose my job, it came out of the blue. - *British*

Out of the blue - Unexpected - I got offered a new job out of the blue. - *British*

Over and done with - Finished - Me and the wife split up, we are over and done with. - *British*

Over my dead body - Used to express disagreement with a proposed course of action - There's no way I will ever let you sell this house, over my dead body! - *British*

Part and parcel - Part of something - Keeping yourself fit is part and parcel of being a professional footballer. - *British*

Parting of the ways - To separate - Susan and Ken weren't getting on, there was a parting of the ways last month. - *British*

Parting shot - To have the final word in an argument - Jorge had the parting shot in the argument. - *British*

Pearly gates - The entrance to heaven - Paul you will see the pearly gates if you don't quit smoking. - *British*

Phoenix from the ashes - To regain your power - I was really ill last year, but I rose like a phoenix from the ashes. - *British*

Pie in the sky - Wishful thinking - Robert wants to be a rock star but that is just pie in the sky. - *British*

Piece of piss - An easy task - That job interview was a piece of piss. - *British*

Pigeon hole - To categorise things, or to stereotype someone and limit their potential - The new boss pigeon holed Keith as a trouble maker. - *British*

Pig's ear - To mess something up - Jack rushed the task and made a pig's ear out of it. - *British*

Pipe down - Be quiet - He was annoying me so I told him to pipe down. - *British*

Piss off - Go away - Piss off! - *British*

Piss poor - Rubbish - The food in the hotel was piss poor. - *British*

General

Pissing in the wind - A futile task - There is no point arguing with him when he is drunk, you may as well piss in the wind. - *British*

Plain sailing - An easy task - Getting to work was plain sailing this morning. - *British*

Play to the gallery - To speak loudly so that others can overhear you - Ron had a disagreement with the boss. He made sure everyone heard it, he was playing to the gallery. - *British*

Plumb the depths - A negative event - The service at the hotel got worse and worse. They were really plumbing the depths. - *British*

Poetic justice - An ironic event that seems to punish or reward someone for their past deeds - The boy racer crashed his car into the ditch. It was poetic justice for the way he raced around the village terrorising pedestrians. - *British*

Poetic Licence - To use words figuratively rather than literally - The teacher used poetic licence by descriving the school as like a zoo and all the kids were animals. - *British*

Poisoned chalice - An unpleasant task - The new boss was given a poisoned chalice, he needed to make savings and redundancies were likely. - *British*

Poker faced - To conceal your true emotions - You could never tell if the boss was serious, he had a poker face. - *British*

Pour cold water on - To reject a plan - I wanted to make changes to the office but the boss poured cold water on my plan. - *British*

Pride goes before a fall - This phrase suggest that arrogance can lead to disaster - It was obvious that Ken's business would fail. He was so cocky and flashy - pride comes before a fall. - *British*

Prodigal son - The return of a loved one - When Hank rejoined the company everyone treated him like the prodigal son. - *British*

Pull a fast one - To trick someone - She tried to pull a fast one. - *British*

Pull one's finger out - Stop being lazy and take action - The boss told Kevin to pull his finger out. - *British*

Pull one's leg - To tease or trick someone - Terry was getting annoyed because everyone was pulling his leg. - *British*

Pull one's weight - To take your fair share of responsibility - Gary never pulled his weight. - *British*

Pull out all the stops - To try your best - I will need to pull out all the stops if I want to finish the project by Friday. - *British*

Pull the other one - To express disbelief - When he told me he was famous, I said, pull the other one! - *British*

Pull the wool over some ones eyes - To lie - Louise tried to pull the wool over my eyes. - *British*

Push the boat out - To put in maximum effort - I will have to push the boat out for my wedding anniversary. - *British*

Push the envelope - To stretch the limits - I will have to push the envelope if I want to finish the project by Friday. - *British*

Pussyfoot around - To avoid getting to the point or to avoid taking action - I wish the boss would stop pussyfooting around and make a decision. - *British*

Put a sock in it - Be quiet - Put a sock in it! - *British*

Put a sock in it - This phrase is used to tell someone to be quiet - I told Frank to put a sock in it when he kept moaning about his job. - *British*

Put on ice - To postpone a decision or activity - The new project was put on ice. - *British*

Put on the back burner - To postpone a decision or activity - The new project was put on the back burner. - *British*

Put one's nose out of joint - To be rebuffed - When the boss dismissed my idea, that really put my nose out of joint. - *America/ British*

Put one's thinking cap on - To think carefully - The boss wanted me to make savings, so I will need to put on my thinking cap. - *British*

Put the dampers on - To reject a plan - The boss put the dampers on my idea. - *British*

General

Put the Kibosh on - To reject a plan - The boss put the Kibosh on my ideas. - *British*

Put the screws on - To increase the pressure - The boss wanted more productivity so he put the screws on us. - *British*

Put through the mill - To have had a torrid experience - I have been put through the mill this year. First I lost my job, then my girlfriend left me. - *British*

Pyrrhic victory - A minor temporary victory before a crushing defeat - The company reported better sales at Christmas, but it was only a pyrrhic victory, by Easter they went bankrupt. - *British*

Rack and ruin - Deteriorated - This company has gone to rack and ruin. - *British*

Rack one's brains - To try to remember something - I racked my brains but I still can't think where I left my car keys. - *British*

Read between the lines - To look for implicit meaning - The boss said he would have to make savings. If you read between the lines this could means redundancies. - *British*

Read the riot act - To reprimand someone - The boss read the riot act to Phillip for his poor customer service. - *British*

Real McCoy - A genuine product - These shoes are the real McCoy, not a cheap copy from down the market. - *British*

Red herring - A misleading piece of information - I was told that Susie was in town but that was a red herring. - *British*

Ridic - Abbreviation of the word ridiculous - That restaurant is ridic. - *British*

Right hand man - To be a close ally - Paul was the boss's right hand man. - *British*

Ring true - Something that sounds correct - It didn't ring true when Peter said that he had already given me his report - *British*

Rise to the bait - To be unable to control your feelings - George was trying to annoy me and I rose to the bait - *British*

Rome wasn't built in a day - Patience - The new boss wants all reports done by Friday, but Rome wasn't built in a day. - *British*

Root and branch - Thorough - The new boss performed a root and branch investigation in order to find efficiency savings. - *British*

Ropey - Poor quality, rubbish - The food in the hotel was ropey. - *British*

Rule of thumb - General rule - As a rule of thumb, I am usually home from work by 9pm. - *British*

Run amok - To lose temper or to act in a wild manner - The children were running amok in the playground. - *British*

Run of the mill - Ordinary - The restaurant was a bit run of the mill, actually. - *British*

Run of the mill - Average - The hotel food was pretty run of the mill. - *British*

Run the gamut - To take a risk - You have to run the gamut if you have any hope of getting into work before 9am. - *British*

Run the gauntlet - To do something dangerous - Driving during rush hour is like running the gauntlet. - *British*

Sack it off - To give up - Kevin hated his job, so he decided to sack it off! - *British*

Salad days - Retirement - Pete was in his salad days. - *British*

Salt of the earth - A reliable, honest person - Pete was the salt of the earth. - *British*

Sandwich short of a picnic - Lacking intellect - Pat is one sandwich short of a picnic. - *British*

Saved one's bacon - To rescue - I was going to be late for work because my car had broken down but luckily Pete picked me up and saved my bacon. - *British*

Saving grace - A redeeming feature - Ulrika can be annoying but her saving grace is that she is very generous. - *British*

Scot free - To avoid punishment - Richard was caught speeding by the police but he got off scot free. - *British*

General

Scrap it - To throw away - I'm going to have to scrap it. - *British*

Seal of approval - An official endorsement - The General Medical Council gave the product its seal of approval. - *British*

Second nature - To practice a skill to the extent that it becomes an unconscious habit - Dealing with customer complaints had become second nature to Steven. - *British*

See a man about a dog - Attend a secret meeting or deal - I went to town to see a man about a dog. - *British*

Send to Coventry - To be shunned by others for your misdeeds - Terry was sent to Coventry after cheating on Rebecca. - *British*

Shagged - To be tired out, or broken - I'm shagged after my long day at work. - *British*

Shambolic - A disorganised mess - The hotel staff were completely shambolic. - *British*

Ship shape and Bristol fashion - Tidy and clean - The nurses made sure the ward was always ship shape and Bristol fashion. - *British*

Ships that pass in the night - To see very little of a loved one due to work commitments - Delroy and Alice were like ships that pass in the night. - *British*

Short shrift - To dismiss an idea - Reforms to working conditions were given short shrift by the management. - *British*

Shot across the bows - A warning - The boss wasn't happy with the way complaints were being handled. In the meeting he fired a shot across the bows by talking about customer service. - *British*

Sick as a parrot - To be disappointed - I was sick as a parrot when I missed out on promotion. - *British*

Six of one and half a dozen of the other - Equal - I'm not sure if it was my fault or Ken's, it was six of one and half a dozen of the other. - *America/British*

Skew whiff - Out of alignment - I was late for work, and my tie was all skew whiff too! - *British*

Sling one's hook - To go away - Sling your hook, Dave. - *British*

Sod off - Go away - Sod off, Pete. - *British*

Sod this for a game of soldiers - An exclamation of defeat - It was impossible to finish the report in time, so I said, sod that for a game of soldiers. - *British*

Soz - Short for sorry - Soz for being late! - *British*

Spick and span - Tidy and clean - The nurses made sure the ward was always ship shape and Bristol fashion. - *British*

Spitting image - A close resemblance - Harold was the spitting image of Tony Blair. - *British*

Start from scratch - To restart an activity - The computer crashed so I had to start the project from scratch. - *British*

Start the ball rolling - To initiate an activity - I wanted to move house so I decided to start the ball rolling. - *British*

Steal a march on - To seize the initiative - I was going to ask Paula out but Ricky stole a march on me and asked her out first. - *British*

Steal one's thunder - To seize the initiative - I was going to ask Paula out but Ricky stole my thunder and asked her out first. - *British*

Stick out like a sore thumb - Unusual and conspicuous - His new hair cut made him stick out like a sore thumb. - *America/British*

Stick to one's guns - To be resolute in the face of opposition - The reforms were not well received by the staff but the boss stuck to his guns. - *British*

Sting in the tail - An unpleasant outcome - I was so happy when I moved into my new flat but the sting in the tail was the neighbours, who were awful. - *British*

Storm in a teacup - A minor dispute - Helen and Kevin had an argument but it was just a storm in a teacup. - *British*

Stumbling block - A barrier to reaching an agreement - The negotiations to takeover the company had began but the stumbling block was staffing levels. - *British*

General

Stump up - To pay for something - I had to stump up a thousand pounds to repair my car. - *British*

Sweet F.A. - Nothing - She got me sweet F.A. for Christmas! - *British*

Sweet Fanny Adams - Nothing. Often shortened to sweet F.A. or S.F.A. - He bought me sweet Fanny Adams for my birthday! - *British*

Sword of Damocles - The threat of punishment for failure - Sue knew she had to perform perfectly during the inspection. She felt as if the sword of Damocles was hanging over her head. - *British*

Take a hike - Go away! - Take a hike! - *British*

Take a leaf out of one's book - To be inspired by another person - I took a leaf out of Joanna's book and tried to be more cooperative at work. - *British*

Take a running jump! - Go away! - Tom was annoying me, so I told him to go and take a running jump. - *British*

Take down a peg - To humiliate someone - Clive is so arrogant he needs taking down a peg, or two. - *British*

Take great pains - To do something thoroughly - Jim took great pains when explaining his decision to the boss. - *British*

Take one's hat off to someone - To show appreciation for someone - I take my hat to Lyn, she is a brilliant worker. - *British*

Take rain check - To postpone a decision or activity - I was too busy for the meeting so we took a rain check. - *British*

Take the biscuit - An action that surpasses all previous ones - Alan was always annoying but it took the biscuit when he tried chatting up my girlfriend. - *British*

Take to task - To be reprimanded - The boss took me to task for missing the deadline. - *British*

Take to the cleaners - To be destroyed - Gary was taken to the cleaners by Rex. - *British*

Take umbrage - To be offended - Flynn took umbrage with David's racist comments. - *British*

Take up the gauntlet - To accept a risky proposition - The boss wanted someone to deal with customer complaints so I decided to take up the gauntlet. - *British*

Take with a pinch of salt - To be sceptical - I wouldn't believe everything Paul tells you; you have to take him with a pinch of salt. - *British*

Taken aback - Surprised - I was taken aback when Ellie said she wanted to leave me. - *British*

Taken for a ride - To be used or conned by someone - I wouldn't trust Paul, he will take you for a ride. - *British*

Talk gibberish - Nonsense - The doctor was talking gibberish. - *British*

Tarred with the same brush - To be negatively perceived due to your association with another - Raymond has got a bad reputation, if you hang around with him you will get tarred with the same brush. - *British*

Tat - Rubbish - That shop just sells a load of old tat. - *British*

Thanks a bunch - Ironic expression of appreciation - All I got was a packet of crisps for Christmas, thanks a bunch! - *British*

Thanks for nothing - Ironic expression of appreciation - Dave got me a packet of peanuts for my birthday, thanks for nothing! - *British*

That doesn't cut the mustard - An unsatisfying or incomplete explanation - He was late because he couldn't find his car keys, but that doesn't cut the mustard. - *British*

That won't wash - An unsatisfying or incomplete explanation - He said he'd only had three pints, but that won't wash with me. - *British*

The American Dream - The American concept that anyone can achieve success because all men are born equal - Is the American Dream still a possibility in modern America? - *British*

The bigger they are, the harder they fall - Used to signify that powerful people can make catastrophic errors - The businessman lost his whole fortune during the banking crisis. The bigger they are, the harder they fall. - *British*

The blind leading the blind - Refers to situation where the leaders are unsure what to do - That man giving advice about relationships, is like the blind leading the blind! - *British*

The chattering classes - Media speculation and public opinion - The chattering classes were all talking about Britain leaving the EU. - *British*

The die is cast - A firm and unalterable conclusion, or to gain a bad reputation - Ian has persistently caused trouble at work, the die is cast now, I think he will be made redundant. - *British*

The icing on the cake - The best or worse bit of a situation that is revealed last - My day got even worse when I missed the bus home from work and had to walk instead in the rain; that was the icing on the cake for me! - *British*

The skinny - The inside story or to tell a quick story about a certain subject - The skinny version is that... we were lost. - *America*

Thick as thieves - Perception that two people are up to mischief or conspiring - When Fin and Alex were together, they were as thick as thieves. - *British*

Thin end of the wedge - An event that leads to an ever worsening trend - The boss talked about cost cutting, but that was just the thin end of the wedge. Redundancies were soon to follow. - *British*

Thin on the ground - Rare - It was a struggle finding a new job, as they were thin on the ground due to the recession. - *America/British*

Third degree - To be interrogated - Sally gave Richard the third degree when he came home late from work. - *British*

Throw in the towel - To give up - I can't do this job anymore, I'm thinking of throwing in the towel. - *British*

Thrown in at the deep end - To be unprepared for a difficult task - I hadn't had much training for my new job, I was thrown in at the deep end. - *British*

Tie the knot - To get married - Sally and Richard tied the knot last year. - *British*

Tit for tat - To retaliate in an argument - The argument went on and on, it was tit for tat. - *British*

To bandy words about - To talk freely or without thinking - Rachel said she hated her boss and was going to quit her job, but I think she was just bandying words about. - *British*

To bank on - To makes plans based on the occurrence of an anticipated outcome - I put in an offer for a new car but I am banking on selling my old one first. - *British*

To be safe and sound - Be safe and secure - It was a bad crash, but we all came out of it safe and sound. - *British*

To cap it all - A final action - It had been a bad day, but to cap it all off, I missed the bus and had to walk home in the rain! - *America/British*

To the manor born - To have a wealthy background - Richard is so posh, he is to the manor born. - *British*

To the nth degree - In great detail - We discussed the new procedure to the nth degree. - *British*

Toe the line - To follow the rules - The new boss made loads of changes and demanded we all toe the line. - *British*

Toe to toe - An argument or physical fight - Richard and Ken went toe to toe. - *British*

Tongue in cheek - To speak in a light hearted or ironic way - Winny was always saying she was going to leave Trent but it was just tongue in cheek. - *British*

Tooth and nail - To fight with determination - I had to fight tooth and nail to make my business a success. - *British*

Top brass - Upper management - The top brass were looking to expand the business. - *British*

Top drawer - Excellent - The food at the hotel was top drawer. - *British*

Touch and go - An uncertain outcome - It was touch and go whether Mabel would survive surgery. - *British*

General

Touch wood - Superstitious act that brings good luck - Touch wood, I seem to be feeling better at the moment. - *British*

Turn up for the books - A surprising outcome - It was a turn up for the book when Jorge got promoted. - *British*

Under the weather - Unwell - I feel under the weather today. - *British*

Up the spout - Broken or not working properly - My TV broke last night, it is up the spout. - *British*

Up to scratch - To reach the required standard - I need to get up to scratch if I want to pass the exam. - *British*

Up to the ears - To be overworked - I can't come out tonight I'm up to my ears in it. - *British*

Up to the mark - To reach the required standard - I need to get up to the mark if I want to pass the exam. - *British*

Upset the apple cart - To cause a problem - When Irene left, it really upset the apple cart. - *British*

Vicious circle - A negative spiral of thoughts or behaviours that is hard to rectify - Huru drinks because he is sad. This doesn't help, it just makes him more depressed: It is a vicious circle. - *British*

The walls have ears - Take care of people who might be listening out for gossip - You can't tell anyone your business around here, the walls have ears. - *British*

Wangle - To use your wits to find a better deal - Simon managed to wangle a better deal. - *British*

Wanksta - Fake gangster, someone who aspires to be a gangsta but fails to make the grade - "Paul is a wanksta," said Tracey. - *American*

Wash one's dirty linen in public - To be indiscreet with your private affairs - Joan and Frank had a row in the restaurant. I hate it when people wash their dirty linen in public. - *British*

Wash one's hands of - To withdraw support for something - I'm fed up with Carol's antisocial behaviour. From now on I wash my hands of her. - *British*

Way to go! - Well done, many congratulations - Way to go, Stephanie, you passed your driving test! - *America*

Wear one's heart on one's sleeve - To show your emotions - You always know how Doug feels, he wears his heart on his sleeve. - *British*

Well heeled - Well behaved - The children were very well heeled. - *British*

Went a pisser - To metaphorically fall badly when things do not go to plan - James tripped over the dog and went a pisser. - *Bristol*

Wet behind the ears - Naive - Susie is wet behind the ears when it comes to men. - *British*

What's his face - To reference a person without their name - I don't remember his name, you know, what's his face? - *British*

Wipe the slate clean - To forgive and forget misdeeds - Lyn and Frank decided to wipe the slate clean. - *British*

Wipe the slate clean - To start again - Debbie forgave Ricardo and they decided to wipe the slate clean. - *British*

With flying colours - To achieve great success - I passed the exam with flying colours. - *British*

Without rhyme or reason - Disorganised - I don't understand how this company survives, there doesn't seem to be any rhyme or reason to it! - *America/British*

Work like a Trojan - To work extremely hard - Yannick works like a Trojan. - *British*

Worth one's salt - To be valuable - Jorge is worth his salt to this company. - *British*

Worth one's weight in gold - To be valuable - Jorge is worth his weight in gold to this company. - *British*

Would not say boo to a goose - Timid or amenable - Lara is great to work with, she wouldn't say boo to a goose. - *British*

Writing is on the wall - Impending doom - The writing is on the wall for this project. - *British*

Wrong side of the tracks - To come from a troubled background - Ian grew up on the wrong side of the tracks. - *British*

General

General

Zilch - Nothing - Katy bought me zilch for my birthday. - *British*

Bushed - Tired - I need to go to bed, I'm bushed. - *Ireland*

Catch some Zs - To get some sleep - I'm tired, I need to catch some Zs. - *America*

Cream crackered - Rhyming slang for knackered- really tired - I need to go to bed, I'm cream crackered. - *cockney*

Duvet day - To stay in bed all day - I was tired, so I decided to have a duvet day. - *British*

Forty winks - Taking a small sleep/ nap - I'm tired, I need to have forty winks. - *British*

Kipping - Taking a small sleep/ nap - I was so tired, I spent all day kipping. - *British*

Nod off - Fall asleep - I might nod off if I sit here too long. - *British*

Out like a light - Went to sleep quickly - I was so tired I went out like a light. - *British*

Sleep in late - To oversleep or to have a long rest - Tomorrow I'm on holiday so I'm going to sleep in late. - *America*

Snooze - A little sleep - In the afternoon, I like a snooze. - *British*

To nod off - To fall asleep - I'm so tired, I'm likely to nod off. - *British*

Glass ceiling - An invisible obstacle that blocks your progress. Typically used in reference to inequalities in the workplace, such as pay - There is a glass ceiling here, women never get promoted! - *British*

Rat race - To put in lots of effort for little reward. Typically used in reference to the strains of life in a materialistic world - Working in London is such a rat race. - *America/British*

A la mode - Code - Hazel and John spoke to each other a la mode so no one else could understand! - *cockney*

A little bird told me - Gossip - Joseph said that a little bird had told him Julia was getting married, but this was only gossip. - *British*

A little birdie told me.. - Someone told me a secret - A little birdie told me that you were pregnant, is it true? - *British*

A load of drivel - Nonsense - The elderly man spoke a load of drivel when describing how good things had been in the past. - *America/British*

Air one's dirty linen/ laundry in public - To discuss private things in public - She has a habit of airing her dirty linen in public when she should be keeping it private. - *British*

All over - The act of verbally insulting another - Sven was all over him, constantly throwing insults his way. - *America/British*

Argue the toss - To disagree and dispute - Simon always argued the toss about everything and found it difficult to agree. - *British*

Backhanded compliment - Good intentions but not expressed well - It was a backhanded compliment when Kev said my girlfriend looked good for her age. - *America/British*

Bad taste in the mouth - A lingering bad feeling after an argument - Me and Jules had made peace, but some of things he said had left a bad taste in my mouth. - *British*

Bang on about - To keep talking about something - Stu always bangs on about football. - *British*

Barking up the wrong tree - To enquire incorrectly - Steve asked me if he could borrow some money, but he was barking up the wrong tree, I was skint. - *British*

Beat around the bush - To talk without getting to the point - Andrew, stop beating around the bush, if you can't come to my party, just admit it! - *British*

Bite your lip - To keep your opinions to yourself in order to avoid an argument - Keith was being rude, I tried to bite my lip but it was tricky. - *British*

Blah, blah - Silly, worthless talk - Meg was so boring, blah blah blah! - *British*

Blather - To talk - Jacob was blathering on about the football. - *Ireland*

Bollocking - A severe telling off - John got a massive bollocking for being late. - *British*

Bring to a head - To allow conflict to be brought into the open - There was a bad atmosphere between us, so I thought we needed to have an honest discussion and bring it to a head. - *British*

Bury the hatchet - To settle an argument - Me and Kate decided to bury the hatchet. - *British*

Chatting shit - To talk nonsense - Billy is always chatting shit! - *British*

Chit chat - Idle talk - We were having a nice chit chat, then the boss came in so we had to get back to work! - *British*

Cock and bull story - A fabricated tale - Dave said he needed to borrow some money to pay for his son's new bicycle but that was a cock and bull story; he spent the money on drugs. - *British*

Codswallop - Nonsense - Jim talks codswallop. - *British*

Curiosity killed the cat - To keep asking questions and find out the truth may not be beneficial - Greg's girlfriend kept asking me where he was, so I said, "you know that curiosity killed the cat, don't you?" - *British*

Cut the crap - Stop talking nonsense - Cut the crap Sue, just be honest! - *British*

Cut the mustard - A compelling argument - He said he was late because his alarm didn't go off, but that doesn't cut the mustard! - *British*

Cut to the chase - To get to the point - Its a long story, but to cut to the chase, Les got fired for persistent lateness. - *America*

Dish the dirt - To reveal gossip - Cam was angry so he decided to dish the dirt on his ex-girlfriend. - *British*

Double Dutch - Incomprehensible - I couldn't understand the doctor, it was like he was speaking double Dutch. - *British*

Drop a bombshell - To reveal shocking information - Stu dropped a bombshell when he said he was leaving. - *British*

Earwig - To eavesdrop - He always earwigs on my conversations! - *British*

Flannel - To talk nonsense or to give a sales spiel - Stop talking flannel! - *British*

Go off half cocked - To enter an argument without all the facts to hand - There is no point going off half cocked, you need to get your facts straight before you challenge the boss. - *British*

Grumble - Complain - Nanny will always find something to grumble about! - *America*

Guff - Ridiculous nonsense talk, or flatulence - Paul talks guff sometimes. - *British*

Hook, line and sinker - To be fooled by a persuasive argument - The salesman made a good pitch and I was sold, hook, line and sinker. - *America/British*

Jackanory - Rhymes with story, but also a cultural reference to a TV programme for children, where the presenters told stories - He tells so many lies, it's all just Jackanory! - *cockney*

Knock - The act of verbally insulting another - He annoyed me so I gave him a knock. - *America/British*

Lace into - To verbally assault someone - He annoyed me, so I laced into him. - *British*

Let us know - Speak up your views - If you have a problem, just let us know. - *America*

Let's not go there - Used to imply that the current topic is not up for discussion - I don't want to talk about that, let's not go there. - *British*

Listen up! - Listen to me! - Ok, listen up, I have an idea. - *America*

Mouth off - To talk in an aggressive or thoughtless manner - He was cross, so he decided to mouth off. - *British*

Piffle - Rubbish - Harry talks a lot of piffle! - *British*

Rabbit - To talk incessantly - Joe doesn't half rabbit on! - *British*

Reem - The act of verbally insulting another person - Ryan likes to reem people. - *America/British*

Rip a new asshole - The act of intentionally, verbally, insulting another - When Pete gets cross, he will rip you a new asshole! - *America/British*

General

Set straight - The act of verbally insulting another - I need to see Liam and set him straight. - *America/British*

Slag off - To talk negatively - Sharon slagged you off yesterday. - *British*

Speak your mind - Say what you really want to or feel - He is very honest, he always speaks his mind. - *British*

Spiel - To talk persuasively - Jermaine went into his usual spiel. - *British*

Talk the hind legs off a donkey - To talk incessantly - Jodie can talk the hind legs off of a donkey. - *British*

Talking out your arse - Rubbish, nonsense - You are talking out of your arse! - *British*

Tear into - The act of verbally insulting another - I will tear into that man, if he carries on being rude. - *America/British*

Throw rocks at - The act of verbally insulting another - Me and Susie had a huge argument, we were throwing rocks at each other. - *America/British*

Tosh - Rubbish, nonsense - Dougie, that is total tosh! - *British*

Total codswallop - Nonsense - Mate, that is total codswallop! - *British*

Verbal diarrhoea - Talking incessantly - She has verbal diarrhoea. - *British*

Waffle - To talk without getting to the point - Sometimes she just waffles on. - *British*

Warts and all - Including everything, be it good or bad - Kieron always tells the truth, warts and all. - *British*

Witter on - Talking incessantly - Dad witters on! - *British*

A grey area - Something unclear - How the plans were going to work was unclear, there was too much of a grey area to sort out. - *British*

A kick - To feel happy/ to get a positive feeling from something - Being top of the class gave me a kick, and made me feel positive about my studies. - *America/British*

Baffled - Confused - I was baffled when the doctor was explaining my condition to me. - *British*

Befuddled - Confused - Sorry, I can't understand this map, I am befuddled. - *British*

Bewildered - Confused - I was bewildered by the instructions; I needed help reading the map. - *British*

Blowed if I know - I haven't got a clue - The man asked me how far it was to London and I said, "I'm blowed if I know!" - *Bristol*

Can't make head or tail of it - Confusing - I don't understand algebra; I can't make head or tail of it! - *British*

Affluential - To have both money and power - The Prime Minister is very affluential having both money and power. - *American*

Kudos - To give someone the congratulations and recognition for their achievements- well done! - Les was so brave, you have to give him kudos for that. - *America*

Bossed it - To be successful in an activity - I bossed that exam. - *British*

Hit the big time - To be successful - If I pass this exam then I will be ready to hit the big time. - *British*

Make it - Succeed - I'm so talented, I'm bound to make it, eventually! - *America*

Make the grade - Succeed - I hope I make the grade. - *America*

Billy Hunt - Play on words of taboo: cunt - Ken, stop being such a Billy Hunt! - *cockney*

Bloomin' - Euphemism for the swear word 'bloody' - I've lost my bloomin' keys, again! - *British*

Bollocks - An exclamation of annoyance - Bollocks, I've lost my keys. - *British*

Casa Blanca - Play on words: wanker - Andy, you are such a Casa Blanca! - *cockney*

Charing Crosser - Rhyming slang : tosser - James is a Charing Crosser! - *cockney*

Sidebar: **General**

Charlie Bucket - Play on swear exclamation: fuck it! - I can't be bothered to do this job anymore, Charlie Bucket! - *cockney*

Chicken plucker - Play on swear word: fucker - Wayne is a chicken plucker. - *cockney*

Clucking bell - Play on swear words: fucking hell - Oh, clucking bell, I'm late for work! - *cockney*

Cupid stunt - Play on the swear words: stupid cunt - Darren is a cupid stunt. - *cockney*

Darius Rucker - Rhyming slang with swear word: fucker - Rylan is a Darius Rucker. - *cockney*

Dog and bone - Phone - I need to use the dog and bone. - *cockney*

The blower - The telephone - I called her on the blower to ask her out. - *America*

Channel surfing - To switch between television stations - I was tired, so I just slumped into the arm chair and did some channel surfing. - *British*

Idiot box - Television - Let's watch the news on the idiot box? - *British*

Ages - A long time - It was ages ago that we met. - *Ireland*

Bang on schedule - On time - The train arrived bang on schedule. - *America*

Blast from the past - Anything that causes a sudden bout of nostalgia - I saw Carol the other day; I haven't seen her for years, it was a real blast from the past! - *British*

Call it a day - Time to stop - It was getting late and I couldn't type anymore, so I decided to call it a day!! - *British*

Early bird catches the worm - To take the initiative - I was the first in the queue for the tickets, the early bird catches the worm or, so they say! - *British*

Early doors - Too soon to cast judgement on a situation - I don't know how quickly I will recover from the operation, it's early doors. - *British*

Fits and starts - Intermittently - I get back pain in fits and starts. - *British*

Flash in the pan - A momentary success that soon disappears - My new healthy lifestyle was a flash in the pan. - *British*

Get a wriggle on - Hurry up - Get a wriggle on or we will be late for the appointment. - *British*

Going through a stage... - Used to describe a time period in life, for example adolescence - I'm sorry about the way I behaved, I'm just going through a stage. - *British*

Hold your horses - Slow down and wait - Hold your horses, I'm not ready to go out yet! - *British*

In donkey's years - A long time - How are you? I haven't seen you for so long, it's been donkey's years! - *British*

Jump the gun - To anticipate an event or to act prematurely - I was too early, I had jumped the gun. - *British*

Make it snappy - Hurry up - Bring me that report, and make it snappy. - *British*

P.D.Q. - Abbreviation of pretty damn quick - They rushed the report to the boss P.D.Q. - *British*

Shake a leg - Hurry up - Shake a leg, or we will be late. - *British*

Twenty four seven - All the time - I'm so tired, I've been working twenty four seven. - *British*

Two secs - A short period of time - Hang on, I will be back in two secs. - *British*

Baptism of fire - To be unprepared for a difficult task - On my first day at work, I was asked to man the phones, it was a baptism of fire. - *British*

Bat on a sticky wicket - To be in a difficult situation - Yasmin was batting on a sticky wicket when she turned up late for work. - *British*

Beggars cannot be choosers - A difficult situation with limited options - I don't want to live with him, he is rude and untidy, but beggars cannot be choosers! - *British*

Between a rock and a hard place - To be stuck in a difficult situation, where all options seem unpleasant - If Lewis moves out I can't afford the rent, if he stays we will fight. I'm stuck between a rock and a hard place. - *British*

General

Big deal - A serious situation - It was a big deal when he took my cigarettes. - *America*

Bite the bullet - To engage in a undesirable task - I had to ask Ken to move out, it wasn't going to be pleasant, but I knew I just had to bite the bullet. - *British*

Bite the dust - something that has come to an unwanted end - I was with Sal for a year, but now that has bitten the dust. - *British*

Bitter pill to swallow - An unpleasant fact someone has to accept - It was a bitter pill to swallow when I found out my girlfriend had cheated on me. - *British*

Catch 22 - To be stuck in a no win situation - I don't want to live with him anymore but I can't afford to live alone, so it's a catch 22 situation. - *British*

Cheek by jowl - To survive in difficult circumstances - We were so poor growing up, we lived cheek by jowl. - *America/British*

Clutch at straws - In a hopeless situation - After Dave was diagnosed with cancer, we tried all sorts of treatments but we were just clutching at straws. - *British*

Cornered - A difficult situation - I was cornered by the boss so I had to agree to stay on late. - *British*

In a bind - In a difficult situation - I don't know what to do for the best, I'm in a complete bind. - *British*

In a spot of bother - In trouble - I'm in a spot of bother because I have spent the rent money on booze. - *British*

In limbo - Stuck in a difficult position - I can't get a car until I get a new job, so I'm in limbo, at the moment. - *British*

Keep your chin up - To remain positive in a difficult situation - I know things look bad right now, but keep your chin up and things will improve. - *British*

Keep your head above water - To struggle in a difficult situation - Since I lost my job, I have spent all my savings and it is really hard to keep my head above water. - *British*

Millstone round your neck - A difficult situation - I am in so much debt, it's like a millstone around my neck. - *British*

No win situation - A difficult situation - I'm not sure what to do for the best; it's a no win situation. - *British*

Run the gauntlet - To undertake a challenging task - Jose ran the gauntlet, when he tried to sneak into work late. - *British*

To the bitter end - To stick with a difficult task - She was determined to battle on until the bitter end! - *America/British*

Up against it - A difficult situation - I don't think the report will be finished today, I am really up against it! - *British*

Gay - Sad and uncool - That music is so gay! - *Bristol*

Adam and Eve - Believe - "Would you Adam and Eve it!" said Pru, when describing her friends upset . - *cockney*

Over my head - Too complicated to be understood - I don't understand algebra, it goes way over my head. - *British*

No joy - To be unsuccessful in an endeavour - I had no joy getting a job. - *British*

A doddle - Easy - My new job is a doddle. - *British*

A good egg - A decent person, fun - Sara is a good egg and will have a go at anything you ask her to do. - *British*

A spot of… - A small amount - Please may I have a spot of tomato sauce on my chips? - *British*

Absolutely ghastly - Horrible - The hat she was wearing was absolutely ghastly and did nothing to complement her outfit. - *British*

Absolutions - Prayers of forgiveness - It was the custom for the congregation to go to church on Sunday to get absolution for their sins. - *British*

Balderdash - Nonsense - Paul, you are talking absolute balderdash! - *British*

Bash - Party - We had a massive bash before I left my old job. - *British*

Beastly - Horrible - The new boss is quite beastly. - *British*

Bettah - Better - I'm feeling so much bettah. - *British*

Blimey o'Reilly - Said in surprise - Blimey o' Reilly, I'm late! - *British*

Botheration - Used to express annoyance - Oh botheration, I'm late. - *British*

Bunkum - Nonsense - John, that is bunkum. - *British*

By George! - Used to express shock surprise or dismay - By George, I'm late! - *British*

By Jove! - Used to express shock surprise or dismay - By Jove, I'm late! - *British*

Chap - Man - I met a new chap at work, today. - *British*

Cheerio - Goodbye - I have got to go now, okay, cheerio. - *British*

Chocks away - Let's go. Derived from the 'chocks' used to stabilise the wheels of an aeroplane and taken away just prior to take off - Are you ready for the party? Okay, chocks away! - *British*

Chuffing - A polite curse word - I tripped over the chuffing door step! - *British*

Clevah - Intelligent - I'm rather clevah, don't you know? - *British*

Cloakroom - Toilet - Where is the cloakroom? - *British*

Corking - Excellent - The food was absolutely corking! - *British*

Cretinous - Idiotic or stupid - Simon is so cretinous! - *British*

Cripes - Polite way of saying 'Christ' - Cripes, I'm late. - *British*

Crumbs - Said in surprise. Polite way of saying Christ - Crumbs, I'm late. - *British*

Daarling - A term of affection - Hello, daarling! - *British*

Darn it - Polite way of saying damn it - Darn it, I'm late! - *British*

Dash it - A polite way of saying god damn it. Can be used to express anger, surprise or happiness - Dash it, I'm late. - *British*

Dicky - Feeling unwell or not working properly - My tummy is a bit dicky! - *British*

Drawing room - The lounge or living room - Where is the drawing room? - *British*

Elevenses - A break for refreshments at 11 am - Are we stopping for elevenses? - *British*

Fagged out - Tired or exhausted - I have been gardening, I'm absolutely fagged out! - *British*

Feaahrs - Fears - Being alone is one of my biggest feaahrs, darling. - *British*

Fish hooks - Nonsense - John, you are talking fish hooks! - *British*

For Pete's sake - Used to express annoyance - Oh, for Pete's sake, I'm late again! - *British*

Frightfully - Means terribly or sometimes a lot - I am frightfully sorry, but I cannot come to your party. - *British*

Fudge - Polite way of saying the swear word fuck - Oh fudge, I'm so very late. - *British*

Golly gosh - Used to express shock surprise or dismay - Golly gosh, I'm late. - *British*

Good sport - A decent person. Fun - Oh, I do love Sally, she is such a good sport! - *British*

Goodness gracious me - Said in surprise - Goodness, gracious me, I'm very late. - *British*

Goodness me - Used to express shock surprise or dismay - Goodness me, I'm so late! - *British*

Gordon Bennet - Polite way of saying good god - Gordon Bennet, I'm late! - *British*

Gosh darn it - A polite way of saying god damn it. Can be used to express anger, surprise or happiness - Gosh, darn it, I just stubbed my toe! - *British*

Grotty - Unpleasant - The hospital is so grotty. - *British*

Hang it all - Used to express annoyance - Hang it all, I'm late! - *British*

Hear, hear - I agree - Well said, hear, hear! - *British*

Heavens to Betsy - Said in surprise - Heavens to Betsy, I'm late. - *British*

Higgledy piggledy - Disorganised - I need to tidy up, my office is all higgledy piggledy. - *British*

Home James and don't spare the horses - Let's go quickly - We are very late. Home James, and don't spare the horses! - *British*

How angry-making - What a nuisance - I stubbed my toe, how angry- making is that? - *British*

How irksome - What a nuisance - I'm late, how irksome! - *British*

I say, old chap - Listen to me - I say, old chap, do you have the time? - *British*

I say - Listen to me - I say, where is the lavatory? - *British*

Jeepers - Said in surprise - Jeepers, I'm late! - *British*

Jolly good show - Good - That meal was excellent, jolly good, show! - *British*

Lorks a lordy - Said in surprise - Lorks a lordy, I'm late! - *British*

Lowah class - Working class - Wayne is lowah class. - *British*

Mwah mwah - Kiss - I have to go now, 'mwah mwah'! - *British*

Oh, blow me out - Said in surprise - Oh, blow me out, I'm very late! - *British*

Oh, golly gosh - Said in surprise - Oh, golly gosh, I'm so late! - *British*

Oh, my dizzy aunt - Said in surprise - Oh, my dizzy aunt, I'm late! - *British*

Oh, what a pip - What a shame - Oh, what a pip, you didn't get that job! - *British*

Ok yah? - Ok or hello - Hello John, ok yah? - *British*

Old bean - A term of affection - How are you, old bean? - *British*

Old chap - A term of affection - How are you, old chap? - *British*

One agrees - I agree - One agrees with you. - *British*

One does not agree - I do not agree - One does not agree with you! - *British*

Othah - Other - What othah options do we have? - *British*

Outright wretched - Not good or feeling ill - I feel outright wretched, today. - *British*

Pip pip - Goodbye - I have to go now, pip pip! - *British*

Plebians - Aggressive 'lower class' people - I do not like it in the town centre, it is full of plebians! - *British*

Rathah - Very much or I agree. The emphasis is on drawing the 'ah' sound out in the word - I have had rathah too much to drink. - *British*

Right ho - Okay - Right ho, I had better be off! - *British*

Ruffians - Aggressive 'lower class' people - The town is full of ruffians tonight! - *British*

Rugger - Rugby - I hurt my arm playing rugger last week. - *British*

Simply dashing - Very attractive - That doctor is simply dashing! - *British*

Simply divine - Good - The food was simply divine, darling! - *British*

Simply marvellous - Good - The hotel is simply marvellous! - *British*

Spend a penny - Go to the toilet - I need to spend a penny. - *British*

Spiffing - Good - That meal was spiffing! - *British*

Squiffy - Feeling sick or drunk - I feel a bit squiffy! - *British*

Starkers - Naked - Percy was starkers and paraded around for all to see! - *British*

Steady on old chap - Careful - Steady on old chap, you might hurt yourself. - *British*

Tadjah - Penis - I have a pain in my tadjah, doc. - *British*

Tally ho - Lets go. Associations with horse riding - Tally ho, I have to go to work. - *British*

Teaahrs - Tears - I'm so sad, I'm full of teaahrs. - *British*

Tish and nonsense - Nonsense - Jane, you are talking tish and nonsense. - *British*

General

To fag - Work hard - I need to really fag, if I'm going to make that deadline! - *British*

Toodle ooh - Goodbye - Toodle ooh, I have to go now. - *British*

Toodle pip - Goodbye - Toodle pip, I have to go now. - *British*

Top notch - Excellent - That meal was top notch! - *British*

Trific work chaps - Old fashioned way to say good work - We finished the project just in time, trific work chaps! - *British*

Twickers - Twickenham - I'm going to Twickers at the weekend, to watch the cricket. - *British*

Utter rot - Nonsense - Steve, you are talking utter rot! - *British*

Vulgaar - Disgusting - That food served was vulgaar. - *British*

Well orf - Affluent - We are very well orf. - *British*

What a bother - What a nuisance - I'm late, what a bother! - *British*

Whippersnapper - Young person - I was mugged by a whippersnapper. - *British*

Whoopsie daisy - Said when you have an accident - Whoopsie daisy, I just spilt the tea! - *British*

You utter rotter - You are a bad person - Colin, you utter rotter! - *British*

Piddle - To urinate - I need to have a piddle. - *British*

Waz - Urination - I need a waz. - *British*

Whizz - Urination - I need to go for a whizz. - *British*

Bog - Toilet - I need to use the bog. - *British*

Bogroll - Toilet paper - We have ran out of bogroll. - *British*

Cat and dog - Rhyming slang for bog- the toilet - I need to find the cat and dog. - *cockney*

Loo - Lavatory - Where is the loo? - *British*

On the throne - On the toilet - He is sitting on the throne. - *America/British*

The little boy's/girl's room - Lavatory/ bathroom/ toilet - I need to use the little boy's room. - *British*

Baltic - Very cold - It is baltic outside today. - *British*

Bucketing - Raining - It's been bucketing all day. - *Ireland*

It's raining cats and dogs - Heavy rain - I got so wet, it's raining cats and dogs out there! - *British*

Mizzley - Cold and wet weather - The weather is stormy today, it is mizzley. - *midlands*

Parky - Cold - It's very parky outside, today. - *British*

110 percent - To put in lots of effort - Archibald put in lots of effort working at 110 percent. - *America/British*

All-nighter - To put in lots of effort - I was on an all-nighter and put in lots of effort to get the project finished. - *America/British*

Between jobs - Unemployed - Zoe has been between jobs for three years now. - *British*

Bust (one's) back - To put in lots of effort - I bust my back on that assignment, I deserve a rest now. - *America/British*

Bust (one's) hump - To put in lots of effort - I bust my hump getting that assignment in on time. - *America/British*

Bust a nut - To put in lots of effort - I bust a nut decorating the flat. - *America/British*

Dole - Social security payments - Kim is on the dole. - *British*

Earner - Profitable - I buy and sell things on eBay, it's a nice little earner! - *British*

Fire on all cylinders - To put in lots of effort - We need to fire on all cylinders, if we want to complete this project on time. - *America/British*

Flog - To over work - The new boss was determined to flog us until bedtime! - *British*

Go all out - To put in lots of effort - I will have to go all out, if I want to pass the exam. - *America/British*

Go the whole hog - To do something to the fullest - When we have a party we go the whole hog. - *British*

Go to town - To do a task meticulously - We intend to really go to town on the new project. - *British*

General

Graft - To work hard - You will have to graft if you want to pass the exam. - *British*

Keener - Someone who works hard and shows great enthusiasm - I can't be bothered to work too hard, not like Mike, he is such a keener! - *Bristol*

Keep (one's) nose to the grindstone - To put in lots of effort - If I want to get promoted, I will have to work really hard, and keep my nose to the grindstone. - *America/British*

Knuckle down - Work hard - You are so lazy, you need to knuckle down and get some work done. - *British*

Nose to the grindstone - Working very hard - I'm so tired, I've had my nose to the grindstone all day. - *Australian*

On the dole - To claim social security benefits - I was on the dole for a long time. - *British*

Piece of cake - An easy task - He finished his job early, it was a piece of cake. - *British*

Piss easy - An easy task - The job was piss easy. - *British*

Rule with a velvet glove - A kind encouraging boss - The boss is very relaxed, she likes to rule with a velvet glove. - *America/British*

Sacked - To have employment terminated - She got the sack after repeatedly turning up late. - *British*

Slave driver - A cruel and unfeeling boss - I hate the new boss, he is such a slave driver. - *America/British*

Slog your guts out - To work hard - You will have to slog your guts out, if you want to finish that report by lunchtime. - *British*

Snowed under - Extremely busy - The boss keeps increasing my workload, I'm completely snowed under. - *America*

Carry the can - To take responsibility for a mistake - I'm a bit worried that I might have to carry the can if the project fails. - *British*

Cheek - Disrespectful - The young lad gave me some cheek. - *Ireland*

Come clean - To admit your own wrong doings - The other driver knew he had caused the accident, so he decided to come clean and tell the truth. - *British*

Cover your tracks - To hide incriminating information in order to evade detection - Keith didn't want to get caught with stolen goods, so he made sure to cover his tracks. - *British*

Fall from grace - To lose your good reputation - It was a fall from grace when the mayor was charged with fraud. - *British*

Foul play - Corrupt or underhand tactics - I went for promotion, but it seems like foul play because the bosses' son got the job. - *British*

In the doghouse - To be in trouble - Karim is in the doghouse because he was late for work. - *British*

It was done under the table - In an underhand way, not by the rules - They cheated me out of that job; it had already been given to John under the table. - *Australian*

Just deserts - A fair reward or punishment for your deeds - If he carries on being rude, he will get his just deserts. - *British*

Red herring - Duped or misled - The instructions suggested making a left turn, but that was a complete red herring. - *British*

Rumbled - To be caught out doing something wrong - He got rumbled when he arrived at work late. - *British*

Shit hits the fan - Bad consequences - The shit will hit the fan when the boss finds out that James is late again! - *British*

Swizz - Swindle - The lottery is a swizz, you never win! - *British*

Taken to the cleaners - To be swindled - I was taken to the cleaners by that con man. - *British*

Busted - Caught doing something wrong - I got busted smoking in the toilets. - *British*

General

Health/illness

'Zonked'
Tired and worn-out

Kick the habit - Break or stop a habit that has potential to cause health issues, e. g smoking or drinking alcohol - The doctor said I should stop smoking, but I don't think I can kick the habit. - *British*

Meat wagon - An ambulance - Linda had a nasty fall, so we called a meat wagon. - *British*

A bundle of nerves - Very anxious person - Caroline was a bundle of nerves when taking her driving test. - *British*

Break out into a cold sweat - To perspire either from nervousness, anxiety or a fever - When the police arrived at the front door, Jimmy broke out into a cold sweat. - *British*

Draw blood - To make someone bleed, perhaps through a scratch or bite. Doctors need to draw blood to test it - The dog bite drew blood. - *British*

Bag of bones - Very thin - Fred had lost a lot of weight, he was a bag of bones. - *British*

Black eye - To get a bruised or blackened eye after being hit in or around the eye socket - Roger had a black eye. - *British*

Dedun - Corpse - "I think he's a dedun," said the paramedic. - *Bristol*

Dicky ticker - Heart problems - Alex has heart problems, he has a dicky ticker. - *British*

Front passage - This phrase can be used to mean the urinary tract - "I've got a problem with my front passage, Doc." said Max. - *British*

It's all gone South - Things are not going well and will probably just get worse still; changes noticed as part of the aging process. For example, sagging breasts - It's all gone South since I hit fifty! - *Australian*

Nothing but skin and bone - Very thin, underweight possibly even emaciated. can be used ironically, depends on context - Kyle has lost a lot of weight, he is nothing but skin and bone now. - *British*

Pins and needles - Tingling and numbness in limbs - "I've got pins and needles in my leg," said Steph - *British*

Spit - To eject saliva from the mouth by force - The patient was told to spit the blood from her mouth into a cup. - *British*

The old ticker - Heart - The old ticker has given me palpitations all day, today. - *British*

Ticker - Heart - My ticker is on its way out. - *British*

To spit up something - To eject something from the mouth, saliva, phlegm etc. - The patient was told to spit something up from her mouth into a cup. - *British*

In remission - A disease, such as cancer, that seems to be getting better - Justin was pleased to hear that he was now in remission. - *British*

Give birth - To have a baby - My wife gave birth to our first baby yesterday. - *British*

In labour - The time when a women is giving birth - Catherine was in labour for about 12 hours and was very tired now. - *British*

Quit smoking - Stop smoking - Elsie had tried many times before to quit smoking but this was the only time she had managed it for the whole week. - *British*

Rollies - Roll your own cigarettes - "Fancy a rollie?" said Jim. - *British*

Tailors - Make of cigarette - "A packet of Tailors, please." said the teenager. - *Australian*

At peace - Dead - Molly died last night. She was really struggling but she is at peace now. - *British*

At rest - Dead - Diane was very poorly and died during the night. She is at rest now. - *British*

Be fender meat - Related to death or dying - Pete is fender meat. - *America/British*

Beyond the grave - After life - I often wonder if anything happens beyond the grave? - *British*

Beyond the veil - After life - We will never see beyond the veil. - *British*

Bite it - Related to death or dying - People are said to bite it when they die. - *America/British*

Bite the big one - Related to death or dying - Bite the big one, means to die. - *America/British*

Bite the dust - To die - I'm not well, I worry I might bite the dust. - *British*

Buy the farm - To die - If you carry on smoking, you are going to buy the farm. - *British*

Cash in (one's) chips - Related to death or dying - Peter, you will cash in your chips, if you keep smoking. - *America/British*

Check out - Related to death or dying - Pedro, you will check out if you keep smoking. - *America/British*

Croak - To die - If you don't lose weight, you are going to croak! - *British*

Dirt nap - Related to death or dying - Pam has gone for a dirt nap! - *America/British*

Done for - Dying - Paul had cancer, he was done for. - *British*

Doornail - Dead - Danny was as dead as a doornail. - *Australian*

Drop dead - To insult someone by telling them to die - Drop dead, Richard. - *British*

Drop like flies - Related to death or dying - The plague was doing the rounds and people were dropping like flies. - *America/British*

Expire - To die - I have to get more healthy or I might expire. - *British*

Final curtain - Dying/ dead - It's time to face the final curtain. - *British*

Floater - A corpse - Kenneth was a floater, he was found in the river last night. - *America/British*

Go belly up - Related to death or dying - Karen, you will go belly up if you keep smoking. - *America/British*

Goner - Dead - Clair had terminal cancer, she was a goner. - *British*

Kick the bucket - Dead - Steve kicked the bucket last night. - *British*

Maggot food - Dead - Alex is maggot food. - *British*

Not with us anymore - Dead - Grandad is not with us anymore. - *British*

On one's deathbed - Dying - It was sad to see grandad on his death bed. - *British*

On one's last legs - Dying - Frank has cancer, he is on his last legs. - *British*

One foot in the grave - Near to death/ elderly - Sybil was very frail, it seemed like she already had one foot in the grave. - *British*

Pass away - To die - Derek could pass away at any moment. - *British*

Pass on - To die - Una might pass on today. *- British*

Passed away - Dead - Lionel passed away last night. *- British*

Peg it - To die - Oliver pegged it last night. *- British*

Pine overcoat - Coffin - Helen is going to get a pine overcoat. *- British*

Pop one's clogs - To die - Alice popped her clogs last week. *- British*

Pushing up the daisies - Dead - She is now pushing up the daisies. *- British*

RIP - Rest in peace - It was sad to hear about Linda, RIP. *- British*

Roadkill - A corpse - Doug was roadkill, he got hit by a truck. *- America/British*

Screw the pooch - Related to death or dying - Yameen, you will screw the pooch, if you keep smoking. *- America/British*

Six feet under - Dead - Gavin is six feet under. *- British*

Snuff - Kill - Karen, you will snuff it, if you don't lose weight. *- British*

Snuffed it - Died - Clive snuffed it last night. *- British*

Snuffed out - Killed - Kevin got snuffed out during the fight. *- British*

Stiff - Dead - Ken is a stiff. *- British*

Take a dirt nap - Related to death or dying - Rick, you will take a dirt nap if you don't lose weight. *- America/British*

The Grim Reaper - Personification of death as a person - Look out or the Grim Reaper will catch you! *- British*

To be about to croak it - Gravely ill and likely to die - Adam is about to croak it, I think. *- British*

To be at Death's door - Gravely ill and likely to die - Eddie was at Death's door. *- British*

To be beyond help - 1. Gravely ill and likely to die or 2. Someone who has gone so far with an addiction or problem that no matter how much help they've had or still might be offered it's too late - Sadly, the man was beyond help due to the extent of his injuries. *- British*

To be living on borrowed time - Gravely ill and likely to die - Sue was living on borrowed time after being diagnosed as terminally ill with cancer. *- British*

To be near the end - Gravely ill and likely to die - "I'm sorry to tell you that Grayson is near the end," said the doctor. *- British*

To be on one's last legs - Gravely ill and likely to die - Robert was on his last legs. *- British*

To be struck down - To die - Fred was struck down last year. *- British*

To be wasting away - 1. Used ironically when someone is hungry. 2. Used to describe a gravely ill person who is becoming frail and fragile and will possibly die - Sally was wasting away due to the lack of nutritious food in her diet. *- British*

To be with god - To die - Frida is with god now. *- British*

To be with the lord - To die - Zoe is with the lord now. *- British*

To breathe one's last breath - To die - Jack breathed his last breath yesterday. *- British*

To cash in one's chips - To die - Keith cashed his chips in last year. *- British*

To come to a sticky end - To die in unfortunate circumstances - Clive came to a sticky end in a car accident. *- British*

To croak it - To die - Rob, you will croak it if you carry on drinking. *- British*

To depart this life - To die - Irene has terminal cancer and will depart this life soon. *- British*

To die a natural death - To die of old age or natural causes, as opposed to accident or violence - The coroner reported that the homeless man had died of natural causes. *- British*

To fade away - To die slowly becoming more fragile with time - Jill was very weak and slowly began to fade away. *- British*

To fall off one's perch - To die - Terry fell off his perch last year. *- British*

Health/illness

To give up the ghost - To die - Gary gave up the ghost last year. - *British*

To go for Burton - Die or be broken beyond repair - Nick went for a Burton. - *British*

To go home in a box - Die, for example in hospital, or on the battlefield, or on holiday - Sadly the soldier came home in a box. - *British*

To go out with one's boots on - To die suddenly but doing something one enjoyed - Jim was having sex when he died. At least he went out with his boots on! - *British*

To go west - To die - Freddy went west last year. - *British*

To keel over - To die - Alan was fine one minute, then he suddenly keeled over. - *British*

To lose one's life - To die - Zara lost her life last year. - *British*

To shuffle off this mortal coil - To die - Walter shuffled off this mortal coil last week. - *British*

To take one's own life - To commit suicide - Sadly, Dave took his own life. - *British*

To turn up one's toes - To die - Rachel turned her toes up last month. - *British*

Ate up - To feel unwell - "I'm feeling completely ate up," said Estelle. - *American*

Rub salt in the wound - Be deliberately unkind to or worsen a situation for someone already suffering - On top of everything else, Valerie rubbed salt into the wound by saying she didn't love me anymore. - *British*

Check up - A medical examination - Kyle wasn't feeling well, so he booked a check up with the Doctor. - *British*

Get a check up - A physical examination by a doctor - Jamie needed to get a check up at the Doctors after finding a lump in his testicle. - *British*

Given a clean bill of health - A discussion or report that confirms a person (animal/ car/ other object) is healthy - Jeremy was given a clean bill of health by the Doctor. - *British*

Quack - Doctor - I need to make an appointment to see a quack as soon as possible. - *British*

Run some tests - To do a thorough check up - The doctor told Jodie that he needed to run some tests to see why she was so tired all of the time. - *British*

Show signs of … - Indication or hints there is an illness present that may need further investigation - The doctor told Henry that he was showing signs of sugar in his urine and this would need further examination. - *British*

Take someone's pulse - To measure the number of beats of a person's pulse rate - The nurse needed to take David's pulse to check how high it was. - *British*

To take someone's temperature - To measure body temperature using a thermometer - The nurse needed to take Maureen's temperature to check how high it was. - *British*

Trouble down there - A problem with the genitals - I've got a problem down there, Doc. - *British*

Delhi belly - A severe stomach upset - I ate something dodgy and now I've got Delhi belly! - *British*

I've got the shits - Vulgar way of describing diarrhoea - I've got the shits today after that spicy chicken. - *British*

Montezuma's revenge - Diarrhoea after spicy food - Justine had a bad case of Montezuma's revenge after eating a very spicy curry. - *British*

Number twos - Faeces- mostly used by small children - I need a number two. - *British*

Poo - Excrement - I need to have a poo. - *British*

Squits - Diarrhoea - I had squits on holiday. - *British*

The runs - Diarrhoea - I had the runs on holiday. - *British*

The trots - Diarrhoea - I had the trots on holiday. - *British*

Runs in the family - To have common characteristics in a family - Asthma runs in the family. - *British*

Woke up with a sore head - A headache hangover due to consuming too much alcohol - Margy woke up with a sore head after the party. - *British*

A flare up - An illness has begun again suddenly - The doctor decided that the patient was suffering from a flare up of a previous illness. - *British*

As pale as a ghost - Extremely pale and looking unwell - The little boy was as pale as a ghost. - *British*

As pale as death - Extremely pale and looking unwell - The woman was as pale as death and looked like she had seen a ghost. - *British*

Blah - To feel unwell - "I feel blah, today." said Alistair. - *American*

Bleugh - To feel unwell - I feel bleugh! - *British*

Break out - To break out in something such as spots, a rash or skin disorder - Eileen had a break out of spots, all over her back. - *British*

Burnt out - To feel unwell, fatigued and generally unable to do anything - Ian had had enough, he couldn't carry on, he was burnt out. - *British*

Catch a cold - To get a cold - "Be careful you don't catch a cold." said Granny. - *British*

Catch your death - To get ill, usually as a result of not looking after yourself properly - Some people say... if you don't wear a coat in winter, you will catch your death. - *British*

Could be better - Implies not totally well in health - I'm not feeling great, I could be better. - *British*

Crook - Feeling unwell - I feel a bit crook. - *Australian*

Crunchy - To feel unwell - "I feel crunchy today." said Grace. - *American*

Eppy fit - Abbreviation for epilepsy - The flashing lights caused Caroline to have an eppy fit. - *British*

Foot and mouth - An illness - Daisy and Dexter both caught foot and mouth from nursery school. - *British*

Foul - Feeling sick - I feel foul. - *British*

Gammy - Inability to function normally due to chronic pain or injury. Example, to have a gammy leg from the war - After the First World War, Granger was left with a gammy leg. - *British*

Get over (something) - To get better/improve from an illness, recover from a shock or disappointment - John had a nasty fall, it will take him a long time to get over it. - *British*

Get sick - Become ill - I always get sick when I travel abroad. - *British*

Get well - To become fit and healthy again - Everyone at the office hoped Coralie would get well soon, and be able to come back to work. - *British*

Gone downhill - Got worse - May has gone downhill lately. - *British*

Green around the gills - Feeling unwell or sick, causing skin pallor changes - Millie felt a bit green around the gills. - *British*

Gut rot - Stomach ache - I have gut rot. - *British*

Gyp - In pain or discomfort - My back is giving me gyp. - *British*

Housemaid's knee - Joint pain and inflammation of kneecap often due to excessive kneeling - Jane has an inflamed knee joint and her doctor thinks that it might be housemaid's knee. - *British*

Iffy - Feeling doubtful or uncertain. For example, my stomach feels a bit iffy today, I hope I'm not sick! - I feel iffy, I think I need to see a Doctor. - *British*

Ill - Malady - I feel really ill. - *British*

Itchy bits - Itchy genitals - I've got right itchy bits, today! - *British*

Jacked up - To feel unwell, perhaps after over indulging in drugs/ alcohol - Fred was jacked up and felt very unwell. - *American*

Look like death warmed up - To appear very ill - Ian looked like death warmed up. - *British*

Lousy - Feel unwell - I feel lousy. - *British*

Lurgey - An illness - Miranda has got the lurgey. - *Australian*

Lurgie - An illness - Margaret has got the lurgie. - *British*

Lurgy - Slang term for an illness, perhaps a contagious one - Andrew has got the lurgy. - *British*

Off - Feeling unwell - I feel really off today. - *British*

Off colour - Feeling unwell - I'm a bit off colour. - *British*

Off sick - Taken time off of work because of illness - Alan hurt his back so he is now off sick. - *British*

Out of sorts - Feeling unwell and in a bad/grumpy/ weird mood - I'm not well, I'm out of sorts. - *British*

Pale around the gills - To look ill - You look really pale around the gills, are you okay? - *British*

Poorly - Malady - I feel really poorly. - *British*

Putrid - Feeling sick - I feel putrid. - *British*

Ropey - To feel unwell - I feel ropey. - *British*

Rough - To feel unwell - I feel rough. - *British*

Run a fever/ temperature - To have a high temperature and be unwell - I am feeling sick and running a high temperature. - *British*

Run down - To be in poor physical condition - I feel run down. - *British*

Seedy - Unwell - I feel quite seedy today. - *British*

Sick - Generic term for being ill or to vomit - I feel sick. - *British*

Sick as a dog - Metaphor used to add emphasis to how very ill one feels - I've been as sick as a dog all night. - *British*

Sick day - Taking time off of work because of illness - Julian needed to take a sick day to recover from the sore throat he had got on holiday. - *British*

Sick in bed - To feel so ill you are unable to get out of bed - I was sick in bed all day, not able to move. - *British*

Sickness benefits - Monies paid to cover time off work when ill - I've been told that I qualify for sickness benefit because I have been ill for so long now. - *British*

Slipped disc - Spinal problems in back - Karen has a slipped disc and it is really painful for her. - *British*

So-so - Way of describing how you are feeling -okay but could be better - I'm feeling so-so today, could be better. - *British*

Stiff as a board - Aching or stiffness in the muscles - After all of that digging at the allotment, I'm as stiff as a board. - *British*

Stuffed up - Injured oneself or messed up a situation, depends on context - Over the years Steve has played a lot of football and this has stuffed his knees up. - *British*

Take a turn for the worse - To begin to decline in health and condition - Sara's health took a turn for the worse. - *British*

Take sick - To become ill with something - Coralie took sick after eating some dodgy prawns last night. - *British*

To be riddled with… - The illness has taken over the body, like wood is riddled with woodworm when it is infected and bad - Paul is absolutely riddled with cancer, it sadly seems. - *British*

To be susceptible to something - To get/ pick up a particular illness easily. e.g., I was susceptible to colds - Daisy is susceptible to colds, especially during the winter months. - *British*

To be susceptible to something - To get/ pick up a particular illness easily. e.g., I was susceptible to colds - Jackie was susceptible to coughs and chest infections. - *British*

To catch one's death from cold - To be very ill with cold/ flu like symptoms - "Come in out of the cold air, you'll catch your death!" said Dad. - *British*

To come down with… - To become ill with something - Karen had come down with a temperature during the day. - *British*

To fall ill - To become ill with something - Lucy had fallen ill during the night. - *British*

To feel broken - To feel unwell, particularly after a heavy session of drinking or drugs - I feel completely broken. - *British*

To feel under the weather - To feel generally unwell - I feel really under the weather today. - *British*

To get sick - To become ill with something - Dave got sick over the weekend and couldn't go to work. - *British*

To pick up a cold - To acquire a cold - I think I picked up a cold last Thursday, on the train home after work. - *British*

Tom and Dick - Rhyming slang for sick, not feeling well - I feel a bit Tom and Dick. - *British*

Tummy ache - Stomach pain - The child had tummy ache and cried all night long. - *British*

Under the weather - A little bit ill - I feel under the weather. - *British*

Unwell - Malady - I feel really unwell. - *British*

Wog: I've had a wog, I've got a wog - A minor illness - "It's just a wog," said the passenger on the bus. - *Australian*

Wonky - Unwell, dizzy - I feel all wonky today. - *Australian*

Woozy - Unwell, dizzy, lightheaded - I feel woozy. - *British*

Lapse into a coma - Go into a coma - Poor bloke lapsed into a coma, and subsequently died. - *British*

To be in a bad way - Gravely ill and likely to die - Jeremy was in a bad way after the car crash. - *British*

Over the worst - Recovering from an illness and improving - I have had a terrible sickness bug, but I'm over the worst now. - *British*

Pull through - Recover from a serious illness, possibly having been close to death - Dylan managed to pull through after suffering a heart attack. - *British*

Take a turn for the better - To begin to improve in health and condition - Jack's health took a turn for the better. - *British*

To be back on one's feet - Used after someone has been ill to imply they are no longer bed bound, but able to stand and move again - I'm back on my feet now after having major surgery on my back. - *British*

To be given a new lease of life - To be given a second chance - Toby was given a new lease of life after his kidney transplant. - *British*

To be nursed back to health - To give someone lots of medical care in order to restore them to fitness - Dexter had to be nursed back to health after a nasty fall. - *British*

To be on the mend - To be getting better, improving in condition - Alice was on the mend now after a nasty cold. - *British*

To bring someone round - To revive someone, restore someone to health or consciousness - The paramedic was able to bring the man around after he had fallen and bumped his head . - *British*

To get something out of your system - To lessen the desire for doing something - I've had a sore throat for over a week now, I'm hoping it will soon be out of my system. - *British*

Up and about - Feeling better so able to get out of bed and move around - Les is up and about now, he is much better than he was last week. - *British*

To be found without a scratch on.. - To survive an accident unmarked - There wasn't a scratch on Ben after the car crash, it's an absolute miracle. - *British*

Throw a sickie - Take a day off work with a pretend illness - Susan didn't want to go to work, so she decided to throw a sickie. - *British*

Throw a sicky - To avoid work by feigning illness - Jill didn't want to go to work so she decided to throw a sicky. - *British*

Fill in a prescription - A request from the doctor to collect some medicine from the pharmacy/ drug store - "Please fill in the back of your prescription," said the receptionist. - *British*

Take one's medicine - To administer medicine orally - Mary had to take her medicine regularly to be pain free. - *British*

Going through the change - Menopause - She is going through the change. - *British*

Got the painters in - Menstruation - Lynda has the painters in and is being so moody. - *British*

Monthlies - Menstruation - Lynda has her monthlies. - *Australian*

On the blob - Menstruation - My wife is on the blob. - *British*

Period - Menstruation - Jackie's periods were really regular. - *British*

Rags - Vulgar term to describe menstruation - Have you got the rags on? - *Australian*

Red flag is flying - Menstruation - Catherine's red flag is flying this week. - *Australian*

Time of the month - Euphemism for the female menstrual cycle - It was Angela's time of the month and she was very tired. - *British*

Visitor - Menstruation - Catherine has a visitor in this week. - *Australian*

A couch doctor - A psychiatrist or psychoanalyst who requires a patient to lie on a couch during their appointment - Gerald was off to see his psychiatrist, known as his couch doctor because he made his patients lie on a couch. - *British*

A vegetable - Vulgar term- implies a person has such severe physical and/ or intellectual difficulties they are unable to communicate with the world - The brain injury that he sustained in the accident, had left Richard a vegetable with severe intellectual disability. - *British*

Breakdown - A nervous episode where someone cannot control their emotions - Barbara was so stressed out, she had a breakdown. - *British*

Spanner - Insulting term used to describe someone with low intelligence - Tony is a right spanner! - *British*

Spazzer - Insulting term used to describe someone with severe physical or intellectual disability - Tony is a right spazzer! - *British*

Tard - Insulting term used to describe someone with severe physical or intellectual disability - Tony is a right tard! - *Australian*

Veggie - Vulgar term- implies a person has such severe physical and/ or intellectual difficulties they are unable to communicate with the world - "He's such a veggie," taunted the nasty boy. - *Australian*

Fat as a pig - Simile to describe being obese/ overweight. Derogatory - Kenneth is as fat as a pig, he needs to go on a diet! - *British*

Fatso - Derogatory term to describe obese or overweight person - Jamie is a fatso. - *British*

Jubba - Insulting term for an overweight person - Look at that jubba over there, he's enormous. - *Australian*

Podgy - Overweight - Martha is quite podgy. - *British*

Porker - Derogatory term for an obese or overweight person - Corrine is a porker. - *British*

Tub of lard - Insulting term for an overweight person - Jade is a tub of lard. - *British*

Tubby - Insulting term for an overweight person - Kayden is tubby. - *British*

Tubs - Insulting term for an overweight person - Alright tubs! - *British*

A frog in my throat - A sore throat and croaky voice - I woke up with a frog in my throat today, it's really sore and my voice is all croaky. - *British*

Black and blue - Bruises, possible from physical harm - John had fallen badly, his face was black and blue. - *British*

216

Crick - A sore neck - Carl cricked his neck whilst decorating the house. - *British*

Crick in one's neck - A bone out of place in the neck - Neil had a crick in his neck. - *British*

Get a charley horse - Cramp in the arm or leg - I keep getting a charley horse in my arm. - *British*

I've put my back out - A sore back - I put my back out lifting the kids into the car this morning. - *British*

Jip - Painful - My back is causing me jip. - *British*

Kink in one's neck - A cramp causing pain in the neck - I've got a kink in one's neck. - *British*

Me 'eds erting - Head hurting - "Me 'eds erting ," said Francis. - *Bristol*

My back is in half - Back pain - My back is in half after too much gardening at the weekend. - *British*

Splitting head - Headache - I've got a splitting head after my shift at school. - *British*

Splitting headache - Severe painful headache - I've got a splitting headache so won't be coming out tonight after all. - *British*

Tennis elbow - Inflammation of the tendons in the elbow joint - Jane has a painful joint and her doctor thinks it might be tennis elbow. - *British*

To be old and decrepit - Aged person - I feel quite old and decrepit today. - *British*

Black out - To lose consciousness - James couldn't remember what had happened, he had had a blackout. - *British*

Out cold - Unconscious but breathing - John hit his head when he fell over, he was out cold. - *British*

Out of it - To appear spaced out or unwell after taking drugs or alcohol, or if delirious with a high temperature - Darren had been drinking all night, he was out of it. - *British*

Pass out - To faint - I need to sit down, I feel like I'm going to pass out. - *British*

Bound up - Constipated - "I'm all bound up, Doc, can you prescribe me some laxatives, please?" - *British*

In the club - Pregnant - My wife is in the club. - *British*

In the family way - Pregnant - My wife is in the family way. - *British*

Knocked up - Pregnant - My sister got knocked up. - *British*

Preggars - Pregnant - My partner is preggars. - *British*

Up the spout - Pregnant - My wife is up the spout. - *British*

With child - Pregnant - My wife is with child and I'm so excited. - *British*

Meds - Short for medication - Kay needed her meds. - *British*

On medication - Taking prescribed medication for specific medical conditions - Chris was on medication for her migraine headaches. - *British*

Take it easy - Go carefully and try to rest - The doctor told Justin to take it easy after his operation. - *British*

An ounce of prevention is worth a pound of cure - It is better to try to prevent something bad happening than deal with the consequences afterwards - Try to use caution when approaching the task because, an ounce of prevention is worth a pound of cure. - *British*

Can't hold (their) drink - Inability to drink a few drinks socially without becoming drunk or ill - He just can't hold his drink. - *British*

Chuck a sickie - Take a day off work with a pretend illness - Bartholomew didn't want to go to work, so he decided to chuck a sickie. - *Australian*

Until one's dying day - To do something worthwhile whilst still alive - I won't give up on my dreams until my dying day. - *British*

A rabbit - A sex toy/ vibrator - Sally owned a rabbit to pleasure herself when her partner was away on business. - *British*

Health/illness

Rabbits - Derogatory way to describe sex, 'they were at it like rabbits' or prolific breeding, 'they had children like rabbits' - The young couple were at it like rabbits when they were first married. - *British*

Rooted - Depending on context can infer having had sex - Jo had just finished rooting Demi when the phone rang. - *Australian*

Sprog - Semen - After having sex, there was sprog on the bed clothes. - *Australian*

Clap - Gonorrhoea - Joe was promiscuous and got the clap. - *British*

The clap - Venereal disease- gonorrhoea - Nick had the clap and had to get special treatment for it from the Sexual Health Clinic. - *British*

I haven't slept a wink - I have had no sleep - Jodie hadn't slept a wink all night. - *British*

In surgery - Undergoing an operation - They are in surgery now, said the nurse to the concerned relatives. - *British*

To go under the knife - To have an operation or surgery - "I'm going under the knife to have a heart bypass operation." said Barry. - *British*

Carked it - To die - "Babe has carked it," said the Vicar. - *Australian*

Blitzed - Tired - I'm absolutely blitzed. - *British*

Burn out - To work too hard causing someone to become extremely fatigued and ill - Mary suffered burn out after having years of stress and overwork. - *British*

Bushed - Tired out - John had worked for three weeks without a rest, he was bushed. - *Australian*

Dead beat - Tired out - Lois was dead beat after such a long day at school. - *British*

Done in - Tired out - I'm very tired, I feel done in. - *British*

Done like a dog's dinner - Tired out - I'm done like a dog's dinner, tonight! - *Australian*

Drained - Tired - I feel drained, I need a rest. - *British*

Fagged out - Tired - Robert was fagged out so he had a rest. - *British*

Flake out - To collapse in exhaustion - I'm so tired, I might flake out in a minute. - *British*

Knackered - Exhausted - I haven't slept, I'm knackered. - *British*

Rooted - Tired out - I'm absolutely rooted, tonight. - *Australian*

Tuckered out - Old fashioned way to say you're tired - I am tuckered out. - *Australian*

Wiped out - Exhausted - I am wiped out. - *British*

Worn out - Tired - I am worn out. - *British*

Zonked - Tired or worn out - I'm completely zonked out. - *British*

Barf - To vomit - "I feel sick, I think I'm going to barf," said Nigel. - *American*

Couch potato - A person who is lazy and does not move far from laying on the sofa watching TV - Miriam is a couch potato. - *British*

Out of condition - Unfit - The old man was out of condition, he realised, as he struggled up the hill. - *British*

Out of shape - Unfit - Andrew is out of shape. - *British*

Number ones - Urine- mostly used by small children - I need a number one. - *British*

Pass water - Old fashioned phrase to describe urinating - I need to pass water, where's the toilet please? - *British*

Pee - Urine - I need a pee. - *British*

Piss - Urine - I need to have a piss. - *British*

Powder my nose - Polite but old fashioned way to imply a woman is going to use the bathroom to urinate - I need to powder my nose. - *British*

Waterworks - Urinary issues - My wife has a problem with her waterworks. - *British*

Wee - Urine - I need a wee. - *British*

Wee wee - Urine- mostly used by small children - Do you need a wee wee? - *British*

Poxy - Derived from pox as in viral disease but in this instance meaning of poor quality and worthless - The portion sizes in the restaurant were quite poxy! - *British*

Chuck up - To vomit - I feel sick, I think I might chuck up. - *British*

Chunder - To vomit - I am going to chunder! - *Australian*

Chundered - To vomit - Christopher was very ill last night and he chundered. - *British*

Dicky - Not strong or healthy. Sometimes used with 'heart' or 'stomach' etc to indicate issues with specific organs - I have a dicky stomach. - *British*

Hurl - To vomit - I feel sick, I think I'm going to hurl. - *British*

Painting the pavement - To vomit - He vomited so hard, he painted the whole pavement. - *British*

Painting the toilet - To vomit - He vomited so hard, he painted the whole toilet. - *British*

Puke - Vomit - "I feel sick, I think I'm going to puke," said Charlotte. - *British*

Pukey - To feel sick - I feel pukey. - *British*

Shit-canned - Drunk and vomiting in rubbish bin/ trash - David was so drunk he ended up shit-canning on the way home - *America*

Speaking Welsh - To vomit - Danny spoke Welsh all night, last night, after drinking too much alcohol. - *British*

Spew - To vomit - I feel sick, I think I'm going to spew. - *British*

Spew ones guts up - To vomit - I drank too much, then I spewed my guts up. - *British*

Spewed - Vomit - "Sorry, I've spewed all over your carpet," said Stuart. - *British*

Technicolour yawn - Vomit - Noreen did a technicolour yawn all over the floor. - *British*

Throw up - Vomit - I think I'm going to throw up. - *British*

Throwing up - Vomit - I was throwing up all night, last night. - *British*

To hurl - Vomit - "I think I am going to hurl!" said Alistair - *Australian*

Vom - Vomit - I think I might vom. - *British*

Yack - To be physically sick - I am going to yack. - *British*

Yack up - To vomit - I ate a massive bowl of chilli and then yacked it all up. - *British*

Alive and kicking - To be well and healthy, often used when someone is elderly - Martha was 100 years old but still alive and kicking. - *British*

Alive and well - To be well and healthy, often used when someone is elderly - The woman was still alive and well, although of a great age now. - *British*

As fit as a fiddle - In good health - The elderly man was as fit as a fiddle. - *British*

Fair to middling - Old fashioned way to say you're okay but not perfect - "I'm fair to middling, thanks for asking." said Kayleigh. - *British*

Feel fit - To feel well and healthy - I feel really fit. - *British*

Fit as a fiddle - Phrase used to describe health condition - Katie is as fit as a fiddle. - *British*

In good shape - Fit and healthy - The doctor said I was in good shape. - *British*

In the best of health - Fit and healthy - For his age, Eric was in the best of health. - *British*

In the pink - Fit and healthy - I feel great, I'm in the pink. - *British*

Look a picture of health - Look fit and healthy - You look really well, a right picture of health. - *British*

On the mend - Improving in health and fitness after an illness, injury or surgery - Tom had had a nasty fall, but he is on the mend now. - *British*

Picture of health - Fit and healthy - Jemma was a picture of health after her holiday. - *British*

Tip-top - Term used to describe being in good health, quite old fashioned - I feel quite tip-top today. - *British*

Health/illness

To be (in) a picture of health - To be in good health - Leighton was a picture of good health. - *British*

To be in the pink - To be in good health - She was in the pink. - *British*

To feel on top of the world - Extremely well - Sandra felt on top of the world today. - *British*

Medical

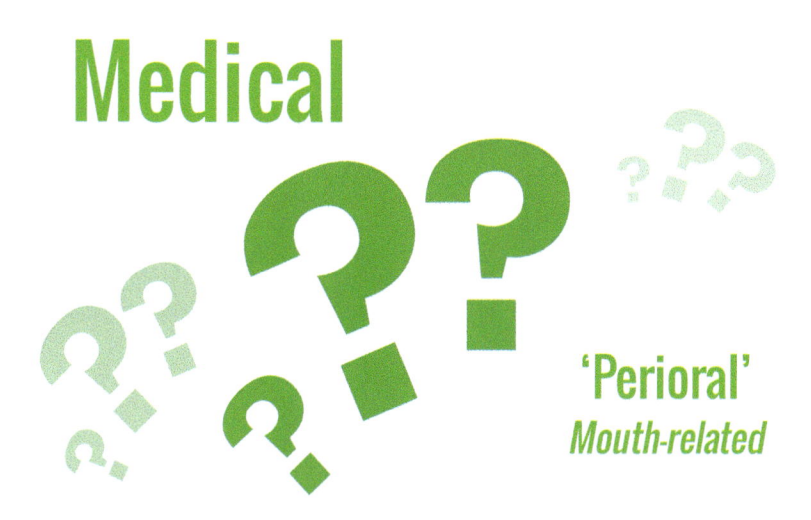

'Perioral'
Mouth-related

Abrupt - Sudden - The speech was a bit abrupt, short and ended quickly. - *British*

Acuity - Sharpness - He was thought of as someone with acuity and very bright. - *British*

Acute - Severe - "The situation is very acute and calls for emergency action," said the boss. - *British*

Analogous - Similar - One diet pill is analogous with another. - *British*

Antecedent - Forerunner - The book was the antecedent to several more which would follow. - *British*

Atypical - Unusual - The spots were atypical in that sort of illness. - *British*

Conservative - Not extreme - She thought her ideas were conservative. - *British*

Depletion - Removal - The medical supplies were subject to depletion. - *British*

Abstinence - Going without - Diane had decided to be abstinent and not drink alcohol until at least Christmas. - *British*

Allergen - Substance causing allergy - The grass pollen was an allergen and causing her to sneeze. - *British*

Anaphylactic - Severe allergic response-related - The child had eaten peanuts and this had produced an anaphylactic reaction. - *British*

Atopic - Allergic reaction - He was very ill, and had an atopic reaction to the peanuts. - *British*

Cross allergy - Multi-allergy - "She has cross allergy and will need careful medication," said the nurse. - *British*

Musophobia - Fear of mice - The fear of mice is: musophobia. - *British*

Ophidiophobia - Fear of snakes - After the incident at the zoo, Yameen was diagnosed with ophidiophobia. - *British*

Ornithophobia - Fear of birds - Some people are really fearful of birds. This is called, ornithophobia. - *British*

Parasitophobia - Fear of parasites - Zena has parasitophobia. - *British*

Pediculophobia - Fear of lice - The teacher had a fear of lice: pediculophobia. - *British*

Batrachophobia - Fear of reptiles - Batrachophobia, is the fear of reptiles. - *British*

Cnidophobia - Fear of insect stings - Carmel has cnidophobia. - *British*

Cynophobia - Fear of dogs - Stuart has a fear of dogs: cynophobia. - *British*

Doraphobia - Fear of fur - A fear of fur is called doraphobia. - *British*

Medical

Entomophobia - Fear of insects - Jenny has entomophobia. - *British*

Helminthophobia - Fear of worms - Helminthophobia is the fear of worms. - *British*

Hippophobia - Fear of horses - If you are frightened of horses, you might have hippophobia. - *British*

Ichthyophobia - Fear of fish - Someone diagnosed with ichthyophobia, has a fear of fish. - *British*

Zoophobia - Fear of animals - John suffers from zoophobia - *British*

Dysphoria - Anxiety - Because she had dysphoria she was very anxious whenever she went out alone. - *British*

Aggregation - Joining - They had aggregated the scores together to get the average. - *British*

Dorsal - Back-related - The issue was dorsal and he needed physiotherapy. - *British*

Bacillus - Bacteria - The test results showed bacillus present. - *British*

Bacteraemia - Bacteria in the blood - There was a high level of bacteraemia present. - *British*

Bactericide - Anti-bacteria drug - The doctor had prescribed a bactericide to combat the infection. - *British*

Bacteriological - Bacteria study-related - They had undertaken a bacteriological study in the laboratory. - *British*

Bacteriostatic - Antibiotic - The nurse was asked to give the patient a bacteriostatic. - *British*

Bacteroid - Bacteria-like - The word bacteroid means 'bacteria-like'. - *British*

Mycobacterium - Bacteria - There was lots of mycobacterium on the wound. - *British*

Colonic flora - Colon bacteria - There was a substantial amount of colonic flora in her gut. - *British*

Commensal - Microorganism - A commensal is a harmless bacteria that lives on the body. - *British*

Decorum - Good taste - He had lots of decorum and everyone liked the way he behaved. - *British*

Biosynthesis - Formation - Biosynthesis is the formation of complex compounds by living organisms. - *British*

Biotransformation - Chemical changes - The matter was undergoing a biotransformation. - *British*

Glycoside - Carbohydrate - Glycosides play important roles in living things. - *British*

In vitro - In a test tube - The baby had been fertilised in vitro. - *British*

Lipid - Fat - Lipid fats are organic compounds. - *British*

Mitosis - Cell division - Mitosis is a type of cell division. - *British*

Albumin - Water-soluble blood protein - They did a blood test to see how much albumin he had in his blood. - *British*

Anastomosis - Connection between two vessels or tubes - Anastomosis is a natural or artificial connection between two blood vessels. - *British*

Anticoagulant - Substance that prevents blood clotting - The doctor gave him an anticoagulant to stop his blood clotting. - *British*

Antifibrinolytic - Drug to stop breakdown of blood clots - The doctor prescribed an antifibrinolytic medication to stop the breakdown of clots. - *British*

Coagulation - Clotting - "We were waiting for coagulation of the wound before proceeding," said the doctor. - *British*

Complement - Collection of around 20 blood proteins - He had a complement of blood proteins. - *British*

Creatinaemia - Excess blood - He has creatinaemia. - *British*

Eosinophilia - Increase in white blood cells - There appeared to be eosinophilia according to the blood test. - *British*

Erythropoiesis - Red cell production - The students were learning about erythropoiesis. - *British*

Extravascular - Outside a vessel - The problem was extravascular. - *British*

Medical

Ferriprive - Anaemic - The blood test showed she was ferriprive. *- British*

Fibrin - A blood-clotting protein - Fibrin is a substance produced in the blood during blood clotting. *- British*

Granulocytopenia - Lack of white blood cells - The blood test had revealed he had granulocytopenia. *- British*

Haematemesis - Vomiting blood - When he was admitted, he was haematemesis. *- British*

Haematological (niet: hemaetological) - Blood study-related - He was undertaking a haematological study. *- British*

Haemolysis - Destruction of red blood cells - The disease has caused haemolysis. *- British*

Haemopathy - Blood disease - She had been diagnosed with a form of haemopathy. *- British*

Haemopoietic - Blood cell formation-related - The word haemopoietic means blood cell formation related. *- British*

Hypercapnia - Excess of carbon dioxide in the blood - The blood test revealed hypercapnia. *- British*

Hyperkalaemia - Excessive potassium in the blood - The blood test revealed hyperkalaemia. *- British*

Hypokalaemia - Low blood potassium - The blood test showed he had hypokalaemia. *- British*

Ischaemia - Inadequate blood flow - He had ischaemia. *- British*

Leukocytic - White blood cell-related - The illness was leukocytic. *- British*

Leukocytosis - Increased white blood cell count - The blood test revealed that he had leukocytosis. *- British*

Leukopenia - Reduced white blood cell count - The blood test revealed that he was suffering from leukopenia. *- British*

Lipoprotein - A group of soluble proteins that combine with and transport fat in the plasma - Lipoprotein allow the transportation of fats in the blood stream. *- British*

Lymphocytic - White blood cell-related - The illness was lymphocytic. *- British*

Megaloblastic - Large abnormal red blood cell - He had a megaloblastic. *- British*

Metrorrhagia - Breakthrough bleeding - He was suffering with metrorrhagia after surgery. *- British*

Microcirculation - Blood flow in fine vessels - His microcirculation was good for his age. *- British*

Neutropenia - Low white blood cell count - The blood test had shown he had neutropenia. *- British*

Normotensive - With normal blood pressure - "The elderly man was normotensive," said the nurse. *- British*

Pancytopenia - Aplastic anaemia - The blood test had shown she had pancytopenia. *- British*

Plasma expander - Blood expander - He was given a plasma expander. *- British*

Plasma protein - Blood protein - Plasma protein is a blood protein. *- British*

Plasminogen - Part of the blood - Protein is a plasminogen. *- British*

Prothrombin - Blood factor II - Prothrombin is blood factor II. *- British*

Septicaemia - Blood poisoning - The ulcer had burst, giving him septicaemia. *- British*

Serological - Blood study-related - The issue was serological. *- British*

Thrombocytopaenia - Low blood platelet count - The blood test revealed he had thombocytopaenia. *- British*

Thrombocytosis - Increased platelets in the blood - The test revealed thrombocytosis. *- British*

Thromboembolism - Blood clotting - He had thromboembolism following his surgery. *- British*

Toxoplasmosis - Blood infection from cat excrement - He had acquired toxoplasmosis from sitting on the grass. *- British*

Valvule - Small valve - There are small valvule in the circulatory system. *- British*

Vascular - Blood vessel-related - His illness was of a vascular nature and needed further investigation. - *British*

Vasculitis - Blood vessel inflammation - He had been diagnosed with vasculitis. - *British*

Vasoactive - Affecting blood vessels - The illness was vasoactive. - *British*

Vasoconstriction - Narrowing of the small arteries - He had been diagnosed with vasoconstriction. - *British*

Vasodilatation - Widening of the blood vessels - Vasodilation is the widening of the blood vessels. - *British*

Vasomotor - Blood flow-related - The word vasomotor means blood flow related. - *British*

Vasopressor - Substance affecting blood flow - Vasopressor is the substance affecting blood flow. - *British*

Venous - Vein-related - His illness was venous related. - *British*

Diastolic - Part of blood pressure - The lower reading when taking blood pressure is called diastolic. - *British*

Hypertension - High blood pressure - Her doctor had given her medication for hypertension. - *British*

Hypovolaemia - Low blood volume - The tests showed hypovolaemia and he needed a transfusion. - *British*

Anatomical - Body-related - The department had produced an anatomical model for the students to practise upon. - *British*

Anus - Back passage - "I will need to examine your anus to see if you have piles," said the doctor. - *British*

Atrium - Part of the heart - The consultant explained that the atrium was part of the heart. - *British*

Cardiogenic - Originating in the heart - The problem seemed to be cardiogenic. - *British*

Caudal - Nearer the tail - "You need to go caudal," said the surgeon. - *British*

Cervical - Womb neck-related - The woman went for a cervical smear test regularly. - *British*

Cervix uteri - Womb neck - The woman had a biopsy of her cervix uteri. - *British*

Cicatrization - Scarring - The injury had left cicatrization. - *British*

Clitoral - Clitoris-related - The itching was clitoral and was very uncomfortable. - *British*

Colorectal - Colon and rectum-related - The illness was colorectal. - *British*

Conjugated - Joined - They were conjugated twins. - *British*

Constitutional - Whole-body - They needed to find a constitutional way forward. - *British*

Defaecation - Emptying the bowels - He was having difficulty with defaecation and needed medication. - *British*

Dilation - Stretching - The cervix needs to dilate to allow the birth of the baby. - *British*

Distal - Further from central - The point was distal from the central room. - *British*

Duct - Passage - A duct is a passageway. - *British*

Duodenum - Gut - He had a duodenum ulcer and needed an operation. - *British*

Endocrine - Internal secretion-related - It was part of the endocrine gland. - *British*

Endothelium - Lining of heart and blood vessels - The issue seemed to be with the woman's endothelium. - *British*

Enterohepatic - Intestine and liver-related - His illness was enterohepatic. - *British*

Epigastralgia - Upper abdomen pain - He had epigastralgia: a pain in his abdomen. - *British*

Epigastric - Upper abdomen-related - The illness appeared to be epigastric. - *British*

Epiphyseal - Bone growth-related - The illness was epiphyseal. - *British*

Epithelium - Covering of internal and external body surfaces - The epithelium cells cover the entire surface of the body. - *British*

Eruption - Breaking out - She had an eruption of spots on her face. - *British*

Excretion - Removal of waste - The wound was excreting pus from the infection. - *British*

Exfoliation - Shedding of cells - Her skin was subject to exfoliation and was very dry. - *British*

Exocrine - Glands which secrete outwards - The exocrine gland secretes substances through a duct on to the inner surfaces of an organ. For example, sweat. - *British*

Exogenous - With an external origin - The disease was exogenous. - *British*

Expiration - Breathing out - He appeared to have difficulty with expiration. - *British*

Extrarenal - Outside the kidney - The problem was extrarenal. - *British*

Femoral - Thigh-related - The problem was femoral and was giving her a lot of pain. - *British*

Flatulence - Wind - After I eat curry I always get flatulence. - *British*

Gastroduodenal - Stomach and gut-related - The illness was gastroduodenal. - *British*

Gastrointestinal - Related to the stomach and intestines - The illness was gastrointestinal. - *British*

Gastrooesophageal - Stomach and gullet-related - The illness was gastrooesophageal. - *British*

Genitourinary - Genital and urinary organ-related - The illness was genitourinary of origin. - *British*

Glottis - Voice box - The problem appeared to be with her glottis. - *British*

Gonadal - Testicle-related - The illness was gonadal related. - *British*

Gonadotropic - Stimulating sperm production - The medication was for gonadotropic. - *British*

Gynaecological - Related to female sex organs - Her G.P. referred her to the gynaecological department. - *British*

Hepatic - Liver-related - The disease was hepatic and needed treatment urgently. - *British*

Hepatobiliary - Liver and bile duct-related - The illness was hepatobiliary. - *British*

Hepatocellular - Liver cell-related - The illness was hepatocellular. - *British*

Homeostasis - Self-regulating information feedback - The body needs to maintain homeostasis. - *British*

Homogeneous - Uniform - The shape of the cells were homogeneous. - *British*

Homologous - Of same essential nature - The wing of a bat and the arm of a monkey are homologous. - *British*

Humeral - Upper arm-related - His injury was humeral. - *British*

Humeroscapular - Shoulder-related - Her injury was humeroscapular. - *British*

Humor - Normal body fluid - For example, the aqueous humor is the fluid in the eye between the cornea and the iris. - *British*

Humoral - Related to bodily fluids and immunity - Humoral immunity is called this as it relates to the humors, or bodily fluids. - *British*

Hypophyseal - Pituitary gland-related - The illness was hypophyseal. - *British*

Idiosyncrasy - Peculiarity - There was an idiosyncrasy in the way the illness was developing. - *British*

In vivo - In the body - In vivo refers to the process of experimentation on a living organism. - *British*

Ingestion - Swallowing - The patient had difficulties with the ingestion of tablets. - *British*

Inguinal - Groin-related - He explained that the problem appeared to be inguinal. - *British*

Inhalation - Breathing in - The little girl had difficulty with inhalation. - *British*

Inhibition - Stopping - The teenager appeared to have an inhibition with public speaking. - *British*

Medical

225

Integrity - A complete structure - Via the ultrasound, the doctor could see the whole of the organ in its integrity. - *British*

Intercostal - Muscles between the ribs - The pain was intercostal and would need an X-ray to determine cause. - *British*

Interstitial - In gaps between tissue - The doctor ordered an interstitial X-ray. - *British*

Interval - Space - There are intervals between breaths. - *British*

Intervertebral - Between two adjacent vertebrae - The pain was intervertebral and he was in a lot of pain. - *British*

Intramuscular - Within the muscle - He had an intramuscular injury caused by too much running. - *British*

Intraocular - Within the eye - He had an intraocular illness which needed treatment. - *British*

Intrathecal - Within the windpipe - He had an intrathecal tumour. - *British*

Intravascular - Within a blood vessel - She had an intravascular disease. - *British*

Intravenous - Within a vein - The doctor carried out an intravenous injection. - *British*

Intrinsic - Belongs naturally, essential or congenital - The behaviour was intrinsic to his personality. - *British*

Jejunum - Part of the small intestine - He had an ulcer in his jejunum. - *British*

Keloid - Raised scar - He had a keloid on his arm. - *British*

Lateral - A side - The pain was lateral. - *British*

Lenticular - Lens-related - The problem was lenticular. - *British*

Limbic - The limbic system is the complex system of nerves and networks in the brain - The limbic system controls basic emotions in human beings. - *British*

Locomotor - Movement-related - The illness was locomotor and she was referred to the physiotherapist. - *British*

Lumen - Inside of a tube - Lumen is the space within a tubular organ such as an intestine. - *British*

Lytic - Cell destruction-related - The illness was lytic. - *British*

Maculopapular - Small spot-related - The issue was maculopapular. - *British*

Mastocyte - Connective tissue cell - He developed a problem with a mastocyte. - *British*

Maxillary - Face bone-related - The issue was maxillary. - *British*

Medullary - Marrow-related - The illness was medullary and difficult to treat. - *British*

Mineralocorticoid - Hormones - She has a problem with her mineralocorticoid. - *British*

Mucosa - Mucous membrane - It was part of the mucosa. - *British*

Musculature - Muscles - Muscle fibres are part of the musculature. - *British*

Mutagenic - Causing genetic mutation - The cells were mutagenic. - *British*

Nasal - Nose-related - The infection was nasal. - *British*

Nasolacrimal - Nose and tear duct related - The illness was nasolacrimal. - *British*

Natriuresis - Excretion of sodium by kidneys - Natriuresis is the excretion of sodium by the kidneys. - *British*

Orchitis - Testicle inflammation - He had orchitis which was very painful. - *British*

Orofacial - Mouth and face-related - The patient had an orofacial illness and needed treatment. - *British*

Orthostatic - Upright posture-related - Her problem was orthostatic and she found difficulty standing straight. - *British*

Ossicle - Small bone - The ossicle is a small bone in the ear. - *British*

Ossification - Bone formation - Ossification is the process by which bone is reformed and repaired. - *British*

Papillary - Nipple-related - The illness was concerned with her papillary. - *British*

Parathyroid - Thyroid-related - She was suffering from a parathyroid illness. - *British*

Medical

Paravenous - Beside a vein - The tumour was paravenous. - *British*

Parenchyma - Functional tissue of an organ - Parenchyma is the functional tissue of an organ. - *British*

Parietal - Outer wall-related - The disease was parietal. - *British*

Peptic - Digestion-related - The doctor diagnosed a peptic problem. - *British*

Perianal - Back passage-related - The disease was perianal and needed further investigation. - *British*

Perineal - Pelvis-related - Her problem was perineal. - *British*

Perioral - Mouth-related - She had a perioral problem and was referred to the dentist. - *British*

Peristalsis - Pushing of food though the body - The peristalsis did not appear to be working. - *British*

Perivascular - Around a vessel - The illness was perivascular. - *British*

Piloerection - Hair standing on end - In the morning he had piloerection. - *British*

Precordial - Heart and chest-related - His illness was precordial and needed urgent treatment. - *British*

Prepuce - Foreskin - He had an infection in the prepuce. - *British*

Prostaglandin - Fatty acid - Prostaglandin is a fatty acid. - *British*

Pylorus - Narrow outlet of stomach - The disease was in the pylorus. - *British*

Renal - Kidney-related - His illness was renal and he saw an urologist. - *British*

Renovascular - Kidney blood vessel-related - The illness was renovascular. - *British*

Retrosternal - Behind the breastbone - The disease was retrosternal. - *British*

Sclera - White of the eye - She had a problem with her sclera. - *British*

Septum - Dividing wall - The septum is the dividing wall between various parts of the body. - *British*

Sequestra - Pieces of bone - The sequestra is a piece of bone. - *British*

Sinusal - Sinus-related - His illness was sinusal and he needed treatment. - *British*

Spermatogenesis - Sperm-formation - He had difficulty with spermatogenesis. - *British*

Sphincter - Bottom - The problem was around the sphincter area. - *British*

Stria - Stretch marks - She had lots of stria across her stomach from her pregnancy. - *British*

Subcapsular - Below a tough outer covering - The infection was subcapsular and difficult to access. - *British*

Synovial - Secreting a clear sticky lubrication in a joint - Synovial means secreting a clear sticky liquid in a joint. - *British*

Testicular - Testicle-related - The disease was testicular and he saw a urologist. - *British*

Thin - Brittle fingernails - She had thin nails and they kept breaking. - *British*

Thoracic - Chest-related - He had a thoracic disease and needed lots of care. - *British*

Torsion - Twisting - Torsion means twisting. - *British*

Torticollis - Twisting of head and neck - He needed to carry out a torticollis to reach the injury. - *British*

Tract - Channel - She had a bilary tract infection. - *British*

Transaminase - An enzyme - Transaminase is an enzyme. - *British*

Transcutaneous - Through the skin - The piercing was transcutaneous. - *British*

Transdermal - Through the skin - The injection was transdermal. - *British*

Trichophobia - Fear of hair - You could not be a hairdresser if you were trichophobic. - *British*

Trivalent - With a valence of three - Trivalent means with a valence of three. - *British*

Medical

Trophic - Nutrition-related - Her condition was trophic because she was not eating sufficient food. - *British*

Tympanum - Ear drum - He had an infection in his tympanum which was very painful. - *British*

Unilateral - One-sided - The argument was unilateral. - *British*

Uraemia - Kidney failure - She had been diagnosed with uraemia. - *British*

Uterus - Womb - The uterus is also known as the womb. - *British*

Uveitis - Eye inflammation - He was diagnosed with uveitis. - *British*

Ventral - Belly-related (stomach) - The illness was ventral. - *British*

Vertebral - Vertebra-related - The disease was vertebral. - *British*

Vesicular - Of small bladders/blisters - The family all had vesicular. - *British*

Virilization - Masculinization - Virilization means masculinization, the development of male physical characteristics in a female. - *British*

Visceral - Relating to an organ in the chest area - The problem appeared to be visceral. - *British*

Vitreous - Glassy - His eyes were vitreous. - *British*

Vulval - Vagina-related - The problem was vulval and she was referred to gynae. - *Rritish*

Xanthopsia - Yellow vision - He had xanthopsia. - *British*

Xerophthalmia - Dry eyes - She needed eye drops because she had xerophthalmia. - *British*

Xerostomia - Dry mouth - She needed water because she had xerostomia. - *British*

Cerebellar - Brain-related - The disease was cerebellar. - *British*

Cerebral - Brain-related - The disease was cerebral. - *British*

Cerebrospinal - Brain and spinal cord-related - The disease was cerebrospinal. - *British*

Cerebrovascular - Brain and blood vessel-related - The disease was cerebrovascular. - *British*

Cognitive - To understand - She was referred for cognitive therapy. - *British*

Commotion - Concussion - He had suffered a commotion when playing rugby. - *British*

Cortex - Outer layer - The disease was in the cortex of the brain. - *British*

Cortical - Cortex-related - The disease was cortical. - *British*

Dura mater - Covering of brain and spinal chord - The dura mater had been damaged in the fall. - *British*

Encephalitis - Brain inflammation - The child had been diagnosed with encephalitis and was very sick. - *British*

Encephalopathy - Brain disease - It was known the patient had encephalopathy. - *British*

Hypothalamic - Brain-related - The illness was hypothalamic. - *British*

Peridural - Outside the brain/spinal cord - The disease was peridural. - *British*

Subarachnoid - In the brain - The tumour was subarachnoid. - *British*

Thalamus - Part of the brain - The thalamus is part of the brain. - *British*

Vegetative - Without consciousness - He was in a vegetative state when he was admitted. - *British*

Carcinogenic - Cancer-causing - Research shows smoking to be carcinogenic. - *British*

Carcinoma - Cancer - The patient was diagnosed with carcinoma. - *British*

Cytotoxic - Cancer drug - The drug prescribed for his cancer was called, cytotoxic. - *British*

Epithelioma - A cancer - She had an epithelioma and was very sick. - *British*

Lymphoma - Cancer - He had been diagnosed with lymphoma six months before. - *British*

Medical

Melanoma - Skin cancer - The patient was diagnosed with a melanoma. - *British*

Metastasis - Disease site transfer - Metastasis is a secondary cancer tumour. - *British*

Myeloma - Bone marrow cancer - She had been diagnosed with myeloma and was very sick. - *British*

Myelomatosis - Bone marrow cancer - She had myelmatosis and was very poorly. - *British*

Oncolytic - Cancer treatment-related - The treatment was oncolytic. - *British*

Cell membrane - Cell surface - A cell membrane regulates the passage of useful substance, such as oxygen, into the cell. - *British*

Cytoplasm - Part of a cell - The cytoplasm is part of a cell. - *British*

Extracellular - Outside cells - They were part of the extracellular. - *British*

Astringent - Toner - She used an astringent to clean her face. - *British*

Catabolism - Chemical breakdown - Catabolism is a chemical process by which foods are broken down. - *British*

Catalyse - Speed up - The pharmacist added a chemical to catalyse the process. - *British*

Caustic - Corrosive - Caustic agents are used to destroy warts. - *British*

Chelation - Chemical combination with heavy metal - He knew about chelation and its effects. - *British*

Derivative - Substance obtained from something else - The substance was a derivative of something else. - *British*

Hydroalcoholic - Solutions containing water and alcohol - The hydroalcoholic solution was used as a vehicle for medicine. - *British*

Hydrolysis (niet: hydrolyse) - Adding water to split a compound - Hydrolysis is a chemical process. - *British*

Hydrophilic - A chemical that can be dissolved, mixed or wetted by water - Hydrophilic substances attract water and absorb it, for example, sugar. - *British*

Hydrophobic - Not readily absorbing water - The substance was hydrophobic. - *British*

Hydroxylation - Chemical process that introduces hydroxyl into an organic compound - He carried out the process of hydroxylation. - *British*

Infuse - Pour in - They decided to infuse the perfume with lavender. - *British*

Inorganic - Non-organic - The food was inorganic. - *British*

Lipophilic - Combine or dissolve in fat - The substance was lipophilic. - *British*

Liposome - Fatty or oily globule - It was a liposome, formed artificially to carry drugs into the tissues. - *British*

Miscible - Mixable - Water and ethanol are miscible. - *British*

Reagent - Reactive substance - Reagent is a chemical substance that reacts with another. - *British*

Distil - Purify - The whiskey was distilled before bottling. - *British*

Amnion - Sack containing the foetus - The amnion was clearly visible on the ultra sound scan. - *British*

Epidural - Painkiller during childbirth - She was given an epidural during her delivery. - *British*

Episiotomy - Cut to vagina in childbirth - The doctor had carried out an episiotomy during her delivery. - *British*

Foetoplacental - Foetus and placenta-related - The problem was foetoplacental. - *British*

Foetotoxic - Toxic to the foetus - The matter was foetotoxic. - *British*

Fontanelle - Soft spot - The baby was born without a fontanelle. - *British*

Galactorrhoea - Excessive milk production - She had galactorrhoea. - *British*

Gestation - Pregnancy - The woman was of 38 weeks gestation and due very soon. - *British*

Medical

Gravidity - Pregnancy- gravida - the number of times a women has been pregnant - Gravidity is the number of times a woman has been pregnant in her life. - *British*

Induction - Inducing - The woman was given an induction to bring on the birth of her baby. - *British*

Lactation - Milk production - She did not start lactation straight away after birth. - *British*

Lochia - Post-birth vaginal discharge - She had lochia after giving birth. - *British*

Mammary - Breast-related - Her problem was mammary and she had difficulty feeding her child. - *British*

Mastitis - Sore breasts - After giving birth she developed mastitis. - *British*

Multiparous - Woman who has had 2 or more babies - "As she is multiparous, she could have her baby at home," said the midwife. - *British*

Neonatal - New baby-related - They had moved the baby to the neonatal unit. - *British*

Nulliparous - Never having given birth - The woman was nulliparous, although she wished for children. - *British*

Obstetrical - Obstetrics-related - Her illness was obstetrical. - *British*

Ovum - Egg - The ovum is the egg cell of reproduction. - *British*

Oxytocic - Inducing a baby - The mum had agreed to an oxytocic procedure to induce her delivery. - *British*

Parturition - Giving birth - Her favourite midwife was there during her parturition. - *British*

Perinatal - Shortly after the birth - The incident happened perinatal and was being investigated. - *British*

Postpartum - After childbirth - The mother was postpartum and was doing well. - *British*

Preeclampsia - Complication of late pregnancy - She had been diagnosed with preeclampsia late in her pregnancy. - *British*

Prenatal - Before birth - She became quite unwell during her prenatal period. - *British*

Puerperium - Time as vagina and uterus return to normal after birth - She was in the puerperium period after giving birth. - *British*

Teratogenic (niet: teratogen) - Producing foetal abnormality - The condition had left the baby teratogenic and had abnormalities. - *British*

Teratological - Early foetus development-related - The issue with the baby was teratological. - *British*

Chromosomal - Chromosome-related - The illness was chromosomal. - *British*

Asepsis - Cleanliness - The nurse was careful to ensure asepsis. - *British*

Aseptic - Clean - The bathrooms were very aseptic. - *British*

Amine - Organic compound containing nitrogen - Amine is an organic compound containing nitrogen. - *British*

Tenosynovitis - Inflammation of a tendon sheath - He had tenosynovitis in his leg which was painful. - *British*

Absence - Mild epilepsy - He was often going absent and was not with us. - *British*

Acidosis - High blood acidity - The patient had been diagnosed as suffering from acidosis with high blood acidity. - *British*

Acrocyanosis - Blueness - The patient had acrocyanosis and looked very blue. - *British*

Adenitis - Gland inflammation - He was suffering from adenitis and his glands were very swollen. - *British*

Adenoma - Non-cancerous tumour - Following the biopsy the patient was diagnosed with an adenoma which was non-cancerous. - *British*

Adhesion - Sticking - Following his operation it was discovered the patient had an adhesion in his stomach. - *British*

Adnexitis - Fallopian tube/ovary inflammation - She was suffering from adnexitis and her fallopian tubes were inflamed. - *British*

Aerophagy - Air swallowing - The patient suffered from aerophagy because he ate too quickly. - *British*

Agammaglobulinaemia - Immune deficiency - The boy was suffering from agammaglobulinaemia. - *British*

Agranulocytosis - Bone marrow poisoning - The boy was admitted being diagnosed with agranulocytosis. - *British*

Akathisia - Ants in your pants - "You have akathisia you can never keep still," said Mum. - *British*

Akinesia - Lack of movement - Jed is suffering with akinesia and finding it difficult to move. - *British*

Alimentary - Digestion-related - Her illness was related to her alimentary canal and gave her severe indigestion. - *British*

Alkalosis - High blood alkalinity - He is suffering from alkalosis with very high blood alkilinity. - *British*

Alopecia - Baldness - The young girl has big patches of baldness in her hair and has been diagnosed with alopecia. - *British*

Alveolitis - Lung inflammation - The patient had alveolitis, a severe lung inflammation. - *British*

Amblyopia - Sight problems - The woman was suffering from amblyopia and was having difficulty seeing. - *British*

Amenorrhoea - Lack of periods - The woman was finding it difficult to conceive as she was suffering from amenorrhoea. - *British*

Anaerobic - Without oxygen - The patient was unconscious and anaerobic. - *British*

Anamnesis - Remembering - He was coming out of the coma and was having moments of anamnesis. - *British*

Aneurysm - Swelling in artery wall - The doctor diagnosed Janet as having an aneurysm in her leg, which was causing her so much pain. - *British*

Angiitis - Blood vessel inflammation - He had been diagnosed with angiitis and his blood vessels were very inflamed. - *British*

Angina pectoris - Angina - The elderly man had severe chest pain that the doctor had diagnosed as being caused by angina. - *British*

Anginal - Angina-related - The pain was anginal and related to a heart condition. - *British*

Angioedema - Skin blistering - Hilary's skin was very blistered and the nurse thought this was probably, angioedema. - *British*

Angioneurotic - Vein neuron disorder - I had been diagnosed as being angioneurotic having as vein neuron disorder. - *British*

Anhydrous - Without water - The patient was anhydrous and was not producing any sweat at all. - *British*

Anisocoria - Different sized eyes - The little girl had anisocoria, having two different sized eyes. - *British*

Anogenital - Anus and genital-related - The rash was anogenital related. - *British*

Anorectal - Back passage-related - The problem was anorectal. - *British*

Anosmia - Lack of sense of smell - Brian had anosmia so did not smell the pan burning. - *British*

Anovulatory - Without producing an egg - The woman did not conceive because she was anovulatory. - *British*

Anoxia - Total lack of oxygen - The patient was diagnosed with anoxia. - *British*

Antacid - Indigestion remedy - "You need to take an antacid for that indigestion," said my mother. - *British*

Aphasia - Stroke - The patient had an aphasia last night. - *British*

Aplasia - Non-development of an organ - The girl was missing a kidney and had aplasia. - *British*

Aplastic anaemia - Severe anaemia - The woman had aplastic anaemia and was very poorly. - *British*

Apnoea - Stopping breathing - The man was blighted by sleep apnoea and would stop breathing whilst asleep. - *British*

Arrhythmia - Irregular heartbeat - Maureen has arrhythmia. - *British*

Medical

Arrhythmogenic - Causing abnormal heartbeat - The doctor diagnosed the patient as having an illness which was making him arrhythmogenic. - *British*

Arterial - Artery-related - He had an arterial disease. - *British*

Arteriolar - Artery-related - The illness he had was arteriolar. - *British*

Arteriosclerosis - Hardening of the arteries - He had arteriosclerosis. - *British*

Arteriovenous - Artery and vein-related - The illness was arteriovenous. - *British*

Arthralgia - Pain in a joint - She had arthralgia in some of her joints. - *British*

Arthropathy - Joint disease - She had been diagnosed with arthropathy. - *British*

Arthrosis - Joint disease - She had been diagnosed with arthrosis. - *British*

Articular - Joint-related - He had articular; joint related problems. - *British*

Ascites - Dropsy - He had been diagnosed with ascites some years earlier. - *British*

Asthenia - Weakness - She was feeling asthenia in her legs. - *British*

Asystole - Heart attack - The doctor diagnosed the patient as having an asystole. - *British*

Ataxia - Lack of coordination - John has ataxia and is always falling over. - *British*

Atheromatosis - Thickening of the arteries - The atheromatosis was acute. - *British*

Athetosis - Cerebral palsy - He had been diagnosed with athetosis. - *British*

Atony - Lack of muscle tone - There was a distinct atony in his arms. - *British*

Atrial - Heart-related - He had an atrial illness. - *British*

Atrioventricular - Heart-related - He had an atrioventricular illness. - *British*

Atrophy - Wasting - There was a degree of atrophy in his muscles. - *British*

Automatism - Repetitive movements - The woman was diagnosed with automatism. - *British*

Autonomic - Unconscious - When the child was admitted he was autonomic. - *British*

Azoospermia - Lack of sperm - He attended the fertility clinic because he had azoospermia. - *British*

Azotaemia - Kidney failure - She had azotaemia and needed dialysis. - *British*

Balanitis - Swollen penis - He had balanitis so the doctor had prescribed antibiotics - *British*

Basal - Base - He had been diagnosed with a basal ganglia. - *British*

Benign - Non-malignant - Mr. Colins had been diagnosed with a benign tumour. - *British*

Biliary - Bile-related - "The problem seems to be in the billiary tract," said the doctor to the patient. - *British*

Blepharitis - Eyelid inflammation - Her G.P. diagnosed her as having blepharitis. - *British*

Blood spots - Bruising and discolouring to skin - She had a number of blood spots on her hand. - *British*

Bradycardia - Slow heartbeat - The doctors diagnosed the patient as having bradycardia. - *British*

Bradykinesia - Sluggishness - The woman had bradykinesia. - *British*

Bradypnoea - Slow breathing - The patient had bradypnoea which was causing concern. - *British*

Bronchiectasis - Widening of the airways - The steroids brought about bronchiectasis. - *British*

Bronchoconstriction - Breathing difficulties due to a tight chest - The little boy had bronchoconstriction due to an infection. - *British*

Bronchopneumonia - Bronchial pneumonia - The elderly woman had bronchopneumonia. - *British*

Bronchopulmonary - Chest-related - The issue appeared to be of a broncopulmonary origin. - *British*

Bronchospasm - Asthma - The little girl was having a bronchospasm attack. - *British*

Medical

Bronchus - Breathing tube - There appeared to be a blockage in the bronchus. - *British*

Buccal - Cheek-related - The problem appeared to be buccal. - *British*

Buccopharyngeal - Mouth and throat-related - The illness appeared to be buccopharyngeal. - *British*

Bulbar - Bulb-related - The tumour was bulbar. - *British*

Bullous - Blistered - The heat had caused the skin to become bullous. - *British*

Bursitis - Housemaid's knee - The doctor diagnosed the man as having bursitis. - *British*

Cachexia - Wasting away - She was cachexia and losing weight rapidly. - *British*

Calcaemia - Excess blood calcium - It was clear from blood results that he had calcaemia. - *British*

Calcification - Hardening - The patient was diagnosed with calcification of the arteries. - *British*

Calciuria - Calcium in the urine - Following his test the nurse identified calciuria. - *British*

Calculus i - Stone - He had a calculus i. - *British*

Calculus ii - Tartar - He had calculus ii. - *British*

Candidiasis - Thrush - The woman had candidiasis. - *British*

Cellulitis - Inflammation of connective tissue - The patient was suffering from cellulitis. - *British*

Cephalalgia - Headache - The man had a cephalalgia. - *British*

Chloasma - Dark patches on the face - The patient had chloasma. - *British*

Cholangitis - Bile duct inflammation - The patient was diagnosed with cholangitis. - *British*

Cholecystitis - Gall bladder inflammation - The patient had cholecystitis. - *British*

Cholelithiasis - Gallstones - The doctor diagnosed the patient as having cholelithiasis. - *British*

Cholestasis - Bile flow stoppage - The patient had been diagnosed with cholestasis. - *British*

Chorea - Huntingdon's Chorea - The patient was diagnosed as having Huntingdon's chorea. - *British*

Cirrhosis - Liver disease - The alcoholic had cirrhosis of the liver. - *British*

Claudication - Limping - The patient had right claudication on entering the department. - *British*

Colitis - Colon inflammation - He had been diagnosed with colitis the year before. - *British*

Colonopathy - Colon disease - She had colonopathy. - *British*

Concomitant - Associated - He had a new problem which was concomitant with his diabetes . - *British*

Conjugation - Linkage - There was a conjugation between the two medical issues. - *British*

Conjunctivitis - Eye inflammation - He had conjunctivitis. - *British*

Contracture - Permanent tissue shortening - Contracture is a deformity caused by shrinkage of the skin etc. - *British*

Conversion - Hysteria - The woman was suffering from conversion. - *British*

Cor pulmonale - Heart failure - The elderly woman had been diagnosed with cor pulmonale. - *British*

Coronary - Heart muscle/artery-related - He had a coronary. - *British*

Coxalgia - Hip pain - She had coxalgia. - *British*

Crystalluria - Crystals in the urine - The test had shown he had crystalluria. - *British*

Cumulative - Increasing - The problem was cumulative and difficult to control. - *British*

Medical

Curarize - Paralyse - The illness was likely to cause curarization if he was not treated urgently. - *British*

Cyclic - Regular - The failure was cyclic and needed addressing. - *British*

Cycloplegia - Eye muscle paralysis - He seemed to have cycloplegia. - *British*

Degenerative - Worsening - The condition was degenerative and there was little that could be done to stop this. - *British*

Degradation - Break-down - The vegetable waste was subject to degradation to make compost. - *British*

Delirium - Being delirious - He was subject to delirium when he had a high temperature. - *British*

Dementia - Loosing your mind - He has been diagnosed with dementia by his G.P. - *British*

Dendritic - Branching - The woman had a dendritic ulcer of the cornea. - *British*

Depersonalization - Dream-like feeling - He had a form of depersonalization and found it hard to focus. - *British*

Deprivation - Loss or lack - Some children live in poverty and are subject to huge deprivation. - *British*

Diaphoresis - Sweating - She suffered badly from diaphoresis. - *British*

Diathesis - Susceptibility to a disease - A bleeding diathesis is present when a person is susceptible to bleeding after an injury. - *British*

Diffusion - Spreading - Radiation is diffused in many directions. - *British*

Diphtheria - An infection caused by the bacterium corynebacterium diptheriae - She was diagnosed as having diphtheria. - *British*

Diplopia - Double vision - The ophthalmologist said he had diplopia. - *British*

Discoid - Disk-shaped - The plate was discoid. - *British*

Dislocation - Moving out of position - His shoulder was very prone to dislocation. - *British*

Distension - Enlarging - The distension of the tumour was pressing on nerves. - *British*

Diuresis - More urine than normal - She was diagnosed with diuresis and needed the toilet often. - *British*

Diverticulitis - Colon inflammation - She had been diagnosed with diverticulitis the previous year. - *British*

Dominance - Ability to influence - He has a lot of dominance with the board and can usually get things done. - *British*

Dysarthria - Speech defect - He had a dysarthria and was not very clear when speaking. - *British*

Dysentery - Extreme case of diarrhoea - She had picked up dysentery when holidaying abroad. - *British*

Dysgenesis - Malformation - The child had a dysgenesis in his foot. - *British*

Dysgeusia - Distortion of sense of taste - She had dysgeusia and struggled with tasting food. - *British*

Dyskinesia - Jerky movements - His illness had given him dyskinesia. - *British*

Dysmenorrhoea - Problems with menstruation - She had dysmenorrhoea and was ill every month. - *British*

Dyspareunia - Painful sexual intercourse - The doctor diagnosed dyspareunia after the woman complained of pain during sex. - *British*

Dysphagia - Difficulty in swallowing - She had dysphagia and, therefore, difficulty with swallowing whole food. - *British*

Dysplasia - Abnormality of development - The baby had dysplasia and was not developing normally. - *British*

Dyspnoea - Laboured breathing - The elderly man had dyspnoea and needed oxygen. - *British*

Dystonia - Muscle disorders - It was a dystonia and needed some treatment. - *British*

Dystrophy - Growth failure in tissue - He had a dystrophy in his arm. - *British*

Dysuria - Painful urination - When he went to the lavatory he complained of dysuria. - *British*

Medical

Ecchymosis - Bruising - He had lots of ecchymosis on his body from the accident. - *British*

Eclampsia - Pregnancy complication - "When she was pregnant she had eclampsia," said the midwife. - *British*

Ectopic - In the wrong place - Her pregnancy was ectopic and needed terminating. - *British*

Embolism - Sudden blocking of an artery - An embolism had caused his heart attack. - *British*

Emesis - Vomiting - She had extreme emesis and was very unwell. - *British*

Emphysema - Lung disease - The elderly man had emphysema. - *British*

Empyema - Collection of pus - The infection had caused an empyema and was very painful. - *British*

Enanthema - Eruption on a mucous surface - She had an enanthema on her nose. - *British*

Endometriosis - Condition related to painful menstruation - She had endometriosis and concieving children might be difficult. - *British*

Enteritis - Small intestine inflammation - She had enteritis following a holiday abroad. - *British*

Enterocolitis - (Small and large) intestine inflammation - She had been diagnosed with enterocolitis. - *British*

Enuresis - Bed wetting - At aged ten, the boy still had a problem with enuresis. - *British*

Epicondylitis - Tennis elbow - The G.P. had diagnosed epicondylitis. - *British*

Epistaxis - Nosebleed - He had suffered an epistaxis as a result of the bump on his nose. - *British*

Eructation - Belching - He suffered with eructation a lot. - *British*

Exacerbation - Worsening - The girl was suffering from an exacerbation of her illness. - *British*

Exophthalmos - Protruding eyes - The doctor noticed her eyes were exophthalmos. - *British*

Extrasystole - Premature heart contraction - He had an extrasystole. - *British*

Extravasation - Escape of blood or fluid into tissue - She had an extravasation where her blood escaped into her tissues. - *British*

Exudate - Cells and fluid leaked out of a blood vessel or an organ - The man had lots of inflammation in his leg caused by exudate. - *British*

Fasciculation - Twitch - He suffers from fasciculation when nervous. - *British*

Febrile - Feverish - He had febrile convulsions and was very unwell. - *British*

Fibrillation - Twitch - Fibrillation is the localised rapid contractions of individual muscles. - *British*

Fibrosis - Fibrous tissue formation - Fibrosis is pain and stiffness in the muscles. - *British*

Fissure - Groove - There was a fissure in the skin. - *British*

Fistula - Abnormal passage - A fistula may be present at birth or acquired. - *British*

Flexion - Displacement of the womb - She had flexion. - *British*

Fluor albus - Vaginal discharge - Her vagina was sore as she had a case of fluor albus. - *British*

Folliculitis - Follicle inflammation - She had folliculitis which was very painful. - *British*

Furunculosis - Boils - The woman had several furunculosis in her armpit. - *British*

Ganglion - Knot - A ganglion is a fluid filled swelling. - *British*

Gastralgia - Colic - The baby had gastralgia and was in great distress. - *British*

Gastritis - Upset stomach - She was diagnosed with gastritis and felt really ill. - *British*

Gastroenteritis - Gastric flu - He had gastroenteritis and felt very unwell. - *British*

Glaucoma - Progressive blindness - The woman had glaucoma and was losing her sight. - *British*

Medical

Glomerulonephritis - Acute kidney inflammation - The young woman had glomerulonephritis. - *British*

Glossitis - Tongue inflammation - The patient had been diagnosed with glossitis. - *British*

Glossodynia - Pain in the tongue - She had glossodynia. - *British*

Gluten - Cereal protein - The woman had a gluten allergy. - *British*

Glycosuria - Sugar in the urine - The urine test showed she had glycosuria. - *British*

Grand mal - Epileptic seizure - She was suffering from grand mal and needed to take medication regularly. - *British*

Gynaecomastia - Development of breasts in men - He had gynaecomastia. - *British*

Haematoma - Bruising - She had a large haematoma on her leg. - *British*

Haematuria - Blood in the urine - Her urine test showed haematuria. - *British*

Haemeralopia - Day blindness - She had haemeralopia. - *British*

Haemoptysis - Coughing up blood - He was haemoptysis when admitted. - *British*

Haemorrhoids - Piles - She was diagnosed as having haemorrhoids. - *British*

Hemiplegia - Paralysis of one side - He had a hemiplegia on his left side. - *British*

Hepatomegaly - Liver enlargement - She was diagnosed as having hepatomegaly. - *British*

Herpes simplex - Cold sore/ genital herpes virus - She was suffering from a herpes simplex on her mouth. - *British*

Herpes zoster - Chickenpox/shingles virus - She had the herpes zoster virus and was infectious. - *British*

Hirsutism - Hairiness - He suffered from hirsutism from a very early age. - *British*

Hydrocephalus - Water on the brain - The child had hydrocephalus and needed urgent treatment. - *British*

Hyperaemia - Excess of blood in the vessels supplying a part of the body or a particular organ - She had hyperaemia in her legs. - *British*

Hyperaesthesia - Increased sensitivity to stimulation - He had hyperaesthesia. - *British*

Hyperalgesia - Excessive sensitiveness to pain - She had hyperalgesia and was very sensitive to pain. - *British*

Hyperemesis - Excessive vomiting - She had hyperemesis. - *British*

Hyperglycaemia - High blood sugar - The blood test revealed hyperglycaemia. - *British*

Hyperhidrosis - Excessive sweating - She had hyperhidrosis, which was embarrassing. - *British*

Hyperkeratosis - Thickening of the skin - She had hyperkeratosis on the bottom of her feet. - *British*

Hyperkinesia - Hyperactivity - The little boy had hyperkinesia and was always on the go. - *British*

Hyperlipidaemia - Increase in blood fat levels - The second blood test revealed hyperlipidaemia. - *British*

Hyperostosis - Abnormal bone thickening - The X-ray revealed she had hyperostosis. - *British*

Hyperplasia - Increase in the number of normal cells in tissue - The doctor decided to carry out tests for hyperplasia. - *British*

Hyperpyrexia - Extreme fever - The little boy had hyperpyrexia on admittance to hospital. - *British*

Hyperreflexia - Exaggerated reflexes - The child had hyperreflexia. - *British*

Hypersecretion - Excessive secretion - The elderly patient appeared to have hypersecretion of saliva. - *British*

Hypersensitivity - Over-sensitivity - The little girl had hypersensitivity to wool. - *British*

Hyperstimulation - Over-stimulation - The child had been subject to hyperstimulation and couldn't keep still. - *British*

Hyperthermia - High body temperature - She had hyperthermia by the time she was found. - *British*

Hyperthyroidism - Over-active thyroid - The tests showed she had hyperthyroidism. - *British*

Hypertonia - Stiffness - He had hypertonia in all of his joints. - *British*

Hypertrichosis - Excess hair - The baby had been born with hypertrichosis. - *British*

Hypertrophy - Increase in the size of an organ - One of her kidneys showed hypertrophy. - *British*

Hyperuricaemia - Gout - They say that drinking port causes hyperuricaemia but that is probably just a myth. - *British*

Hypervitaminosis - Vitamin overdose - The doctor thought she had hypervitaminosis and told her to stop taking them immediately. - *British*

Hypervolaemia - Abnormal increase in blood volume - She had hypervolaemia and needed urgent treatment. - *British*

Hypoacusis - Slight deafness - He had hypoacusis and found it difficult to hear. - *British*

Hypochondriasis - Being hypochondriac - She was diagnosed with hypochondriasis, as she was always visiting her doctor. - *British*

Hypoglycaemia - Low blood sugar - She did not eat enough and often had hypoglycaemia. - *British*

Hypogonadism - Sterility - Unfortunately, he had been diagnosed with hypogonadism. - *British*

Hypoplasia - Tissue or organ under or incomplete development - The child had enamel hypoplasia and might lose his teeth early. - *British*

Hypotension - Low blood pressure - My G.P. has said I have hypotension. - *British*

Hypotensive - With low blood pressure - The patient was hypotensive and needed medication. - *British*

Hypothyroidism - Under active thyroid - She had been diagnosed with hypothyroidism and would need to take medication. - *British*

Hypotonia - Muscle wastage - After the accident the patient had hypotonia where his leg had been plastered. - *British*

Hypotrophy - Enlargement of organ or tissue due to enlargement of component cells - Hypotrophy is seen in the enlargement of the cells of the uterus during pregnancy. - *British*

Hypouricaemia - Lack of uric acid in the blood - The blood test showed hypouricaemia. - *British*

Hypoventilation - Holding your breath - The child often hypoventilated and went red in the face. - *British*

Hypovitaminosis - Vitamin deficiency - The little girl had hypovitaminosis because her diet was insufficient. - *British*

Hypoxaemia - Blood oxygen deficiency - The blood test showed hypoxaemia so she was put on oxygen. - *British*

Hypoxia - Tissue oxygen deficiency - She was hypoxic. - *British*

Iatrogenic - An illness caused by medical exam or treatment - Iatrogenic illnesses should be avoided as much as possible. - *British*

Icterus - Jaundice - The baby had icterus at birth and needed treatment. - *British*

Idiopathic - Of unknown cause - The illness was idiopathic and difficult to explain. - *British*

Ileitis - Crohn's disease - She had been diagnosed with ileitis the previous year. - *British*

Ileus - Intestinal blockage - She had an ileus which needed urgent treatment. - *British*

Immobilization - Stopping movement - The patient was subject to immobilization and found it difficult to walk. - *British*

Medical

Incarceration - Hernia - He had been diagnosed with an incarceration that could not be manipulated. - *British*

Incidental - Minor - The injuries were incidental and did not cause concern. - *British*

Induration - Sclerosis or hardening - The patient had induration of the arteries. - *British*

Influenza - Flu - She was suffering from influenza and was very poorly. - *British*

Inotropic - Affecting muscular contractions - The patient was suffering from an illness which was inotropic. - *British*

Insomnia - Sleeplessness - He had always suffered from insomnia. - *British*

Inspiration - Breathing in - She was having difficulty with inspiration and needed assistance. - *British*

Intention tremor - Shakiness - "He has an intention tremor," said the nurse. - *British*

Intertrigo - Chaffing - The patient had intertrigo on his thighs. - *British*

Iridocyclitis - Eye inflammation - The elderly man had iridocyclitis. - *British*

Iritis - Eye irritation - The sand blowing had caused him to have iritis. - *British*

Keratitis - Conjunctivitis - She had picked up keratitis from somewhere. - *British*

Keratoconjunctivitis - Conjunctivitis - She had keratoconjunctivitis. - *British*

Kinetic - Motion-related - His problem was kinetic and caused by motion. - *British*

Labile - Unstable - She was very labile on her feet. - *British*

Laceration - Tear, wound or cut - He had a laceration in his leg where he fell over. - *British*

Lacrimal - Tear producing glands - The problem was with his lacrimal glands. - *British*

Laryngitis - Sore throat - He had laryngitis and so, stayed away from work. - *British*

Lassitude - Weariness - He had a real lassitude and did not feel like working. - *British*

Latent period - Inactive period between infection and onset of symptoms - The latent period had lasted for 4 days before he had developed the rash. - *British*

Lesion - Injury - She had a lesion on her leg. - *British*

Leukoplakia - White patch in the mouth - The test revealed a leukoplakia in his mouth. - *British*

Leukorrhoea - Vaginal discharge - She had a leukorrhoea. - *British*

Lichenification - Skin hardening and thickening - She had lichenfication on her feet. - *British*

Lipodystrophy - A problem with the way the body produces and stores fat - He was suffering from lipodystrophy. - *British*

Livedo - Mottling - She had livedo of the skin. - *British*

Luxation - Dislocation - He had luxation of his shoulder which was very painful. - *British*

Lymphadenopathy - Lymph node disease - She had lymphadenopathy. - *British*

Lymphangitis - Lymphatic vessel inflammation - She had been diagnosed with lymphangitis. - *British*

Malabsorption - Poor digestion - He had difficulty with malabsorption of food. - *British*

Malaise - Vague illness - "He always has some sort of malaise," said the manager. - *British*

Mastoiditis - Ear infection - The little boy had mastoiditis and was referred to the ENT Department. - *British*

Megacolon - Colon enlargement - "He has a megacolon," said the doctor. - *British*

Mesenteric - Involving the skin attaching various organs to the body - Mesenteric illness can affect children. - *British*

Metaplasia - Abnormal tissue change - He had metaplasia which was concerning. - *British*

Meteorism - Abdominal gas - He had meteorism and kept passing wind. - *British*

Mononucleosis - Glandular fever - He was diagnosed with mononucleosis. - *British*

Mutism - The inability or unwillingness to speak aloud, as in elective mute, where the individual chooses not to speak, Or it can be the result of brain damage or deafness - The young boy was diagnosed with mutism. - *British*

Myasthenia - Muscle weakness - Having her arm in plaster had caused myasthenia. - *British*

Mycosis - Fungal disease - He had a mycosis and needed to be treated. - *British*

Mycotic - Caused by a fungus - The illness was mycotic. - *British*

Myopathy - Muscle disease - He had myopathy and was finding it difficult to walk. - *British*

Myositis - Muscle inflammation - He had myositis and needed treatment. - *British*

Necrolysis - Gangrene - He had necrolysis in his toes, which might lead to amputation. - *British*

Necrosis - Gangrene - He had necrosis in his leg which needed treatment. - *British*

Neoplastic - Tumour-related - Her illness was neoplastic and needed further investigation. - *British*

Nephritis - Kidney inflammation - He had had nephritis since he was a very young child. - *British*

Nephrolith - Kidney stone - The man had a nephrolith, which the doctor was hoping he would pass without surgery. - *British*

Nephropathy - Kidney disease - He had been diagnosed with nephropathy. - *British*

Nephrotic - Kidney disorder-related - His illness was nephrotic. - *British*

Nodose - With nodes - The tumour was nodose. - *British*

Nosocomial - Disease contracted in hospital - He acquired a nosocomial whilst in hospital. - *British*

Obstipation - Severe constipation - He had obstipation which was causing him a lot of discomfort. - *British*

Oedema - Swelling due to fluid - She had oedema of the feet and legs. - *British*

Oesophagitis - Gullet inflammation - He had oesophagitis and found it difficult to swallow. - *British*

Oncotic - Swelling related - Her illness caused her to be oncotic. - *British*

Opisthotonos - Spasm - He was regularly having opisthotonos. - *British*

Opportunistic - Disease usually excluded by body defences - It was an opportunistic disease which the body would usually deal with. - *British*

Osteodystrophy - Defective bone formation - "He has osteodystrophy," said the doctor. - *British*

Osteolysis - Bone dissolving - He had osteolysis in his spine, which was very painful. - *British*

Osteomalacia - Bone softening - He had osteomalacia in his leg, which made it difficult for him to walk. - *British*

Osteomyelitis - Bone inflammation - He had osteomyelitis in his leg, which was very serious. - *British*

Otitis - Ear inflammation - He was suffering from otitis, which was very painful. - *British*

Otorrhoea - Weeping ear - He had otorrhoea. - *British*

Otosclerosis - Progressive deafness - He had otosclerosis and needed treatment. - *British*

Ovarian - Ovary-related - The scan had shown an ovarian cyst. - *British*

Pancreatitis - Inflammation of the pancreas - She had been diagnosed with pancreatitis. - *British*

Panniculitis - Inflammation of fat under the skin - He had panniculitis. - *British*

Paraesthesia - Pins and needles - He had paraesthesia in his legs. - *British*

Paraplegia - Paralysis - After the accident he had paraplegia. - *British*

Paresis - Partial paralysis - He was suffering from paresis. - *British*

Parkinsonism - Parkinson's disease - He had parkinsonism. - *British*

Medical

239

Paronychia - Inflammation of the nail skin - The chiropodist diagnosed that she had paronychia. - *British*

Parotitis - Swollen glands - He had parotitis and was feeling unwell. - *British*

Pediculosis - Lice - All of the children had pediculosis in their hair. - *British*

Peptic ulcer - Stomach ulcer - He had a peptic ulcer. - *British*

Periarthritis - Joint inflammation - She had periarthritis. - *British*

Pertussis - Whooping cough - The little boy was diagnosed with pertussis. - *British*

Petit mal - Minor epilepsy - She often had petit mal attacks. - *British*

Pharyngitis - Sore throat - He was diagnosed with pharyngitis. - *British*

Phlebitis - Vein inflammation - The doctor diagnosed that she had phlebitis. - *British*

Phlegmon (niet: flegmone) - Phlegm - She was always coughing up phlegmon. - *British*

Photophobia - Intolerance to light - He had photophobia and did not like the light on. - *British*

Photosensitivity - Over-sensitivity to light - He had photosensitivity and did not like daylight. - *British*

Photosensitization - Development of over-sensitivity to sunlight - He had developed photosensitization to light. - *British*

Poliomyelitis - Polio - He had contracted poliomyelitis as a child. - *British*

Polyarthritis - Severe arthritis - He had polyarthritis. - *British*

Polydipsia - Chronic thirst - He had polydipsia and needed to keep drinking. - *British*

Preclinical - Before the disease becomes recognisable - The illness was preclinical and was not recognisable. - *British*

Preload - Heart muscle tension - "The preload is pretty high," said the cardiologist. - *British*

Priapism - Continuous erection - He had a priapism which was very embarrassing. - *British*

Proctitis - Sore bottom - He had proctitis and had a job walking. - *British*

Prostatism - Prostate trouble - He had prostatism and had discussed the various treatments with the doctor. - *British*

Prostatitis - Prostate inflammation - He had prostatitis. - *British*

Pruritic - Itchy - The rash was pruritic and very irritating. - *British*

Pruritus - Itching - She had pruritus. - *British*

Pseudotumour - Tumour-like growth - He had a pseudotumour on his leg. - *British*

Pustular - Boil-like - He had lots of pustular spots on his face. - *British*

Pyelitis - Inflammation of kidney pelvis - She was suffering from pyelitis and needed medication. - *British*

Pyelonephritis - Inflammation of the kidney and its pelvis - She had pyelonephritis and needed treatment urgently. - *British*

Pyoderma - Skin disease resulting in pustules - He had been given medication for pyoderma. - *British*

Pyrosis - Heartburn - She always got pyrosis at night. - *British*

Raucousness - Hoarseness - She had raucousness and could hardly speak. - *British*

Raynaud's phenomenon - Chilblains - He had Raynaud's phenomenon on his toes. - *British*

Reflux - Return flow - The baby was suffering from reflux and kept vomiting his milk back. - *British*

Regurgitation - Bringing back - The patient suffered regurgitation and kept bringing back her food. - *British*

Rhagade - Fissures, cracks or scars in the skin. There is a connection to congenital syphilis - There were rhagades around his mouth and nose. - *British*

Rhinitis - Hay fever - In the summer, she always got rhinitis. - *British*

Rhinopharyngitis - Inflammation of the space behind the nose - She had rhinopharyngitis. - *British*

Medical

240

Rhinorrhoea - A runny nose - He had rhinorrhoea. - *British*

Rhonchus - Wheezing - He had really bad rhonchus and needed treatment. - *British*

Rigidity - Stiffness - There was a lot of rigidity in her arm. - *British*

Rubella - German measles - The little girl had contracted rubella. - *British*

Salpingitis - Inflammation of the fallopian tubes - She had salpingitis which needed treatment. - *British*

Sarcoma - Tumour - He had a sarcoma in his lung and was seen by the oncologist. - *British*

Scarlatina - Scarlet fever - The child had been diagnosed with scarlatina. - *British*

Singultus - Hiccup - He had a singultus and needed a drink of water. - *British*

Somnambulism - Sleep-walking - It was clear that he had somnambulism. - *British*

Souffle - Puff - His face would souffle up when he suffered allergy. - *British*

Spasticity - Muscle rigidity - He was suffering spasticity in his right leg. - *British*

Splenomegaly - Spleen enlargement - He had a splenomegaly. - *British*

Spondylitis - Vertebrae inflammation - He was suffering with spondylitis in his neck. - *British*

Steatorrhoea - Excess fat in the motions - She had steatorrhoea which needed further investigation. - *British*

Steatosis - Fatty degeneration - He had steatosis. - *British*

Stenosis - Duct narrowing - She had stenosis in the arteries. - *British*

Stomatitis - Mouth inflammation - She had stomatitis preventing her from eating. - *British*

Struma - Thyroid enlargement - She was suffering with struma, which needed further investigation. - *British*

Sublingual - Under the tongue - She had sublingual ulcers, which were very painful. - *British*

Surdity - Deafness - He had surdity in the right ear. - *British*

Syncope - Fainting - She was prone to syncope attacks. - *British*

Synovitis - Inflammation of a joint-lubricating membrane - She had synovitis in her knee joint. - *British*

Telangiectasia - Broken veins - She had telangiectasia. - *British*

Tendinitis - Inflamed tendons - She had been diagnosed with tendinitis in her wrist. - *British*

Tenesmus - The runs/diarrhoea - He had tenesmus all morning, and could not leave the toilet. - *British*

Tetany - Muscle spasm - He often had tetany in the night, which gave him cramp in his leg. - *British*

Thrombolytic - Dissolving blood clots - He was prescribed thrombolytic medication. - *British*

Thrombophlebitis - Vein inflammation plus blood clotting - He had thrombophlebitis in his leg. - *British*

Thrombus - Blood clot - He had a thrombus following his surgery. - *British*

Thyrotoxicosis - Overactive thyroid - She had thyrotoxicosis. - *British*

Tinea pedis - Foot infection - He had a tinea pedis and was finding it difficult to walk. - *British*

Tinnitus - Ringing in the ears - He had been diagnosed as suffering from tinnitus. - *British*

Tophus - Gout - He has tophus in his feet. - *British*

Trismus - Lockjaw - He had been diagnosed with trismus. - *British*

Ulcus cruris - Foot ulcer - He had an ulcus cruris on his foot. - *British*

Urticaria - Hives - From time to time, she suffered with urticaria. - *British*

Vaccinia - Cowpox - He had been diagnosed with vaccinia. - *British*

Varicella - Chicken pox - He had been diagnosed with varicella. - *British*

Medical

Medical

Xanthoma - Fatty skin tumour - He had been diagnosed with a xanthoma. - *British*

Empiric - Based on experience - The treatment was based on empiric data. - *British*

Endemic - Occurring continuously in a population - The spread of measles was endemic. - *British*

Epidemiological - Involving study of epidemics - They had undertaken an epidemiological study. - *British*

Histological - Microscopic study of body-related - She was undertaking a histological study. - *British*

Hypothesis - Theory - The trainee had written his hypothesis and now needed to do the research. - *British*

Immunological - Immunity study-related - They had carried out an immunological study in the past. - *British*

Incidence - Number of cases - There were a number of incidences of measles in the area. - *British*

Accumulation - Build-up - There was an accumulation of plaque on the patient's teeth that the dentist needed to deal with. - *British*

Caries - Decay - The little girl had caries in her teeth that required dental treatment. - *British*

Cavity - Hollow - She had lots of cavities in her teeth. - *British*

Dentition - Set of teeth - "He needs a new dentition," said the dentist. - *British*

Gingivitis - Gum inflammation - "You have gingivitis," said the dentist. - *British*

Masticatory - Chewing-related - His problem was masticatory and he was losing weight because he could not eat. - *British*

Vestibular - Inside tooth surface-related - The dentist diagnosed a vestibular problem. - *British*

Causal - Cause-related - The causal diagnosis was difficult to determine. - *British*

Endogenous - Without obvious external cause - The infection was endogenous and was difficult to diagnose. - *British*

Interpretation - Explanation - He gave us his interpretation of what he thought the cause of the patient's illness was. - *British*

Adverse - Harmful - If you take drugs, you are likely to get an adverse reaction and could become quite poorly. - *British*

Neuroleptanalgesia - Altered awareness of pain due to drugs - Due to his drugs, he had neuroleptanalgesia. - *British*

Opiate (niet: opioid) - Opium-like drug - He had been taking opiates for a long time. - *British*

Toxicomania - Drug addiction - He had toxicomania from the number of drugs he took. - *British*

Chrysophobia/aurophobia - Fear of gold - Sue has been diagnosed as having a fear of gold or chrysophobia or aurophobia. - *British*

Heliophobia - Fear of sun - Heliophobia is the fear of the sun. - *British*

Hydrophobia - Fear of water - Some people have a fear of water: hydrophobia. - *British*

Mysophobia - Fear of dirt - Margaret has a fear of dirt. This is called mysophobia. - *British*

Photophobia - Fear of light - The fear of light is called: photophobia. - *British*

Thermophobia - Fear of heat - Job had thermophobia. - *British*

Aura - Warning sensation - The nurse had an aura that something bad was about to happen. - *British*

Dyscrasia - Bad temper - I have dyscrasia and can get in a bad mood easily! - *British*

Zelotypophobia - Fear of jealousy - Tracey has zelotypophobia. - *British*

Biodegradation - Bio-degrading - The waste material was being tested for its bio-degradable properties. - *British*

Bioequivalent - Equivalent - We will need to get a bioequivalent. - *British*

Arteriography - Artery x-ray - The doctor referred him for arteriography. - *British*

Assay - Analytical test - The nurse wanted to undertake an assay before making comment. - *British*

Auscultation - Listening with a stethoscope - The doctor carried out ausculation on the little boy's chest. - *British*

Cholangiography - Bile duct x-ray - The doctor referred the patient for a cholangiography. - *British*

Contrast medium - Barium or iodine - Barium or iodine, is a contrast medium. - *British*

Cranial - Skull-related - The injury was cranial and needed a CT scan. - *British*

Cystoscopy - Bladder examination - The G.P. referred him for a cystoscopy. - *British*

Dark - Blood-stained stools or vomit - "He has dark stools and vomit," said the doctor. - *British*

Echography - Scan - He was sent for an echography to examine his heart. - *British*

Electrocardiography - Heart monitor - They had connected him to electrocardiography to monitor his heart. - *British*

Electroencephalography - Brain scan - The consultant referred him for a electroencephalography. - *British*

Electrophysiological - Involving study of electrical phenomena in living bodies - They undertook an electrophysiological study. - *British*

Endoscopy - Internal examination using fibre optic tube - The G.P. referred the patient for an endoscopy to aid his diagnosis. - *British*

Flaccid - Soft - Her stomach was flaccid and did not show signs of infection. - *British*

Gonioscopy - Eye examination - The G.P. referred her for a gonioscopy. - *British*

Intact - Whole - The area around his hip appeared to be intact following his accident. - *British*

Micrography - Microscope examination - He was undergoing micrography. - *British*

Phlebography - Vein x-ray - The doctor referred her for a phlebography. - *British*

Qrs complex - Part of heart monitor readout - Qrs complex is part of the heart monitor readout. - *British*

Radiography - X-ray - He was referred to radiography. - *British*

Radiological - X-ray-related - The error was radiological and needed investigation. - *British*

Rectal - Bowel-related - He underwent a rectal examination which was uncomfortable. - *British*

Tomography - CT scanning - He was undergoing tomography to identify the problem. - *British*

Urography - Urinary tract x-ray - The doctor referred him for a urography. - *British*

Vital capacity - Lung capacity - "Can you measure his vital capacity please? " asked the doctor. - *British*

Miotic - Eye drops - "Can you please put some miotic in her eyes?" said the ophthalmologist. - *British*

Myopia - Short-sightedness - The ophthalmologist had diagnosed myopia. - *British*

Nystagmus - Wonky eyes - The little girl had nystagmus and needed assessment. - *British*

Ocular - Eye-related - His illness was ocular and he was referred to the eye hospital. - *British*

Oculogyric - Involving circular eye movements - The assessment was oculogyric. - *British*

Oculomucocutaneous - Mucous membrane and skin around eyes-related - The oculomucocutaneous relates to the skin around the eyes. - *British*

Ophthalmic - Eye-related - The disease was of an ophthalmic nature. - *British*

Ophthalmological - Eye treatment-related - The treatment was ophthalmological. - *British*

Optic - Eye-related - The problem was in her optic nerve. - *British*

Medical

Orbital - Eye socket-related - The issue was orbital and needed further assessment. - *British*

Palpebral - Eyelid-related - Her illness was palpebral and she needed to see the ophthalmologist. - *British*

Papillitis - Optical disk inflammation - Papillitis is optical disc inflammation. - *British*

Papilloedema - Swollen optical disk - Papilloedema is a swollen optical disc. - *British*

Periorbital - Eye socket-related - His illness was periorbital. - *British*

Proptosis - Protruding eyes - She had proptosis. - *British*

Ptosis - Droopy upper eyelid - She had a ptosis which was very noticeable. - *British*

Pupillary dilation - Wide eyes - He had pupillary dilation. - *British*

Retinal - Eye-related - The disease was retinal and she needed to go to the eye hospital. - *British*

Retinopathy - Eye-disease - He had retinopathy and needed treatment. - *British*

Retrobulbar - Eyeball - Retrobulbar means behind the eyeball. - *British*

Scotoma - Blind spot - He had a scotoma in one corner of his eye. - *British*

Strabismus - Squint - He had a strabismus in his left eye. - *British*

Subconjunctival - Under the white of the eye covering - The disease was subconjunctival and she needed to be seen by the ophthalmologist. - *British*

Trachoma - Eye infection - Her eye was swollen from a trachoma. - *British*

Affinity - Attraction - I felt I had an affinity with the other girls in my class. - *British*

Androgenic - Masculine - The model looked very androgenic in his smart suit. - *British*

Localization - Locating - "We are hoping for localization near the hospital," said the manager, referring to the new paediatrician. - *British*

Maceration - Soaking - Maceration is to soften by soaking. - *British*

Manifest - Visible - The lump had only begun to manifest the week before. - *British*

Manifestation - Sign - The manifestation of the problem had been very recent. - *British*

Median - Average - The median is the middle value in a frequency distribution. - *British*

Mediate - Indirect - He usually took the mediate route to work. - *British*

Metabolite - Substance produced by metabolism - Metabolite is a substance produced by metabolism. - *British*

Microsporum - Type of fungus - Miscrosporum is a type of fungus. - *British*

Microvillus - Bump on a cell - Microvillus is a bump on a cell. - *British*

Mime (niet: mimicry) - Facial expression - "Just look at this mime," said the physiotherapist. - *British*

Morbidity - Diseased state - The morbidity of the area was researched. - *British*

Motility - Ability to move spontaneously - She had motility and could move unassisted. - *British*

Mucocutaneous - Mucous membrane and skin-related - Mucotaneous is a region of the body where mucosa transitions to skin. - *British*

Mucopurulent - Containing mucus and pus - The wound was mucopurulent. - *British*

Mycological - Fungus study-related - They were undertaking a mycological study. - *British*

Nadir - Low point - He was at the nadir and from here it could only be up. - *British*

Nidation - Fertilisation - She wanted to undertake a nidation treatment but it was very costly. - *British*

Occlusion - Closing - The surgeon had reached the point of occlusion of the wound. - *British*

Occult - Concealed - The occult involves mystical powers or phenomena - *British*

Odour - Smell - There was a strange odour in the room. - *British*

Oligoelement - Trace element - There was an oligoelement found. - *British*

Opalescent - Opal-like - The jewellery was opalescent. - *British*

Orientation - Awareness of your environment - His orientation was poor following his accident. - *British*

Osmotic - Osmosis-related - The osmotic pressure is the minimum amount of pressure needed to prevent water, for example, flowing in across a semipermeable membrane. - *British*

Ototoxic - Damaging hearing - The loud music was ototoxic but the young people enjoyed it. - *British*

Oxidation - Adding oxygen - The patient needed oxidation and was connected to a respirator. - *British*

Paediatric - Paediatric- children - She was referred to the paediatric department for assessment. - *British*

Palliative - Giving relief but not cure - There was no cure for her illness so she was referred for palliative care. - *British*

Parasitic - Parasite-related - The doctor thought she had a parasitic infection under the skin. - *British*

Parenteral - Not by mouth - "No food parenteral, until after surgery," said the doctor. - *British*

Paroxysmal - In sudden attacks - The fits came paroxysmal. - *British*

Pathogen - Disease-producing organism - A pathogen is a disease producing organism. - *British*

Pathological - Disease study-related - They undertook a pathological study for their research. - *British*

Percutaneous - Through the skin - The incision was made percutaneous. - *British*

Perennial - Persistent - "Lack of resources is a perennial problem," said the nurse. - *British*

Perfusion - Through passage of fluid - The medication was administered through perfusion. - *British*

Periodic (niet: periodical) - Periodic - The issue was periodic and only happened occasionally. - *British*

Perioperative - Immediate pre and post-operative - The problem usually occurred perioperative. - *British*

Pernicious - Fatal - The disease was pernicious. - *British*

Peroral - By mouth - The medication was given peroral. - *British*

Phagocytosis - Destruction of bacteria - The medication was phagocytosis. - *British*

Pharmacodynamics - Study of biochemical and physiological effects of drugs - They were undertaking a pharmacodynamics study. - *British*

Pharmacological - Drug science-related - The study was pharmacological. - *British*

Physicochemical - Physics and chemistry-related - The research was physicochemical. - *British*

Physiological - Normal - The outcome of the physiological studies were widely discussed. - *British*

Plexus - Network - The plexus is a network of blood vessels. - *British*

Polymorphic - In a variety of shapes - The illness was polymorphic and passed through many different stages. - *British*

Polypeptide - Amino acid polymer - A polypeptide consists of many peptides. - *British*

Polyvalent - With more than one valence - Polyvalence means active against several toxins or pathogens. - *British*

Postprandial - After dinner - "We will give her more medication postprandial," said the doctor. - *British*

Postural - Posture-related - Her illness was postural and she needed physiotherapy. - *British*

Precursor - Forerunner - The symptoms were the precursor to the full blown disease. - *British*

Predisposition - Tendency - He had a predisposition to getting chest infections. - *British*

Presentation - Angle - The illness presentation was different than he had seen before. - *British*

Primary - First - She was part of the primary care team at the hospital. - *British*

Primary vaccination - First vaccination - It was the child's primary vaccination and he did not know what was happening. - *British*

Prognosis - Outlook - The prognosis was not looking good. - *British*

Proliferation - Multiplication - There had been a proliferation of MRSA in the hospital. - *British*

Prophylaxis - Disease prevention - The public health department was concerned with prophylaxis. - *British*

Propulsive - Driving - He was the propulsive force behind the scheme. - *British*

Prosthesis - Artificial limb - He was going to the hospital to have his prosthesis fitted today. - *British*

Protease - Enzyme - Protease is an enzyme. - *British*

Protective - Protector - She was asked to wear protective clothing when undertaking some procedures. - *British*

Proteolytic - Able to split molecules - Proteolytic is an enzyme that digests proteins. - *British*

Protozoon - Single-cell creature - Protozoon is a single cell creature. - *British*

Proximal - Nearest - The proximal surgery was many miles away. - *British*

Purulent - Pustules - The infection was purulent and needed urgent treatment. - *British*

Pyrexia - Fever - He had pyrexia and a high temperature. - *British*

Pyrogenic (niet: pyrogen) - Fever-inducing - The illness was pyrogenic and he needed medication to control his temperature. - *British*

Qt interval - Space between two seizures - "The Qt interval is very short" said the nurse. - *British*

Quaternary - Fourth - The meeting is in the quaternary every year. - *British*

Quiescent - Inactive - The illness is quiescent at the moment. - *British*

Reabsorption - Absorbing again - Reabsorption means absorbing again. - *British*

Recidivist - Person who lapses back into old habits - He was a known recidivist who regularly relapsed into bad habits. - *British*

Recombinant - Produced from more than one source - The medication was a recombinant and produced from more than one source. - *British*

Reconstitution - Regeneration - They had carried out the reconstitution of the department and it was looking good. - *British*

Reconvalescence - Convalescence - He was being sent for reconvalescence, which he was looking forward to. - *British*

Recurrent - Recurring - The illness was recurrent and did not appear to be manageable with medication. - *British*

Refractory - Not responding to treatment - "The illness is refractory," said the doctor. - *British*

Renin - Enzyme - Renin is an enzyme involved in the regulation of blood pressure. - *British*

Replication - Duplication - The prescription had been the subject of replication. - *British*

Retard - Delay - The child was considered 'a retard' and had delayed development, although this term is not PC today. - *British*

Retardation - Delaying - The child had retardation which was delaying his development. - *British*

Retraction - Moving backwards - The surgeon retracted his original diagnoses having carried out more tests. - *British*

Retrograde - Backwards - He was taking retrograde steps which were taking him nowhere. - *British*

Revulsive - Causing revulsion - "The pus that came out of his wound was revulsive," said the HCA. - *British*

Routinely - Usually - "Routinely, the tests come back fairly quickly," said the rheumatologist. - *British*

Saline - Salty - She had been given a saline drip as soon as she was admitted. - *British*

Salivation - Salivating - He was salivating at the smell coming from the canteen. - *British*

Saluric - Salutetic drugs encourage the excretion of sodium and chlorine salts in urine - Saluric means encouraging sodium and chlorine excretion in the urine. - *British*

Saprophyte - Organism living on dead, decaying matter - There were lots of saprophyte on the dead body. - *British*

Sclerosis - Hardening - The woman was diagnosed with sclerosis. - *British*

Senility - Old age - The woman was senile and needed care. - *British*

Sensory - Sense-related - They had built a sensory room at the hospital. - *British*

Sequelae - Complication - The sequelae is the complication that follows a disease. - *British*

Somatic - Body-related - She needed somatic care, from her carers. - *British*

Sputum - Phlegm - He was coughing up lots of sputum and needed a nebuliser. - *British*

Stasis - Keeping in check - "In order to stasis, we will see him regularly," said the doctor in clinic. - *British*

Stomatological - Involving the study of mouth inflammation - They had undertaken a stomatological study. - *British*

Subacute - Somewhat acute - "The illness is subacute," said the doctor. - *British*

Subclinical - Mild - Subclinical means mild. - *British*

Substrate - Substance on which an enzyme acts - Substrate is a substance on which an enzyme acts. - *British*

Superinfection - Secondary infection - The little boy had a superinfection that also needed treatment. - *British*

Supine - Laying down - She was supine when brought in by the paramedics. - *British*

Suppressive - Suppressing - He prescribed a suppressive drug. - *British*

Suppuration - Discharging pus - The wound was suppuration and was not good to look at. - *British*

Symptomatology - Study of symptoms - They were undertaking symptomatology. - *British*

Synergistic - Combined - The group became synergistic and worked well together. - *British*

Systemic - Whole body-related - The disease was systemic and affected her whole body. - *British*

Systolic - Part of blood pressure reading - The systolic is part of your blood pressure reading. - *British*

Tardive - Late - He was always tardive and left us waiting. - *British*

Tensioactive - Affecting surface tension - Tensioactive means affecting surface tension. - *British*

Titre - Concentration of a substance in solution - Titre is the concentration of a substance in a solution. - *British*

Transitory - Brief - He was only here for a transitory moment. - *British*

Tubercular - Nodular - The disease was tubercular. - *British*

Congenital - From birth - The illness was congenital and was apparent when the child was born. - *British*

Inherent - Natural - It was inherent to his personality. - *British*

Abrasion - Graze - The little boy had an abrasion on his knee caused by his falling over. - *British*

Habitual - Usual - It was habitual for her to miss lunch. - *British*

Auditory - Hearing-related - His giddiness was auditory and he was referred to ENT. - *British*

Aural - Heard - Aural issues are hearing related. - *British*

Auricular - Ear-related - The illness was auricular and so he was referred to the ENT Department. - *British*

Cerumen - Earwax - The patient had lots of cerumen which needed treatment. - *British*

Cochlear - Acoustic nerve-related - The problem seemed to be in his cochlear. - *British*

Cardiological - Heart study-related - The research was cardiological. - *British*

Cardiomegaly - Heart enlargement - The child had cardiomegaly and was very unwell. - *British*

Cardiomyopathy - Chronic heart disease - The elderly man was suffering from cardiomyopathy. - *British*

Cardiopathy - Heart disease - The woman had cardiopathy. - *British*

Cardiopulmonary - Heart and lung-related - The disease appeared to be of a cardiopulmonary nature. - *British*

Cardiorespiratory - Heart and lung-related - The disease appeared to be of a cardiorespiratory nature. - *British*

Cardioselective - Affecting the heart most - The disease was cardioselective. - *British*

Cardiotonic - Heart tonic - The Doctor prescribed a cardiotonic. - *British*

Cardiotoxic - Poisonous to the heart - The medication was cardiotoxic. - *British*

Cardiovascular - Heart and blood vessel-related - His illness was cardiovascular. - *British*

Defibrillation - Restoring heart beat - There were a number of defibrillation machines installed in the school. - *British*

Endocarditis - Heart (lining and valve) inflammation - She had endocarditis. - *British*

Infarction - Heart attack - He had suffered an infarction and was admitted to the heart hospital. - *British*

Myocarditis - Heart inflammation - He was assessed as suffering from myocarditis. - *British*

Pericarditis - Heart inflammation - She had pericarditis. - *British*

Supraventricular - Above the heart chambers - The disease was supraventricular. - *British*

Tachyarrhythmia - Irregular heartbeat - She had tachyarrhythmia. - *British*

Tachycardia - Racing heart - After surgery she had tachycardia. - *British*

Torsade de pointes - Irregular heartbeat - He had a torsade de pointes, which left him breathless. - *British*

Ventricular - Heart chamber-related - The problem was ventricular and needed urgent treatment. - *British*

Oestrogen - Female hormone - The tablets the doctor prescribed contained oestrogen. - *British*

Progestogen - Female hormone - Her HRT medication contained the drug progestogen. - *British*

Somatotrophin - Growth hormone - The doctor prescribed somatotrophin. - *British*

Disinfectant - Disinfectant - The floors were regularly washed with disinfectant. - *British*

Borborygmus - Rumbling tummy - All the way through the lecture she had a borborygmus! - *British*

Billy Rae Cyrus - Virus - Jack has got a Billy Rae Cyrus and needs some paracetamol. - *cockney*

Antigen - Foreign substance - An antigen is a substance that can trigger an immune response. - *British*

Contractility - Ability to contract - She was not sure about their contractility with regards to malaria in Africa. - *British*

Contusion - Bruise - The little boy had multiple contusions to his head. - *British*

Agalactia - Not producing milk - The lamb was agalactia and was unable to feed its offspring. - *British*

Correlation - Association - There seemed to be a correlation between his lifestyle and his condition. - *British*

Mucolytic - Main part of mucous - Mucolytic drugs make spit less sticky, and easier to cough up. - *British*

Pneumopathy - Lung disease - He was diagnosed with pneumopathy several weeks before. - *British*

Mucociliary - Mucous membrane and hair-related. Lungs - The Mucociliary Transport System consists of cilia (hairs) which line the airways and move mucus. - *British*

Medical

Peak flow - Lung power - "Can you measure his peak flow please," said the G.P. to the practice nurse. - *British*

Pulmonary - Lung-related - He had a pulmonary illness. - *British*

Tracheitis - Bronchitis - She had been diagnosed with tracheitis. - *British*

Ventilation - Breathing - He needed ventilation to assist him with his breathing. - *British*

Approximate - Rough - My approximate time of arrival is 12 noon. - *British*

Belonephobia - Fear of needles - It is unfortunate to be belonephobic if you need an injection. - *British*

Bromidrosiphobia - Fear of body odour - Karen has been diagnosed with bromidrosiphobia. - *British*

Carcinophobia - Fear of cancer - Lots of people have a real fear of cancer: carcinophobia. - *British*

Cardiophobia - Fear of heart disease - John has been diagnised with cardiophobia. - *British*

Coitophobia - Fear of coitus - Some people have a fear of sex; coitophobia. - *British*

Coprophobia - Fear of faeces - The doctor diagnosed, coprophobia. - *British*

Coprostasophobia - Fear of constipation - After taking so many laxatives, the doctor decided the patient had coprostasophobia. - *British*

Dermatosiophobia - Fear of skin disease - A fear of contracting a skin disease is called, dermatosiophobia. - *British*

Emetophobia - Fear of vomiting - Emetophobia is a fear of vomiting. - *British*

Erythrophobia - Fear of blushing - Erythrophobia is the fear of blushing. - *British*

Febriphobia - Fear of fever - Febriphobia is the fear of falling sick with a fever. - *British*

Haemophobia - Fear of blood - The fear of blood is called, haemophobia. - *British*

Hydrophobophobia - Fear of rabies - A fear of rabies is called: hydrophobophobia. - *British*

Hypnophobia - Fear of sleep - The fear of sleep is called: hypnophobia. - *British*

Kopophobia - Fear of fatigue - Kopophobia is the fear of fatigue. - *British*

Leprophobia - Fear of leprosy - The fear of leprosy is called: leprophobia. - *British*

Lyssophobia/maniphobia - Fear of insanity - The fear of insanity can be defined either as lyssophobia or maniphobia. - *British*

Nosophobia - Fear of illness - Mary has nosophobia. - *British*

Odontophobia - Fear of teeth - You would not become a dentist if you had odontophobia! - *British*

Ommetaphobia - Fear of eyes - You would not become an opthalmist if you had ommetaphobia! - *British*

Pathophobia/nosophobia - Fear of disease - If you have a fear of disease it is called: pathophobia or nosophobia. - *British*

Patroiophobia - Fear of heredity - Jodie has patroiophobia. - *British*

Phagophobia - Fear of swallowing - Jim has phagophobia, which makes eating almost impossible. - *British*

Pharmacophobia - Fear of drugs - Alice has pharmacophobia. - *British*

Phthisiophobia - Fear of tuberculosis - If you are fearful of tuberculosis, it is called: phthisiophobia. - *British*

Potophobia - Fear of drink - To have a fear of drinking is called: potophobia. - *British*

Scabiophobia - Fear of scabies - Carol has scabiophobia. - *British*

Selaphobia - Fear of flesh - Demelsa has selaphobia. - *British*

Syphilophobia - Fear of venereal disease - The fear of venereal disease is called, syphilophobia. - *British*

Thanatophobia - Fear of death - Frank has thanatophobia. - *British*

Tocophobia - Fear of childbirth - You could not be a midwife if you had tocophobia. - *British*

Toxiphobia - Fear of poison - To have a fear of poison is called, toxiphobia. - *British*

Medical

Traumatophobia - Fear of injury - Conrad has traumatophobia. - *British*

Trypanophobia/vaccinophobia - Fear of inoculation - You would have difficulty being a nurse, if you were trypanophobic or vaccinophobic. - *British*

Adsorption - Sticking to a surface - The plaster was known to have adsorption and would stick to the skin. - *British*

Dysfunction - Malfunction - There had been a dysfunction in the medical equipment. - *British*

Hermetic - Airtight - The bag needed to be hermetically sealed. - *British*

Urogenital - Urinary and genital apparatus-related - They had ordered some new urogenital apparatus. - *British*

Vial - Small bottle - The blood was collected in a small vial. - *British*

Acth - Hormone - "I have decided to give her the right acth," said the doctor. - *British*

Adjuvant - Stimulator - The doctor had prescribed an adjuvant in order to stimulate the patient. - *British*

Adrenergic - Acting like adrenaline - "That drug is adrenergic," said the doctor. - *British*

Adrenolytic - Adrenaline-blocking - "That drug is adrenolytic," said the doctor. - *British*

Agent - Substance - He had mixed the drugs with some other agent to reduce the toxicity. - *British*

Aggravation - Worsening - The medication was causing me aggravation, and making my illness worse. - *British*

Alkylate - Anti-cancer treatment - The woman was being treated with alkylate for her breast cancer. - *British*

Ampoule - Small sealed flask - The medication was in an ampoule and needed to be injected. - *British*

Anabolic - Body-building - Doug knew that if it was discovered he was using anabolic steroids, he would be suspended. - *British*

Anaesthesia - Deadening of sensation - Before the operation the patient was given anaesthesia to deaden the pain. - *British*

Anaesthetic - Drug to deaden sensation - The girl was given a general anaesthetic before the operation. - *British*

Analeptic - Pick-me-up - The doctor prescribed an analeptic for the girl. - *British*

Analgesic - Pain-killer - Aspirin is an analgesic and will kill pain. - *British*

Antacid - Indigestion remedy - There are some very good antacids you can take for indigestion. - *British*

Antagonist - Substance tending to nullify effects of another - An antagonist is a substance which will nullify the effects of another. - *British*

Anthelmintic - Anti-worm drug - Some anthelmintic drugs produce side effects. - *British*

Antiallergic - Bacteria-destroying substance - The medicine was an antiallergic and was for destroying bacteria. - *British*

Antibiogramme - Part of cancer treatment - Antibiogramme is part of cancer treatment. - *British*

Antibiotherapy - Treatment with antibiotics - The doctor decided on a course of antibiotherapy for her infection. - *British*

Anticonvulsant - Substance to stop convulsions - The doctor gave him an anticonvulsant to stop his convulsions. - *British*

Antidepressant - Tranquiliser - When I was depressed, my G.P. prescribed anti-depressants to lift my mood. - *British*

Antidiabetic - Diabetes drug - To stabilize his diabetes, Joshua took an antidiabetic drug. - *British*

Antidiuretic - Substance to slow urine formation - To slow down his urine formulation, Brendan took an antidiuretic drug. - *British*

Antiemetic - Substance to stop vomiting - The doctor prescribed an antiemetic to stop the patient vomiting. - *British*

Antiepileptic - Epilepsy drug - To help control his epilepsy, the doctor prescribed an antiepileptic drug. - *British*

Medical

Antiexudative - Anti-inflammatory - To help with his arthritis, Bill took an antiexudative. - *British*

Antifibrinolytic - A drug to prevent the breakup of fibrin and maintain clot stability - The doctor prescribed an antifibrinolytic. - *British*

Antifungal - Fungus-killer - To cure his athletes foot fungus, Barry used an anti-fungal cream. - *British*

Antihypertensive - High blood pressure drug - To manage her high blood pressure, Diane took an antihypertensive drug. - *British*

Antiinfective - Disinfection - In order to reduce the infection, the doctor prescribed an antiinfective medicine. - *British*

Anti-inflammatory - Substance to reduce swelling - To reduce the swelling, the nurse prescribed an anti-inflammatory drug. - *British*

Antimicrobial - Substance to kill microorganisms - What was needed was an antimicrobial treatment to kill microorganisms. - *British*

Antimitotic - Anti-cancer drug - As part of her treatment for cancer, the doctor prescribed an antimitotic drug. - *British*

Antimycotic - Fungus treatment - To treat his fungus infection, the doctor prescribed an antimycotic. - *British*

Antineoplastic - Anti-cancer drug - The doctor prescribed an antineoplastic drug for the treatment of the woman's cancer. - *British*

Antioestrogenic - Oestrogen suppressant - In order to suppress the development of oestrogen, the doctor prescribed antioestrogenic medication. - *British*

Antiphlogistic - Swelling and fever treatment - "To stop the swelling and bring the fever down, we will use an antiphlogistic treatment," said the doctor. - *British*

Antiproliferative - Substance to stop spread of illness - "To stop the spread of infection, we will use an antiproliferative treatment," said the emergency doctor. - *British*

Antipruritic - Itch treatment - "To calm the itchiness, I will prescribe an antipruritic treatment," said the nurse. - *British*

Antipsychotic - Tranquiliser - In order to calm the patient, the psychiatrist prescribed an antipsychotic drug. - *British*

Antipyretic - Fever treatment - "The fever treatment I recommend is an antipyretic medication," said the doctor. - *British*

Antispasmodic - Spasm treatment - To help my IBS, the doctor gave me antispasmodic medication. - *British*

Antithrombotic - Blood clotting treatment - Following my stroke, the doctor prescribed an antithrombotic medication. - *British*

Antitoxin - Vaccine - I was given an antitoxin vaccine to help with my treatment. - *British*

Antitumour - Anti-cancer drug - The doctor recommended I take antitumour medication for my cancer. - *British*

Antitussive - Cough medicine - To help manage the cough, the pharmacist recommended an antitussive medication. - *British*

Antiviral - Virus treatment - I was given an antiviral treatment by the doctor. - *British*

Anxiolytic - Tranquiliser - "I will give him an anxiolytic to calm him down," said the psychiatrist. - *British*

Bioavailability - Effectiveness - "We will need to test this drug for its bioavailability," said the research chemist. - *British*

Bronchodilatation - Drug to help breathing - The doctor had prescribed a bronchodilatation. - *British*

Collyrium - Eye wash - The pharmacist recommended a collyrium for her sore eye. - *British*

Contraindication - Reason not to prescribe - The medication had several contraindications. - *British*

Corticosteroid - Hormone - The medication contained corticosteroid. - *British*

Cytostatic - Substance to stop cell growth - The doctor prescribed a cytostatic medication. - *British*

Medical

Diuretic - Drug to increase urine output - Her G.P. had prescribed a diuretic medication. - *British*

Dyspepsia - Indigestion - He needed some medication for dyspepsia. - *British*

Emetic - Substance to cause vomiting - The doctor gave the child an emetic after she had swallowed her mother's medication. - *British*

Entericcoated - Coating on tablets - The coating on some tablets is called enteric. - *British*

Excipient - Inactive part of drug - The excipient is the inactive part of the drug. - *British*

Expectorant - Cough medicine - The pharmacist recommended an expectorant medicine for her cough. - *British*

Fibrinolytic - Thrombylitic drug - Fibrinolytic was used to disperse the blood clot. - *British*

Fungistatic - Inhibiting the growth of fungus - The medication was fungistatic. - *British*

Germicide - Germ-killer - The ward had used lots of germicide in an attempt to stop the infection. - *British*

Hypnotic - Sleeping tablet - She had taken too many hypnotics and needed treatment. - *British*

Immunosuppressant - Drug to stop immune response - The doctor had prescribed an immunosuppressant. - *British*

Keratolytic - Product to produce skin shedding - She had applied a keratolytic to her arm. - *British*

Loading dose - Initial dose - "We will give him a loading dose in the first instance," said the doctor. - *British*

Medicament - Medicine - "Can you give her the medicament please?" asked the doctor. - *British*

Microgram - Millionth of a gram - She was unclear how many micrograms of medication he should be having. - *British*

Micronize - Reduce to fine powder - The medication had been micronized. - *British*

Monocomponent - One molecule drug - It was a monocomponent. - *British*

Morphinomimetic - Simulating effects of morphine - The doctor prescribed a morphinomimetic. - *British*

Mydriatic - Pupil-dilating drug - The doctor prescribed a mydriatic. - *British*

Myelosuppression - Stopping bone marrow activity - She had been prescribed a drug for myelosuppression. - *British*

Myelotoxicity - Destructive to bone marrow - The drug was myelotoxic. - *British*

Narcotic - Morphine-like drug - He was prescribed a narcotic. - *British*

Nephrotoxic - Destructive to the kidneys - The substance he was using was nephrotoxic. - *British*

Neuroleptic - Tranquiliser - The doctor had prescribed a neuroleptic drug. - *British*

Overdosage - Overdose - He was suffering from an overdosage of medication. - *British*

Penicillinase - Penicillin-destroying enzyme - The medication contained a penicillinase. - *British*

Pharmacokinetic - Action of drugs in body - The result was pharmacokinetic. - *British*

Pharmacon - Drug - The doctor prescribed pharmacon. - *British*

Polytherapy - Treatment using several drugs - She was being treated with polytherapy to attempt to halt the disease progressing. - *British*

Potentialization - Joint action of two drugs - The potentialization of the drugs was interesting. - *British*

Potentiation - Joint action of two drugs - The potentialization of the drugs was interesting. - *British*

Premedication - Pre-med - Medication given before an operation - He was given a pre-med before surgery. - *British*

Purgative - Strong laxative - The doctor had prescribed a purgative, and he had just got to the toilet in time! - *British*

Salicylism - Pain-killer poisoning - He had salicylism from taking too many tablets. - *British*

Medical

Sigmoid - S-shaped - The sigmoid colon is the lowest part of the colon. - *British*

Spasmolytic - Anti-spasm - "I have prescribed a spasmolytic," said the doctor. - *British*

Standard dosing - Standard dose - "We will dispense standard dosing," said the pharmacist. - *British*

Steroid - Steroid - He had been taking steroid medication for some time now. - *British*

Thyrostatic (niet: thyreostatic) - Anti thyroid product - He had ordered a thyrostatic from the pharmacy. - *British*

Topical - Applied to the surface - He was prescribed a topical medication. - *British*

Tricyclic - Drugs used to treat depression - He had been prescribed a tricyclic drug to treat his depression. - *British*

Tuberculostatic - Anti-TB drug - He was prescribed a tuberculostatic. - *British*

Ulcerogenic - Ulcer-causing - The medication was ulcerogenic. - *British*

Unitdose - Single dose - He was prescribed a unitdose. - *British*

Uricosuric - Drug to promote uric acid excretion - He was prescribed an uricosuric drug. - *British*

Menarche - First period - She was eleven when she had her first menarche. - *British*

Menorrhagia - Heavy periods - She had suffered with menorrhagia all of her life. - *British*

Menstruation - Periods - Some say that girls start menstruation earlier these days. - *British*

Oligomenorrhoea - Infrequent periods - She had oligomenrrhoea. - *British*

Postmenopausal - Postmenopausal - After the menopause - The woman was postmenopausal. - *British*

Agitation - Anxiety - The young man had a high level of agitation and was very anxious. - *British*

Dissociation - Separation or detachment from reality - Dissociation is commonly seen on a continuum. - *British*

Hypomania - A mild form of mania shown through hyperactivity and over the top happiness - His behaviour suggested hypomania. - *British*

Psychogenic - Caused by mental factors - His illness was psychogenic. - *British*

Psycholeptic - Hopelessness and inertia-related - His illness was psycholeptic. - *British*

Psychological - A condition that is rooted in the mind - The doctor thought his illness was psychological. - *British*

Psychomotor - Involving motor effects of mental activity - The illness was psychomotor and involved motor effects of mental activity. - *British*

Psychosis - Mental illness - The psychiatrist had diagnosed psychosis. - *British*

Psychotropic - Mood-altering - The psychiatrist had prescribed psychotropic drugs. - *British*

Coenzyme - Organic non protein molecule - There were a number of coenzymes in the food. - *British*

Antioxidant - Substance to stop decay - Antioxidants are mostly found in fruit and vegetables. - *British*

Ambulant - Walking - "There is no need for a wheelchair because the patient is quite ambulant," said the nurse. - *British*

Anergia - Inactivity - The youngster was suffering from anergia and was always tired. - *British*

Chronotropic - Speed-related - His accident had been chronotropic and he was badly injured. - *British*

Sideeffect - Side effect - There were lots of side effects to the medication. - *British*

Chemoreceptor - Nerve ending - The pain was felt in the chemoreceptor. - *British*

Depolarization - Nerve impulses - Depolarization occurs in nerves. - *British*

Innervation - Nerve distribution - Innervation is about how the nerves are distributed. - *British*

Neural - Nerve-related - The illness was neural. - *British*

Medical

Neuritis - Nerve inflammation - She had neuritis in her hand. - *British*

Neurological - Nervous system-related - Her problem was neurological and needed assessment. - *British*

Neuromuscular - Muscle and nerve-related - He had a neuromuscular disease. - *British*

Neuronal - Neuron-related - Neuronal describes a nerve related matter. - *British*

Neuropathy - Nervous system disorder - He had a neuropathy which needed treatment. - *British*

Neurotoxic - Destructive to nerve tissue - The substance was neurotoxic. - *British*

Neurotransmitter - Chemical released by nerve endings - The chemical released by nerve endings is called a neurotransmitter. - *British*

Neurovegetative - Nervous system-related - Neurovegetative is nervous system related. - *British*

Polyneuritis - Inflammation of the nerves - He had been diagnosed with polyneuritis the previous week. - *British*

Presynaptic - Before a nerve/organ joint - Presynaptic means before an organ joint. - *British*

Extrapyramidal - Part of central nerve system - The extrapyramidal is part of the nervous system. - *British*

Vagal - Nerve-related - The disease was vagal and needed treatment. - *British*

Vagotonia - A nerve complaint - She had been diagnosed with vagotonia. - *British*

Triskaidekaphobia - Fear of thirteen - You would not live at number 13 if you had triskaidekaphobia. - *British*

Bilateral - Two-sided - Mr. Jones had bilateral issues with his legs. - *British*

Oophorectomy - Removal of an ovary - She was undergoing an oophorectomy later in the day - *British*

Osteotomy - Cutting a bone - The surgeon undertook an osteotomy. - *British*

Preoperative - Before an operation - The nurse carried out preoperative procedures on the patient. - *British*

Resection - Removal of any part of the body - The surgeon carried out a resection of the kidney. - *British*

Transplantation - Transplantation - If she was lucky, she was hoping for a kidney transplantation. - *British*

Aerobic - With oxygen - The patient was advised to undertake aerobic exercise. - *British*

Abdomen - Gut - She has a pain in her gut and is constantly complaining of stomach ache. - *British*

Abdominal - Gut-related - Julia is suffering from abdominal pain. - *British*

Aberrant - Irregular - The pain was aberrant and came and went. - *British*

Mastodynia - Breast pain - She had mastodynia and needed to see her GP. - *British*

Myalgia - Muscle pain - His illness was some form of myalgia. - *British*

Sporadic - Random - The pain was sporadic, it came and went. - *British*

Vulvovaginitis - Vagina inflammation - She had vulvovaginitis which was very painful. - *British*

Anionic - With an anion - An anion is an ion with a negative charge. - *British*

Decubitus - Lying down - "He is decubitis, at the moment," said the nurse. - *British*

Disposition - Tendency - He had a disposition towards eating too much. - *British*

Diurnal - Daytime - Some animals are diurnal and very active in the daytime. - *British*

Effusion - Escape of fluid - There was an effusion of fluid from the drip. - *British*

Elective - Non-urgent - He was due for elective surgery next week. - *British*

Evacuation - Emptying - He had an evacuation of his bowels yesterday. - *British*

Extracorporeal - Outside the body - The cause was extracorporeal. - *British*

Indicate - Show - "Perhaps you could indicate whether you are free to come?" asked the nurse. - *British*

Indication - Sign - "Could you please give me an indication of your availability?" asked the doctor. - *British*

Infaust - Unfavourable - He had had an infaust reaction to the treatment. - *British*

Insufficiency - Inadequacy - They were concerned about the insufficiency of the equipment they had. - *British*

Interindividual - Between individuals - "The argument is interindividual and they must resolve it," said the medical director. - *British*

Intraindividual - Within the individual - The issue was intraindividual. - *British*

Agonist - Prime mover - He was the agonist in strike action over Doctor's pay. - *British*

Anterograde - Moving forward - He was anterograde and making progress. - *British*

Demophobia/ochlophobia - Fear of crowds - A fear of crowds is called: demophobia or ochlophobia. - *British*

Gamophobia - Fear of marriage - Gamophobia is the fear of marriage. - *British*

Gynophobia - Fear of women - Some people have gynophobia. - *British*

Hagiophobia - Fear of saints - If you are afraid of saints you might be hagiophobic. - *British*

Harpaxophobia - Fear of robbers - Harpaxophobia is the fear of robbers. - *British*

Hierophobia - Fear of priests - A fear of priests is called, hierophobia. - *British*

Homophobia - Fear of homosexuals - People with a fear of homosexuals are said to have homophobia. - *British*

Italophobia - Fear of Italy, its people and things - A fear of all things Italian, might be described as: italophobia. - *British*

Necrophobia - Fear of corpses - Necrophobia is the fear of corpses. - *British*

Ochlophobia - Fear of mobs - James has ochlophobia. - *British*

Onomatophobia - Fear of names - Yasmin has onomatophobia. - *British*

Paedophobia - Fear of children - You could not become a teacher if you had paedophobia. - *British*

Papaphobia - Fear of pope - Joe has papaphobia. - *British*

Phasmophobia - Fear of ghosts - Bert has phasmophobia. - *British*

Pogonophobia - Fear of beards - I have a fear of beards; pogonophobia. - *British*

Russophobia - Fear of Russian people and things - Derek has russophobia. - *British*

Satanophobia - Fear of satan - Ahmed is satanophobic. - *British*

Scotophobia - Fear of Scottish people and things - Benjamins is scotophobic. - *British*

Sinophobia - Fear of chinese people and things - Jack is sinophobic. - *British*

Teratophobia - Fear of monsters, giving birth to - Dexter and Daisy have teratophobia. - *British*

Theophobia - Fear of god - Jackie has theophobia. - *British*

Tyrannophobia - Fear of tyrants - John has tyrannophobia. - *British*

Xenophobia - Fear of foreigners - Ivor has xenophobia. - *British*

Vertigo - Fear of heights - He suffered badly with vertigo and did not like flying. - *British*

Acarophobia - Fear of itching - John has been diagnosed with acarophobia. - *British*

Acarophobia - Fear of mites - David has been diagnosed with acarophobia. - *British*

Acerophobia - Fear of sourness - Kevin has been diagnosed with acerophobia. - *British*

Acousticophobia - Fear of sound - Les has been diagnosed with acousticophobia. - *British*

Aichmophobia - Fear of sharp things - Stephanie has been diagnosed with aichmophobia, the fear of sharp things such as needles. - *British*

Medical

Acrophobia/hypsophobia - Fear of high places - Justin has been diagnosed with acrophobia or hypsophobia. - *British*

Aerophobia - Fear of air travel - Jane has been diagnosed with aerophobia. - *British*

Agoraphobia - Fear of open places - Catherine has agoraphobia. - *British*

Ailurophobia - Fear of cats - Graham has a fear of cats, it is called, ailurophobia. - *British*

Algophobia - Fear of pain - Emma has a fear of pain, algophobia. - *British*

Americophobia - Fear of American people and things - Joe has Americophobic. - *British*

Androphobia - Fear of men - A fear of men is called, androphobia. - *British*

Anemophobia - Fear of wind - A fear of wind is called, anemophobia. - *British*

Anginophobia - Fear of narrowness - A lesser known fear is, anginophobia, the fear of narrow spaces. - *British*

Anglophobia - Fear of English people and things - Anglophobia, is the fear of English people and things. - *British*

Anthophobia - Fear of flowers - Jonathan has been diagnosed with anthophobia. - *British*

Anthropophobia - Fear of people - Anthropophobia is the fear of people. - *British*

Antlophobia - Fear of floods - Antlophobia is a fear of floods. - *British*

Apeirophobia - Fear of infinity - Melanie has apeirophobia. - *British*

Apiphobia - Fear of bees - Lewis has a fear of bees, apiphobia. - *British*

Arachnophobia - Fear of spiders - Some people have a real fear of spiders. This is called, arachnophobia. - *British*

Asthenophobia - Fear of weakness - Asthenophobia, is the fear of weakness. - *British*

Astrapophobia - Fear of lightning - Val has a real fear of lightning, astrapophobia. - *British*

Atelophobia - Fear of imperfection - Peter has been diagnosed with atelophobia. - *British*

Atephobia - Fear of ruin - Andy has a fear of being ruined. This is called, atephobia. - *British*

Autophobia/ermitophobia - Fear of loneliness - Some people are fightened of being lonely. This is called autophobia or ermitophobia. - *British*

Bacillophobia/microbiophobia - Fear of microbes - A fear of microbes is called: bacillophobia or microbiophobia. - *British*

Bacteriophobia - Fear of bacteria - A fear of bacteria is called: bacteriophobia. - *British*

Ballistophobia - Fear of bullets - Some people have a real fear of bullets: ballistophobia. - *British*

Biphasic - Two-phase - The project was biphasic. - *British*

Chronophobia - Fear of time - Chelsea has chronophobia. - *British*

Dikephobia - Fear of justice - Andrew has dikephobia. - *British*

Eleutherophobia - Fear of freedom - Eleutherophobia is a fear of freedom. - *British*

Eremophobia - Fear of solitude - If you are diagnosed with eremophobia, you are afraid of solitude. - *British*

Ergophobia - Fear of work - Ergophobia is the fear of work. - *British*

Erotophobia - Fear of sex - Jessica is erotophobia, having a fear of sex. - *British*

Geumatophobia - Fear of taste - Sandu has geumatophobia. - *British*

Graphophobia - Fear of writing - Wellington has graphophobia. - *British*

Gymnophobia - Fear of nudity - Candice had gymnophobia when she was a small child. - *British*

Hamartophobia - Fear of sin - If you are very frightened of being sinful, you might be diagnosed with hamartophobia. - *British*

Haptophobia - Fear of touch - A fear of touch is called, haptophobia. - *British*

Medical

Hedonophobia - Fear of pleasure - Hedonophobia is the fear of pleasure. - *British*

Hormephobia - Fear of shock - The fear of shock is called, hormephobia. - *British*

Hypegiaphobia - Fear of responsibility - John has been diagnosed with hypegiaphobia. - *British*

Ideophobia - Fear of ideas - A fear of ideas is called, ideophobia. - *British*

Kakorrhaphiaphobia - Fear of failure - Kakorrhaphiaphobia is the fear of failure. - *British*

Katagelophobia - Fear of ridicule - Kim has katagelophobia. - *British*

Kinetophobia - Fear of motion - Davy has kinetophobia, a fear of motion. - *British*

Kleptophobia - Fear of stealing - Kleptophobia is the fear of stealing. - *British*

Lalophobia/laliophobia - Fear of stuttering - Some people have a fear of stuttering. This is called lalophobia or laliophobia. - *British*

Lalophobia/laliophobia/ glossophobia/phonophobia - Fear of speech - There are many ways to describe a fear of speech: lalophobia or laliophobia or glossophobia or phonophobia. - *British*

Logophobia - Fear of words - Logophobia is the fear of words. - *British*

Mastigophobia - Fear of beating - Gemma has mastigophobia. - *British*

Musicophobia - Fear of music - Those that are fearful of music, could have musicophobia. - *British*

Neophobia - Fear of new things - A fear of new things is called, neophobia. - *British*

Olfactophobia/osmophobia - Fear of smell - The fear of smell is olfactophobia or osmophobia. - *British*

Oneirophobia - Fear of dreams - Candy has oneirophobia. - *British*

Panophobia/pantophobia - Fear of everything - To have panophobia/ pantophobia would be severely debilitating. - *British*

Peniaphobia - Fear of poverty - Ken has peniaphobia. - *British*

Philosophobia - Fear of philosophy - Susie had philosophobia. - *British*

Phobophobia - Fear of fear - To have phobophobia, is to be afraid of fear itself. - *British*

Phronemophobia - Fear of thinking - The fear of thinking is phronemophobia. - *British*

Pinaciphobia/katastichophobia - Fear of lists - Having a fear of lists can be called: pinaciphobia or katastichophobia. - *British*

Pnigerophobia - Fear of smothering - Kath has pnigerophobia. - *British*

Poinephobia - Fear of punishment - Will has poinephobia. - *British*

Politicophobia - Fear of politics - Dwayne is politicophobic. - *British*

Rhabdophobia - Fear of magic - A magician could not have rhabdophobia. - *British*

Siderodromophobia - Fear of rail travel - The fear of rail travel is called: siderodromophobia. - *British*

Stasophobia - Fear of standing - Sherry has stasophobia. - *British*

Symmetrophobia - Fear of symmetry - Barb has symmetrophobia. - *British*

Tachophobia - Fear of speed - Janey has tachophobia. - *British*

Taphephobia - Fear of burial alive - Max has taphephobia, the fear of being buried alive. - *British*

Thassophobia - Fear of idleness - Nora has thassophobia. - *British*

Conduction - Transfer - Deafness is caused by the faulty conduction of sound. - *British*

Electrolyte - Solution which conducts electricity - An electrolyte is a solution which conducts electricity. - *British*

In situ - In the normal place - The equipment was found in situ for the nurses to access. - *British*

Accommodation - Adjustment - "We will make accommodation in order to fit him in," said the receptionist. - *British*

Medical

Bathophobia - Fear of depth, such as those found in stairwells or caves - Some people are too frightened of deep caves. They might have bathophobia. - *British*

Batophobia - Fear of high buildings - Batman does not have batophobia! - *British*

Claustrophobia - Fear of enclosed places - Lots of people do not like enclosed places, they suffer from claustrophobia. - *British*

Cremnophobia - Fear of precipices - Someone with a fear of the edge, the precipice, is described as cremnophobic. - *British*

Cyrnophobia - Fear of waves - Joanne has cyrnophobia. - *British*

Ecclesiophobia - Fear of church - A fear of churches is called, ecclesiophobia. - *British*

Eosophobia - Fear of dawn - Steve has been diagnosed with, eosophobia. - *British*

Francophobia/gallophobia - Fear of the French words, people and things - James has been diagnosed as having francophobia or gallophobia, a fear of the French. - *British*

Germanophobia/teutophobia - Fear of German, people and things - Germanophobia or teutophobia, are the fear of all things German. - *British*

Hadephobia/stygiophobia - Fear of hell - A fear of hell is called hadephobia or stygiophobia. - *British*

Hodophobia - Fear of travel - A fear of travel is called, hodophobia. - *British*

Kenophobia - Fear of voids - Carrie Anne has kenophobia. - *British*

Limnophobia - Fear of lakes - If you have a fear of lakes, it is called: limnophobia. - *British*

Nyctophobia - Fear of night - Stephanie has nyctophobia. - *British*

Oikophobia - Fear of home - John has oikophobia. - *British*

Potamophobia - Fear of rivers - Lesley has potamophobia. - *British*

Thalassophobia - Fear of sea - You could not be a sailor if you had thalassophobia. - *British*

Topophobia - Fear of places - The fear of places is called: topophobia. - *British*

Uranophobia - Fear of heaven - Fred has uranophobia. - *British*

Toxaemia - Blood poisoning - She had toxaemia. - *British*

Toxicity - Poisonousness - The level of toxicity in her body was high. - *British*

Toxicological - Poison study-related - They were undertaking a toxicological study. - *British*

Toxin - Poison - His liver was not dealing with the toxins any more. - *British*

Amino acid - Protein building block - Amino acids form the basic structure of all proteins. - *British*

Aetiology - Study of disease causation - I am interested in the study of disease formation so will include aetiology in my studies. - *British*

Coitus - Intercourse - "How often do you have coitus?" asked the therapist. - *British*

Condyloma - Genital warts - After being quite promiscuous, she was now suffering from a nasty bout of condyloma. - *British*

Contraception - Birth control - The young couple did not use any contraception and that is how she got pregnant. - *British*

Locoregional - Syphilitis-related - His illness was locoregional. - *British*

Potency - Sexual ability - His potency had reduced substantially since taking the medication. - *British*

Spermicide - Sperm-killing contraceptive - He used a spermicide when having sexual intercourse. - *British*

Urethritis - An STD - He was referred to the STI clinic with urethritis. - *British*

Venereal - Sexually transmitted - He had a venereal disease and was referred to the STI clinic. - *British*

Nausea - Feeling sick - She was having bouts of nausea and could not work. - *British*

Vomitus - Vomit - There was a whole lot of vomitus to clear up. - *British*

Medical

Comedone - Blackhead - The teenager had developed a comedone just before the disco. - *British*

Cutaneous - Skin-related - The problem was cutaneous. - *British*

Cyanosis - Bluish skin - He had cyanosis. - *British*

Depigmentation - Loss of normal pigment - There were several areas on the man's arms which had depigmentation. - *British*

Dermatitis - Skin problems - He was diagnosed with dermatitis on his hands. - *British*

Dermatological - Skin-related - The problem he had was dermatological. - *British*

Dermatomycosis - Fungal skin infection - She had dermatomycosis. - *British*

Dermatophytosis - Ringworm - The child had a dose of dermatophytosis. - *British*

Dermatosis - Skin disease - He had dermatosis. - *British*

Dermographia - Using pressure or friction to write on skin - The teenagers often practised dermographia. - *British*

Desquamation - Flaky skin - Her face was often subject to desquamation. - *British*

Epidermal - Skin-related - The treatment was for an epidermal problem. - *British*

Erysipelas - Skin infection - He had been diagnosed with erysipelas. - *British*

Erythema - Skin redness - Erythema can have many causes. - *British*

Erythrasma - Bacterial skin infection - He had erythrasma. - *British*

Exanthema - Skin rash - He had an exanthema and the doctor prescribed ointment. - *British*

Hypodermic - Under the skin - He inserted an hypodermic needle. - *British*

Ichthyosis - Scaly skin - She was prescribed an ointment for her ichthyosis. - *British*

Integumentary - Of skin - The issue seems to be integumentary and will need treatment. - *British*

Melanosis - Abnormal pigmentation - The patient had melanosis on his arm. - *British*

Neurodermatitis - Skin damage caused by scratching - She had neurodermatitis in her head. - *British*

Papule - Mole - He had a papule on his arm. - *British*

Pemphigus - Serious skin disease - He had pemphigus. - *British*

Pigmentation - Skin colouring - The pigmentation of his skin had been affected by the disease. - *British*

Pityriasis - Scaling of the skin - She was suffering from pityriasis. - *British*

Seborrhoea - Oily skin - She had seborrhoea which gave her spots. - *British*

Squamous - Scaly - His skin was very squamous and needed moisturising. - *British*

Subcutaneous - Below the skin - The disease was subcutaneous and needed further tests to establish cause. - *British*

Somnolence - Sleepiness - Somnolence is another way of saying sleepiness. - *British*

Soporific - Sleep-inducing - The drug was soporific and he could not keep awake. - *British*

Aromatic - Scented - The herbs were very aromatic and flavoured the pie well. - *British*

Asymptomatic - Without symptoms - The patient was asymptomatic. - *British*

Blennophobia - Fear of slime - I am blennophobic, having a fear of slime. - *British*

Brontophobia/tonitrophobia/keraunophobia - Fear of thunder - A fear of thunder can be known as brontophobia, tonitrophobia, or keraunophobia. - *British*

Cheimaphobia - Fear of cold - Lynda has cheimaphobia. - *British*

Chionophobia - Fear of snow - Suprisingly, there is a fear of snow, chionophobia. - *British*

Chrematophobia - Fear of money - Chrematophobia is the fear of money. - *British*

Chromophobia - Fear of colour - Hollie has chromophobia. - *British*

Medical

Cibophobia/sitophobia - Fear of food - Ben has cibophobia or sitophobia. - *British*

Clinophobia - Fear of bed - Sandip has clinophobia and so sleeps on the sofa. - *British*

Cometophobia - Fear of comets - Macca has cometophobia. - *British*

Cryophobia - Fear of ice - Cryophobia is the fear of ice. - *British*

Cyberphobia - Fear of computers - Cyberphobia is the fear of computers. - *British*

Eisoptrophobia - Fear of mirrors - Tony has been diagnosed as eisoptrophobic, as he has a fear of mirrors. - *British*

Electrophobia - Fear of electricity - A fear of electricity is called: electrophobia. - *British*

Enetophobia - Fear of pins - Enetophobia is a fear of pins. - *British*

Epistolophobia - Fear of correspondence - Epistolophobia is a fear of correspondence, such as letters. - *British*

Gephyrophobia - Fear of bridges - Gephyrophobia is the fear of bridges. - *British*

Homichlophobia - Fear of fog - John was diagnosed with homichlophobia. - *British*

Hygrophobia - Fear of dampness - Hygrophobia is the fear of dampness. - *British*

Iconophobia - Fear of religious works of art - If you have a fear of religious works of art, you are iconophobic. - *British*

Koniophobia - Fear of dust - Mabel has koniophobia, a fear of dust. - *British*

Linonophobia - Fear of string - Kev has linonophobia, a fear of string. - *British*

Mechanophobia - Fear of machinery - Penny has mechanophobia. - *British*

Metallophobia - Fear of metal - Rupert has metallophobia, a fear of metals. - *British*

Microphobia - Fear of small things - Some people have a fear of small things. This is called: microphobia. - *British*

Nelophobia - Fear of glass - Darren has a fear of glass, nelophobia. - *British*

Nephophobia - Fear of clouds - Some people have a fear of clouds. This is called: nephophobia. - *British*

Ochophobia - Fear of vehicles - Wayne has ochophobia. - *British*

Pteronophobia - Fear of feathers - The fear of feathers is called: pteronophobia. - *British*

Pyrophobia - Fear of fire - To be afraid of fire, is to be pyrophobic. - *British*

Sciophobia - Fear of shadows - Melissa has been diagnosed as having sciophobia. - *British*

Scotophobia - Fear of darkness - Sholto has scotophobia. - *British*

Siderophobia - Fear of stars - Lewis has a fear of stars; siderophobia. - *British*

Technophobia - Fear of technology - Some people are frightened of technology. This is called: technophobia. - *British*

Telephonophobia - Fear of telephone - Justin is telephonophobic. - *British*

Alkaloid - Bitter plant poison - The plant was known to produce an alkaloid. - *British*

Atoxic - Non-poisonous - The substance he had swallowed was atoxic. - *British*

Endotoxic - Heat stable toxin-related - Endotoxins that are released in infected people cause fever. - *British*

Ergotism - Poisoning (from ergot fungus) - The man had ergotism from infected cereals. - *British*

Haemoperfusion - Method of removing poison from blood - She was undergoing haemoperfusion. - *British*

Hepatotoxic - Poisonous to liver cells - The medication was hepatotoxic. - *British*

Intoxication - Poisoning - He was debilitated from intoxication with alcohol. - *British*

Aspiration - Breathing in - He was told to undertake aspiration more slowly. - *British*

Bolus injection - Big injection - He was given a bolus injection. - *British*

Cannula - Thin tube - The doctor decided to insert a cannula before taking blood. - *British*

Catheter - (Urine) bag, fitted by a tube directly into the bladder to drain away - After his operation the patient had a catheter inserted. - *British*

Catheterization - Fitting a (urine) bag - The nurse was learning how to do catheterization. - *British*

Chemotherapeutic - Chemotherapy - The doctor had prescribed a chemotherapeutic treatment. - *British*

Conventional - Normal - It was not the conventional way forward but he thought it was worth a try. - *British*

Curative - Curing - The therapy was thought to be curative. - *British*

Demulcent - Soothing - "This ointment is demulcent," reassured the nurse. - *British*

Detoxication - Drug addiction treatment - Her G.P. referred her for detoxication at the re-hab unit. - *British*

Diathermy - Heat treatment - The doctor recommended diathermy. - *British*

Diffuse - Widely distributed - The medicine was diffused throughout the tissue. - *British*

Digitalization - Giving heart failure drugs - The doctor prescribed digitalization. - *British*

Douching - Washing out - The nurse undertook to cleanse the wound by douching with water. - *British*

Emollient - Soothing - The cream acted as an emollient and calmed the irritation. - *British*

Emulsify - Turn into an emulsion - "Can you emulsify that?" said the cook. - *British*

Emulsion - Suspension of one liquid in another - An emulsion is usually used for the treatment of chickenpox. - *British*

Extension - Movement to draw apart parts of a joint or realigned with each other - He had to have a buck's extension to his leg. - *British*

Extraction - Removal - He had been to the dentist for the extraction of two teeth. - *British*

First pass - First pass effect/ metabolism is the degradation or alteration of a drug or substance seen after absorption - They analysed the drug after first pass. - *British*

Galenical - Relating to Galen's methods; he was a Greek philosopher and physician - They used galenical methods. - *British*

Haemodialysis - Dialysis - She was referred by her doctor for haemodialysis. - *British*

Haemostasis - Stopping bleeding - He was concerned with haemostasis before further treatment. - *British*

Hydration - Adding water - She was in need of hydration so they attached a drip. - *British*

Hyperbaric - Involving a gas at a higher pressure than normal - The doctor recommended hyperbaric oxygen treatment. - *British*

Immunogenic - Producing immunity - The flu jab is immunogenic. - *British*

Implantation - Implant - The woman had undergone an implantation of breast tissue. - *British*

Impregnation - Making pregnant - The nurse had the right equipment to ensure the woman's impregnation. - *British*

Incision - Cut - "I will make an incision into his chest," said the surgeon. - *British*

Incisive - Cutting - Her remark was incisive and everyone sat up and listened. - *British*

Incorporation - Inclusion - The smaller trust was due for incorporation into the larger hospital organisation. - *British*

Infusion - Transfusion, not of blood - The doctor decided to give her an infusion of antibiotics. - *British*

Insertion - Inserting - The patient needed to agree to the insertion of a cannula. - *British*

Medical

Instillation - The administration of a liquid, slowly, drop by drop - The nurse took the instillation procedure to administer the medicine. - *British*

Intubation - Inserting a tube - The medication was administered through intubation. - *British*

Invasive - Involving an operation - The treatment was invasive and involved an operation. - *British*

Irrigation - Washing - The doctor recommended irrigation to deal with the eye problem. - *British*

Liquifilm - A liquid used as a substitute for real tears - She used a liquifilm to protect her eyes. - *British*

Lyophilisate - Freeze-dry - He agreed they should lyophilisate the skin. - *British*

Monotherapy - One drug therapy - "We will treat him with monotherapy," said the doctor. - *British*

Orthopaedic - Correcting deformity - His G.P. referred him to the orthopaedic department. - *British*

Otorhinolaryngology - E.N.T - He was referred to otorhinolaryngology. - *British*

Paracentesis - Fluid removal - The doctor undertook paracentesis which made him feel more comfortable. - *British*

Seroconversion - Development of resistance - He was developing a seroconversion to the medication. - *British*

Shunt - Bypass - The patient had a shunt inserted to form a bypass. - *British*

Sympathomimetic - Substance to simulate sympathetic nervous system - He was prescribed a sympathomimetic. - *British*

Tachyphylaxis - Rapid immunisation - "We need to book her in for tachyphylaxis," said the G.P. - *British*

Thermoregulation - Heat regulation - "We need to undertake thermoregulation," said the ward nurse. - *British*

Micturition - Urination - His micturition was very frequent. - *British*

Nocturia - Frequent urination at night - She was nocturia which was very annoying. - *British*

Oliguria - Abnormally small urine output - "He has oliguria," said the nurse. - *British*

Polyuria - Going to the toilet a lot - He had always had polyuria and spent a lot of time in the toilet. - *British*

Transurethral - Through the urine tube - He passed urine transurethral. - *British*

Urgency - Needing to go to the toilet - He suffered with urgency and needed to be close to a toilet. - *British*

Urinary - Urine-related - He was diagnosed with an urinary infection. - *British*

Anuria - Non-production of urine - The patient had anuria and was not producing urine. - *British*

Disseminate - Scatter - She was asked to disseminate the information to staff. - *British*

Aqueous - Watery - His eyes were very aqueous so he was given lots of tissues. - *British*

Medical

Mental Health

'Tuned to the moon'
Mentally unstable

A basket case - Someone behaving oddly - Shelly is a basket case. - *British*

A shrink - A psychiatrist - Jeremy needs to see a shrink. - *British*

A snag short of a barbie - Lacking intellect - The psychologist thought the patient was a snag short of a barbie. - *Australian*

Ape shit - Lacking in sanity. To be unable to control thoughts and feelings - John went ape shit. - *America/British*

Around the bend - Mentally unwell - Dave is around the bend. - *British*

Bacon butty - Nutty- mental illness - John is bacon butty. - *cockney*

Barking mad - Mentally unstable - Doug is barking mad. - *British*

Basket case - A mad person - Sarah is a basket case. - *British*

Bat-shit crazy - Lacking in sanity. To be unable to control thoughts and feelings - Jodie is bat-shit crazy. - *America/British*

Black dog - Depression - Mike has the black dog. - *British*

Blaine - Insane - Alex is Blaine. - *cockney*

Blow a fuse - Lacking in sanity. To be unable to control thoughts and feelings - Mal might blow a fuse. - *America/British*

Blow a gasket - Lacking in sanity. To be unable to control thoughts and feelings - Dexter might blow a gasket. - *America/British*

Blow up - Lacking in sanity. To be unable to control thoughts and feelings - Dee might blow up. - *America/British*

Blue - Feeling sad or depressed - Karim feels blue. - *British*

Bobo - Lacking in sanity. To be unable to control thoughts and feelings - Steph is bobo. - *America/British*

Bonkers - Mentally unwell/ unstable - Freddie is bonkers. - *British*

Brake fluid - Psychiatric medication - The psychiatrist prescribed some brake fluid for the patient. - *American*

Bug juice - Intoxicants or depressant drugs - "Give him some bug juice," said the doctor. - *American*

Bug out - Lacking in sanity. To be unable to control thoughts and feelings - Careful, they might bug out. - *America/British*

Bunny boiler - A psychotic person, usually an ex-girlfriend or a deranged woman, who feels unjustally treated and seeks revenge - Zoe is a bunny boiler. - *British*

Cabbage - A brain damaged person - Marilyn is a cabbage. - *British*

Certifiable - Lacking in sanity. To be unable to control thoughts and feelings - I think he is certifiable. - *America/British*

Chicken jalfrezi - Crazy- mentally unstable or wild - Eric is chicken jalfrezi. - *cockney*

Chicken oriental - Mental- suffering some kind of mental illness/ behaviour - Harry is chicken oriental. - *cockney*

Completely hatstand - A crazy person - Russell is completely hatstand. - *British*

Crack up - Lacking in sanity. To be unable to control thoughts and feelings - Lee might crack up. - *America/British*

Crackass - Lacking in sanity. To be unable to control thoughts and feelings - Dave is a crackass. - *America/British*

Cracked out - Lacking in sanity. To be unable to control thoughts and feelings - Carol is cracked out. - *America/British*

Crackers - Referring to someone as if they are mentally ill - Jon is crackers. - *British*

Crackpot - A mentally deranged person - The man was mentally deranged and described as a crackpot. - *British*

Cra-cra - Lacking in sanity. To be unable to control thoughts and feelings - Bobby is cra-cra. - *America/British*

Cray - Lacking in sanity. To be unable to control thoughts and feelings - Glenn is cray. - *America/British*

Crazier than a run-over dog - Lacking in sanity. To be unable to control thoughts and feelings - Candice is crazier than a run-over dog. - *America/British*

Crazier than a shit-house rat - Lacking in sanity. To be unable to control thoughts and feelings - Fabian is crazier than a shit-house rat. - *America/British*

Craziness - Lacking in sanity. To be unable to control thoughts and feelings - Leroy, that is craziness. - *America/British*

Crazy - Mentally unwell/ angry - Ahmed is crazy. - *British*

Crazy-pants - Lacking in sanity. To be unable to control thoughts and feelings - Tosh is crazy-pants. - *America/British*

Creepy - Lacking in sanity. To be unable to control thoughts and feelings - John is creepy. - *America/British*

Cuckoo for cocoa puffs - Lacking in sanity. To be unable to control thoughts and feelings - Tracey is cuckoo for cocoa puffs. - *America/British*

Cut snake - Mentally unwell - "Meredith is a cut snake," said the psychiatrist. - *Australian*

Dad's Army - Barmy- mentally ill - Leighton is in the Dad's Army. - *cockney*

Delusions of grandeur - A person who believes that they are more important than they really are - Esther suffers delusions of grandeur. - *British*

Ding-a-ling - Lacking in sanity. To be unable to control thoughts and feelings - Pascale is a ding-a-ling. - *America/British*

Doe - Lacking in sanity. To be unable to control thoughts and feelings - Pedro is a doe. - *America/British*

Doolally - Insane - Lucy went doolally. - *British*

Down - Sad - Anna feels down. - *British*

Down in the dumps - Depressed - Elsa feels down in the dumps. - *British*

Downer - Depressing - Stuart is on a downer. - *British*

Epi - Lacking in sanity. To be unable to control thoughts and feelings - Edgar is an epi. - *America/British*

Flaky - Unstable - George is a bit flaky. - *British*

Flat as a tack - Depressed - I feel as flat as a tack. - *Australian*

Flip your lid - Lacking in sanity. To be unable to control thoughts and feelings - Paul sometimes flips his lid. - *America/British*

Flip out - Lacking in sanity. To be unable to control thoughts and feelings - Chris might flip out. - *America/British*

Mental Health

Freak - Lacking in sanity. To be unable to control thoughts and feelings - Nobby is a freak. - *America/British*

Freak'n - Lacking in sanity. To be unable to control thoughts and feelings - Robert is freak'n. - *America/British*

Freaky-deaky - Lacking in sanity. To be unable to control thoughts and feelings - Bob is freaky-deaky. - *America/British*

Frost (one's) muffin - Lacking in sanity. To be unable to control thoughts and feelings - Cathy don't frost your muffin. - *America/British*

Fruit cake - A crazy person - Lois is a fruit cake. - *British*

Fruitcake - Lacking in sanity. To be unable to control thoughts and feelings - Lucy is a fruitcake. - *America/British*

Funny farm - Mental institution - Katie needs to go to the funny farm. - *British*

Gaga - Insane - Ben is gaga. - *British*

Ga-ga - Mentally unstable or unwell - Jen is ga-ga. - *British*

Gert and daisy - Crazy- mentally unstable or wild - I don't understand Nicky, I think he might be a bit gert and daisy. - *cockney*

Get (one's) goat - Lacking in sanity. To be unable to control thoughts and feelings - When Jaz stole my wallet, I was furious; that really got my goat. - *America/British*

Get (one's) knickers in a twist - Lacking in sanity. To be unable to control thoughts and feelings - Lyn, don't get your knickers in a twist. - *America/British*

Get a rise out of - Lacking in sanity. To be unable to control thoughts and feelings - Justin was being really obnoxious, I think he was trying to get a rise out of me. - *America/British*

Get bent - Lacking in sanity. To be unable to control thoughts and feelings - When Si is rude, I get bent. - *America/British*

Go around the bend - Lacking in sanity. To be unable to control thoughts and feelings - Mikey is stressed out, he needs to be careful or he might go around the bend. - *America/British*

Go batshit - Lacking in sanity. To be unable to control thoughts and feelings - When Sammy is annoyed, he goes batshit. - *America/British*

Go bejesus - Lacking in sanity. To be unable to control thoughts and feelings - When Tyrone is annoyed, he goes bejesus. - *America/British*

Go bitchcakes - Lacking in sanity. To be unable to control thoughts and feelings - When Samir is annoyed, he goes bitchcakes. - *America/British*

Go bonkers - Lacking in sanity. To be unable to control thoughts and feelings - When Ricky is annoyed, he goes bonkers. - *America/British*

Go Nam - Lacking in sanity. To be unable to control thoughts and feelings - When Ian is annoyed, he goes Nam. - *America/British*

Go nuclear - Lacking in sanity. To be unable to control thoughts and feelings - When Henry is annoyed, he goes nuclear. - *America/British*

Go off the deep end - Lacking in sanity. To be unable to control thoughts and feelings - When Harry is annoyed, he goes off the deep end. - *America/British*

Go over the edge - Lacking in sanity. To be unable to control thoughts and feelings - When Jon is annoyed, he goes over the edge. - *America/British*

Go trench coat - Lacking in sanity. To be unable to control thoughts and feelings - When Lisa is annoyed, she goes trench coat. - *America/British*

Got a screw loose - Mentally unwell or unstable - Steve has got a screw loose. - *British*

Grind (one's) gears - Lacking in sanity. To be unable to control thoughts and feelings - When Ralph is rude, it really grinds my gears. - *America/British*

Mental Health

Hack off - Lacking in sanity. To be unable to control thoughts and feelings - When Ruth is rude, it really hacks me off. - *America/British*

Have a meltdown - Lacking in sanity. To be unable to control thoughts and feelings - Adam is stressed, he is having a meltdown. - *America/British*

Have a screw loose - Lacking in sanity. To be unable to control thoughts and feelings - Paddy has a screw loose. - *America/British*

Head case - Lacking in sanity. To be unable to control thoughts and feelings - Patricia is a head case. - *America/British*

Head doctor - Psychiatrist - Janet is stressed, she needs to see a head doctor. - *British*

Head shrinker - Psychiatrist - Brian is stressed, he needs to see a head shrinker. - *British*

Headcase - Mentally unstable person - The nurse thought the patient was a headcase. - *British*

Insane in the membrane - Lacking in sanity. To be unable to control thoughts and feelings - Sarah is insane in the membrane - *America/British*

Jam butty - Nutty- mental illness - Claire is a jam butty. - *cockney*

John McCane - Insane - I am John McCane. - *cockney*

Klepto - Abbreviation of kleptomaniac - The teenager was a klepto, he is always taking stuff. - *British*

Kook - Lacking in sanity. To be unable to control thoughts and feelings - Emily is a kook. - *America/British*

Loon - Abbreviation of lunatic - Tony is a loon. - *British*

Loony - Abbreviation of lunatic - Nargis is a loony. - *British*

Loony bin - Mental institution - Yameen should be sent to the loony bin. - *British*

Looper - Lacking in sanity. To be unable to control thoughts and feelings - Dan is a looper. - *America/British*

Loopy - Mentally unwell/ crazy - May is loopy. - *British*

Lose (one's) cool - Lacking in sanity. To be unable to control thoughts and feelings - When Dev is rude, I lose my cool. - *America/British*

Lose (one's) head - Lacking in sanity. To be unable to control thoughts and feelings - When Samantha is rude, I lose my head. - *America/British*

Lose (one's) marbles - Lacking in sanity. To be unable to control thoughts and feelings - When I get old, I will probably lose my marbles. - *America/British*

Lose (one's) shit - Lacking in sanity. To be unable to control thoughts and feelings - When Daisy is rude, I lose my shit. - *America/British*

Lose your marbles - To go mad - I worry that Andrew could lose his marbles. - *British*

Lost it - To describe someone who loses their temper - Toby has lost it. - *British*

Lost the plot - Mentally unwell or a rage - Lily has lost the plot. - *British*

Mad - Lacking in sanity. To be unable to control thoughts and feelings - Lo is mad. - *America/British*

Mad as a box of frogs - Mentally unwell / eccentric - Hannah is as mad as a box of frogs. - *British*

Mad as a hatter - Mentally unwell - Yasmin is as mad as a hatter. - *British*

Mad whack - Lacking in sanity. To be unable to control thoughts and feelings - Katy is mad whack. - *America/British*

Madcap - Lacking in sanity. To be unable to control thoughts and feelings - Craig is madcap. - *America/British*

Mad-cow - Lacking in sanity. To be unable to control thoughts and feelings - Deb is a mad-cow. - *America/British*

Mental - Crazy or insane - Simone is mental. - *British*

More cuckoo than a clock - Lacking in sanity. To be unable to control thoughts and feelings - Benjie is more cuckoo than a clock. - *America/British*

More cuckoo than a clock factory - Lacking in sanity. To be unable to control thoughts and feelings - Ally is more cuckoo than a clock factory. - *America/British*

Noid - Lacking in sanity. To be unable to control thoughts and feelings - Paranoid - Sam gets noid, he thinks we are talking about him. - *America/British*

Not the full packet - Mentally unstable or unwell - Valerie isn't quite the full packet. - *British*

Not the full quid - Intellectually impaired - "Pamela is not the full quid," said her friend. - *Australian*

Nucking futs - Lacking in sanity. To be unable to control thoughts and feelings - Barbara is nucking futs. - *America/British*

Nut - Eccentric person - Dianna is a nut. - *British*

Nut job - Lacking in sanity. To be unable to control thoughts and feelings - Ellie is a nut job. - *America/British*

Nutcase - An insane person - Pat is a nutcase. - *British*

Nuthouse - A psychiatric hospital (lunatic asylum) - Em needs to go to the nuthouse. - *British*

Nuts - Mentally unwell/ unstable - Simon is nuts. - *British*

Nutso - Lacking in sanity. To be unable to control thoughts and feelings - Zoe is nutso. - *America/British*

Nutter - A crazy or insane person - Julian is a nutter. - *British*

Nuttso - Lacking in sanity. To be unable to control thoughts and feelings - Sharon is nuttso. - *America/British*

Nutty - An insane person - Jane is nutty. - *British*

Off (one's) box - Lacking in sanity. To be unable to control thoughts and feelings - Jim is off his box. - *America/British*

Off (one's) nut - Lacking in sanity. To be unable to control thoughts and feelings - Jack is off his nut. - *America/British*

Off (one's) rocker - Lacking in sanity. To be unable to control thoughts and feelings - Lewis is off his rocker. - *America/British*

Off me head - Mentally unwell/ unstable - I'm off me head. - *British*

Off one's head - Mad or delirious - Cameron is off of his head. - *British*

Off one's nut - Crazy or foolish - Colin is off his nut. - *British*

Off the deep end - Lacking in sanity. To be unable to control thoughts and feelings - Chloe went off the deep end. - *America/British*

Off their trolley - Mentally unwell - Ian is off his trolley. - *British*

Off your rocker - Insane or crazy - Karim is off of his rocker. - *British*

One fry short of a happy meal - Lacking in sanity. To be unable to control thoughts and feelings - Jermaine is one fry short of a happy meal. - *America/British*

One sandwich short of a picnic - Insane - Betty thought he was one sandwich short of a picnic. - *British*

Out of (one's) mind - Lacking in sanity. To be unable to control thoughts and feelings - David is out of his mind. - *America/British*

Out of hand - Lacking in sanity. To be unable to control thoughts and feelings - Adam is out of hand. - *America/British*

Out of one's head - Mentally unwell - "He is always out of his head," said the rehab worker. - *British*

Out of one's tree - Mentally unwell - "Fred is out of his tree," said the nurse. - *British*

Out of the box - Lacking in sanity. To be unable to control thoughts and feelings - Tom is out of his box. - *America/British*

Mental Health

Mental Health

Out there - Lacking in sanity. To be unable to control thoughts and feelings - Tim is out there. - *America/British*

Out to lunch - Mentally vacant - "That woman is out to lunch," said the psychiatric nurse. - *British*

Para - Paranoid - Simon gets para, he thinks we are talking about him. - *British*

Postal - Lacking in sanity. To be unable to control thoughts and feelings - Marcus sometimes goes postal. - *America/ British*

Potty - Crazy - The little boy's behaviour was potty. - *British*

Psycho - Lacking in sanity. To be unable to control thoughts and feelings - John is a psycho. - *America/British*

Raving - To talk incessantly - The patient wasn't well, he was raving. - *British*

Scatty - Mentally unwell/ unstable - There was one girl at school who was really scatty. - *British*

Schizo - Schizophrenic - "Brenda is schizo," said her father. - *British*

Screwy - Lacking in sanity. To be unable to control thoughts and feelings - Marlin is screwy. - *America/British*

Section 8 - Lacking in sanity. To be unable to control thoughts and feelings - Jordan is section 8. - *America/British*

Sectioned - To be detained under the Mental Health Act - The doctor thought the man needed to sectioned. - *British*

Shrink - Psychiatrist - Ellie needs to see a shrink. - *British*

Spaced out - Affected by drugs, marijuana - Karen is spaced out. - *British*

Spaz out - Lacking in sanity. To be unable to control thoughts and feelings - When Colin is stressed, he is likely to spaz out. - *America/British*

Trip out - Lacking in sanity. To be unable to control thoughts and feelings - Lynn is likely to trip out, if she finds out I stole her cigarrettes. - *America/British*

Tuned to the moon - Mentally unstable - Pete is tuned to the moon. - *British*

Two cans short of a six pack - Lacking in sanity. To be unable to control thoughts and feelings - Jin is two cans short of a six pack. - *America/British*

Unhinged - Mentally unstable - James is unhinged. - *British*

Wacked out - Lacking in sanity. To be unable to control thoughts and feelings - Ken is wacked out. - *America/British*

Wacko - Insane - Ben is wacko. - *British*

Wacky - Mentally unwell/ unstable - Joe is wacky. - *British*

Went bananas - Mentally unwell/ unstable - John went bananas. - *British*

Whack job - Lacking in sanity. To be unable to control thoughts and feelings - Chris is a whack job. - *America/British*

Whacked out - Lacking in sanity. To be unable to control thoughts and feelings - Candy is whacked out. - *America/British*

Wig out - Lacking in sanity. To be unable to control thoughts and feelings - When Nick is stressed he is likely to wig out. - *America/British*

Wigged out - Lacking in sanity. To be unable to control thoughts and feelings - Mal got stressed and wigged out. - *America/ British*

Window licker - Derogatory term for a mentally handicapped person - Kay is a window licker. - *British*

Nursing

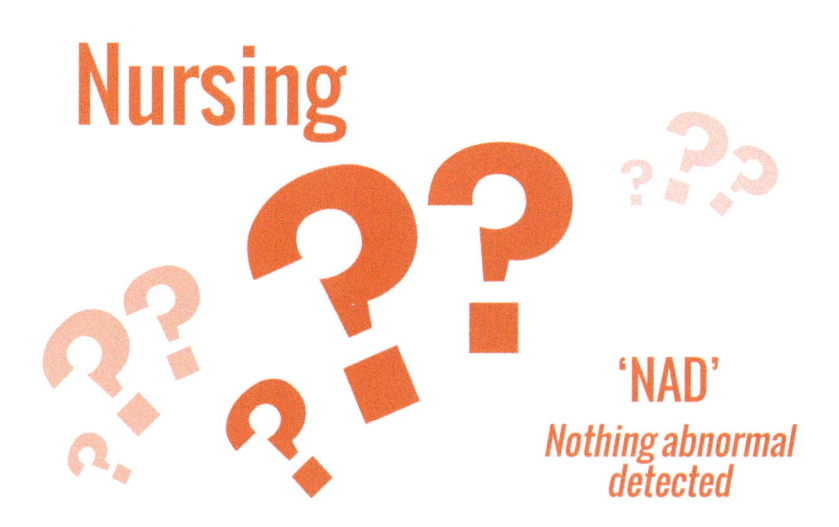

'NAD'
Nothing abnormal detected

 # - Fracture sign - The doctor put # on the patient's notes signifying he had a fracture. - *British*

AAA - Abdominal Aortic Aneurysm - The elderly man had been diagnosed with an AAA. - *British*

Abduction - Moving the limb away from the midline of the body - The doctor carried out abduction and moved the limb away from the central line of the body. - *British*

ABG - Arterial blood gas - The nurse had recorded the ABG on the patient's notes. - *British*

Abscess - Collection of pus in a localized area - The woman had an abscess on her bottom which was very painful. - *British*

Accommodation - Adjustment, as the accommodation of the lens of the eye - To make focusing on a nearer object possible, an adjustment called accommodation is carried out. - *British*

ACS - Acute Coronary Syndrome - Colin had ACS and was very unwell. - *British*

Acuity - Clearness; or a disorder's level of severity; minimum level or need for healthcare services that must be met for a client to be admitted to an acute care facility - Her visual acuity was very poor. - *British*

Acute disease - Disease or illness that develops suddenly and runs its course in days or weeks; illnesses that interfere with the continuum for a short period of time - Her disease was acute and she expected to recover quickly. - *British*

Acute pain - Acute pain; a pain sensation that results abruptly - He was in acute pain and the doctor diagnosed he was having a heart attack. - *British*

Adduction - The opposite of abduction - The doctor carried out an adduction and moved the limb towards the central line of the body. - *British*

Adjuvant - Assisting or enhancing therapy given, especially in cancer, to prevent further growth or pain; therapy used which was originally intended for another purpose - The term adjuvant is usually used to describe an ingredient added to a vaccine. - *British*

ADLs - Activities of daily living - The occupational therapist discussed the ADLs with the patient. - *British*

AF - Atrial fibrillation - Nicky had been diagnosed with AF. - *British*

AK POP - Above knee plaster of paris - The technician was asked to apply AK POP to the patient's leg. - *British*

Alias - An assigned name under which certain clients are admitted to (and records kept in) a healthcare facility in order to maintain anonymity - The Prime Minister was given an alias when he was admitted to the hospital. - *British*

Anaesthesia - Complete or partial loss of sensation - She would be given anaesthesia whilst the procedure was carried out. - *British*

Analgesics - An agent that relieves pain without causing unconsciousness - Her G.P. recommended she take analgesic to manage her painful leg. - *British*

Anti-embolism stockings - Also called ted socks; elastic stockings that cover the foot (not the toes) and the leg, up to the knee or mid-thigh - During surgery she wore anti-embolism stockings. - *British*

ANTT - Aseptic Non Touch Technique - The nurse had used ANTT when caring for the patient. - *British*

Anuria - Complete suppression of urine secretion in the kidney - He had anuria which had caused a complete cessation of urine output. - *British*

AO - Arbeitsgemeinshaft fur osteosynthesefragen. This is German for ASIF (Association for the study of Internal Fixation) which develops instruments and implants for the fixation of fractures - He had worked for AO for some years having an interest in instruments and implants for the fixation of fractures. - *British*

Aphasia - An abnormal neurologic condition in which a person is unable to express oneself through speech or writing - He had aphasia and was showing a complete lack of language skills. - *British*

Apical pulse - Pulse normally heard at the heart's apex, which usually gives the most accurate assessment of pulse rate - To get an accurate apical pulse it is necessary to listen to the pulse at the heart's apex. - *British*

Apnea - Cessation of breathing - The elderly man was diagnosed with sleep apnea. - *British*

Aquathermia pad - Pad which produces a dry heat by the use of temperature-controlled water flowing through a waterproof shell - The doctor decided to prescribe an aquathermia pad as part of his treatment. - *British*

ARF - Acute renal failure - Robert had been diagnosed with ARF and was very unwell. - *British*

Arthritis - Any inflammation of any joint - Caroline had arthritis in her knees making it painful to walk. - *British*

Arthro- - A prefix meaning 'relating to a joint' - Arthro is a prefix which relates to a joint. - *British*

Arthrodesis - An operation to fuse a joint - The surgeon carried out an arthodesis on David's knee. - *British*

Arthroplasty - Artificial joint as in hip arthroplasty (THR) where the head and neck of the femur and acetabulum are replaced - Sylvia had agreed to have an arthroplasty to assist her arthritis. - *British*

Arthroscopy - To look inside the joint with an arthroscope - In order to diagnose the problem in her knee, Pat agreed to undergo an arthroscopy. - *British*

Assertiveness - Confidence without aggression or passivity, an important skill for a nurse to possess in interpersonal communication - The nurse had training in assertiveness so she was skilled at managing her patients. - *British*

Atelectasis - Collapse of all or part of a lung - The woman had atelectasis and had difficulty breathing. - *British*

Auscultation - Externally listening to sounds from within the body to determine abnormal conditions, as auscultation of blood pressure with a stethoscope - The doctor carried out auscultation using a stethoscope. - *British*

Avascular necrosis - Also known as septic necrosis. Bone death without infection such as in fractured neck of femur when the fracture interrupts the blood supply to the bone - Following the fall when Susie had fractured her femur, she had developed avascular necrosis. - *British*

Nursing

Axillary - The underarms - She often had problems in her axillary, probably caused by shaving her underarm hair. - *British*

AXR - Abdominal x-ray - The doctor referred Tom for a AXR. - *British*

Base of support - Balance or stability provided by the feet and their positioning - As a ballet dancer she was very aware of her base of support. - *British*

BD - Twice daily (Latin) - The medication had been prescribed BD for the patient. - *British*

Bed cradle - A frame used to prevent bedclothes from touching all or part of a person's body - The nurse erected a bed cradle over the woman's bed. - *British*

Biopsy - Removal of a sample of body tissue or fluid for diagnostic examination, usually microscopic; most often used to detect the presence of cancer - The consultant carried out a biopsy of the lump in Margaret's breast. - *British*

BK POP - Below knee plaster of paris - The technician was asked to apply BK POP to the patient's leg. - *British*

BM - Near patient testing (capillary blood glucose monitoring) - The doctor had requested BM for the patient. - *British*

Body language - Impressions one conveys through body movements and posture, eye contact, and other non-verbal means - The nurse could tell from her body language that the woman was not telling her the whole truth of the situation. - *British*

Body mechanics - Use of safe and efficient methods of moving and lifting - All of the nurses had been trained in the body mechanics of moving and lifting patients. - *British*

BP - Blood pressure - "Can you take his BP please?" said the G.P. to the nurse. - *British*

Bradycardia - Abnormally slow heart; slow pulse - The doctor had diagnosed bradycardia from her very slow pulse. - *British*

Bradypnea - Condition in which breaths are abnormally slow and fall below ten per minute - The nurse saw from the patient's notes that the doctor had diagnosed bradypnea. - *British*

C Diff - Clostridium difficile - She had picked up the C Diff bug whilst in hospital. - *British*

C/O - Complaining of - "The patient is C/O chest pain," said the HCA. - *British*

C1 - C7 - Cervical vertebrae 1-7 - The patient was diagnosed with arthritis in C1-C7 joints. - *British*

CABG - Coronary Artery Bypass Graft - He had undergone a CABG the previous year. - *British*

Calculi - An abnormal concretion usually composed of mineral salts, occurring in the hollow body organs; a "stone," as a calculus in the kidney (pl: calculi); deposit on the teeth (tartar). - The young girl had calculi forming around her teeth. - *British*

Cancer pain - Specific type of pain identified by IASP, caused by a malignancy; often intractable and severe; usually chronic - She had severe cancer pain and her medication was not working. - *British*

Carotid pulse - Pulse felt on either side of the neck, over the carotid artery - He felt her carotid pulse in her neck. - *British*

CCF - Congestive Cardiac Failure - He had been diagnosed with CCF and was very unwell. - *British*

Celsius - Temperature scale in which water boils at 100 degrees and freezes at zero (formerly centigrade). "Normal" oral body temperature is 37 degrees Celsius. Celsius scale most often used in health care facilities. - The Celsius on the thermometer was above normal. - *British*

Centre of gravity - The centre of one's weight; half of one's body weight is below and half above, and half to the left and half to the right of the centre of gravity. This concept is important in body mechanics - The centre of gravity is important in body mechanics. - *British*

Chronic disease - A disease of long duration that generally manifests itself in an individual as recurring problems that tend to worsen in severity over time - The elderly man had chronic disease of the lungs, which was worsening as time went by. - *British*

Nursing

271

Chronic pain - Pain that lasts more than six months; neuropathic pain - The child had chronic pain, which had been the case for more than six months. - *British*

Circumduction - Circular movement of a limb or the eye - The circumduction of his arm was causing him a great deal of pain. - *British*

Client reminder device - Piece of equipment, most often a vest or a belt, used to ensure the safety of the client (i.e., helping client to remain in a chair without falling); - The patient was fitted with a client reminder device, to prevent her falling from the chair. - *British*

Client-oriented - Focused on meeting individualized needs - The treatment plan put in place was client-oriented. - *British*

Closed bed - Bed used when preparing a unit for a new client or an unoccupied bed - They had three closed beds on the ward which she knew would be full by the end of the day. - *British*

Closed fracture - When the skin remains intact - The patient had a closed fracture of the leg following his accident. - *British*

Closed-ended question - Questions that can usually be answered by one word, such as "yes" or "no" also called close-ended questions - When interviewing children about abuse, you should not use closed -ended questions. - *British*

Cognitive function - Ability to think and reason - The accident had damaged his cognitive function and this was causing great difficulties for him. - *British*

Collaborative problem - Problem in which nurses work with physicians or other healthcare providers - The team acknowledged this was a collaborative problem that they needed to work on together. - *British*

Comminuted fracture - Where there are small fragments of bone - Dexter had a comminuted fracture of the arm after falling off the slide at the playground. - *British*

Communication - Giving, receiving, and interpreting information (maybe verbal or nonverbal) - The nursing staff thought they were good at communication with patients. - *British*

Complication - An unexpected event in a disease's course that delays a person's recovery - Brian was having to stay in hospital longer because he had a complication in his illness. - *British*

Compound fracture - Where the skin is broken, more often called open fracture - The woman, who had been involved in the road traffic accident, had a compound fracture of the leg. - *British*

Conduction block - A form of regional anaesthesia - The surgeon decided to use a conduction block to treat the patient's abscess. - *British*

Conjunctivitis - Commonly called pinkeye; inflammation of the conjunctiva - The little boy had acquired conjunctivitis from a friend at school. - *British*

Conscious sedation - Condition in which internal sedative medications are used alone or in conjunction with local anaesthetics and the client has a depressed level of consciousness but is still able to breathe and respond to verbal stimuli. - The operation was carried out using conscious sedation. - *British*

Constipation - Difficult or infrequent and hardened bowel movements - The medication that John was taking caused constipation as a side effect. - *British*

Contracture - Abnormal shortening of muscles with resultant deformity - The girl had been born with a contracture of the leg which caused her difficulty walking. - *British*

Contralateral - The opposite side - The disease was not on the contralateral side of the patient's body. - *British*

COPD - Chronic Obstructive Pulmonary Disease also known as COAD - Chronic Obstructive Airways Disease - Arthur knew he had COPD and had difficulty breathing. - *British*

Nursing

COSHH - Control of substances hazardous to health - The Health and Safety Officer was responsible for training staff in COSHH. - *British*

CPR - Cardio-pulmonary resuscitation - The paramedics had undertaken CPR on the patient before he reached hospital. - *British*

Crackle - On auscultation, an abnormal discontinuous non-musical respiratory sound heard on inspiration; formerly called rale - The elderly woman had a crackle in her chest. - *British*

CRF - Chronic renal failure - The man was suffering CRF and was very unwell. - *British*

Critical thinking - Mix of inquiry, knowledge, intuition, logic, experience, and common sense - The team had applied critical thinking to the issue. - *British*

CSU - Catheter specimen of urine - The doctor had requested a CSU from the patient in his notes. - *British*

CT - CAT scan and computerised axial tomography - Lynn's G.P. had referred her for a CT to aid his diagnosis of her illness. - *British*

CVE - Cerebral Vascular Event - The elderly man had a CVE before reaching hospital. - *British*

CVP - Central venous pressure - The doctor wanted to measure the patient's CVP. - *British*

CXR - Chest x-ray - Before diagnosing his illness, the boy was sent by the doctor for a CXR - *British*

Cystitis - Inflammation of any bladder (most often refers to urinary bladder) - The young woman had been diagnosed with cystitis and passing urine was painful. - *British*

D&V - Diarrhoea & vomiting - We had been up all night with D&V and felt really tired. - *British*

D/W - Discussed with - The matter has been D/W the patient's relatives in relation to his diagnosis. - *British*

Dangling - Positioning of a client so that he or she is sitting on the edge of the bed with legs down and feet supported by a footstool or the floor. This is an exercise in preparation for sitting in a chair and/or walking - The nurse had assisted the patient into the dangling position, before moving her to the chair. - *British*

Data analysis - Analysing each piece of information to determine its relevance to a client's health problems and its relationship to other pieces of information - The doctor had carried out data analysis on all of the test results. - *British*

DCS - Dynamic Condylar Screw - He had a DCS inserted. - *British*

Debridement - The removal of debris from a wound - The doctor asked the nurse to carry out debridement of the wound. - *British*

Defecation - Discharge of solid waste matter (faeces) from the intestines - The patient was having problems with defecation and the doctor prescribed medication for this. - *British*

Dehiscence - Opening or separation of the surgical incision - The surgeon carried out dehiscence when undertaking the operation. - *British*

Dehumanization - To make a person/client feel like an object, to remove one's dignity - The nurses were taught to be careful of dehumanization and to preserve a patient's dignity when bathing them. - *British*

Dental cavities - The formation of cavities in the teeth by the action of bacteria; tooth decay - Miriam had several dental cavities in her teeth which needed filling. - *British*

DHS - Dynamic Hip Screw - The doctor had inserted a DHS during the patient's operation. - *British*

Diarrhoea - Abnormal frequency and fluidity of discharge from the bowels - Cyril had a tummy upset which gave him diarrhoea. - *British*

Diplopia - Double vision - The ophthalmologist said she had diplopia. - *British*

Dislocation - Where the components of a joint become separated - Jane had caused a dislocation of her toe by hitting a hidden rock buried on the beach. - *British*

Distention - Swelling or fullness, as in urinary distention - She had been diagnosed with distention of the bladder which was very uncomfortable. - *British*

DNAR/DNR - Do not attempt resuscitation - The elderly woman had agreed to DNAR in the event of her condition deteriorating substantially. - *British*

DVT - Deep vein thrombosis - Following her operation she had developed a DVT in her leg. - *British*

Dysphasia - Difficulty in understanding or expressing language - The child had dysphasia and was behind in her speech. - *British*

Dysuria - Difficult or painful urination or voiding - The woman had dysuria and was finding urination difficult. - *British*

Ecchymosis - Bleeding into the tissue under the skin, leaving small bruise - Where she had bumped her arm, Susan had ecchymosis. - *British*

ECG - Electrocardiogram - He had undergone an ECG in an attempt to diagnose his illness. - *British*

ED/E+D - Eating and drinking - The patient was ED/E+D. - *British*

EDD - Estimated date of discharge - The nurse asked the doctor for the EDD of the patient. - *British*

Egg crate mattress - A foam pad, shaped like an egg carton, which is used on top of a regular bed mattress to provide comfort and to prevent pressure areas - The nurse arranged for an egg crate mattress to be put on the bed, to prevent the elderly man getting bed sores. - *British*

Elective - Case in which the client's condition is not life-threatening and may choose whether or not to have surgery; also called optional surgery - The patient was to undergo elective surgery on Tuesday. - *British*

Emaciation - A wasting away of the flesh, causing extreme leanness, starvation. (adj: emaciated) - The young girl had emaciation where she was failing to eat enough food. - *British*

Embolus - A foreign substance, blood clot, fat globule, piece of tissue, or air bubble carried in a blood vessel, which partially or completely obstructs blood flow (embolism; pl. emboli) - Albert had an embolus caused by a blood clot in one of his blood vessels. - *British*

Endorphins - A naturally occurring analgesic that the body produces in response to exercise and other stimuli - Sylvia liked the feeling following exercise when her endorphins were high. - *British*

Endoscope - A tube-shaped, lighted device used to visualize or operate on hollow organs or within body cavities. Specialized endoscopes include the gastroscope, broncho-scope, and proctoscope. (process of visualization using this tool is called endoscopy.) - Her G.P. had referred her to have an endoscope examination. - *British*

Enema - An injection of fluid or medication into the rectum, usually to induce evacuation of the bowel - Before giving birth it used to be common practice to give the mother an enema. - *British*

Enuresis - Involuntary urine discharge, usually occurring during sleep; bedwetting - The little boy suffered with enuresis which caused him embarrassment when going on sleepovers. - *British*

Erythema - Skin redness produced by capillary congestion, as may follow a tuberculin test; bright red colour associated with capillary dilation, can indicate fever or infection - The young girl had erythema indicating that she had a fever. - *British*

EUA - Examination Under Anaesthetic - The consultant undertook an EUA of the woman's bowel. - *British*

Evaluation - In nursing process, measuring the effectiveness of the other steps - The nurse carried out an evaluation of the treatment so far. - *British*

Eversion - Turning inside out; turning outward - The doctor performed eversion and turned the foot outwards. - *British*

Evisceration - The protrusion of the intestines through an abdominal wound; removal of the internal body contents - The man had an evisceration in his stomach where he had received a body wound. - *British*

Expected outcome - Measurable behaviour that indicates whether a person has achieved the expected benefit of nursing care - The patient had received the expected outcome following the nursing care he had received. - *British*

Expectorate - Spitting out and coughing up mucus or other fluid from the lungs and the throat - The man was expectorate and had a significant lung problem. - *British*

Exudate - Material that escapes from blood vessels and is deposited in tissues or on tissue surfaces; usually contains protein substances - The exudate had escaped into the surrounding tissue. - *British*

Eye contact - Looking another person in the eye, as in "making eye contact." - The psychiatric patient failed to make eye contact with the nurse. - *British*

F1 - Newly qualified doctor - He was in his F1 year and needed supervision. - *British*

F2 - Senior house officer - He had been appointed to F2 the previous year. - *British*

FD - Free drainage (for catheters) - It was important to ensure FD for the catheter. - *British*

Fecal impaction - Accumulation of hardened stool in the rectum - The woman had fecal impaction and was very uncomfortable. - *British*

FIB - Fibula - He was told he had a fracture of the FIB. - *British*

Fistula - An abnormal tube-like passage or channel, as an anal fistula or sinus tract - The young boy had a fistula at the bottom of his spine which needed treatment. - *British*

Flatus - Gas in the intestines or stomach; gas expelled through the anus - The elderly woman had lots of flatus which was embarrassing. - *British*

Flotation mattress - Mattress or pad filled with a gel-type material which supports the body in a way to provide comfort and avoid creating pressure points, thereby helping to prevent skin breakdown - In order to avoid skin breakdown, the nurse ordered a flotation mattress for the patient. - *British*

FOB - Faecal occult blood - The nurse was requested to watch for FOB. - *British*

Foot drop - Contracture deformity that prevents the client from putting the heel on the ground - Pauline had foot drop and could not put her heel on the ground. - *British*

Footboard - Vertical support at the foot of a bed, helps to prevent foot drop - The nurse had put a footboard at the end of the patient's bed. - *British*

Fowler's position - Examination position in which the client is lying on his or her back with the head elevated - The physiotherapist put the patient in the Fowler's position. - *British*

Friable - Fragile; easily broken - Her bones were very friable as a result of her illness. - *British*

FWB - Full weight bearing - It took a long time for the patient to become FWB. - *British*

Gait - Manner or style of walking - His gait was upright and military style. - *British*

Gait belt - Sturdy webbed belt used by the nurse to help provide support to the weak or unsteady person - The nurse had put him into a gait belt to assist his walking. - *British*

General anaesthesia - The blockage of all body sensations, causing un-consciousness and loss of reflexes - The anaesthetist had given him general anaesthesia. - *British*

Goal-oriented - Establishment of objectives or specific desired outcomes early in the nursing process - The treatment plan was goal-oriented and the nurse was aware of the desired outcomes for the patient. - *British*

Nursing

GORD - Great Ormond Street Reflux Disease - The baby had been diagnosed with GORD. - *British*

Granulation tissue - New tissue that forms when old destroyed tissue is sloughed off - She was aware that granulation tissue would form where the old tissue had been sloughed off. - *British*

Gravital plane - Direction of gravitation pull; an imaginary vertical line through the top of the head, centre of gravity, and base of support - The nurse was aware of the gravital plane when moving a patient. - *British*

Guaiac - Stool examination for blood; also known as hemoccult - The patient underwent a Guaiac examination. - *British*

Guided imagery - A process through which the client receives a suggestion that helps control his or her pain or disease. The person learns to visualize himself or herself as powerful and able to conquer pain or disease - The therapist had carried out a course of guided imagery with the patient in order to give her more pain control. - *British*

Gurney - Wheeled cart, wheeled stretcher. A litter scale is used to weigh clients who cannot stand - The patient was moved on a gurney to the operating theatre. - *British*

Haemorrhage - Excessive bleeding (internal or external); escape of blood from non-intact blood vessels - The young mother had a haemorrhage following the birth of her baby. - *British*

Halitosis - Bad breath - Jules suffered from halitosis which affected her relationships. - *British*

HCA - Health Care Assistant - The Trust had employed some new HCAs in the past week. - *British*

Health interview - Way of soliciting information from the client; may also be called a nursing history - The nurse undertook a health interview with the patient. - *British*

Hematest - A test for occult (hidden) blood in stool or body secretions - The patient underwent a hematest to reveal whether he had blood in his stools. - *British*

Hemiarthroplasty - Half an artificial joint (Thompson prosthesis). Only the head and neck of femur is replaced - Brian had agreed to undergo a hemiarthroplasty to remove the head and neck of his femur. - *British*

Hemiplegia - Paralysis on one side of the body - After her stroke, Maisie had hemiplegia on her left side. - *British*

Hemoccult - A test for occult (hidden) blood in stool or body secretions - The patient underwent a hemoccult to reveal whether he had blood in his stools. - *British*

Herniation - Abnormal protrusion of an organ or tissue through the structure usually containing it, as an inguinal hernia or hiatal hernia; rupture; condition is called herniation - His herniation needed surgery. - *British*

Homans' sign - A test for thrombophlebitis in which pain occurs behind the knee when the foot is hyper flexed upward (dorsiflexion) - The doctor looked for Homans' sign when testing for thrombophlebitis. - *British*

HTN - Hypertension - The woman was given medication for HTN. - *British*

Hydrometer - Urinometer (used to measure specific gravity of a liquid, such as urine) - The nurse set up a hydrometer to measure the patient's output of urine. - *British*

Hypothermia - Low body temperature; also a syndrome (accidental hypothermia), caused by exposure to cold, which may be fatal. Hypothermia may also be induced for therapeutic purposes such as surgery, or pathologic as a result of faulty thermoregulation (temperature control) - The elderly man had been on the floor all night and was suffering from hypothermia. - *British*

Hypothermia blanket - Cooling blanket - The nurse, as instructed by the doctor, applied an hypothermia blanket to the patient. - *British*

Hypoxemia - Interference with blood oxygenation - The patient had hypoxemia which was causing an inadequate supply of oxygen to his tissues. - *British*

Nursing

Hypoxia - Abnormal reduction of oxygen in the tissues - The patient had hypoxia which was causing an abnormal reduction in oxygen in her tissues. - *British*

IDDM - Insulin dependent diabetes mellitus - Paul had been diagnosed with IDDM. - *British*

IHD - Ischaemic Heart Disease - "My wife has IHD," said Rob. - *British*

IM - Intramuscular - The problem appeared to be IM. - *British*

Implementation - In nursing process, the carrying out of nursing care plans; also called interventions - The nurse carried out the implementation of the care plan for the patient. - *British*

Incentive spirometer - A device used to force the client to concentrate on inspiration and promote full inhalation of the lungs, while providing immediate feedback; used particularly after surgery and in lung disorders - The nurse carried out an incentive spirometer procedure. - *British*

Incontinence - Inability to control urination or defecation (adj: incontinent) - There were several elderly patients on the ward suffering with incontinence. - *British*

Induration - A hardened place, a lump, as in the skin, in a positive reaction to a tuberculin test - He had an induration in the skin where the needle had been inserted for the tuberculin test. - *British*

Infection - The invasion and multiplication of infective agents in body tissues with a resultant reaction (illness or injury) to their presence and/or their toxins - Anne had a raging infection in her throat and felt very poorly. - *British*

Inflammation - A condition resulting from irritation in any body part, marked by pain, heat, redness, and swelling - The mosquito bite had caused an inflammation of the skin and was very painful. - *British*

INR - International Normalised Ratio - She had measured it according to the INR. - *British*

Inspection - Careful, close, and detailed visual examination of a body part - The doctor carried out an inspection of the area where Jill said she had pain. - *British*

Interview - A goal-directed conversation in which one person seeks information from the other - It was usual to carry out an interview with the patient's relatives in order to seek information. - *British*

Intractable pain - That which cannot be relieved; continuous, relentless - Maurice had intractable pain in his neck for which he was seeking medication. - *British*

Intramedullary - Within the medullary cavity of the bone. Intramedullary nails most often used for femoral and tibial fractures - The surgeon had used intramedullary nails during the operation. - *British*

Intraoperative - Occurring during a surgical operation - The bleed occurred intraoperative and was difficult to stop. - *British*

Inversion - Turning inside out; reversing - The surgeon carried out an inversion of the nipple. - *British*

Isometric - Having the same length or dimensions, as isometric exercises (pushing against stable resistance); also called muscle setting - The physio carried out a treatment plan including isometric exercises. - *British*

ITU or ITC - Intensive Treatment Unit/Centre - Following his operation, Norman had been admitted to the ITU. - *British*

IV - Intravenous - He was given an intravenous injection with his medication. - *British*

IVAB - Intravenous antibiotics - The infection needed urgent treatment and so she was given IVAB. - *British*

IVI - Intravenous Infusion - She was very dehydrated and the doctor prescribed an IVI. - *British*

Nursing

IVU - Intravenous Urogram. Previously known as IVP (intravenous pyelogram) - Her G.P. had referred her to hospital for an IVU. - *British*

Kardex - A medical information system, with card slots or a notebook for each client on a unit or nursing care team; a system for recording background information and care related to a client's treatment - The nurse inserted the patient's notes in the Kardex system on her desk. - *British*

Kegel exercises - Exercises designed to increase sphincter tone by tightening, holding, and releasing the muscles of the pelvic floor and sphincter, used to improve incontinence - The patient was given a treatment plan which included Kegel exercises in order to improve her incontinence. - *British*

Keloid - Scar or scar tissue - A keloid scar is usually hard, irregularly shaped and itchy. - *British*

Kerlix - Type of stretchy gauze used to hold dressings in place - The nurse applied Kerlix when dressing the wound. - *British*

K-NAIL - Kuntscher nail, an intramedullary fixation device - She had a K-NAIL inserted as part of her treatment. - *British*

K-WIRE - Kirschner wire, a narrow wire to hold the position of healing bones - During surgery, the surgeon had inserted a K-WIRE to hold the bones in position whilst they were healing. - *British*

Kyphosis - An abnormal increase in the thoracic curvature of the spine, giving a hunchback appearance, commonly as a result of osteoporosis - Joanna had kyphosis as a result of her osteoporosis. - *British*

L - Left - The problem is in her L hand. - *British*

L1 - 5 - Lumbar vertebrae 1-5 - The x-ray showed the problem to be with his L1-5. - *British*

Lateral - Side-lying - The wound was lateral. - *British*

Lithotomy - Examination position in which the client is lying on his or her back with the feet in stirrups - The gynaecologist carried out a lithotomy in order to examine the woman's womb. - *British*

Litter - Same as gurney - The nurse used a gurney to transport the patient to another ward. - *British*

Local anaesthesia - Disruption of sensation to a specific body area without causing unconsciousness; caused by infiltration or topical application of anaesthetic, usually to a small area; not general - She underwent local anaesthesia to have the wart removed. - *British*

Logroll turn - Method of turning a client that keeps the body in straight alignment, used for clients with injuries to the back and/or spinal cord - The nurses had all been trained how to logroll turn patients with back or spinal cord injuries. - *British*

Long-term goal - An outcome or goal that a client hopes to achieve but may require an extended amount of time to do so - The doctor discussed the long-term goal with the nurse. - *British*

Long-term objective - An outcome or goal that a client hopes to achieve but may require an extended amount of time to do so - The patient was given the long-term objective of his treatment by the doctor. - *British*

Lordosis - An abnormal increase in the thoracic curvature of the spine, giving a hunchback appearance, commonly as a result of osteoporosis - Belinda had lordosis as a result of osteoporosis. - *British*

LVF - Left ventricular failure - He had been diagnosed with LVF. - *British*

Maceration - Softening of a solid due to soaking - Caroline found the maceration of her food difficult unless she drank lots of water. - *British*

Macule - Fibres are dissolved, such as maceration of the skin under a cast or bandage - When Alan had a cast on his leg, his skin went macule. - *British*

Medical diagnosis - Statement formulated by a primary healthcare provider that identifies the disease a person is believed to have, which provides a basis for prognosis and treatment decisions - Martha was given a medical diagnosis by the doctor. - *British*

Melena - Passage of dark-coloured stools containing partially or fully digested blood; also used to mean abnormal blood in the stool or vomitus - Her G.P. identified a melena which she shared with the patient. - *British*

MI - Myocardial infarction - He had a MI and was admitted to hospital. - *British*

Micturition - Passage of urine from the urinary bladder; also called voiding, urinating - The nurse observed the patient was in no pain during micturition. - *British*

Mitered (corners) - The type of bevelled corners used when making a hospital bed - The nurse mitered the corners of the sheets when making the bed. - *British*

Montgomery straps - Easily removable straps that stay in place to facilitate dressing removal - The nurse had been trained in using Montgomery straps. - *British*

MRI - Magnetic Resonance Imaging - He needed an urgent MRI following his accident, to ascertain the extent of his injuries. - *British*

MRSA - Methicillin-resistant staphylococcus aureus - The hospital had great difficulty in eradicating the MRSA infection. - *British*

MSU - Mid-stream urine - The doctor had asked for a MSU from the patient. - *British*

MUA - Manipulation under anaesthetic - The emergency doctor referred the little boy for MUA for his dislocated shoulder. - *British*

N/G - Nose tube - A N/G tube is passed through the nose and down into the stomach. - *British*

NA - Nursing Assistant - The NA was of great help on the ward. - *British*

NA - Not applicable - Some of the information requested was NA to the patient. - *British*

NAD - Nothing abnormal detected/ diagnosed - The doctor had written NAD on the patient's notes. - *British*

NBM - Nil by Mouth - no food or drink to be given to patient - The nurse had put a NBM notice over the patient's bed. - *British*

Necrosis - Tissue death - The nurse noticed some necrosis when dressing the patient's wound. - *British*

Neuropathic pain - Chronic pain or discomfort that continues for six months or longer and interferes with normal functioning - The patient had neuropathic pain as a symptom of his illness. - *British*

NEWS - New Early Warning Score - The patient's notes contained NEWS information. - *British*

NH - Nursing Home - The elderly patient was waiting for a place in a NH to become free. - *British*

NIDDM - Non insulin dependent diabetes mellitus - The patient had NIDDM. - *British*

NKDA - No known Drug Allergy - Upon admission the young woman had NKDA. - *British*

Nociceptive pain - Normal pain transmission - The transmission of his pain was nociceptive. - *British*

Nocturia - Excessive voiding (urination) during the night - Gill had nocturia which meant he was up a lot in the night. - *British*

Nodule - Type of skin lesion appearing as a small knot or protuberance - Zoe had a nodule on her back. - *British*

NOF - Neck of femur - The elderly woman had a fracture of the NOF caused when she fell. - *British*

NOH - Neck of humerus - May had a fracture of the NOH caused by falling from her chair. - *British*

NOK - Next of Kin - The name of her NOK was available in her admission notes. - *British*

Nursing

Non-verbal communication - Conveying information or messages without speaking or writing. Components include items such as therapeutic touch, gestures, body language, facial expression, and eye contact - By watching the woman's non-verbal communication carefully the nurse could pick up lots of information. - *British*

Normal blood pressure parameters for adults - 120/80 - Her blood pressure was within the normal range. - *British*

Normal pulse rate for adults - 60-80 bpm (beats per minute) - Her pulse rate was high and of concern. - *British*

Normal range oral temperature - 35.5-37.5 c (95.5-99.5 f) - The elderly woman's temperature was on the high side. - *British*

Normal range respiratory rates adult - 16-20 - Carol's respiratory rate was within normal range. - *British*

Nursing assessment - Systematic and continuous collection and analysis of information about the client - The nurse had completed her nursing assessment on the patient. - *British*

Nursing Care Plan - Guidelines used by healthcare facilities to plan the care for clients - The nurse was aware of the Nursing Care Plan she needed to use for the patient. - *British*

Nursing diagnosis - A statement about the client's actual or potential health concerns that can be managed through independent nursing intervention - There was a nursing diagnosis in place for them to follow. - *British*

Nursing history - Way of soliciting information from the client; may also be called a health interview - Freda undertook a nursing history with the patient's relatives. - *British*

Nursing process - Systematic method in which the nurse and client work together to plan and carry out effective nursing care. (The steps include assessment, nursing diagnosis, planning, implementation, and evaluation.) - Gwen carried out the nursing process with Angela for her care at home. - *British*

Nursing progress notes(nurses' notes): - Documentation by nurses of care given and observations made; charting data input - It was important for nurses to fill in the nursing progress notes. - *British*

OA - Osteoarthritis - John had been diagnosed with OA in his neck. - *British*

Objective data - All measurable and observable pieces of information about a client and his or her overall state of health - She was very aware of the objective data she needed to collect about the patient. - *British*

Observation - Assessment tool that relies on the use of the five senses to discover objective information about the client - The doctor had asked that the nursing staff undertook observation of the patient for the rest of the day. - *British*

Occult - Hidden - The blood in the faeces was occult and she did not notice it. - *British*

Occupied bed - Bed holding a client that is unable to get up as a result of his or her condition or generalized weakness - There were five patients in occupied beds on the ward. - *British*

OD - Once a day - The prescription noted that she should be given her medication OD. - *British*

Oliguria - Deficient urinary secretion or infrequent urination - She had been diagnosed with oliguria that morning. - *British*

OPA - Outpatient Appointment - He had received his next OPA for two weeks time. - *British*

Open bed - Bed that allows linens to be turned down, making it easier for a person to get into or out of - They had put the patient in an open bed which made it easier to nurse her. - *British*

Open-ended question - Questions used in therapeutic communication and interviews that promote in-depth answers and encourage clients to talk about themselves and their concerns - The doctor had asked many open-ended questions in order to elicit information about June. - *British*

Nursing

ORAB - Oral antibiotics - His G.P. had prescribed ORAB to treat his infected foot. - *British*

ORIF - Open Reduction Internal Fixation - The surgeon had carried out ORIF. - *British*

Orthopneic position - Difficult breathing, relieved by sitting or standing erect; orthopneic position: sitting and leaning forward, to facilitate breathing - The patient was put in the orthopneic position in order to aid his breathing. - *British*

OT - Occupational Therapist - "I will ask the OT to come and see you," said the nurse to the patient. - *British*

PACU - Post Anaesthetic Care Unit - She was admitted to the PACU following her procedure. - *British*

Pain - Feeling of suffering, distress or agony, caused by stimulation of specialized nerve endings, a protective device of the body; a subjective sensation (reported by the client) - Kate was in a lot of pain due to her illness. - *British*

Pain threshold - Lowest intensity of a stimulus that causes a subject to recognize pain - Catherine had a high pain threshold. - *British*

Pain tolerance - Point at which a person can no longer tolerate pain - He had reached the top end of his pain tolerance and needed medication. - *British*

Pallor - Absence of skin pigment; paleness - The little girl had a pallor which denoted she was unwell. - *British*

Palpation - The act of feeling with the hand, placing the fingers on the skin to determine the condition of under-lying parts - The doctor carried out palpation of the child's skin to aid his diagnosis. - *British*

Papule - Small, solid, circumscribed skin elevation, less than 0.5-1.0 cm in diameter - The girl had a papule on her arm. - *British*

Paralysis - Motion loss or impairment of sensation in a body part - As a result of his stroke Arthur had paralysis. - *British*

Paraplegia - Paralysis of the legs and sometimes the lower part of the body; a person with this condition is called a paraplegic - Following the road traffic accident, Colin had been left with paraplegia and was in a wheelchair. - *British*

PC - Presenting Condition - Her PC was causing concern to the emergency doctor. - *British*

PDD - Predicted date of discharge - Her PDD had been written on her notes by the doctor. - *British*

PE - Pulmonary embolism - He had been diagnosed with a PE. - *British*

Pediculosis - Infested with lice - The girl's hair was pediculosis and needed treatment urgently. - *British*

Percussion - Tapping a body part with short sharp blows to elicit sounds or vibrations that aid in diagnosis; often refers to the use of a percussion hammer to elicit a reflex - The therapist used a percussion hammer to elicit a reflex. - *British*

Perineal care - Bathing genitals and surrounding area - Susan needed perineal care which she found embarrassing. - *British*

Perioperative - The period surrounding surgery; includes the preoperative, intraoperative, and postoperative periods - The patient was in the perioperative period and needed high intensity care. - *British*

Peripheral neurovascular assessment - Method for evaluating the status of an extremity in a bandage or case - The nurse undertook a peripheral neurovascular assessment of the man's condition. - *British*

Personal space - An invisible, mutually understood area or zone around a person that is considered inappropriate for strangers to violate (varies between cultures). If a person invades another's personal space (comes too close), it may cause discomfort. much nursing care must occur within the client's personal space. - The junior doctor was known for invading the personal space of the nursing staff. - *British*

PICC line - Peripherally Inserted Central Catheter - She had inserted a PICC line into the patient. - *British*

Planning - In nursing process, developing goals to prevent, reduce, or eliminate problems and identifying nursing interventions that will assist in meeting these goals - The ward staff were always involved in the planning process for patients. - *British*

Plantar Fasciitis - Flexion of the foot - Millie had plantar fasciitis and so difficulty in flexing her foot. - *British*

PMH - Past medical history - They always took PMH when admitting a patient to the hospital. - *British*

Pneumonia - Lung inflammation, with consolidation and drainage - The elderly woman had been diagnosed with pneumonia in Emergency Medicine. - *British*

PO - Per oral - The prescription was for the medication to be given PO. - *British*

POC - Package of Care - The team had put together a POC ready for the patient's discharge. - *British*

Polyuria - Voiding an excessive amount of urine - He had polyuria, which was very annoying. - *British*

POP - Plaster of Paris - The boy had invited all of his friends to write on his leg POP. - *British*

Postoperative - After surgery - The patient did well in the postoperative period. - *British*

Postoperative bed - Bed prepared for a client who is returning from surgery or another procedure that requires transfer into the bed from a stretcher or wheelchair - She needed a postoperative bed following her operation. - *British*

Potential needs - In the nursing process, needs which may occur; identified as at risk for - The potential needs of the patient became part of the plan. - *British*

PR - Per rectum - The prescription was for the medication to be given PR. - *British*

Preoperative - Before surgery - The patient was nervous during the preoperative period. - *British*

Primary disease - A disease that occurs independently, not related to another disease - Her primary disease was not related to her current illness. - *British*

Prioritization - Prioritizing: in the nursing process, following specific steps to determine the client's most important needs - The staff undertook prioritization of the patient's needs. - *British*

PRN - Pro Re Nata (Latin for as needed/required) - Jillian's medication was to be taken PRN when the pain increased. - *British*

Prognosis - Projected client outcome - The prognosis did not look good for Bernard. - *British*

Projectile vomiting - Emesis expelled with great force - The baby had projectile vomiting and could not keep her milk down. - *British*

Pronation - Turning the hand so that the palm faces downward or backward - The nurse carried out pronation on the woman's hand. - *British*

Prone - Positioning a client so that he or she is lying on the stomach - The patient was put in the prone position. - *British*

Prosthesis - An appliance to replace a missing limb or other part of the body such as a total hip prosthesis - Graham was being fitted for his prosthesis today. - *British*

Protective device - Same as client reminder device - The client had a protective device installed. - *British*

Proxemics - The use of space in relationship to communication - The man had not learnt the art of proxemics in communication. - *British*

Purulent - Consisting of or secreting pus - The wound was purulent and needed a clean dressing. - *British*

Pustule - A small elevation of the skin filled with pus or lymph - Caroline had a pustule on her hand which needed treatment. - *British*

PV - Per vagina - The instrument was inserted PV to obtain a smear test. - *British*

PWB - Partial weight bearing - He was only PWB since fracturing his leg. - *British*

Nursing

Pyorrhea - Copious discharge of pus - The woman had pyorrhea and her wound needed urgent treatment. - *British*

QDS - Four times daily (Latin) - The medication was to be taken QDS. - *British*

R - Right - The fracture was in his R leg. - *British*

Reduction - Pulling a fracture or dislocation into the correct position - The emergency doctor performed a reduction on the fracture in the arm of the little girl. - *British*

Referred pain - (Referring to pain) pain that is felt at a location other than its origination; when one physician sends (refers) a client to another physician or specialist - Catherine had referred pain in her back which was not the source of the problem. - *British*

Regional anaesthesia - Interruption of sensory nerve conductivity to specific area of the body (includes conduction block, field block, nerve block) - The surgeon undertook regional anaesthesia to carry out the procedure. - *British*

Renal colic - Severe, penetrating lower back pain, caused by a stone becoming lodged in the ureter - Mike had renal colic and needed surgery to remove the stone. - *British*

Residual urine - Amount of urine that remains in the bladder after voiding at least once - They were concerned about the amount of residual urine after he had voided. - *British*

RH - Residential Home - The elderly man had been admitted to hospital from a RH. - *British*

Rhonchi - Rattling sounds in the throat that resemble snoring (singular, rhonchus) - He was really unwell and had rhonchi. - *British*

Risk factor - A factor that increases a person's likelihood of developing a certain disease - It was well known that smoking was a risk factor in cardiac disease. - *British*

RN - Registered nurse - She had qualified as a RN the summer before. - *British*

Rotation - Process of turning about an axis, as rotation of the hand - He was able to undertake rotation of his hand which was a good sign. - *British*

RTC - Road Traffic Collision - The woman had been involved in a RTC. - *British*

S/B - Seen by - She had been S/B the aneasthetist before her operation. - *British*

S/C - Subcutaneous. Sub cut - The surgeon had carried out a S/C when performing the operation. - *British*

S1 - S5 - Sacral vertebrae 1-5 - The issue appeared to be in his S1-S5. - *British*

SATS - Oxygen Saturation Levels in the blood - Her SATS were normal and not raising concern. - *British*

Scientific problem-solving - Precise method of investigating problems and arriving at solutions - The laboratory undertook scientific problem-solving. - *British*

Scoliosis - Lateral curvature of the normally straight, vertical line of the spine, sometimes is s-shaped ("curvature of the spine") - Lois had scoliosis of the spine which required surgery. - *British*

Secondary disease - A disease that directly results from or depends on another disease - The tumour in her lungs was a secondary disease to her breast cancer. - *British*

Sequela - An illness or injury that follows as a direct result of a previous condition or event - The sequela to her torn meniscus was arthritis. - *British*

Serosanguinous - Fluid drainage composed of serum and blood - The serosanguinous was measured by the nurse. - *British*

Serous - Containing clear fluid; drainage made up of serum - The discharge was serous. - *British*

Short-term goal - An expected outcome or goal that a client can reasonably meet in a matter of hours or days - The physiotherapist discussed with Marsha her short-term goals. - *British*

Short-term objective - An expected outcome or goal that a client can reasonably meet in a matter of hours or days - The doctor had set out in the treatment plan, the short-term objectives for the patient. - *British*

Sign - Objective evidence of disease that another person can note (As opposed to symptom, which only the client can describe) - There were many signs which pointed to the illness. - *British*

Sims' position - Examination position in which the client is lying on his or her left side with right knee flexed - The patient was put in the Sims' position for the examination. - *British*

Sitz bath - A bath used to apply heat to the pelvic area - The physio used a sitz bath as part of the treatment plan. - *British*

Slough - To shed; to cast off (noun: slough of mass of dead tissue) - The ointment helped the patient to slough the dead skin. - *British*

Smegma - Sebaceous gland secretion that may collect under foreskin of penis in an uncircumcised male - Chris had smegma under the foreskin of his penis. - *British*

SN - Staff nurse - She had been promoted to SN and really enjoyed her job. - *British*

SOB - Shortness of breath - The elderly woman had SOB when admitted to the ward. - *British*

Sordes - Foul, dark matter that collects around the teeth and lips in low grade fever - Chrissie had sordes as a result of his fever. - *British*

Specific gravity - A substance's weight, as compared with another. Fluids, such as urine, are compared to (pure water, which has a specific gravity of 1.000) and (urine 1.010-1.025) - The specific gravity of the urine was heavier than water. - *British*

Spinal anaesthesia - Anaesthetic injected into the subarachnoid space of the spinal cord providing an extensive conduction block. Many types of surgery can be performed in this manner - In order to carry out the surgery, the surgeon administered a spinal anaesthesia. - *British*

Splinting - Use of a pillow or large towel to provide support along a suture line - The nurse carried out splinting on the woman's hand. - *British*

Steatorrhea - The excretion of abnormal quantities of fat with the faeces owing to reduced absorption of fat by the intestine - Basil had noticed steatorrhea in his stools for some time. - *British*

Strabismus - A deviation of the eye; squint. (convergent strabismus is called cross-eye; divergent strabismus is called exotropia or walleye. Other types include cyclotropia ,esotropia, hypertropia, and hypotropia.) - Convergent strabismus is more commonly called 'cross-eyed'. - *British*

Striae - Stretch marks - Following the birth of her baby, the young woman had lots of striae on her stomach. - *British*

Stridor - A shrill and harsh sound (usually refers to the inspiratory sound that occurs when the larynx is obstructed) - The girl had a stridor in her throat. - *British*

Subjective data - Information that consists of the client's opinions and feeling about what is happening, conveyed to the nurse either directly or through body language - Paula was known to offer the nurses lots of subjective data about her condition. - *British*

Supine - Lying on back - The woman was supine in the road following the accident. - *British*

Suppuration - Formation or discharge of pus (adj: suppurative) - Freda has suppuration from the site of her operation. - *British*

Suture - Thread used to hold an incision together while it heals; also called stitches - Following his operation, Johnny had lots of sutures. - *British*

SVT - Supra-ventricular tachycardia - She had been diagnosed with SVT by the cardiologist. - *British*

Symptom - Functional evidence of a disease or condition that a client perceives subjectively (as opposed to signs, which the examiner or others perceive) - The doctor was able to diagnose Brenda's illness from the symptoms she described. - *British*

T1 - T12 - Thoracic vertebrae 1 - 12 - The disease was in the area of T1-T12. - *British*

TDS - Three times a day - The medication was prescribed for TDS. - *British*

Tepid sponge bath - Bath with water below body temperature, 70 to 85°f, used to reduce fever - The child was given a tepid sponge bath to bring his temperature down. - *British*

Therapeutic communication - Communication (usually verbal) with a client that is helpful and beneficial; creating a healing, curative, and safe milieu by using communication - The nurse had a therapeutic communication with the patient. - *British*

THR - Total Hip Replacement - The woman needed a total hip replacement to help her to walk again. - *British*

Thrombolytic - Type of medication designed to dissolve a clot and clear a blocked blood vessel - Patients are often given a thrombolytic medication after having a heart attack. - *British*

Thrombophlebitis - Formation of a blood clot in a vein, with inflammation - He had a thrombophlebitis in his leg. - *British*

TIA - Transient ischaemic attack - A TIA is a brief interruption of the blood supply to part of the brain. - *British*

TIB - Tibia - He had broken his TIB when he fell. - *British*

TKR - Total Knee Replacement - The elderly man needed a TKR because of his arthritis. - *British*

TPR - Temperature, pulse, respiration - It was routine to do TPR on all patients in the ward. - *British*

Traction - Exertion of a pulling force; an apparatus attached to the client to maintain stability of a joint or aligned fracture or to exert a pulling force elsewhere, as in the lower back, to relieve pressure. - May was put in traction when she was admitted to the hospital. - *British*

Transfer belt - Sturdy webbed belt used by the nurse to help provide support to the weak or unsteady person - The nurse fitted a transfer belt to the patient to support her. - *British*

Transfer board - Board made of hard plastic used to move patients who are unable to stand from the side of the bed to a chair - The ambulance crew had put Joan on a transfer board. - *British*

Trapeze - Horizontal bar suspended above and attached to the bed, which is used to pull up to a sitting position or to lift the shoulders and hips off the bed - Sarah was able to use the trapeze to pull herself up in the bed. - *British*

Trial and error problem-solving - Experimental problem solving, that tests ideas to decide which methods work and which do not - They had deployed a trial and error problem solving approach, to the patient's illness. - *British*

Trochanter roll - Padding placed on sides of legs and feet of a client in bed, to prevent abnormal outward rotation and related sequela - The nurse had placed trochanter roll, down the sides of the patient's legs. - *British*

TTA/TTO - Patient medication to take away/home - The patient waited a long time for the pharmacy to bring her medication to TTA. - *British*

Tumour - An abnormal new tissue growth that has no physiologic use and grows independent of its surrounding structures. May be benign or malignant - Carol had a malignant tumour in her breast. - *British*

Turgor - Skin resiliency and plumpness; also called skin turgor - The patient did not have much turgor in her skin. - *British*

TWOC - Trial without catheter - The doctor had written TWOC on the patient's notes. - *British*

Nursing

Us & Es - Urea and electrolytes - The urine sample was used to measure Us & Es. - *British*

Ulcer - Open sore on an external or internal body surface that causes gradual disintegration of tissues, often an ulcer of the stomach (peptic ulcer) or a pressure sore (decubitus ulcer). - My father had been diagnosed with an ulcer. - *British*

Unoccupied bed - Bed that is empty, at the time it is made up - The nurses made up the unoccupied bed expecting more patients to be admitted. - *British*

Urgency - Desire or sensation of needing to void immediately - Tom had urgency and needed the bed pan in a hurry. - *British*

Urinalysis - Examination of urine - His urine sample was sent off for urinalysis. - *British*

Urinary catheter - Tube inserted into the bladder through the urethra to remove urine - The nurse inserted a urinary catheter which made him more comfortable. - *British*

Urinary frequency - Voiding more often than usual without an increase in total urine volume - The woman had urinary frequency which was annoying for her. - *British*

Urinary retention - Inability to empty the bladder of urine - Craig had urinary retention which was giving him a lot of discomfort. - *British*

Urinary suppression - Stopping or inhibition of urination. Suppression of secretion urine is not formed. Suppression of excretion urine is not expelled - The doctor had diagnosed urinary suppression. - *British*

Urinometer - An instrument that determines urine's specific gravity; also called urometer, hydrometer - The nurse had used an urinometer to determine the urine's specific gravity. - *British*

USS - Ultrasound Scan - She had been able to see her baby during her USS. - *British*

UTI - Urinary Tract Infection - Her G.P. had diagnosed a UTI and prescribed antibiotic. - *British*

Venipuncture - Puncture of a vein, usually with a needle. May be used to obtain a blood specimen or to start an intravenous infusion (IV) - The nurse had used venipuncture in order to obtain a blood sample. - *British*

Venous access lock - Catheter used to maintain an open route to a client's venous system to give fluids and/or medications - The doctor had inserted a venous access lock to the patient's arm. - *British*

Verbal communication - Giving information, news, or messages by speaking or writing - They liked to use verbal communication on the ward, and this was often done at ward rounds. - *British*

Vesicle - Small sac containing liquid; small blister - She had a vesicle on her hand where she had burnt it on the stove. - *British*

Vital signs - Measurements of temperature, pulse, respiration, and blood pressure - The nurse was monitoring the patient's vital signs. - *British*

Voiding - To cast out wastes, as to urinate, micturate - The patient was voiding urine without any difficulty. - *British*

Vomitus - The partly digested food and drink ejected in vomiting - There was a lot of vomitus on the bathroom floor. - *British*

Wheal - A smooth, slightly elevated skin area, usually pale in the centre with a reddened periphery, often accompanied by severe itching when caused by an allergic reaction; small elevation caused by injection of an intra-dermal medication, such as the ppd test for tuberculosis or other skin test - He had wheals all over his body after an injection of intra-dermal medication. - *British*

Wheeze - A whistling respiratory sound, typical of asthma - Lois always had a wheeze after exercise. - *British*

Wound sinus - A wide channel that contains blood or to an abnormal infected tract - Fred had developed a wound sinus following his operation. - *British*

ZF - Zimmer frame - The occupational therapist recommended the patient used a ZF. - *British*

ZF+1 - Patient requires a Zimmer frame plus the help of 1 person - The occupational therapist had assessed the patient as needing a ZF+1 - *British*

Personal

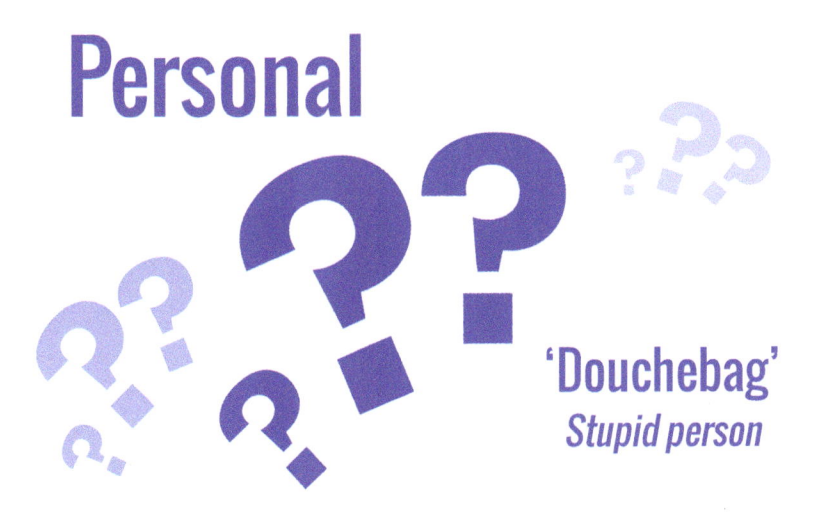

'Douchebag'
Stupid person

All ears - Listen carefully - The children were all ears when the author read them his book. - *British*

Bad vibes - A negative feeling - I get bad vibes about Jim, I'm not sure you should trust him... - *America*

Beat a hasty retreat - Leave a place or situation quickly, for fear of something bad happening - The couple beat a hasty retreat when they realised that they had been spotted by the farmer, trespassing on his land. - *British*

Chillax - Relax - I like to chillax when I'm on holiday. - *British*

Get yourself together - Get organised - Amy your life is chaotic, you need to get yourself together! - *British*

Have no truck with - To have no patience - I have no truck with Tim, when he is drunk. - *British*

Let your hair down - Relax - I like to let my hair down by going to the pub after work. - *British*

A bone to pick - Anger, prepared for a confrontation - Fred said to Anne, "I have a real bone to pick with you, over what you said to Gertrude." - *British*

A red rag to a bull - Something which provokes anger - Suggesting to Lois that her work was not good enough after all her effort, was like showing a red rag to a bull and, made her very angry. - *British*

An axe to grind - Anger, prepared for a confrontation - You need to watch her, she has an axe to grind about past situations and is waiting for a confrontation with you. - *British*

Apeshit - Angry - John went apeshit when he got a parking ticket! - *British*

At the end of (one's) rope - Very angry - Pat was at the end of his rope with the noisy neighbours. - *America/British*

'Avin a head fit - A temper tantrum - Justin was 'avin a head fit because he had lost his keys. - *Bristol*

Baity - Annoyed - Dave got baity because he didn't get his own way! - *Bristol*

Bite your head off - To react angrily - If you upset Ian, he will bite your head off! - *British*

Bristle - Annoyance - It made me bristle when James was rude to me. - *British*

Cranky - Very angry and at the end of your patience with something or someone - Katy got cranky with the noisy neighbours. - *America/British*

Dirty look - Very angry - Rob gave me a dirty look because I forgot his birthday. - *America/British*

Dogging up - To look angrily at another person - Joe was dogging me up because I was flirting with his girlfriend. - *Bristol*

Eggy - Angry - I got eggy when Lois took my cigarettes. - *British*

Eppy fit - Angry - I had an eppy fit when Peter stole my cigarettes. - *British*

Evil - Annoyed - It made me evil when Kay took my cigarettes. - *British*

Evils - look on someone with contempt - Gary gave me evils when I was talking to his girlfriend. - *British*

Fed up - Very angry and at the end of your patience with something or someone - I am fed up with my job, I think I am going to quit. - *America/British*

Fly off the handle - Lose your temper - If you annoy Barry, he is likely to fly off the handle. - *British*

Foam at the mouth - Angry - If Andy is rude again, I might foam at the mouth. - *British*

Gets my goat - Makes me annoyed - It really gets my goat when Emma is late for work. - *British*

Gets on my tits - It annoys me - Vaughan is so rude, he really gets on my tits. - *British*

Gets up my nose - It annoys me - Cam is so rude, he really gets up my nose. - *British*

Go spare - Get angry - I will go spare if Caf is late. - *British*

Hacked off - Annoyed - I'm really hacked off with Joe, he is so rude! - *British*

He went apeshit - He lost his temper - When Sam heard that his girlfriend had cheated on him, he went apeshit! - *British*

Hissy fit - Temper tantrum - I had a hissy fit when Sammy took my cigarettes. - *British*

Hot and bothered - To be very angry - Seule got hot and bothered when he couldn't find his keys. - *America/British*

I felt evil - Annoyed - I felt evil when Stephanie was rude to me. - *British*

In a huff - Very angry - Neil is in a huff because he missed the football match. - *America/British*

In a snit - Very angry - Yasmeen is in a snit because she couldn't go to the pub. - *America/British*

Irked - Annoyed - I'm irked because Candy has used all of the milk up. - *British*

Jarred off - Annoyed - I'm jarred off with Sam, he is so untidy! - *British*

Like a red rag to a bull - Something which provokes anger - When Jamie borrowed my razor without asking, it was like a red rag to a bull. - *British*

Lose your rag - To get angry - I will lose my rag with you, if you carry on being so rude to me. - *British*

Miffed - Annoyed - I'm proper miffed because I've run out of cigarettes. - *British*

Naffed off - Annoyed - I'm naffed off with my old car, and would love to get a new one. - *British*

Narked - Annoyed - I was narked when Julie took the last chocolate. - *British*

Narky - Annoyed - Sam gets narky if he doesn't get his own way! - *British*

Off on one - In a rage - When he was rude to me, I went off on one! - *British*

Peed off - Annoyed - I'm really peed off with Yameen, he is always late to work. - *British*

Peeved - Very angry - I'm really peeved; how dare you take my last cigarette! - *America/British*

Pissed off - Annoyed - I am really pissed off with you!! - *British*

Play merry hell - Angry - I will play merry hell if I find she has been unfaithful to me. - *British*

Raging - Angry - I was raging when Joanna was rude to me. - *British*

Ranting and raving - Angry - Billy was really unhappy with the boss; he was ranting and raving all night about it! - *British*

Riled up - Very angry - I got riled up when Steve was rude to me. - *America/British*

Personal

288

Road rage - Very angry - I got road rage when that old lady pulled out in front of me. - *America/British*

Roid rage - Very angry - I got roid rage when my wallet was stolen at the gig. - *America/British*

Scream blue murder - To shout in an angry and exasperated manner - Stuart will scream blue murder if you touch his stuff! - *British*

Screamed the place down - Very angry or/ and frightened so yelled out - Joe screamed the place down when I moved his books. - *British*

Screaming abdabs - A temper tantrum - I had the screaming abdabs when Emma took my last cigarette. - *British*

Spit your dummy out - To have a temper tantrum - If Dave doesn't get his own way, he will spit his dummy out. - *British*

Spitting feathers - Very angry - I was spitting feathers because Maureen took my last cigarette. - *British*

Steamed up - Very angry - I was steamed up because Caf was rude to me. - *America/British*

Strop - Temper tantrum - I was in a strop because Emma hadn't tidied the flat. - *British*

T'd off - Very angry - I was t'd off because Phil had broke my favourite vase. - *America/British*

Teed off - Annoyed - I am teed off with Dexter's bad attitude! - *British*

The straw that broke the camel's back - The final thing which causes severe emotional upset - When Smithy took my last cigarette, I got really angry; that was the straw that broke the camel's back! - *British*

Throw a wobbly - To have a temper tantrum - I will throw a wobbly if Daisy doesn't tidy up this mess! - *British*

Vexed - Very angry - I got vexed because Jane was rude to me. - *America/British*

Work up - To be very angry - Don't get worked up Kate, it is not worth it. - *America/British*

Wound up - Annoyed - I got wound up because Jim left me with all the washing up to do! - *British*

Kiss ass - To act in a sycophantic manner - Jane is a real kiss ass! - *America*

B.A.E. - A term of endearment which is an acronym, meaning - before anyone else - She is my B.A.E. - *America*

A balancing act - Trying to satisfy two or more people or areas of your life and keep everything stable and happy - I am constantly carrying out a balancing act, trying to keep everything stable between my husband and my children. - *British*

A bit down in the mouth - Sad - The events of the past week have made me very sad, and a bit down in the mouth. - *British*

A cat on hot bricks - A very anxious, nervous feeling - Brenda was like a cat on hot bricks and very nervous waiting for her biopsy results. - *British*

A face like a wet weekend - Look sad and depressed, miserable - Miriam had a face like a wet weekend and was very miserable that her lesson had been cancelled. - *British*

A fit of pique - When your pride has been hurt and you feel insulted, you might show this through an verbal and physical outburst of annoyance and frustration - Barbara had a fit of pique because her friends had hurt her feelings so badly. - *British*

A guilty pleasure - Enjoying something that is not held in high regard and so feel guilty for doing so because it brings you pleasure - Everyone has a guilty pleasure, such as eating chocolate which you have hidden, because you know you are overweight and should not be doing it! - *British*

A lump in your throat - Feeling a strong emotion, your throat constricts and feels tight because you are so upset - I was so overwhelmed by what I saw, I felt I had a lump in my throat. - *British*

Accidently on purpose - Doing something on purpose but claim it was an accident - Diana spilt the milk on the new carpet, accidently on purpose, to annoy her mother. - *British*

Personal

Acting up - Showing off or throwing a tantrum for attention - The little boy was always acting up and looking for attention. - *British*

Afeared - Very frightened - I was very afeared that something awful was about to happen. - *America/British*

Afraid of (one's) shadow - Very frightened - "That girl is afraid of her own shadow." said my grandmother. - *America/British*

Afraid of my/ one's shadow - Easily frightened/ nervous - I was so scared, I was afraid of my own shadow by the time I got home! - *British*

As pleased as punch - Very proud and delighted about something - I was as pleased as punch when I got my new job. - *British*

Bare your heart and soul - Be extremely open and honest, revealing your innermost private thoughts and feelings - Sara bared her heart and soul to her best friend, Tom. - *British*

Bent out of shape - To become upset or annoyed about something that normally wouldn't upset you - " I feel all bent out of shape by that sad news," said the pensioner, on finding out that his neighbour had died suddenly. - *British*

Bite (one's) nails - Very frightened. Sometimes used metaphorically to infer fear felt - I will bite my nails, waiting for my exam results. - *America/British*

Blarg - Feeling sad and /or disappointed - I feel blarg today. - *America/ British*

Blues, the - Feeling sad and /or disappointed - I've got the blues at the moment. - *America/British*

Bored to tears - Very bored! So much so, you could cry - Emma was bored to tears by the speaker at the conference. - *British*

Bottle up your feelings - Suppress your emotions and fail to express them - Justin tends to bottle up his feelings, preferring to suppress them internally, rather than share them. - *British*

Break out in a cold sweat - Real or not, perspiration from fear/ anxiety felt - Andy broke out into a cold sweat when he realised that he had been caught out having an affair with another woman. - *British*

Bricking it - Frightened - I was bricking it when that car crashed into me! - *British*

Bricking myself - Frightened - I was bricking myself when the police stopped me. - *British*

Browned off - Annoyed - I am browned off with my job. - *British*

Bummed out - Feeling sad and /or disappointed - I was really bummed out when I lost my job. - *America/British*

Burst (one's) bubble - Feeling sad and /or disappointed - I wanted a promotion but the boss soon burst my bubble. - *America/ British*

Butterflies in my stomach - A very anxious, nervous feeling - When Andy saw Steph coming down the aisle, he had butterflies in his stomach. - *British*

Butt-hurt - Feeling sad and /or disappointed - Dave got butt- hurt when his friend forgot his birthday. - *America/British*

Can't stand the pace - Feeling the pressure or stress of a situation, which leads to a feeling of not coping well - "If you can't stand the pace of the organisation then it might not be for you," said the boss. - *British*

Change of heart - To change your attitude or feelings about something - Kahlil had a change of heart and decided not to travel around Europe this summer but to study for his exams instead. - *British*

Cheesed off - Fed up and upset - Mary was really cheesed off with her six children, as they never came to see her. - *British*

Chicken out - Very frightened - I wanted to ask her for a date, but I chickened out! - *America/British*

Chicken-shit - Very frightened - Toby would never stand up to a bully, he is a chicken-shit. - *America/British*

Chuffed - Pleased - I was really chuffed with my birthday present. - *British*

Ciced - Energised and enthusiastic - I was ciced about getting my new car. - *America/British*

Climbs the walls - Very worried or frustrated - When my mum went into hospital, I was climbing the walls. - *British*

Cold feet - Very frightened about committing to something or someone - I was going to go to the party, but I got cold feet. - *America/British*

Cork up your feelings - Suppress your emotions and fail to express them - He never was one to speak openly, tending to cork up his feelings instead. - *British*

Couldn't give a hoot! - To not care about something at all - Grayson couldn't give a hoot about Jane's feelings. - *British*

Crabby - Moody - Les gets crabby when he is tired. - *British*

Cry one's eyes out - Cry a lot and for a long time, very sad - I cried my eyes out when my dog was hit by a car. - *British*

Down in the mouth - To look sad, depressed and miserable - Greg was down in the mouth because his girlfriend had left him. - *British*

Emo - Emotional - I got a bit emo when I watched that movie. - *British*

Feels - Feeling sad and /or disappointed - I got the feels when Stu said I couldn't go to his party. - *America/British*

Fish out of water - Feeling uncomfortable in new or unfamiliar surroundings/ situations - Kieron was like a fish out of water in his new job as a barman. - *British*

Full of the joys of spring - Happy and enthusiastic - I was so pleased with my new car, I was full of the joys of spring. - *British*

Get a grip of yourself - Control your emotions and feelings - "Get a grip of yourself!" said the headmaster to the teacher. - *British*

Get cold feet - To be very frightened about committing to something or someone - John was going to buy a house, but he got cold feet. - *America/British*

Get it off your chest - Express your emotions freely - If the boss is upsetting you, you need to talk to him about it; you will feel better when you get it off your chest. - *British*

Get your fingers burnt - A situation that has ended badly and makes you anxious about trying it again - We've had our fingers burnt before, so now we need to learn from our mistakes. - *British*

Go ape shit - Get very angry - Susan went ape shit went she found out that Colin loved Max, not her anymore. - *British*

Go ballistic - Get very angry - Allan went ballistic, when he found out that Ahmet was cheating on him. - *America*

Go bananas - Get very angry - The security guard went bananas running after a thief, that stole from the shop. - *America*

Go mental - lose control of oneself - If they change my medication, I will go mental! - *British*

Go off on one - To lose control of oneself - I will go off on one if Steph is late again! - *British*

Gobsmacked - Amazed and astounded - I was gobsmacked when the company offered Jon a promotion, he is the worst employee ever! - *British*

Goppin - Ugly or disgusting - Dave is goppin. - *British*

Gopping - Disgusting - It was absolutely gopping when the man was sick in the back of the taxi! - *British*

Green eyed monster - Jealousy - I get the green eyed monster if I see Greg flirting with my girlfriend! - *British*

Grief - Something that gives you trouble and causes frustration - My bad back has given me grief for a long time, now. - *British*

Grin from ear to ear - Very happy and satisfied - When Jim was promoted, he had a grin from ear to ear. - *British*

Grin like a cheshire cat - Very happy and satisfied - When John was promoted, he had a grin like a Cheshire cat. - *British*

Personal

Happy go lucky - Happy and content, cheerful and carefree attitude in life - Harry doesn't worry about anything, he is so happy go lucky. - *British*

Heart sinks - Sad and despondent about a situation - My heart sinks every time the boss comes to talk to me. - *British*

Het up - Worried, frustrated or angry - My nan is getting het up about her operation. - *British*

High as a kite - In an ecstatic state, often used to describe the results of drugs use - Tony was as high as a kite when he got promoted. - *British*

Hold your breath - A feeling of waiting for something to happen, possibly something exciting or frightening - Don't hold your breath, I'm not sure we have the right recipe for success here. - *British*

Huff - Bad mood - Dave was in a huff because he had to work late. - *British*

Hump - Bad mood - Sanjay got the hump because he had to work late. - *British*

I bricked myself - Frightened - I bricked myself when the police stopped my car. - *British*

I cacked myself - Really scared - I cacked myself when that lorry was speeding towards me. - *British*

Ignorance is bliss - If you don't know about something then it cannot upset or worry you - Ignorance is bliss, or so they say! - *British*

In a funk - Feeling sad and/ or disappointed - Julian is in a funk because he lost the bet. - *America/British*

In rapture - Very pleased and delighted with a situation, or very enthusiastic about something - That food was delicious, I am in rapture. - *British*

In seventh heaven - Very pleased - My new car is great, I am in seventh heaven. - *British*

In stitches - Laughing uncontrollably - I was in stitches when John was doing impressions of the boss; it was so funny. - *British*

In the dumps - Feeling sad and/ or disappointed - Brian is in the dumps because his girlfriend left him. - *America/British*

Jitters - Nervous - I have the jitters about going to hospital. - *British*

Jump for joy - Feel elated (very happy) about something and may express this through body language and movement - I jumped for joy when I was told I had got the job. - *British*

Kick in the teeth - An unexpected disappointment - It was a kick in the teeth, when he was promoted instead of me! - *British*

Last straw - The final thing which causes severe emotional upset - When Louise used my razor without asking, it was the last straw, we had a massive argument and I asked her to move out! - *British*

Like a dog with two tails - Happy and excited - When Andrew got his new car, he was like a dog with two tails. - *British*

Look blue - Look sad and depressed/ miserable - Don't look so blue, it'll be alright. - *America*

Lose your bottle - lack courage - I was going to confront the boss but I lost my bottle. - *British*

Low - Sad - I feel low today. - *British*

Lump in your throat - A physical reaction when moved by emotion - After watching the sad film, I had a right lump in my throat. - *British*

Makes me sick to my stomach - Makes them upset, ill, disgusted with a situation - The sight of you, makes me sick to my stomach! - *British*

Makes your blood run cold - Something frightening, very scary feeling - The noises in the dark creepy house, made her blood run cold. - *British*

Makes your flesh crawl - Something that makes you feel disgusted and nauseous, possibly scared too - The sight of the maggots made her skin crawl. - *British*

Mardy - Moody - Ahmed gets mardy if he is tired. - *British*

Personal

Misty-eyed - Feeling sad and/ or disappointed - John was a bit misty-eyed when he went to his mum's funeral. - *America/ British*

Music to your ears - Happy information or news - It was music to my ears when I was told that I had got the job. - *British*

Never looked back - The feeling that your life has changed for the better after an event and you are pleased - I'm so glad I left my job to retrain; I have never looked back. - *British*

No hard feelings - To leave a situation without any animosity, bitterness or resentment - "No hard feelings?" said the man to another, after he took his business away from him. - *British*

Not give a hang - To feel indifferent about someone or something - Kev didn't give a hang about Liverpool losing the game, he supported Chelsea! - *British*

Not turn a hair - To show no emotion in a situation, where emotion was expected - Joe didn't turn a hair when the large spider jumped up on to his lap! - *British*

On cloud nine - Very happy - I've been on cloud nine since I found out my partner is pregnant. - *British*

On edge - Very frightened - I find the new boss is very strict, he puts me on edge! - *America/British*

On the edge of one's seat - A situation that could be exciting, thrilling or/ and nerve wracking, making you nervous and restless - The audience were on the edge of their seats watching the horror film at the cinema. - *British*

On top of the world - Enjoying yourself a lot, life could not be better - I've been on top of the world since I won the lottery! - *British*

One hundred percent - Feeling good - I'm really well; I feel one hundred percent. - *British*

Over the moon - Very pleased - I am over the moon with my new car. - *British*

Pissy - In a bad mood - Mark is pissy because he can't go to the football match on Saturday. - *British*

Play it cool - Keep calm - If the boss moans about my work, I will try to play it cool. - *British*

Pour your heart out - To express feelings openly and freely - Jane poured her heart out to her sister so that she would understand why she was so upset. - *British*

Puss out - Very frightened - I was going to challenge the boss over it, but in the end I decided to puss out. - *America/British*

Ratty - Irritable - I get ratty if I am tired! - *British*

Really cheesed off - Fed up or annoyed - I'm really cheesed off with my job, it is so boring! - *British*

Save face - To manage to stay dignified and avoid being embarrassed or humiliated, keeping the respect of others - To save face, Shelia pretended that she meant to fall off the chair for a joke. - *British*

Scaredy cat - Very frightened - I was too much of a scaredy cat to confront the boss. - *America/British*

Shit (one's self) - Very frightened - When the police arrived, I nearly shit myself! - *America/British*

Shit scared - Frightened - I was shit scared when that lorry crashed into my car! - *British*

Sick as parrot - Disappointed - I was as sick as a parrot when they gave the job to Jim, instead of me! - *British*

Soul-sucking - Feeling sad and /or disappointed - This job is completely soul-sucking! - *America/British*

Sour-puss - Feeling sad and/ or disappointed - Andy is a sour puss because he has to work late. - *America/British*

Tail between your legs - Frightened or told off - The boss gave Bill a warning for being late, and he left the office with his tail between his legs. - *British*

Personal

Taking the Michael - Making fun of someone - Are you taking the Michael? - *British*

Taking the Mick - Making fun of someone - Are you taking the Mick? - *British*

Taking the Micky - Making fun of someone - Are you taking the Micky? - *British*

The heebie jeebies - A situation of apprehension, nervousness or anxiety; sometimes can't be explained rationally, just felt. - This place gives me the heebie geebies. - *British*

The waterworks - Feeling sad and / or disappointed - Gary put on the waterworks when he was told his girlfriend had left him. - *America/British*

The willies - Very frightened - That film was scary, it gave me the willies! - *America/British*

Thrilled to bits - Extremely pleased about something/ news - I'm thrilled to bits with my new car! - *British*

Ticked off - Annoyed - I am ticked off with my job, it is so boring! - *British*

Tickled pink - Extremely pleased about something - I'm tickled pink with my new car! - *British*

To badger someone - To annoy someone by persistently nagging or pestering them - The salesman badgered the old man to buy his wares, despite his protestations. - *British*

To be as proud as a peacock - Extremely proud - Jane is as proud as a peacock of her beautiful family. - *British*

To be as proud as punch - Absolutely delighted - Jane is as proud as punch of her family. - *British*

To be beside yourself (with emotion) - Very upset, to the point of losing control of your emotions - John was beside himself when he was told his mother had passed away. - *British*

To be hot under the collar - To be annoyed, embarrassed or indignant about a situation - John was hot under the collar, after being found out, for taking pennies from the tea fund. - *British*

To be in a stew - Worried or anxious about something - Toby was in a stew after looking at his bank balance and not understanding where all of his money had gone! - *British*

To be reduced to tears - Be made to cry by thoughtless and unkind behaviour - The mean teacher reduced the little boy to tears on his first day in school. - *British*

To breath easy - To be relieved - You can breathe easy now the perpetrator has been caught. - *British*

To get worked up - To lose one's temper, become annoyed or, to be overly excited or upset - Len got really worked up at work today and nearly had a heart attack! - *British*

To go off the deep end - To lose one's temper so badly one is unable to control one's emotions or behaviour - The man was so cross at seeing the graffiti the children had left on the wall, that he completely went off the deep end shouting at them, and making such a scene! - *British*

To go to pieces - To be so upset or shocked by an event, that you are no longer able to lead a normal life - Val went to pieces after Graham died. - *British*

To groan inwardly - A situation where you would like to groan out loud because you are distressed or disappointed, but you hold it in because it wouldn't be appropriate - Jane groaned inwardly at the prospect of watching yet another football match on TV. - *British*

To have mixed feelings about something - To have two points of view about something, you can see both the benefits and the drawbacks - I have mixed feelings about cous cous, sometimes I love it, and sometimes I hate it! - *British*

To have your heart in the right place - To have good intentions even if the resulting actions come to no good - My heart was in the right place but I knew I'd got it wrong when everyone laughed at my efforts. - *British*

To keep a stiff upper lip - To suppress feelings and not show distress - Roger and the rest of the crew knew they must keep a stiff upper lip for their tour of duty. - *British*

Personal

To let off steam - To express anger, frustration or disappointment openly - Steph needed to let off steam after looking after two small children all day without a break. - *British*

To lick one's wounds - Trying to regain confidence and spirits after a bad situation, involving disappointment or failure - Jane needed to be on her own for a while, in order to lick her wounds. - *British*

To open an old wound - To revive a painful memory of something distressing or bad that happened - When Jim saw Miranda again, for the first time in many years, it opened up old wounds for him. - *British*

To put nose out of joint - To offend or annoy someone - Dave's nose was put out of joint when Andy didn't choose him to be his best man. - *British*

To put your foot in mouth - Say something rude or embarrassing, because of insensitivity and lack of forethought - The woman put her foot in her mouth by mistaking the little boy for a girl! - *British*

To regain one's composure - To calm down and control emotions after a stressful or upsetting event - Pat needed to regain her composure after losing the tennis match on the last point of the match. - *British*

Too close to home - A situation, comment or behaviour upsets you because it reflects something true that may have happened to you, making you feel uncomfortable - "That situation was too close to home," said the man, after the car crash happened in front of his house. - *British*

Ugh - Feeling sad and or disappointed - Ugh, another day doing this boring job! - *America/British*

Uptight - Stressed - I got uptight because Justine took my last cigarette! - *British*

Whatever floats your boat - Do what makes you happy, make your own choices - Margaret loves drinking, I prefer a smoke. Whatever floats your boat, I suppose? - *British*

Your heart misses/ skips a beat - You are nervous or excited, potentially affecting your heart rate/ rhythm - I was so scared, my heart skipped a beat! - *British*

Your heart's in your mouth - Faced with danger or fearful situation, your heart beat increases and you become anxious - I was so scared, my heart was in my mouth! - *British*

A Freudian slip - A verbal mistake that is said to show truest, innermost thoughts and feelings, so named after Sigmund Freud, Austrian Neurologist and Psychoanalyst - "That was a Freudian slip," said Arthur, "and really shows your true feelings." - *British*

Fick - Colloquial phonetic speech for 'thick' - Jim is so fick. - *Bristol*

A chip on your shoulder - Arrogant or having a bad attitude - Yaz is so annoying, he has a chip on his shoulder. - *British*

Bark up the wrong tree - To be misled, mistaken or wrong about something - "You are barking up the wrong tree there," said the woman to her husband, on being accused of infidelity. - *British*

My ears are burning - To believe people are talking/ gossiping about you - My ears are burning! I wonder who is talking about me? - *British*

To have a chip on your shoulder - To feel resentful about the way you are treated. (Often linked to background, race/ ethnicity, gender etc.) - Jermaine had a chip on his shoulder after having a particularly difficult upbringing. - *British*

Hang up - An emotional problem - Dave has a hang up about commitment because his parents split up when he was small. - *British*

Headfuck - Something that is mentally disturbing - I can't believe she left me, what a headfuck. - *British*

In bits - In a state of mental turmoil - Kev is in bits because his girlfriend left him. - *British*

Screwed up - Emotionally disturbed - She is really screwed up by her childhood. - *British*

A diamond in the rough - A good thing found in an unusual place - I like Ant, he is a diamond in the rough. - *British*

Airy fairy - To do a task in a half hearted manner. Or to be effeminate - Ryland is a bit airy fairy. - *British*

Anorak - A person who is slightly strange or obsessive about particular things; like collecting or counting things, or knowing and remembering random statistics - Roy is strange, he is a bit of an anorak. - *British*

Arse - Someone who acts in a stupid or incompetent way - He is a total arse. - *British*

Arse licker - A sycophant who agrees with everything someone says in order to gain their favour, or for their own benefits/ gains - Patricia is a real arse licker. - *British*

Baby mother - A derogatory term for a woman whose role is purely to rear children - She is my babymother. - *Jamaican*

Bad egg - A criminal, someone not to be trusted - Watch out for Dave, he is a bad egg. - *British*

Ball breaker - A tough and uncompromising person - Rylan is a difficult person to work for, he is a ball breaker. - *America*

Berk - A stupid person - Stephen is a total berk. - *British*

Bestie - Friend - Jim is my bestie. - *British*

Bezzy mates - Best friends - Me and Jenny are bezzy mates. - *British*

Big bollocks - Someone who is over confident or cocky - Ahmed likes to act big bollocks. - *British*

Big cheese - Important person, the boss - David is the big cheese. - *America*

Big girl's blouse - A derogatory phrase to describe a weak person - Dexter is a big girl's blouse. - *British*

Big head - An arrogant person - Fred is big head. - *British*

Big man - An arrogant person - Alex is always acting the big man. - *British*

Bimbo - An attractive but stupid woman - She is a total bimbo. - *America*

Bird brain - Stupid - She is a bird brain. - *British*

Bit of fluff - Derogatory term for a woman - Phillip's got a new bit of fluff. - *British*

Bit of skirt - Derogatory term for a woman - Garth's got a new bit of skirt! - *British*

Bit of stuff - Derogatory term for a woman - Antonio's got a new bit of stuff. - *British*

Bro - Friend - John is my bro. - *America*

Bruddah - A close friend - Ahmed is my bruddah. - *America/British*

Buddy - Friend - Sholto is my buddy. - *America*

Buffoon - A fool or a clown - Sven is a buffoon. - *British*

Camp - To act in an effeminate manner - Leo is a bit camp. - *British*

Charity case - A pitiful and desperate person - Jazbah is a charity case. - *British*

Chav - A derogatory word for a person from the working class or 'under class' - Dwayne is a chav. - *British*

Chief - A term of respect towards one considered important - How are you, chief? - *British*

Chum - A close friend - Pete is my chum. - *America/British*

Clan - Group of friends - Tom, do you want to join the clan? - *British*

Clot - A fool or a clown - Brian is a clot. - *British*

Cloth ears - Someone who doesn't pay attention - Daniel has cloth ears. - *British*

Cowboy - Unscrupulous person in business without the proper qualifications. i.e. shoddy work of cowboy builders - I wouldn't trust Percy, he is a cowboy. - *British*

Cuz - A close friend - How you doin', cuz? - *America/British*

Daft as a brush - A silly person - Jermaine is as daft as a brush. - *British*

Dame - Woman - Dan met this gorgeous dame at the bar last night. - *America*

Dark horse - A person with unexpected or hidden qualities - Ethan is a dark horse. - *British*

Diamond geezer - A good person - Alli is a diamond geezer. - *British*

Dogg - A close friend - How you doin', dogg? - *America/British*

Douchebag - Stupid person - Manfred is a bit of a douchebag! - *America*

Eager beaver - Enthusiastic - Angel is an eager beaver. - *British*

Egg head - An intelligent person (derogatory) - Simmy is an egg head. - *British*

Essex girl - Derogatory term for female with low intelligence and morals - She is a stereotypical Essex girl. - *British*

Fancy Dan - A person who is extravagant - Paul is a fancy Dan. - *British*

Flash Harry - Ostentatious - Lee is a real flash Harry. - *British*

Freeloader - A person who takes items and offers nothing in return - Ian is a freeloader. - *British*

Frenemy - A close friend - Me and Ian love to hate each other, we are frenemies. - *America/British*

Gal - Woman - Joe met a gorgeous gal down the pub last night. - *British*

Gee-dog - A close friend - How you doin', Gee -dog? - *America/British*

Gimp - An idiot - He is a gimp. - *British*

Gobby - A loud annoying person - He can be really gobby sometimes! - *British*

Good egg - A trustworthy person - I like him, he is a good egg. - *British*

Goody two shoes - A virtuous person - Dee is a goody two shoes! - *British*

Guv - Abbreviation of governor. A term of respect - How are you, guv? - *British*

Guy - Man - I bought a new phone off this guy down the pub. - *British*

Has been - A derogatory expression used to describe someone who is past their peak - She is such a has been! - *British*

Hench - Strong - Robert is hench! - *British*

Home dog - A close friend - How you doin', home dog? - *America/British*

Home slice - A close friend - How you doin', home slice? - *America/British*

Homes - A close friend - What's up, homes? - *America/British*

Homey - A close friend - What's up, homey? - *America/British*

Homie - A close friend - What's up, homie? - *America/British*

Honey - Friend - How are you, honey? - *British*

Hun - Short for honey, a term of endearment - How are you, hun? - *British*

Jobsworth - A pedantic person, unhelpful and unmoving with regards to rules and regulations - Coleen is so petty, she is a real jobsworth. - *British*

Jumped up - Arrogant person - Sam gets on my nerves, he is a jumped up idiot. - *British*

Kemo sabe - A close friend - What's up, kemo sabe? - *America/British*

Kid - A close friend - How you doin', kid? - *America/British*

Knuckle head - Stupid person - Wayne is a knuckle head. - *British*

Kooky - Eccentric - Jo is so kooky! - *British*

Low life - A person who is believed to be a criminal or immoral - Darren is a low life. - *British*

Luvver - Friend - Alright, me luvver? - *Bristol*

Mate - Friend - Alright, mate? - *British*

Me babber - Term of affection or endearment - Alright, me babber? - *Bristol*

Meat head - Derogatory phrase for a muscly man - Coby is such a meat head! - *British*

Personal

Misery guts - A moody person - Nan is a misery guts! - *British*

Mrs - Wife or partner - Ian and his Mrs went to a show. - *British*

Muppet - A foolish person - Leigh is a muppet! - *British*

My boy - A close friend - Alright, my boy? - *America/British*

My man - A close friend - Alright, my man? - *America/British*

Nasty piece of work - A bad person - Wilma is a nasty piece of work! - *British*

Newb - Inexperienced - derived from the word, newbie - Alice is a total newb. - *America*

Nigga - A close friend - What's up, nigga? - *America/British*

Nuts - An insane person - Ryan is nuts! - *British*

Pal - Friend - Justin is my pal. - *British*

Partna - A close friend - What's up, partna? - *America/British*

Partner - A close friend - What's up, partner? - *America/British*

Pig headed - Arrogant or obstinate - Don't be pig headed, why won't you compromise? - *British*

Pig ignorant - Rude and obnoxious person - Karen is pig ignorant. - *British*

Pilchard - Idiot - Layla is a pilchard. - *British*

Plank - idiot - He is such a plank. - *British*

Pleb - A derogatory term for a 'lower class' person - Neil is a pleb. - *British*

Pond life - Disgusting person - Daz is pond life. - *British*

Potty mouth - A person who uses foul and crude language - Smithy has a potty mouth. - *British*

Prat - Idiot - Mark is a prat. - *British*

Quack - Doctor. (Can be used in a derogatory way to imply untrained) - That doctor is a quack. - *British*

Radge - Unscrupulous character - Dwayne is a radge. - *Scotland*

Retard - A derogatory phrase used to imply someone is mentally deficient - She is a retard. - *British*

Runt - A weak person - Sue is a runt. - *British*

Sad sack - Hopeless person - Ray is a sad sack. - *British*

Saddo - Pathetic or unpopular person - Carole is a saddo. - *British*

Scum bag - A despicable person - John is a scum bag. - *British*

Shit stirrer - To spread rumours or to gossip - I wouldn't tell him anything, he is a shit stirrer. - *British*

Sick note - Derogatory term for someone who is ill, implies they are pretending to be ill. (A sick note is a colloquial way of describing the document signed by patient and/ or doctor to certify a bout of illness) - Chris is always off work, we call him sick note! - *British*

Sister from another mister - A close friend - She is my sister from another mister. - *America/British*

Slapper - A sexually promiscuous person - She is a bit of a slapper. - *British*

Slob - Untidy or unclean - Davina is a slob. - *British*

Smart arse - Clever person - Don't be a smart arse, Justin! - *British*

Snidey - An untrustworthy person - Eliza is a bit snidey. - *British*

Son - A close friend - How you doin', son? - *America/British*

Squad - A group of friends - Can I invite the squad to your party? - *British*

Sucker - A gullible person - Ian is a complete sucker. - *British*

Suit - A businessman/ office worker/ corporate person - The party was so boring, it was full of suits. - *British*

Sweetie - Friend - Alright, sweetie? - *British*

Trainspotter - Derogatory term for anyone perceived as odd - Jock is a bit of a trainspotter. - *British*

Twonk - Fool - Pat, you are a complete twonk! - *British*

Weasel - An untrustworthy person - Don't trust Ken, he is a weasel! - *British*

Weedy - A slim or physically weak person - Dec is weedy! - *British*

Weirdo - Odd or eccentric person - Bob is a weirdo! - *British*

Whinger - Someone who persistently complains - Dad is such a whinger! - *British*

Wide boy - A stereotypically streetwise male, who may prove untrustworthy - John is a bit of a wide boy. - *British*

Wimp - Feeble, pathetic, emotionally over sensitive. (Or can mean effeminate) - Owen is a wimp! - *British*

Wingman - A close friend - John is my wingman. - *America/British*

Wrong un - Bad person - Doug is a wrong un! - *British*

Wuss - Feeble, pathetic, emotionally over sensitive. (Or can mean effeminate) - Danny is a wuss! - *America*

Yellow belly - Coward - Tony is a yellow belly. - *British*

Carry a torch for… - To have strong feelings for someone but you aren't in a relationship with them - Ian carried a torch for Sue but, kept his feelings a secret. - *British*

Head over heels - People use this expression about lovers being in love - Karim was head over heels in love with Nargis. - *British*

Look on the bright side - Stay positive - Look on the bright side, you can get a dog now! - *British*

Love me, love my dog - If you truly love me then you will accept me for who I am and love everything about me including other people I love - If you love me, love my dog too, we come as a pair! - *British*

Plenty more fish in the sea - Used when unlucky in love and have been left by a partner to imply there will be other potential lovers in the future - There are plenty more fish in the sea, don't worry about it. - *British*

Put a ring on it - Ask someone to marry them - It was about time he put a ring on it and asked her to marry him! - *British*

The bit on the side - A mistress to a married man - David had a bit on the side for years, until his wife found out and went mad! - *British*

To have a soft spot for - To have a special liking for someone or something - Julie has a soft spot for kittens! - *British*

Ear bashing - To reprimand someone verbally - Pete got an ear bashing because he was late for work! - *British*

Earache - Incessant talking that causes the hearer some discomfort - The boss was giving me an earache about my appearance. - *British*

A fish out of water - To be out of your comfort zone - Togi just doesn't fit in here, he is like a fish out of water. - *British*

A legend in one's own mind - A person who over estimates their own importance - John is a legend in his own mind. - *British*

Actions speak louder than words - What you do is more important than what you say - "If you want to prove how good you are, then do something to show me, because actions speak louder than words," said Tom. - *British*

Add fuel to the flames - Make a situation worse by saying or doing something to aggravate further - "That will only add fuel to the flames and make the situation worse," said the nurse. - *British*

As straight as a die - Honest - I like Joe, he is as straight as a die. - *British*

At loggerheads - An ongoing dispute - Me and Jo are at loggerheads, we can't seem to find any common ground. - *British*

Personal

Away with the fairies - A dreamer, or someone who is mentally ill - Kyle finds it hard to concentrate for too long, he is away with the fairies. - *British*

Bad blood - A feud or ongoing argument - There is a lot of bad blood between me and Keith. - *British*

Ball and chain - A derogatory term for a person's wife - I can't go out because the ball and chain wants me to stay in tonight! - *British*

Bare the brunt - The person or thing that suffers the most when something bad happens to them/ it - Leighton bared the brunt of the force in the car crash. - *British*

Billy No -Mates - A solitary person who has no friends - Sandy is a real Billy No-Mates! - *British*

Bit on the side - An affair in addition to ones usual sexual relationship - It is not a serious relationship, she is just my bit on the side. - *British*

Black sheep of the family - A person who is a family outcast - Toby is an outcast, he is the black sheep of the family. - *British*

Bone idle - Lazy - Luke is bone idle, he won't do anything to help. - *British*

Brain dead - Stupid person - Ernie is brain dead. - *British*

Break the ice - To reduce tension in a relationship or situation - Phil wanted to break the ice, so he bought her some flowers. - *British*

Breathing down your neck - Refers to someone who is continually monitoring you - The new boss is always breathing down your neck. - *British*

Bromance - A close friend - Me and James have a bromance going on! - *America/ British*

Brother from another mother - A close friend - Leighton is my brother, from another mother. - *America/British*

Build bridges - To assist cooperation between people with opposing opinions, and help them to understand each other better - Paul, if you want to build bridges with your missus, you need to apologise! - *British*

Butter wouldn't melt - A seemingly nice person who is in fact hiding a darker side - Be careful of Ali, he acts as if butter wouldn't melt but he is usually up to something. - *British*

Cack handed - A person without manual dexterity - Marcus is cack handed. - *British*

Call a spade a spade - To talk the simple truth - You know where you stand with Tom, he is very straight forward, he calls a spade a spade. - *British*

Catch on quick - To be a fast learner - Maninder is really smart, if you explain something to him, he catches on quickly. - *British*

Chat up - To make sexual advances towards someone - Eric loves to chat up the ladies down the pub! - *British*

Clued up - To be knowledgeable - Albert is clued up. - *British*

Comes apart at the seams - Someone who is under a lot of pressure/ stress and does not cope well with it, becomes very upset or is affected mentally - Their relationship was coming apart at the seams. - *British*

Common as muck - An uncultured person - Delia is as common as muck. - *British*

Couldn't organize a piss up in a brewery - An incompetent person - Egbert is hopeless, he couldn't organise a piss up in a brewery! - *British*

Crackers - Crazy - Dave is crackers! - *British*

Crocodile tears - To cry in an insincere manner - Andy said he was upset, but they were just crocodile tears. - *British*

Cut loose - To stop allowing someone to control and influence you, where you cut ties with them - Neil, if you don't love her, you ought to cut her loose. - *British*

Do the dirty - To betray someone - Cameron did the dirty on his missus, last night. - *British*

Don't know your ass from your elbow - Stupid or confused - Jackson, you are hopeless, you don't know your ass from your elbow! - *British*

Don't hold your breath - A feeling of hopelessness about a situation, like it's never going to happen - Don't hold your breath, I'm not sure we have the right recipe for success here. - *British*

Double cross - To betray trust in you - I wouldn't trust him, he might double cross you. - *British*

Faff - To be indecisive or fussy - Vicky, stop faffing about! - *British*

Fair-weather friend - Someone who is there for you during the good times but not supportive of you during the bad - I like Stu, but he is more of a fair-weather friend than a best buddy. - *British*

Flashy - Ostentatious - Eric acts all flashy. - *British*

Flesh and blood - Used in reference to those you are genetically related to - I always treated Lewis like my own flesh and blood. - *British*

Foul mouth - To speak using expletives (swearing and crude language) - Justin has a foul mouth. - *British*

Get on like a house on fire - People who become friends quickly, get on with each other really well and have a lot in common - Me and Kerry get on like a house on fire. - *British*

Go with the flow - To be easy going and happy to please others - I don't mind what we do, I'm happy to go with the flow. - *British*

Good riddance - Used to express pleasure that someone has left a situation; implies they are not very nice - I'm glad he has moved out, good riddance! - *British*

Ham fisted - Clumsy - Caroline is so ham fisted. - *British*

Hard as nails - Tough and resilient, finds it difficult to show emotion - Danny is as hard as nails. - *British*

Have your head examined - To doubt the beliefs of another - Sweetie, you need to have your head examined! - *British*

He was all over the shop - Disorganised and chaotic - Margy is so disorganised, she is all over the shop! - *British*

Henpecked - To be verbally controlled by one's partner - Les is totally hen pecked by his wife. - *British*

Her indoors - One's wife or partner - Her indoors won't like it, if I stay at the pub all night! - *British*

In the palm of my hand - To have control another person - Steve had this girl eating out of the palm of his hand! - *British*

Left in the lurch - Abandoned, or to be unwillingly burdened with responsibility - When Susan moved out, I was left in the lurch, I had to cover all the bills on my own. - *British*

Level headed - Sensible, calm - Marge is very level headed. - *British*

Lick ass - To act in a sycophantic manner - Steph is a lick ass! - *British*

Like a shot in the arm - Given a boost of energy - It was like a shot in the arm, when Lewis moved out. - *British*

Main ho - Friend - She is my main ho. - *British*

Massive - A term used by youths for a collection of people from the same area, often uses postcodes - We are the Bristol Massive! - *British*

Mend fences - Reconciliation after a dispute - It's time Henry and his wife tried to mend fences. - *British*

Not all there - Used to imply that someone is crazy or mentally incapable - Pat is strange, he's not all there. - *British*

Not backwards at coming forward - Brash or confident - Justin is not backwards at coming forwards! - *British*

Not batting on a full wicket - Mentally unstable person - Caz is not batting on a full wicket! - *British*

Off the wall - Unusual - Mike is off the wall! - *British*

Peas in a pod - People who are similar are drawn to each other, and naturally spend time together - Me and Kate are like peas in a pod! - *British*

Personal

301

Raving mad - Crazy - He is raving mad. - *British*

Round the bend - Crazy - He is round the bend. - *British*

Round the twist - Crazy - She is round the twist. - *British*

Sarky - Sarcastic - Joe, there's no need to be sarky! - *British*

Scatty - Illogical - Em Jay is a bit scatty! - *British*

See eye to eye with someone - To agree with someone - Me and Jane see eye to eye on most things. - *British*

Short fuse - Quick to anger - Dan has a short fuse, you never know when he will explode. - *British*

Sober as a judge - Metaphor to emphasise no alcohol consumed; judges must be sober in terms of taking things very seriously so metaphor implies very serious, sober nature - Andrew was as sober as a judge. - *British*

Soft in the head - Mentally unsound - Ken is a bit soft in the head. - *British*

Stick in the mud - An old fashioned and unadventurous person - Trish can be a bit of a stick in the mud. - *British*

Suited and booted - Smartly dressed and highly motivated to succeed - He was suited and booted, ready for his job interview. - *British*

Take to heart - To feel something, to listen to advice, or to be hurt by a comment made by someone - If you criticise Ben, he really takes it to heart. - *British*

Taking the piss - Making fun of someone - Are you taking the piss? - *British*

Tapped - Mentally unstable - Sammy is tapped. - *British*

Thick as thieves - A close friend - Me and you, are as thick as thieves! - *America/ British*

Thick as two short planks - Stupid - He is as thick as two short planks. - *British*

To know someone inside out - To know someone really, really well - We are so close, I know her inside out. - *British*

Toffee nosed - A derogatory term for someone from the 'upper classes' - Greg is a bit toffee nosed! - *British*

Tough cookie - A strong person - Dave is a tough cookie. - *British*

Wacky - Crazy or unusual - Kay is really wacky! - *British*

Walking disaster area - A clumsy or unfortunate person - Lew is a walking disaster area, everything he touches goes wrong! - *British*

Wear the trousers - Used to indicate the dominant partner in a relationship - Jake's wife wears the trousers. - *British*

Wet blanket - A miserable person, a spoiler of a good atmosphere - Don't invite Jack to the party, he is a wet blanket. - *British*

Wet lettuce - Feeble, pathetic, emotionally over sensitive. (Or can mean effeminate.) - Yameen is a wet lettuce, he can't cope with stress at all. - *British*

Wouldn't be seen/caught dead with - To detest someone, be embarrassed or ashamed of them so much you would not even want to be seen with them if you were dead. A snob - I wouldn't be seen dead wearing anything but designer sun glasses! - *British*

Your face speaks volumes - Reading expressive facial reactions, there is no need for words to understand what the person is truly thinking - You don't need to speak another word, your face speaks volumes! - *British*

Hit the hay - Go to sleep - I'm tired, I need to hit the hay. - *America*

Acid tongue - To speak cruelly - Neil can be mean, he has an acid tongue. - *British*

Back seat driver - An annoying passenger who continually criticises the driver of the vehicle - Dad is such a back seat driver, always making little comments on how I should manoeuvre! - *British*

Personal

Cut to the quick - To upset someone deeply by saying or doing very hurtful things - Larry's words cut Gill to the quick. - *British*

If you can't stand the heat, get out of the kitchen - If you are finding a situation too stressful, then leave - "If you can't stand the heat, get out of the kitchen," said Tim to Jim, during a pressurised meeting. - *British*

Make no bones about it - Speak plainly and directly about something - Make no bones about it, their relationship won't last. - *British*

(one's) nuts off - Energised and enthusiastic - Robert was so enthusiastic and energised, he worked his nuts off! - *America/British*

A fool's paradise - False belief that something will happen - Uncle Brian was living in a fool's paradise, believing that he could win the lottery. - *British*

Amped up - Energised and enthusiastic - The boys were amped up and enthusiastic about their game of football. - *America/British*

Banging - A description of something exciting - The party was banging! - *British*

Buzzing - Enthusiastic - I was buzzing when I got my new car. - *British*

Chomp at the bit - Energised and enthusiastic - When I was offered a new job, I was chomping at the bit! - *America/British*

Deep down - People use this expression to describe innermost feelings - Simon knew, deep down, that he loved Elie, very much. - *British*

Fired up - Energised and enthusiastic - I was fired up when I was given tickets to the concert. - *America/British*

Flummox - To confuse - I tried to build the furniture but I was completely flummoxed by the instructions! - *British*

Game on - Expression of excitement and anticipation - Lets go down the pub, game on! - *British*

Get your head together - To collect your thoughts and compose yourself - I was shocked when my girl friend left me. I need some time to get my head together. - *British*

Having the time of your life - Enjoying yourself a lot - I'm having the time of my life in Spain! - *British*

Hyped up - Over excited - I'm really hyped up, I can't wait for my holiday! - *British*

Hyper - Over excited - Calm down, you are getting hyper! - *British*

Lose the plot - Confused - I lose the plot if I drink too much! - *British*

Mad for it - Enthusiastic - I can't wait for the weekend, I'm mad for it! - *British*

Mind blowing - Astonishing, unimaginable - I couldn't believe that Katy had been promoted, it was mind blowing. - *British*

Mind fuck - Confusing, mentally disturbing - When my girlfriend left me, it was a real mind fuck. - *British*

Mixed up - Confused - Ian struggles to fit in, he is a bit mixed up. - *British*

Painted the town red - Enjoying a lively night out in bars and nightclubs - We all went out last night for a party; it was great, we painted the town red! - *British*

Scrambled - Confused - Sorry, I don't understand what you mean, my head is scrambled! - *British*

To bamboozle - Confuse or deceive - The salesman tried to bamboozle the old lady into buying his wares. - *British*

Top of the world - Enthusiastic - I am on top of the world today, I feel great! - *British*

Up for it - Enthusiastic - We are going to the pub after work, Les is really up for it! - *British*

Walking on air - Excited and happy about something - I have been walking on air since I got my new job. - *British*

One's best bet - Choosing a course of action most likely to be successful - I think going to Spain is your best bet, if you want sunshine at that time of year? - *British*

Personal

Bated breath - Anxious or/ and excited about a forthcoming event - Carol waited with bated breath to find out if she had passed her final exams. - *British*

Bide your time - Wait for a good/ better opportunity to come along - If we bide our time, the shares might go up in value. - *British*

Answer the call of nature - Need to go to the toilet - I need to answer a call of nature and to find a toilet, desperately. - *British*

Gob off - To verbally attack someone - Why are you gobbing off at me? - *British*

On the warpath - Prepared for an argument - Watch out, the new boss is on the warpath! - *British*

Personal